lonely

Colorado

Rocky Mountain National Park
& Northern Colorado
p140

Boulder, p100

DENVER, p52

Vail, Aspen &
Central Colorado
p178

Mesa Verde &
Western Colorado
p249

Southeast Colorado &
the San Luis Valley
p299

Liza Prado, Nicole Hagg, Christopher Pitts

CONTENTS

FROM TOP: LANA2011/GETTY IMAGES; SL-PHOTOGRAPHY/SHUTTERSTOCK

Plan Your Trip

The Guide

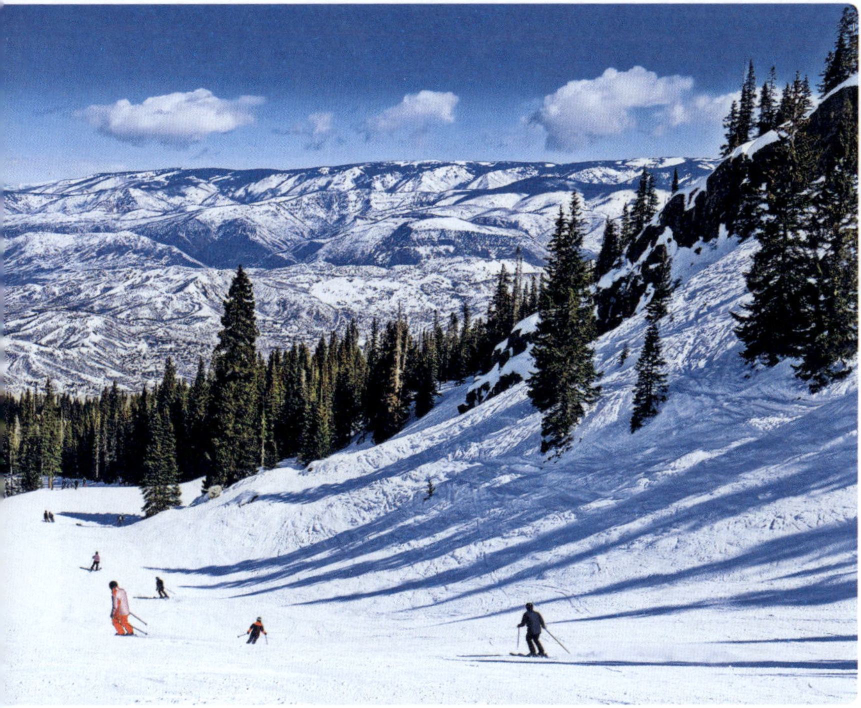

Aspen (p218)

Mesa Verde National Park (p254)

Toolkit

Storybook

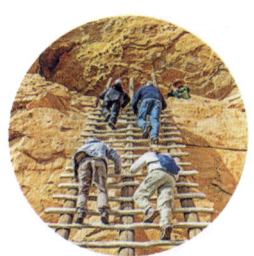

Ute Mountain Ute Tribal Park (p258)

COLORADO
THE JOURNEY BEGINS HERE

When I moved to Denver, I thought of it as a one-, maybe two-year whim to live someplace new. Sixteen years later, I'm still here and have no plans to leave. I'd only been to Colorado once before, a brief stopover on a cross-country road trip. But once I moved here, those snowcapped mountains, they pulled me in hard and fast. Anytime I looked west, they were there. A constant in the city's ever-changing landscape, a reminder that time is long and slow, a promise of adventure hidden within. And with each passing year, the mountains have lived up to their promise, revealing landscapes I'd never imagined in Colorado – red rock canyons, towering sand dunes, high desert mesas. And hot springs! So many hot springs. Even after 16 years, Colorado has the power to surprise me. I have no doubt 40 years from now, I'll feel exactly the same way.

Liza Prado

@liza.prado

Liza Prado is a corporate lawyer turned travel writer and the author of over 60 books. She wrote the Denver and Mesa Verde & Western Colorado chapters.

My favorite experience is being guided through the starkly beautiful Ute Mountain Ute Tribal Park (p258), the dirt roads, narrow trails and teetering ladders revealing little-visited cliff dwellings, still spectacularly intact.

WHO GOES WHERE

Our writers and experts choose the places that, for them, define Colorado.

HAVESEEN/SHUTTERSTOCK

Rocky Mountain National Park (p146) is a microcosm of everything I love about Colorado: otherworldly nights in the high country watching the dancing lights of distant thunderstorms, spine-tingling adventures up gorgeous granite peaks, and crisp fall days, when the aspens blaze gold and the eerie sound of bugling elks carries across the valleys.

Christopher Pitts

christopherpitts.net

Chris is the author of over two dozen Lonely Planet guides as well as a forthcoming novel. He lives in Boulder.

KELLY VANDELLEN/SHUTTERSTOCK

The **Great Sand Dunes** (p313) are an unexpected metaphor for life. Their magnificence and duality take time to process: serene and wild, staid and ever-changing, ancient and new. Navigating trails that change with the wind feels like one step forward and two back. Imagined 'paths' lead to questions rather than a finish line: 'Where am I? Can I do this? What's my best next step?' A powerful reminder to pause and embrace the wonder that surrounds you now!

Nicole Hagg

nicolebhagg.com

Nicole, having performed most jobs short of smelting copper, is a full-time raconteuse, humorist and travel writer.

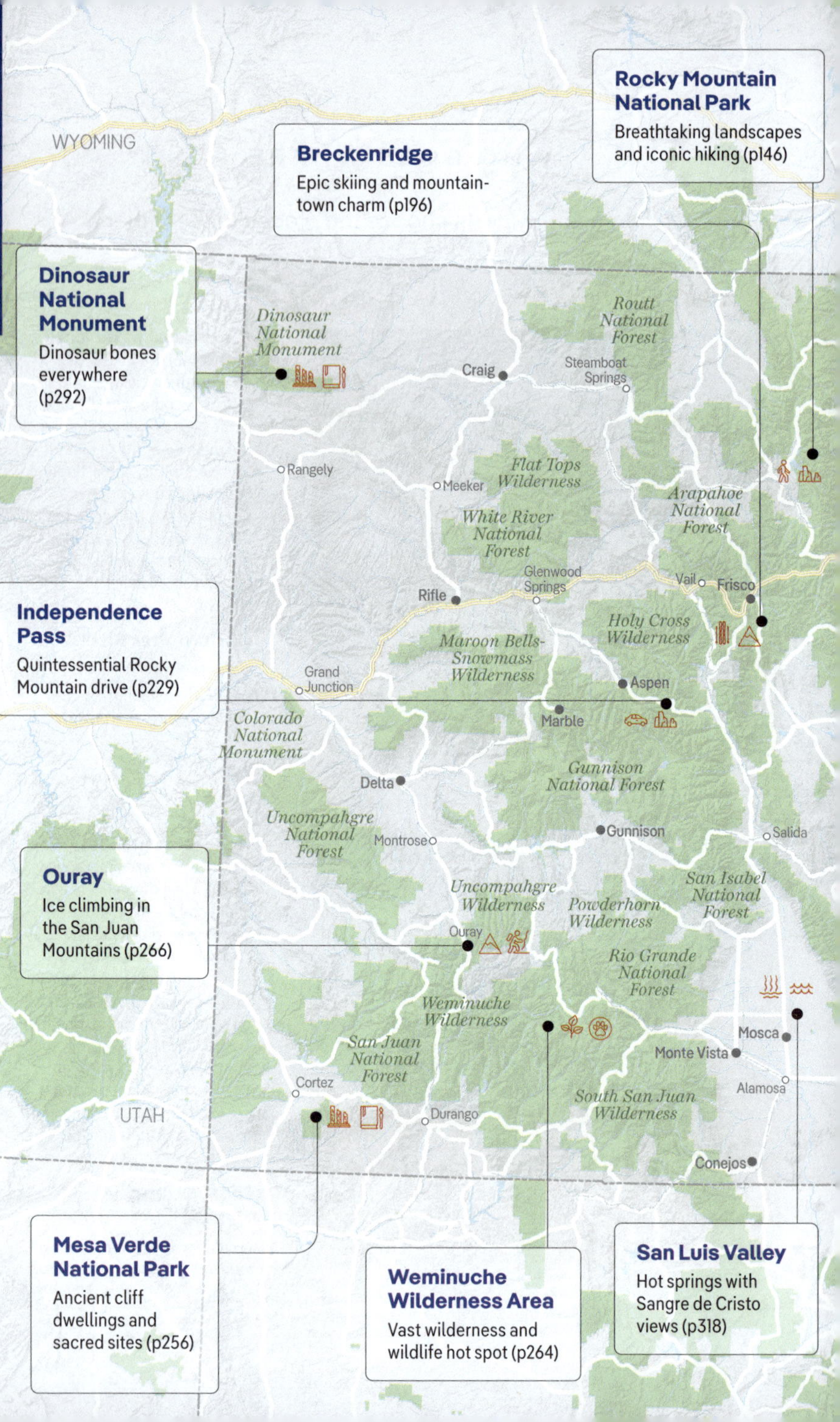

WYOMING

Rocky Mountain National Park
Breathtaking landscapes and iconic hiking (p146)

Breckenridge
Epic skiing and mountain-town charm (p196)

Dinosaur National Monument
Dinosaur bones everywhere (p292)

Dinosaur National Monument

Craig

Steamboat Springs

Routt National Forest

○ Rangely

Flat Tops Wilderness

Meeker ○

White River National Forest

Arapahoe National Forest

Independence Pass
Quintessential Rocky Mountain drive (p229)

Rifle

Glenwood Springs

Vail ○ Frisco

Maroon Bells-Snowmass Wilderness

Holy Cross Wilderness

Grand Junction ○

● Aspen

Colorado National Monument

Marble

Delta ●

Gunnison National Forest

Uncompahgre National Forest

Montrose ○

● Gunnison

○ Salida

Ouray
Ice climbing in the San Juan Mountains (p266)

Uncompahgre Wilderness

Powderhorn Wilderness

San Isabel National Forest

Ouray ●

Rio Grande National Forest

Weminuche Wilderness

Mosca

Monte Vista ●

UTAH

San Juan National Forest

Cortez ○

○ Durango

South San Juan Wilderness

Alamosa ○

Conejos ●

Mesa Verde National Park
Ancient cliff dwellings and sacred sites (p256)

Weminuche Wilderness Area
Vast wilderness and wildlife hot spot (p264)

San Luis Valley
Hot springs with Sangre de Cristo views (p318)

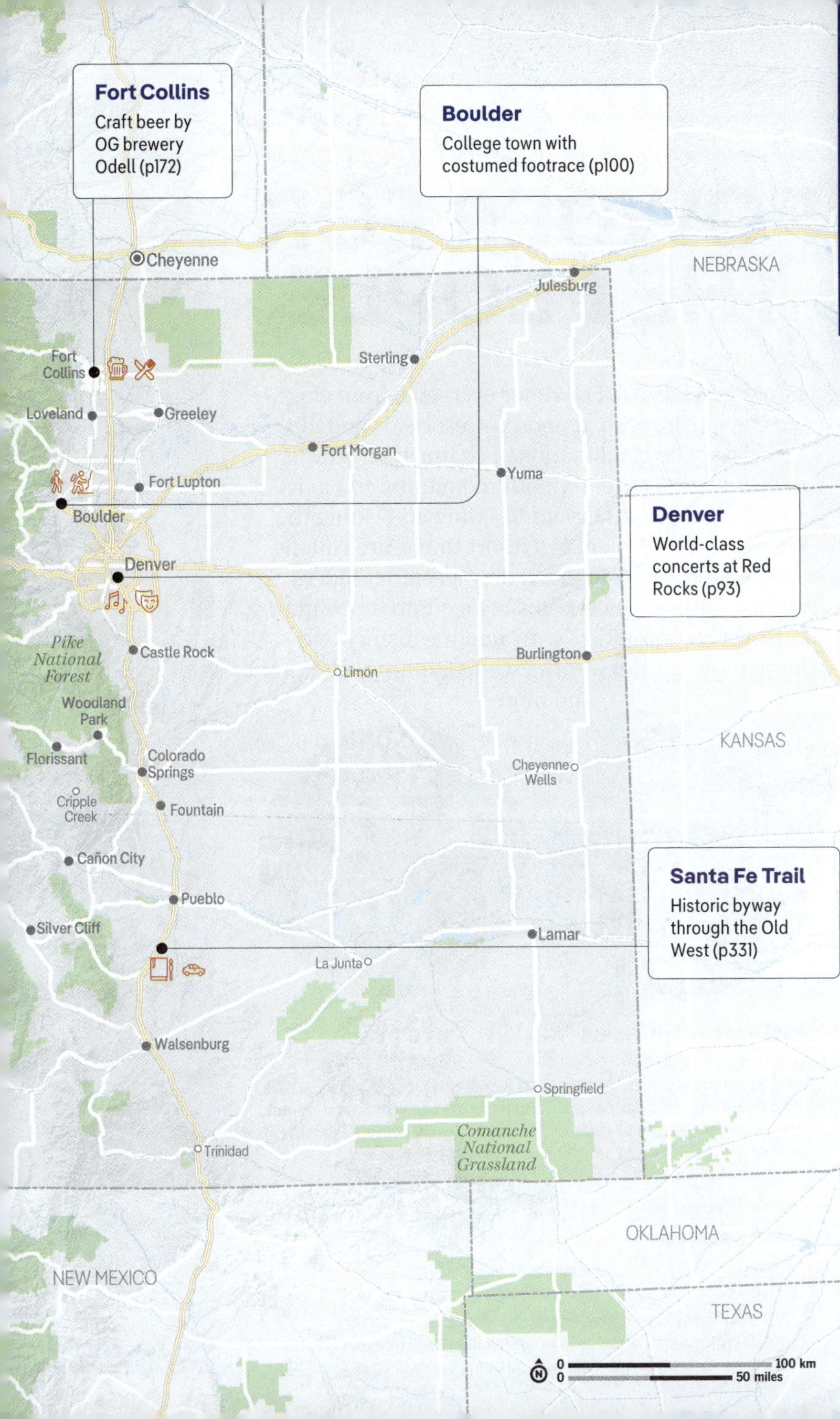

Fort Collins
Craft beer by OG brewery Odell (p172)

Boulder
College town with costumed footrace (p100)

Denver
World-class concerts at Red Rocks (p93)

Santa Fe Trail
Historic byway through the Old West (p331)

Cheyenne

NEBRASKA

Julesburg

Sterling

Fort Collins

Loveland

Greeley

Fort Morgan

Yuma

Fort Lupton

Boulder

Denver

Pike National Forest

Castle Rock

Limon

Burlington

KANSAS

Woodland Park

Florissant

Colorado Springs

Cheyenne Wells

Cripple Creek

Fountain

Cañon City

Pueblo

Silver Cliff

Lamar

La Junta

Walsenburg

Springfield

Trinidad

Comanche National Grassland

OKLAHOMA

NEW MEXICO

TEXAS

N

0 ————— 100 km
0 ————— 50 miles

POWDER FOR THE PEOPLE

Colorado has a ski town for everyone, from chic to cheap(ish), with glamorous resorts or no-frills getaways. The combination of champagne powder, endless blue skies, mammoth mountains and a live-to-ski ethos makes Colorado skiing and riding the stuff of legend. Colorado's resort towns are equally appealing, many founded over a century ago as mining outposts, now transformed into welcoming resort communities, with genuine history and character to go along with excellent dining, nightlife and more.

Ski Pass vs Lift Ticket

Available in various prices, the Epic, Ikon or resort-specific day passes or multipacks are typically less expensive than lift tickets, which can top $275/day.

BYO Boots

If there's one piece of personal gear to bring, make it your boots – rentals rarely fit as well, and aching feet can ruin your day.

Après-Ski

Ski towns have turned end-of-the-day drinks into an art form. 'Après' ('after,' in French) specials range from pub grub to fine cocktails, ski boots optional.

BEST SKI TOWN EXPERIENCES

Have it all in ❶ **Breckenridge**, the best combination of epic skiing, mountain-town charm and easy access from Denver. (p196)

Get your glam on in ❷ **Aspen**, a stylish, star-studded mountain town with world-class skiing and riding to boot. (p218)

Prepare to be stunned by ❸ **Telluride's** sheer beauty, an iconic town and ski resort deep in the gorgeous San Juans. (p272)

Soak at one of the local hot springs after a day of pitch-perfect tree skiing at quintessentially cowboy ❹ **Steamboat Springs**. (p164)

Enjoy ❺ **Crested Butte**, a laid-back and historic town home to a small-but-mighty resort with Colorado's steepest inbound run. (p243)

TRAVIS J. CAMP/SHUTTERSTOCK

Browns Canyon (p238)

ADRENALINE RUSH

Some travelers need more than to simply admire Colorado's natural wonders: they want to engage with them, to scale, hike, bike, raft them. And the state is perfectly happy to oblige, with a virtually endless supply of high-adrenaline adventures to be had throughout Colorado's wilderness, whether it's in summertime or the depths of winter.

Cover Up

The sun shines hard in Colorado, both summer and winter. Slather on sunscreen, wear your hat and shades, and don't forget the SPF-infused lip balm.

Nature Always Wins

Avalanches kill more people in Colorado than any other state, and all adrenaline sports – climbing, biking, rafting – have inherent dangers. Know your limits.

BEST ADVENTURE SPORT EXPERIENCES

Brace yourself for the icy splash and roaring waves as you descend through ❶ **Browns Canyon**. (p238)

Keep your balance as you sandboard down the shifting sandscape of ❷ **Great Sand Dunes National Park**. (p313)

Test your climbing skills on the beautifully veined cliffs of ❸ **Black Canyon of the Gunnison**; guide recommended. (p279)

Swing that ice axe and set those crampons to reach the top of the gorgeous ice walls of ❹ **Ouray Ice Park**. (p268)

Let it rip over 450 miles of mountain-biking trails in ❺ **Crested Butte**. (p243)

EPIC DRIVES

For mind-blowing drives, you've come to the right place. Colorado has over two dozen nationally designated Scenic & Historic Byways, and several more that aren't on the official list but should make yours. Some will take all day, while others are short hops to little-visited mountain passes; all are sure to leave you speechless but smiling.

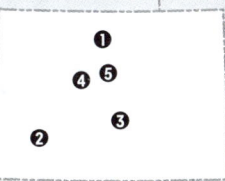

Car Rentals

Save cash by booking your car rental at an off-airport location – a cab ride can typically save about 20% on airport taxes and fees.

I-70

On weekends, the I-70 can move at a snail's pace, packed with metro-Denverites headed to and from the mountains. Travel midweek to avoid the traffic.

Weather Alerts

Check for weather alerts before you set out – roads can close! If you're headed to the mountains, carry a set of auto-socks and have provisions.

BEST DRIVE EXPERIENCES

Take in outrageous alpine vistas on ❶ **Trail Ridge Road** in Rocky Mountain National Park, the highest continuously paved road in North America. (p151)

Experience the priceless views of the ❷ **Million Dollar Highway**, 25 miles of hairpin turns along the incomparable Uncompahgre Gorge between Silverton and Ouray. (p271)

Drive back in time on the ❸ **Gold Belt Byway**, an unpaved former stagecoach road that winds along sheer cliffs and through piñon tree forests. (p326)

Explore along the ❹ **Top of the Rockies Scenic Byway**, crossing iconic Independence Pass, three national forests and historic Colorado towns. (p212)

Be wowed by ❺ **Guanella Pass Scenic Byway**, a stunning high-elevation road known for its alpine lakes, autumn colors and access to Mt Bierstadt. (p290)

FROM LEFT: DMITRY PICHUGIN/SHUTTERSTOCK, SEAN XU/SHUTTERSTOCK

FIRST PEOPLES

Numerous tribes trace their lineage to present-day Colorado, including Cheyenne, Arapaho, Apache, Pueblo and especially the Ute. The Ute are a large and diverse tribe, composed of numerous bands and spanning centuries. They traditionally lived in the mountains, where much of their mythology is centered, and have two reservations in southwestern Colorado today. Several locations around the state honor and illuminate the experience of Utes and other Native tribes in Colorado, from ancient sights to modern-day celebrations.

Sacred Sites

Remember that places like Mesa Verde, Canyon Pintado and Chimney Rock are not just tourist attractions; they are sacred ground to several modern-day tribes.

Unexpected Places

Some non-Native museums have excellent and informative displays on Native American life, history and art, including Denver Art Museum and History Colorado.

Indian Reservations

Colorado has two established tribal nations: the Ute Mountain Ute Reservation and the Southern Ute Reservation, both located in the state's southwest corner.

BEST FIRST PEOPLES EXPERIENCES

Tour the spectacular cliff dwellings at ❶ **Mesa Verde National Park**, including plying stone paths and scaling wooden ladders. (p256)

Delve into the history and culture of the Ute Tribe, Colorado's primary Indigenous group, at Montrose's ❷ **Ute Indian Museum**. (p283)

Commemorate the horrors inflicted on Cheyenne and Arapaho people at the ❸ **Sand Creek Massacre National Historic Site**. (p331)

Enjoy traditional Native dances, music and storytelling at the ❹ **Denver March Powwow**, one of the country's largest. (p87)

Admire the treasure trove of rock art along ❺ **Canyon Pintado**, a 15-mile stretch of lonely road with petroglyphs dating to 100 CE. (p289)

Red Rocks (p93)

THE CREATIVES

Seen as more athlete than artist, Colorado isn't an obvious place for a flourishing arts scene. But by some alchemy of its natural beauty, scrappy history and rich ferment of local and transplanted talent, Colorado is deeply artistic. The perfect summer weather, too, has allowed for outstanding cultural events and performances to be taken outdoors.

Street Art

Urban art is booming in Colorado, alleys and underpasses gleaming with amazing aerosol art. Don't miss Street Wise Boulder and DENVER WALLS, both marquee events.

First Fridays

Denver and Boulder host fun First Friday events where galleries and art studios stay open late, and the sidewalks fill with a party atmosphere.

BEST ART & CULTURE EXPERIENCES

Rock out at ❶ **Red Rocks Park & Amphitheater**, arguably the world's best natural amphitheater and concert venue. (p93)

Be inspired at ❷ **Denver Art Museum**, with an impressive Native American collection and fabulous exhibits. (p70)

Test your limits at the ❸ **Aspen Art Museum**, known for edgy, contemporary installations. Admission is always free. (p227)

Catch a show at Telluride's historic ❹ **Sheridan Opera House**, a beautifully restored vaudeville theater. (p274)

Admire the excellent Latin American and Colonial art collection at the ❺ **Colorado Springs Fine Arts Center**. (p305)

THE OLD WEST

There's something captivating about the Old West: the sheer number of Western movies are proof enough. The reality of that era was less cinematic: fortunes were lost, mining camps were short-lived, and innumerable Native people were displaced and killed. Learning about their true histories makes Colorado's Old West sites all the more evocative and memorable.

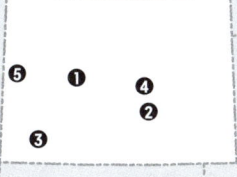

FROM LEFT: BOB POOL/SHUTTERSTOCK, DAVID B. PETERSEN/SHUTTERSTOCK

Mining Towns

Colorado owes its beginning to mining. Many modern-day mountain towns like Aspen, Telluride and Crested Butte (and most ghost towns) started out as mining camps.

Pan for Gold

Learn first-hand how tough it is to pan for gold – and have some fun too! – at mines-turned-tourist attractions in Fairplay, Idaho Springs, Breckenridge and Silverton.

Ghost Town Visits

Treat Colorado's ghost towns as you would any historic site: be careful not to damage the structures and leave artifacts where you find them.

BEST OLD WEST EXPERIENCES

Imagine yourself a 19th-century silver miner in **❶ Ashcroft Ghost Town**, a scenic collection of abandoned wood homes and structures outside Aspen. (p224)

Retrace the **❷ Santa Fe Trail**, with stops at the fascinating Bent's Old Fort and wrenching Sand Creek Massacre National Historic Site. (p221)

Ride the historic **❸ Durango & Silverton Narrow Gauge Railroad**, an impossibly scenic round-trip journey to Silverton, with astounding mountain vistas. (p261)

Learn the lore of Colorado cowboys – and all about rodeo history – at **❹ ProRodeo Hall of Fame and Museum of the American Cowboy**. (p306)

Tour a frontier town at **❺ Museum of the Mountain West** with over two dozen 19th-century buildings filled with memorabilia plus staff in period dress. (p283)

15

CHEERS!

Coloradans love them a good IPA, the hoppier the better. But with 400 breweries and counting, and home to the Great American Beer Festival, Colorado's tap list runs deep: stouts, ales, wheats, lagers and more. You can also find terrific locally brewed ciders, plus creations like Green Chile Ale and, recently, marijuana-infused seltzers. And, of course, the state has been making fine wine longer than craft beer, and we can't forget the 100+ distilleries!

Acronym 411

Vocab lesson! ABV = alcohol by volume (the higher, the stronger). IPA = India Pale Ale, a bitter hoppy style. NV = non-vintage (wine made from a blend).

Mega Batch Beer

If you must drink a Big Beer, make it a Coors, which is brewed in-state. It'll sting locals a little less.

High-Altitude Wineries

Located 4000ft to 7000ft above sea level, Colorado's wine country is the highest in North America and second only to Argentina in the world.

BEST DRINKING EXPERIENCES

Drink a pint of history at **❶ Odell**, the first craft brewery in the state's capital of craft brewing, Fort Collins. (p87)

Follow the aroma of hops to the award-winning **❷ Broken Compass Brewing**, known for its Coconut Porter and pooch-friendly taproom. (p200)

Mountain views and skyscrapers are the twin signatures of **❸ 54thirty**, a swanky rooftop bar 20 stories up, Denver's highest. (p64)

Bike or book a pedicab to visit the small family-run wineries along the Palisade **❹ Fruit and Wine Byway**. (p293)

Sip a quinoa vodka cocktail at **❺ Dune Valley Distillery**, a one-time school gymnasium turned homegrown distillery and community space. (p318)

EFRAIN PADRO/ALAMY STOCK PHOTO

Aspen Music Festival (p223)

FESTIVAL FUN

Coloradans know how to throw a festival. Some are low-key and local, while others draw massive international crowds. Many festivals are focused on food and music, but there are plenty of off-the-wall ones as well. No matter what's being celebrated, festivals are a fun way to get to know the town and the people hosting it.

Sold Out!

Many ticketed festivals, like the Great American Beer Festival and the Telluride Bluegrass Festival, require tickets and can sell out in minutes. Plan accordingly.

Wacky Festivals

Not every festival is about beer or wildflowers: Colorado has some far-out festivals celebrating everything from frozen guys to headless chickens. Save the date!

BEST FESTIVAL EXPERIENCES

Attend the ❶ **Aspen Music Festival** with over 400 classical musical events over an eight-week season. (p223)

Join the costumed runners at ❷ **Bolder Boulder**, a 10K footrace-party with live music and sideline antics. (p133)

Have a cold one with 40,000 buddies at the ❸ **Great American Beer Festival**, the US' largest beer festival. (p64)

Fly away to the ❹ **Telluride Bluegrass Festival**, where banjo and guitar music fills this scenic San Juan Mountains town. (p274)

Warm up your pitching arm for the ❺ **Great Fruitcake Toss**, a lighthearted fest celebrating the bemoaned baked good. (p311)

SOAK IT UP

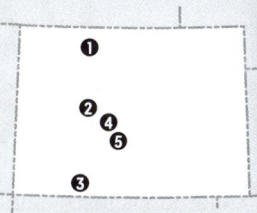

Colorado is a soaker's paradise, with countless natural hot springs throughout the Rocky Mountain region. Rain and snow seep deep into the earth and resurface in sublime pools, steaming and infused with healing minerals. From remote backcountry pools to steam-enveloped luxury resorts, Colorado has a healing, natural hot spring with your name on it.

BEST HOT SPRINGS EXPERIENCES

Soak it up at famous **❶ Strawberry Park Hot Springs** in Steamboat, set beside a rushing mountain stream with acres of wilderness surrounding you. (p167)

Reward yourself with a soak at the gorgeous **❷ Conundrum Hot Springs**, located at the end of a long wildflower-filled hike near Aspen. (p224)

Pamper yourself at the **❸ Springs Resort & Spa** in Pagosa Springs, fed by the Mother Spring, the world's deepest known geothermal spring. (p264)

Find the perfect pool at **❹ Mt Princeton Hot Springs**, a four-star resort with dozens of natural pools dotting its mountainside property. (p240)

Stay overnight at **❺ Joyful Journey Hot Springs Spa**, a sanctuary of pools and accommodations with stunning views of the Sangre de Cristo Mountains. (p318)

Water Temperatures

The water temperature at most public hot springs is 95°F to 110°F (35–43°C). Some scorchers top 120°F (49°C), while family pools average 80°F to 90°F (26°C to 32°C).

Safety First

Soaking is a beneficial pastime, but a few rules apply: stay hydrated, cool off every 20 minutes, and, if you're pregnant, consult your doctor first.

Naked Soaking

Prepare to see fellow soakers in the buff at hot springs. It's not a given but it's common at resorts and in the wild.

HAPPY TRAILS

Colorado is justly famous for its hiking. For mountain adventure, there are alpine lakes, wildflower-strewn valleys and the country's highest concentration of fourteeners (over 50 in all). For something more horizontal, there are high desert mesas, slot canyons and grassland vistas. And everywhere, excellent trails and wildlife abound. Naming Colorado's best hikes is like ranking the greatest sunsets. But here goes, with an eye toward showcasing the state's impressive variety in terrain and difficulty.

Come Prepared

Weather conditions can change quickly, especially in high country. Carry layers, a hat and plenty of water, and don't rely on cell service for maps.

Gray Clouds

Afternoon lightning above the timberline is a real danger, especially in the summer. Start summit hikes early so you'll be off exposed ridgelines by noon.

Tread Lightly

Help protect Colorado! Heed fire bans, stay on trails and pack out your trash (yes, even poop). And please, don't scratch your name onto trees.

BEST HIKING EXPERIENCES

Hike your heart out at ❶ **Glacier Gorge Trailhead**, jumping-off point for iconic hikes like Lake of Glass and Flattop Mountain. (p149)

Brave the crowds at ❷ **Maroon Bells**, one of the state's most beautiful short hikes despite being so busy. (p222)

Stretch your legs at ❸ **Chautauqua Park**, with gorgeous Front Range views and hikes for all levels. (p115)

Circumnavigate the 'Switzerland of America' on Ouray's ❹ **Perimeter Trail**, a 6-mile loop with aspen groves, waterfalls and a quartzite canyon. (p266)

Roam through otherworldly red-rock formations on the stark and beautiful high-desert trails of ❺ **Colorado National Monument**. (p290)

ZACK FRANK/SHUTTERSTOCK

Dinosaur National Monument (p292)

FOSSIL FEVER

Although dinosaurs dominated the planet for over 100 million years, relatively few places in the world had the proper geological and climatic conditions to preserve their bones as fossils and their tracks as permanent evolutionary placeholders. Colorado is happily near the top of that list. If you're a dinophile, you've come to the right state.

Name Change

Dinosaur, Colorado (population 246), was originally called Baxter Springs but changed its name in 1966 to capitalize on Dinosaur National Monument, located 2 miles north.

Cartoon Inspiration

Stegosaurus, Colorado's official state fossil, has a spiky tail called a 'thagomizer.' A Denver paleontologist got the name from a *Far Side* cartoon.

BEST PALEONTOLOGICAL EXPERIENCES

Visit ❶ **Dinosaur National Monument**, whose quarry wall has over 1500 bones still embedded in it. (p292)

Play paleontologist on a full-day dig in Mygatt-Moore Quarry, part of the ❷ **Trail Through Time** outside Fruita. (p289)

Walk in the footsteps of giants at ❸ **Picketwire Dinosaur Tracksite**, containing over 1300 prints. (p332)

Examine fossils and hike past petrified redwood stumps at ❹ **Florissant Fossil Beds National Monument**. (p325)

Bone up on dinosaur basics at ❺ **Denver Museum of Nature & Science**, a family-friendly museum and research center. (p90)

WHERE THE WILD THINGS ARE

Colorado is home to a wealth of wildlife, including moose, elk, antelope, bighorn sheep, black bear, mountain lion, cutthroat trout and bald eagles. In 2023 Colorado also reintroduced gray wolves, which had been eradicated almost a century ago, to the state. Like wildlife everywhere, spotting critters is a mix of skill, timing and luck.

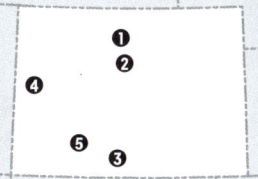

FROM LEFT: JOHN BOLAND/SHUTTERSTOCK, GEORGIA EVANS/SHUTTERSTOCK

Keep Your Distance

No selfie is worth being chased or gored. Don't approach wild animals! It's dangerous and can end in harm to the animal too.

Ask a Park Ranger

Park rangers have tips for encounters with big animals like moose, bears and mountain lions. In general, don't run, back away slowly and avoid eye contact.

Viewing Times

You have the best chances of spotting wildlife in the early morning or late afternoon, when they're most active. Plan accordingly!

BEST WILDLIFE-SPOTTING EXPERIENCES

Spot moose wading through wetlands and elk grazing in high-country meadows in spectacular **❶ Rocky Mountain National Park**. (p146)

Keep your eyes peeled for bighorn sheep and mountain goats on **❷ Guanella Pass**, a scenic byway close to Denver. (p190)

Treat your ears to the incredible soundscape of birdsong in the protected wetlands of **❸ Alamosa National Wildlife Refuge**. (p317)

Just try to drag yourself away from the bands of wild horses at **❹ Little Book Cliffs**, outside of Grand Junction. (p293)

Go wild at **❺ Weminuche Wilderness Area**, a vast and remote wildland in the San Juan Mountains, home to elk, black bears, eagles and more. (p264)

REGIONS & CITIES

Find the places that tick all your boxes.

Rocky Mountain National Park & Northern Colorado

ACROSS THE GREAT DIVIDE

Grazing elk, jewel-like lakes, wildflower meadows, majestic mountains and a sky-high road traversing it all...it's no wonder Rocky Mountain National Park is one of Colorado's most captivating destinations. Nearby Steamboat Springs adds a cowboy vibe, champagne powder and hot springs, while youthful Fort Collins is all about craft brews and bikes.
p140

Vail, Aspen & Central Colorado

LIFE AT 110%

From glamorous to historic, fast and furious to quiet and secluded, central Colorado is the stuff of dreams. Come for epic mountain snow and après-ski, thrilling river runs and singletrack fun. Or bliss out in a hot spring or in the backcountry. Whatever your happy place, you're sure to find it here.
p178

Mesa Verde & Western Colorado

HISTORY AND OUTDOOR ADVENTURE

Western Colorado is big, bold and diverse. It's home to ancient cliff dwellings and epic ski areas, plunging canyons and wine country, relaxing hot springs...even dinosaur bones. There are chic destinations, historic ghost towns and everything in between. And yet none are exactly as you expect – prepare to be surprised.
p249

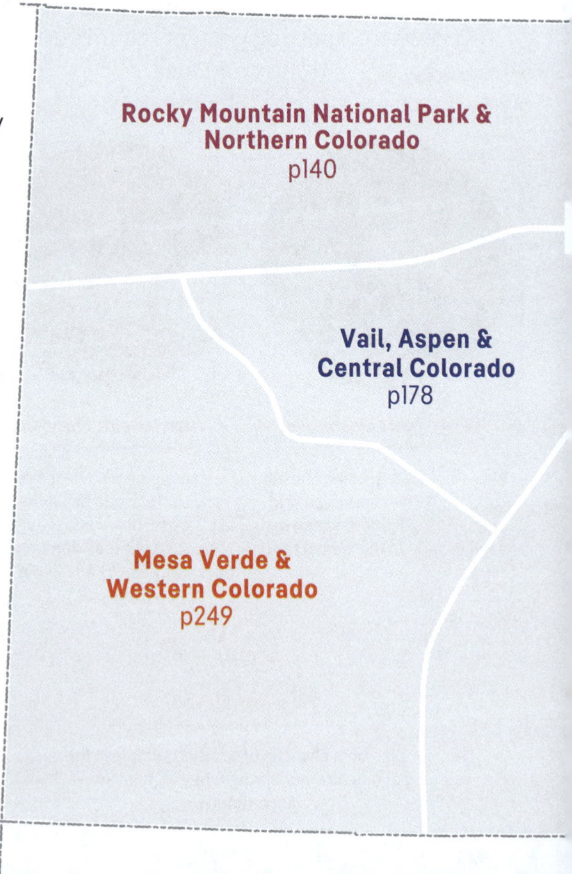

Rocky Mountain National Park & Northern Colorado
p140

Vail, Aspen & Central Colorado
p178

Mesa Verde & Western Colorado
p249

Boulder

TWENTY-FIVE SQ MILES SURROUNDED BY REALITY

A city of contrasts, ultra-liberal Boulder is known for its hippie-chic vibe and million-dollar homes. It's a party-hard college town that happens to have a vibrant art scene. And did we mention the 150-plus miles of trails or those dramatic Flatiron rock formations that look made for climbing?

p100

Denver

URBAN, ARTSY AND SPORTY

Colorado's biggest city, Denver buzzes with activity, with seemingly countless museums and performing arts venues plus a hopping restaurant and nightlife scene. Mix in five pro sports teams and a distinct outdoorsy ethos (not to mention all the street art), and the Mile High City is a destination to be enjoyed year-round.

p52

Boulder
p100

Denver
p52

Southeast Colorado & the San Luis Valley

PEAKS AND VALLEYS OF POSSIBILITY

Don't be fooled by the (relative) lack of hype given to southeast Colorado. This high-desert region boasts beauties like Pikes Peak, Great Sand Dunes National Park and the rushing waters of Royal Gorge. Plus, it's home to the state's second-largest city, Colorado Springs, and the historic Santa Fe Trail.

p299

Southeast Colorado & the San Luis Valley
p299

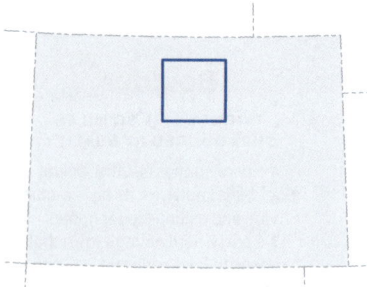

Rocky Mountain National Park (p146)

ITINERARIES

Big Cities & the Northern Rockies

Allow: 7 days   **Distance**: 170 miles

Denver and Boulder have genuine city appeal – museums, pro sports, nightlife – plus easy access to Rocky Mountain adventures. Start with Denver and Boulder, then prepare for mountain peaks, alpine lakes and abundant wildlife in and around iconic Rocky Mountain National Park.

❶ DENVER ⏱ 1½ DAYS

Start in **Denver** (p52), walking its neighborhoods, and taking in the museums, a traveling Broadway show or a Rockies game. (Or all three!) Great food can be had in pretty much every corner of town, though for nightlife, head to RiNo. Before leaving, take in local life at one of the city's parks or drive to Red Rocks to walk among the dramatic red sandstone formations. 🚗 *35 minutes*

❷ BOULDER ⏱ HALF-DAY

After lunch, head north to the heart of downtown **Boulder** (p100) to wander along pedestrian-only Pearl St Mall, to shop and watch the ever-present street performers. Or instead, see what's on at historic Colorado Chautauqua – a guided walk, a concert, a talk – or just DIY it with a hike on one of the myriad trails there, many with gorgeous views of Boulder's quintessential Flatirons. 🚗 *25 minutes*

❸ PEAK TO PEAK HIGHWAY ⏱ 1 DAY

Bright and early, take the gorgeous **Peak to Peak Highway** (p162) to Rocky Mountain National Park; it takes you through the forested Indian Peak Wilderness and southern sections of the park. Stop along the way in the hippie town of Nederland, hike the wilderness around Brainard Lake or take in the waterfalls of Wild Basin. Pick up provisions in Estes Park. 🚗 *1 hour*

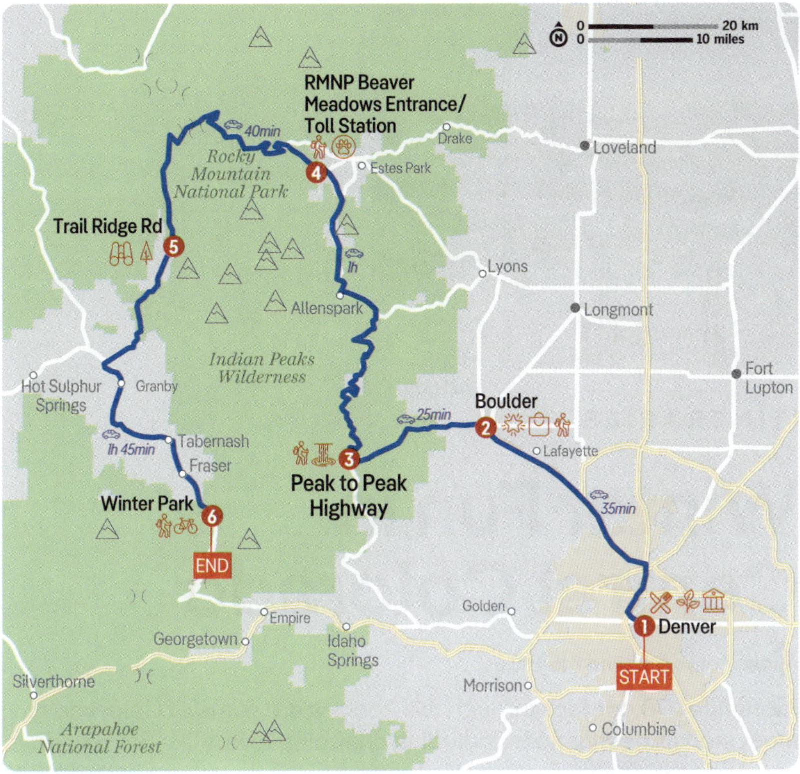
0 20 km
0 10 miles
RMNP Beaver Meadows Entrance/ Toll Station
Drake
Loveland
40min
Rocky Mountain National Park
Estes Park
4
Trail Ridge Rd
5
1h
Lyons
Allenspark
Longmont
Indian Peaks Wilderness
Fort Lupton
Hot Sulphur Springs
Granby
Boulder
25min
2
Lafayette
1h 45min
Tabernash
Fraser
3
Peak to Peak Highway
35min
Winter Park
6
END
Golden
Empire
1 Denver
Georgetown
Idaho Springs
START
Silverthorne
Morrison
Arapahoe National Forest
Columbine

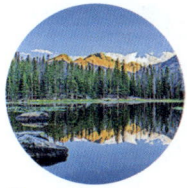

4

ROCKY MOUNTAIN NATIONAL PARK 2½ DAYS

Spend the next few days soaking in the majestic **Rocky Mountain National Park** (p146). A 415-sq-mile giant with granite peaks, shimmering alpine lakes and myriad opportunities to see wildlife. There are hiking trails of all lengths and for all levels. In the backcountry, hundreds of thousands of acres of wilderness await. *40 minutes*

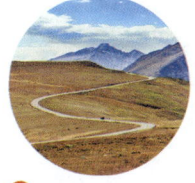

5

TRAIL RIDGE ROAD HALF-DAY

Leave the park along **Trail Ridge Road** (p151), the highest continuously paved road in the US, climbing to a high point of 12,183ft. The drive offers sweeping mountain vistas; numerous turnoffs allow visitors to step out of their cars to take in the magnificent views or explore tundra trails spotted with wildflowers and whistling marmots. *1¾ hours*

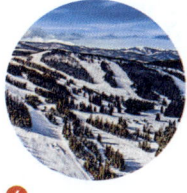

6

WINTER PARK 1 DAY

Spend your last day in **Winter Park** (p192), a favorite hiking and biking destination. Rent a bike in town and take your pick of singletrack trails, from mellow to technical, or check out the Trestle Bike Park at the local ski resort. For organized activities, the posh Devil's Thumb Ranch or family-friendly Snow Mountain Ranch offer horseback riding, fly-fishing, ziplining and much more.

FROM LEFT: SEAN XU/SHUTTERSTOCK, PIER-PHILIPPE CHEVIGNY/SHUTTERSTOCK, JACOB BOOMSMA/SHUTTERSTOCK

MARGARET.WIKTOR/SHUTTERSTOCK

Vail (p207)

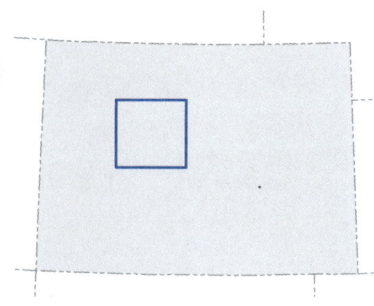

ITINERARIES

Winter Fun in Central Colorado

Allow: 7 days **Distance**: 154 miles

Along the I-70 corridor through the Rockies are some of Colorado's most storied destinations, including charming towns like Breckenridge and Aspen plus world-class ski resorts.

1 BRECKENRIDGE ⏱ 2 DAYS

Begin in **Breckenridge** (p196), enjoying the views from the gondola to Peak 7. Spend the day downhill skiing or boarding, or head to the Nordic Center for cross-country skiing. The next day, hit the trails mushing a team of huskies through the Swan River Valley. Time your visit to coincide with Breck's Viking-inspired Ullr Fest or Snow Sculpture Championship. 🚗 *20 minutes*

2 KEYSTONE ⏱ HALF-DAY

Head to **Keystone Resort** (p205), skipping the slopes and straight-shotting to its namesake lake, transformed into a 5-acre ice rink; ice-skate rentals including helmets (as well as hockey sticks and pucks) are available at the Keystone Adventure Center. If you're traveling with little ones, check out the world's largest snow fort, with loads of tunnels, caves, slippery slides and even a tubing hill. 🚗 *25 minutes*

3 COPPER MOUNTAIN ⏱ 1 DAY

Stop at local fave **Copper Mountain** (p204), a world-class mountain with a down-home vibe. Spend the day on the slopes or terrain parks. Consider stopping in Woodward Barn, the US Ski Team's training center, to practice on trampolines and foam pits first! 🚗 *25 minutes*

🚙 *Detour: Learn about the Old West in Frisco's Historic Park (p202) with fascinating museum exhibits and several original structures.*

FROM LEFT: SEAN PAVONE/SHUTTERSTOCK, PENNI L. LEVINE/SHUTTERSTOCK, RODCLEMENTPHOTOGRAPHY/SHUTTERSTOCK

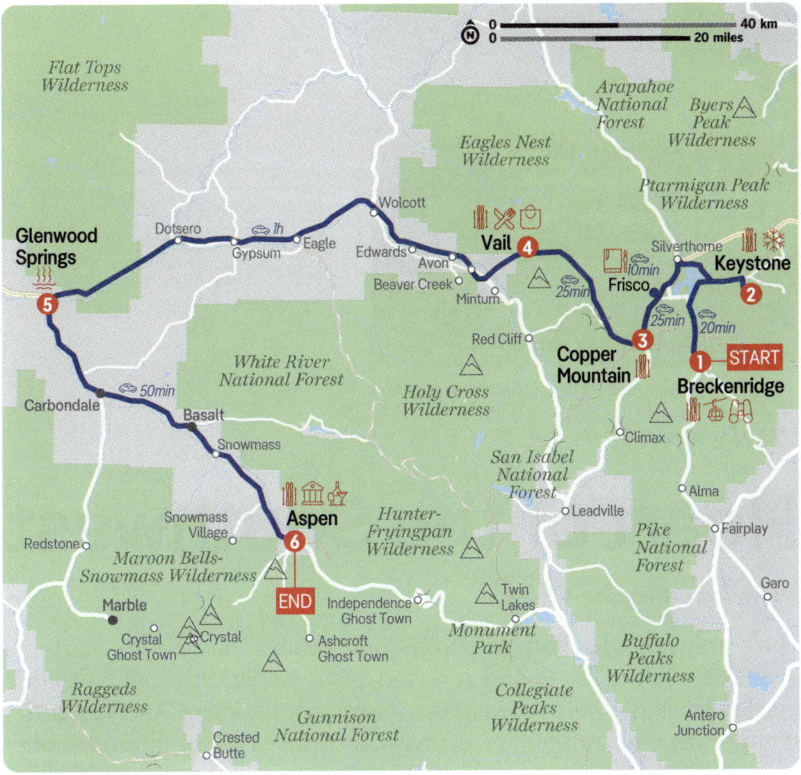

The map shows the route with numbered stops:

- Glenwood Springs **5**
- Flat Tops Wilderness
- Dotsero
- Gypsum
- Eagle
- Edwards
- Avon
- Beaver Creek
- Minturn
- Wolcott
- Vail **4** · 25min
- Eagles Nest Wilderness
- Arapahoe National Forest
- Byers Peak Wilderness
- Ptarmigan Peak Wilderness
- Silverthorne
- Keystone **2**
- Frisco · 10min
- 25min · 20min
- Copper Mountain **3**
- Breckenridge **1** START
- Red Cliff
- White River National Forest
- Holy Cross Wilderness
- Climax
- Carbondale · 50min
- Basalt
- Snowmass
- Snowmass Village
- Redstone
- Maroon Bells-Snowmass Wilderness
- Marble
- Crystal Ghost Town
- Crystal
- Aspen **6**
- END
- Independence Ghost Town
- Ashcroft Ghost Town
- Hunter-Fryingpan Wilderness
- San Isabel National Forest
- Leadville
- Alma
- Fairplay
- Pike National Forest
- Garo
- Twin Lakes
- Monument Park
- Buffalo Peaks Wilderness
- Collegiate Peaks Wilderness
- Antero Junction
- Raggeds Wilderness
- Crested Butte
- Gunnison National Forest

0   40 km
0   20 miles

4

VAIL ⏱1 DAY

If you only ski once, make it **Vail** (p207), a mammoth mountain with second-to-none slopes. For some outdoorsy alternatives, take your pick at this glitzy resort: ice-skating, snowshoeing, snowmobiling, even sleigh rides. When the sun sets, mountainside glam awaits in Vail's Bavarian-style village with fine dining, mountain-chic bars and designer boutiques. 🚗 1 hour

5

GLENWOOD SPRINGS ⏱HALF-DAY

Soak in the thermal waters of **Glenwood Springs** (p230). Choose from the family-friendly Glenwood Hot Springs Resort, home to the world's largest hot springs pool, or the understated and soothing pools at Iron Mountain Hot Springs. Open year-round, water temperatures range from 90°F to 108°F (32–42°C), keeping you toasty despite the snow. 🚗 50 minutes

6

ASPEN ⏱2 DAYS

Take a day to enjoy **Aspen** (p218) by strolling through the historic downtown, stopping in museums or people-watching at its farm-to-table cafes. Afterwards, choose between Aspen's world-class slopes (it is a ski town after all), a guided snowshoeing trip with an ACES naturalist or a cross-country ski trip to the iconic Maroon Bells Lake. Be sure to make time for après (fur blankets included).

JEREMY JANUS/SHUTTERSTOCK

Colorado National Monument (p290)

ITINERARIES

Heart of the Southwest

Allow: 7 days **Distance**: 305 miles

The southwest of Colorado is truly spectacular. The itinerary starts in pleasantly low-key Grand Junction, but gets big fast: soaring cliffs, gorgeous hikes, ancient dwellings, relaxing hot springs. And you can pamper yourself in Telluride, an eye-candy town if ever there was one, deep in the San Juan mountains.

❶ GRAND JUNCTION ⏱1 DAY

Base yourself in **Grand Junction** (p285), spending the morning in the dramatic red-rock landscape of Colorado National Monument; stop at overlooks along Rim Rd or take short hikes deeper into the park. In the afternoon, go wine tasting in Palisade or check out its lavender and alpaca farms. Back in Grand Junction, have dinner on Main St, enjoying the public art all around.
🚗 1½ hours

❷ BLACK CANYON OF THE GUNNISON NATIONAL PARK ⏱1 DAY

Start early for **Black Canyon of the Gunnison National Park** (p279), its sheer 2000ft cliff walls a jaw-dropping sight. Take in the views at 11 spectacular overlooks along the edge of the canyon, some reached via short trails off the park's South Rim Rd. 🚗 1½ hours
🔎 *Detour: Make time for the Ute Indian Museum in Montrose.*

❸ TELLURIDE ⏱2 DAYS

Spend a couple of glorious days in the box canyon town of **Telluride** (p272), where you can splurge on a luxe hotel or camp right in town. Take your pick of breathtaking hikes surrounded by 13,000ft peaks or push your comfort zone on the via ferrata. Post-adventure, good food and drink abound. Time your visit for festival season...just book your tix and accommodations early!
🚗 1 hour

FROM LEFT: JEREMY JANUS/SHUTTERSTOCK, GALYNA ANDRUSHKO/SHUTTERSTOCK, MELISSAMN/SHUTTERSTOCK

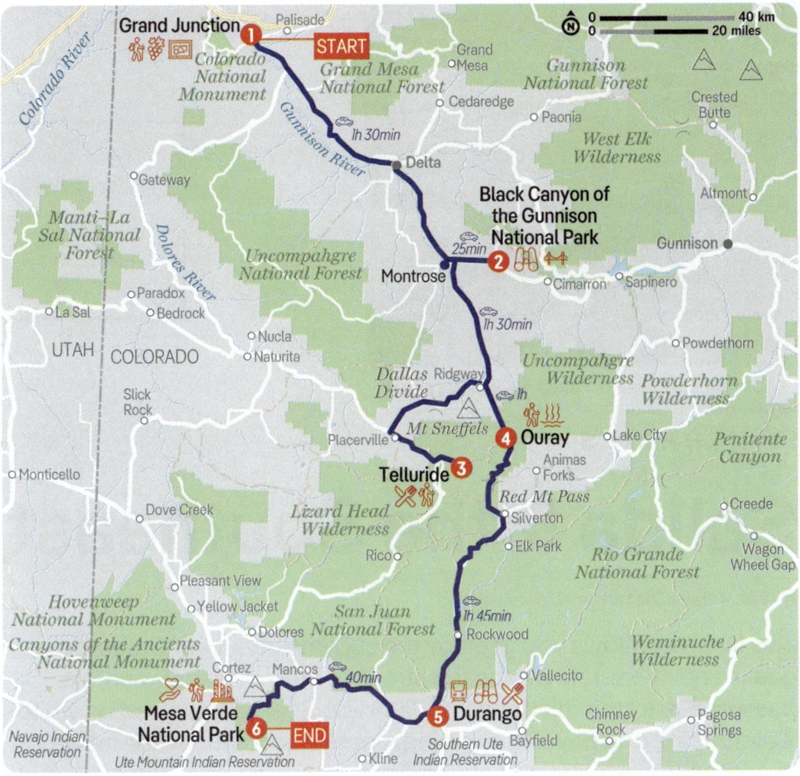

The map:

Grand Junction ① START
Palisade
Colorado River
Colorado National Monument
Grand Mesa
Grand Mesa National Forest
Cedaredge
Paonia
Gunnison National Forest
West Elk Wilderness
Crested Butte
1h 30min
Delta
Gunnison River
Gateway
Altmont
Manti-La Sal National Forest
Dolores River
Uncompahgre National Forest
Montrose
Black Canyon of the Gunnison National Park ②
25min
Gunnison
Cimarron
Sapinero
Powderhorn
1h 30min
UTAH COLORADO
Paradox
Bedrock
La Sal
Nucla
Naturita
Dallas Divide
Ridgway
Uncompahgre Wilderness
Powderhorn Wilderness
Slick Rock
1h
Mt Sneffels
Ouray ④
Lake City
Penitente Canyon
Monticello
Placerville
Telluride ③
Animas Forks
Red Mt Pass
Silverton
Creede
Dove Creek
Lizard Head Wilderness
Rico
Elk Park
Rio Grande National Forest
Wagon Wheel Gap
Pleasant View
Yellow Jacket
San Juan National Forest
1h 45min
Rockwood
Weminuche Wilderness
Hovenweep National Monument
Dolores
Vallecito
Canyons of the Ancients National Monument
Cortez
Mancos
40min
Durango ⑤
Chimney Rock
Pagosa Springs
Mesa Verde National Park ⑥ END
Kline
Bayfield
Navajo Indian Reservation
Ute Mountain Indian Reservation
Southern Ute Indian Reservation

0 40 km
0 20 miles

④ OURAY ⏱ 1 DAY

Hike the alpine wonderland of **Ouray** (p266) – the 6-mile Perimeter Trail loop has several access points, or take Silvershield Trail to the world's longest-known dinosaur trackway. Afterwards, soak in one of the town's hot springs; the historic water park has lots of pools or try Wiesbaden vapor cave instead. Head out on the Million Dollar Hwy, a sinuous and steep journey over three mountain passes. 🚗 1¾ hours

⑤ DURANGO & SILVERTON ⏱ 1 DAY

Catch the **Durango & Silverton Narrow Gauge Railroad** (p261), a day of gorgeous vista after gorgeous vista on a 19th-century steam locomotive that cuts through the San Juan wilderness to the tiny town of **Silverton** (p276); stroll the historic streets, stopping at the excellent Mining Heritage Center Museum. Enjoy a good dinner and brews in Durango's historic downtown corridor. 🚗 40 minutes

⑥ MESA VERDE NATIONAL PARK ⏱ 1 DAY

Plan on a full day exploring the magnificent **Mesa Verde National Park** (p254), the best-preserved Native American archaeological site in the US and one-time home of the Ancestral Puebloans. Brimming with stunning cliff dwellings, surface sites and trails, the best way to experience it is via a ranger-led tour or two. Book online and well in advance to guarantee a spot.

31

FROM LEFT: JACOB BOOMSMA/SHUTTERSTOCK, PATRICK E PLANER/SHUTTERSTOCK, DOMINIC GENTILCORE PHD/SHUTTERSTOCK

ANDRIY BLOKHIN/SHUTTERSTOCK

Great Sand Dunes (p313)

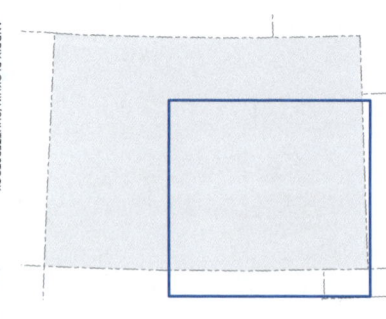

ITINERARIES

Salida & the Southeast

Allow: 4 days **Distance**: 475 miles

This itinerary allows you to enjoy the sublime beauty of Colorado's peaks and rivers, and avoids the stress of driving major mountain passes. You'll start in appealing Colorado Springs, followed by white-water rafting one day and climbing massive sand dunes the next. End by retracing the historic Santa Fe Trail.

① COLORADO SPRINGS ⏱ 1 DAY

Spend your day in **Colorado Springs** (p304) museum-hopping, feeding giraffes at the zoo and touring the Olympic and Paralympic Training Center. Stroll through Garden of the Gods, a spectacular red-rock park; or head straight to Pikes Peak, a 14,000ft behemoth that you can summit by foot, car or cog railway. In January, make time for the Great Fruitcake Toss fest. 🚗 *2 hours*

② SALIDA ⏱ 1 DAY

Get up early for rafting in **Salida** (p236) on the Arkansas River, Colorado's best-known white water. Depending on the season and your comfort level, you can find everything from extreme rapids to chilled-out floats. If you have energy afterwards, explore the epic bike trails of S Mountain. In the evening, stroll through the pleasant redbrick downtown, filling up on elk brats and IPAs. 🚗 *1½ hours*

③ GREAT SAND DUNES NATIONAL PARK ⏱ 1 DAY

Prepare to be awe-stricken at the **Great Sand Dunes National Park** (p313), an undulating sea of sand bounded by jagged peaks and scrubby plains. Hike to the top of the tallest dune in North America (no easy task!), making your way down on wooden sleds. For a couple of months in spring, snowmelt creates Medano Creek – perfect for water play afterwards. 🚗 *2½ hours*

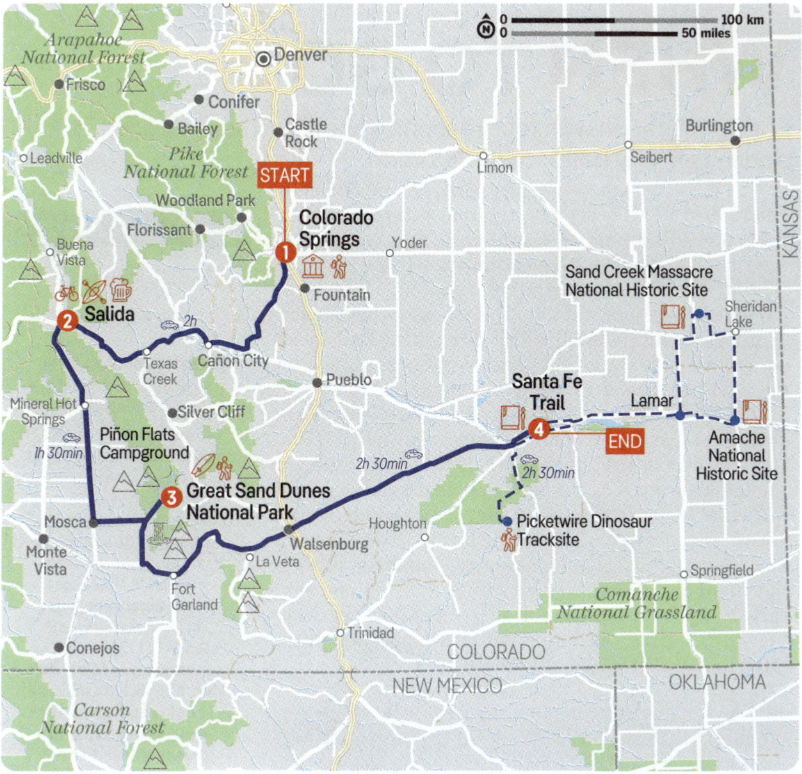

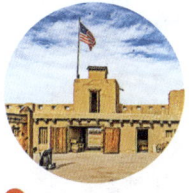

4

SANTA FE TRAIL 1 DAY

Spend the day driving the **Santa Fe Trail** (p331), making stops to learn about the Old West at places like the beautifully recreated Bent's Old Fort and Sand Creek Massacre National Historic Site. Make time for a visit to Amache National Historical Site, a WWII Japanese internment camp.

Detour: *If time permits, visit the Picketwire Dinosaur Tracksite to see over 1300 dino tracks.*

KIT LEONG/SHUTTERSTOCK

Garden of the Gods (p308)

ZACK FRANK/SHUTTERSTOCK

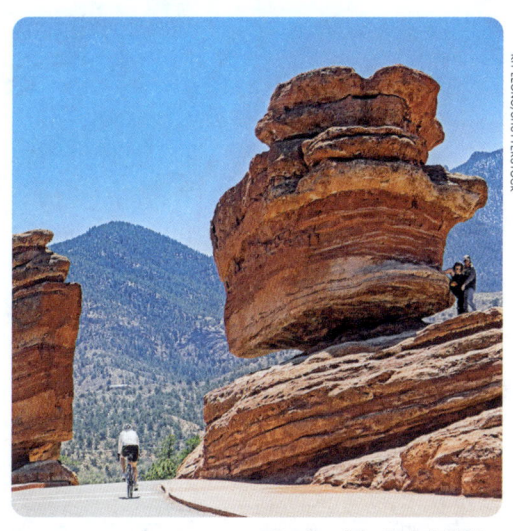

WHEN TO GO

For a destination with four seasons, year-round sun included, it doesn't get any better than Colorado.

Colorado is a four-season destination with endless sunshine and low humidity. Elevation drives much of the weather here, and with destinations from 3315ft to 14,433ft, there's lots of variation.

Winter brings snow throughout Colorado. The temperatures are relatively mild, which lures skiers and shredders to the mountains. At lower elevations, snow often melts within a day, even in Denver, which is a mile high. Spring can be unpredictable, bringing wildflowers and green landscapes, but sometimes snowstorms as late as May. The fluctuation brings mud at almost every elevation.

Summer means long sunny days, high daytime temperatures and temperate evenings; dramatic thunderstorms are afternoon hallmarks and hailstorms occasionally follow, especially along the Front Range. Autumn is all about the changing leaves, typically from mid-September to early November. And like spring, temperatures can fluctuate dramatically, bringing the occasional snowstorm, often followed by muddy conditions.

⌖ I LIVE HERE

WINTER FREEDOM

Paisley Johnson, DNP, ANP at Denver Health Cardiology

Growing up in Boulder, skiing Eldora was a social scene. Saturdays my friends and I would take a city bus packed with other middle schoolers through the winding canyon to the resort. We'd mingle and move around the bus, and step off at the base. The mountain was filled with kids, our parents at home. The ski conditions were always questionable – bluebird days to snow blasting in your face – but skiing didn't feel like weather. It felt like independence.

POWDER

Thank the dry air and cold temperatures for Colorado's legendary powder. Low water content makes for large airy snowflakes, while cold temperatures keep them from collapsing and melting together. The result is a blanket of snow that's light as a feather.

JAKOB HELBIG/GETTY IMAGES

Aspen (p218)

Weather through the Year

    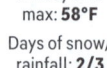

JANUARY	FEBRUARY	MARCH	APRIL	MAY	JUNE
Av. daytime max: **49°F**	Av. daytime max: **49°F**	Av. daytime max: **58°F**	Av. daytime max: **65°F**	Av. daytime max: **73°F**	Av. daytime max: **86°F**
Days of snowfall: **6**	Days of snowfall: **7**	Days of snow/rainfall: **2/3**	Days of snow/rainfall: **2/5**	Days of rainfall: **8**	Days of rainfall: **4**

WALKING ON SUNSHINE

Colorado boasts 300 days of sunshine each year, though some quibble with whether that figure should include partly cloudy days. (It does.) Whichever way you measure it, count on seeing blue skies and sun most days, even if it's between puffy white clouds.

Big Colorado Festivals

Denver's PrideFest (p74) is one of the largest LGBTIQ+ celebrations in the country, a two-day event when rainbow revelry, free performances and joyful parades fill the city streets and parks. ☀ **June**

The revered **Colorado Shakespeare Festival** (p122) brings the Bard's works to CU Boulder's Mary Rippon Outdoor Theatre on summer nights, rain or shine. Come early for pre-show talks with the artistic director. ☀ **June–August**

The **Colorado State Fair and Rodeo** (coloradostatefair. com), held since 1872, is one of the state's biggest events, a carnival combined with all sorts of competitions, concerts, parades and rodeo events. ☀ **August**

Telluride Film Festival (p274) showcases indie films in venues all around its box canyon community, transforming the tiny mountain town into a cinephile paradise, red carpet included. ☀ **September**

Quirky Colorado Festivals

Durango's Snowdown (p262) is a zany festival with different annual themes, where costumes and eccentric events (ski kickball, anyone?) coax people onto the city's wintery streets. ❄ **February**

Fabulously macabre, **Frozen Dead Guy Days** (p149) in Estes Park celebrates a cryogenically frozen Norwegian awaiting his thaw in a shed. Come for the coffin races and polar plunge but stay for the Royal Blue Ball, a costume party and concert. ❄ **March**

Celebrating a creepy-crawling migration, La Junta's **Tarantula Fest** (p331) combines lively parades, spider costumes and hairy leg contests with tours to check out these furry arachnids crossing Comanche National Grassland. ☀ **September**

Breckenridge's raucous **Ullr Fest** (p200) celebrates the Norwegian snow god, Ullr. Expect polar plunges and raging bonfires plus an annual attempt to break the world record for longest shotski. Horned Viking helmets encouraged. ❄ **December**

HAIL ALLEY

Colorado's Front Range lies in the heart of 'Hail Alley,' where the nation's highest number of hailstorms occur. Take cover if one hits! In 2017 a storm of baseball-sized hail hit metro Denver, causing a record-breaking $2 billion in damages in just minutes.

☀	☀	☀	☁	🌧	❄
JULY	**AUGUST**	**SEPTEMBER**	**OCTOBER**	**NOVEMBER**	**DECEMBER**
Av. daytime max: **92°F**	Av. daytime max: **90°F**	Av. daytime max: **82°F**	Av. daytime max: **68°F**	Av. daytime max: **57°F**	Av. daytime max: **47°F**
Days of rainfall: **6**	Days of rainfall: **4**	Days of rainfall: **4**	Days of snow/rainfall: **1/4**	Days of snow/rainfall: **2/2**	Days of snow/rainfall: **4/3**

FROM LEFT: DON MAMMOSER/SHUTTERSTOCK, AJ PICS/ALAMY STOCK PHOTO

Colorado National Monument (p290)

GET PREPARED FOR COLORADO

Useful things to load in your bag, your ears and your brain.

Clothes

Jeans and puffer jackets Casual dress rules in Colorado – jeans and puffy jackets are the unofficial state uniform. In fact, pretty much the only place jeans don't work are on the slopes.

Billed hats The sun is no joke here, and the elevation makes it that much stronger. Wear a billed hat, especially if you'll be outdoors for an extended period.

Boots If you'll be hiking, bring good, broken-in hiking boots. (If they're brand new, bring moleskin padding in case you get blisters.) Likewise, if you'll be here in winter, bring warm, waterproof boots.

Layers Colorado weather can change quickly year-round, and summer evenings

Manners

Use tact when talking politics. Despite voting blue in recent presidential elections, opinions run the gamut in Colorado.

Haggling isn't common. If you're at a farmers market, though, low-key and polite bargaining is accepted.

Don't compare Colorado to the Midwest. Coloradans identify with the West, the mountains and a degree of sophistication they perceive as lacking in the Midwest.

can be chilly too, especially in the mountains. Bring layers! A waterproof shell, fleece and warm hat are a good idea any time of the year.

📖 READ

Corina and Sabrina (Kali Fajardo-Anstine; 2019) Collection of short stories about Latinas of Indigenous descent living in Denver.

Abandon (Blake Crouch; 2009) Time travel thriller set in a fictional Colorado ghost town, integrating survival and the Old West.

House of Rain (Craig Childs; 2007) Travelogue about the Ancestral Puebloans, with adventure and scholarly research baked in.

Plainsong (Kent Haruf; 1999) Heartstrong tale about a Colorado farming community on the eastern plains.

Words

Après-ski (*ah*-pray ski) A French term meaning 'after-skiing,' a happy hour when people meet up to drink and eat after a day on the slopes.

Backcountry Any remote mountain area, away from roads, resorts, campgrounds or other development. It's used in conjunction with outdoors activities (eg backcountry skiing or hiking).

Colorado Cologne Refers to the skunky smell of marijuana.

Colorado Kool-Aid A can of Coors beer.

Dispensary A business where marijuana and other cannabis products are sold. In Colorado, there are recreational and medicinal-only (prescriptions required) dispensaries plus hybrids.

420 (four twenty) refers to marijuana or its use. You'll see '420-friendly' at hotels that allow pot smoking.

Fourteener (14er) A mountain that exceeds 14,000ft. Depending on who you ask, Colorado has either 53 or 58 fourteeners.

Freshies Coveted ski- or snowboarding runs through fresh untouched powder, also called 'first tracks.'

Front Range The corridor of cities that lie along the eastern edge of the Rockies, from Fort Collins to Trinidad.

Hill Shorthand for a ski mountain (eg 'A-Basin may be small but it's a great hill.')

LBS Shorthand for 'local bike shop.'

Peak Bagger Someone who climbs mountains to cross them off a bucket list, often with a focus on epic climbs.

Western Slope The region west of the Continental Divide, generally central and southwest Colorado.

Yard Sale A wipeout when a skier loses their skies and poles.

🎬 WATCH

The Hateful Eight (pictured; Quentin Tarantino; 2015) Wild West action movie filmed near Telluride.

Bowling for Columbine (Michael Moore; 2002) Documentary examining gun proliferation and the mass shooting at Columbine High School in Littleton.

South Park (Trey Parker, Matt Stone and Eric Stough; 1997–present) Animated TV satire set in a fictional Colorado town.

The Shining (Stanley Kubrick; 1980) Psychological horror film inspired by the Stanley Hotel in Estes Park.

Snowball Express (Norman Tokar; 1972) Comedy about a family fixing up a dilapidated hotel in the Colorado Rockies.

🎧 LISTEN

Colorado Matters (Colorado Public Radio; 2001–present) Six-day-a-week radio program and podcast focused on the state's people and issues.

City Cast Denver (Bree Davis; 2021–present) Daily podcast covering everything Denver, from culture to politics.

South of Here (Nathaniel Rateliff and the Night Sweats; 2024) Latest album by popular Denver-based Americana band.

Rocky Mountain High (John Denver; 1972) Hit folk rock album; its title track is one of Colorado's official state songs.

ERIKA NUSSER/ALAMY STOCK PHOTO

Colorado-style pizza

THE **FOOD** SCENE

Fresh, locally grown food combined with a culture that caters to specialized preferences make Colorado a delicious place to eat.

A one-time meat and potatoes state, Colorado's food scene has bloomed into a celebration of the state's natural bounty. From farm-to-table fare to vegan options and everything in between, there's something for just about everyone to enjoy. Fresh produce, free-range meats and fish from the state's mountain rivers form the backbone of the local cuisine; meals are delicious, healthy and sustainable. Southwestern flavors and traditional Mexican dishes are threaded through the cuisine. Colorado's thriving craft beer and distillery industries also play a major role, with most restaurants and food halls offering extensive drink menus or, at least, a couple of local brews on tap. Colorado is also home to a thriving farmers market scene, with plenty of opportuni-

ties to sample locally grown foods. If you're a wine lover, the state's Western Slope is ground zero for wineries and vineyards. Quickly growing into a foodie's paradise, Colorado will indulge your senses and invite you to explore the state through its flavors.

Farm-to-Table Dining

Colorado takes great pride in sustainable dining, and with close to 40,000 farms and ranches in the state, there are plenty of opportunities to buy locally grown and sourced foods. There are terrific farmers markets found around the state, most bustling from May to October with rows of vendors selling fresh fruits and vegetables plus ethically produced meat like lamb and bison. The explosion of gourmet

Best Colorado Dishes

GREEN CHILE
Roasted chili sauce, often with pork, poured over Mexican dishes.

ROCKY MOUNTAIN OYSTERS
Bull testicles, breaded and deep fried, served with dipping sauce.

ELK BRATS
Gourmet sausages, often mixed with cheddar and jalapeño.

food halls, too, showcase the state's offerings with aspiring chefs testing their recipes and new concepts. And in towns like Denver, Boulder, Aspen, Telluride and Vail, auteur restaurants increasingly feature flavorful local ingredients as the new gold. Go ahead, treat your taste buds!

Alt Eating

With the lowest rate of obesity of any state, Coloradans know how to eat. They're a discerning crowd, which can make your wait in a deli line a game of patience. But, if you have a special diet or are simply a picky eater, you'll feel at home in Colorado. No one will bat an eye at any food allergies or restrictions. And it's de rigueur to find gluten-free, vegan and vegetarian items on menus in urban and tourist areas – even at local steakhouses. Many restaurants also nod to the latest food fads, so keto followers and fans of kombucha will do just fine.

Happy-Hour Dining

Coloradans take happy hour seriously and restaurants comply by competing fiercely and offering incredible deals on both food and drink. Nowhere is this more apparent than in Colorado's fine-dining establishments, which may be out of reach for many

during dinner hour, but offer incredible small-plate deals during happy hour that are often cheaper than pizzerias – and far more delectable. In general, happy-hour menus are offered in pubs and restaurants from 4pm to 6pm. Go early to get a table. Weekend deals are rare, though some spots offer late-night happy hours from 10pm until closing time during the week.

MICHAEL BERLFEIN/SHUTTERSTOCK

FOOD & DRINK FESTS

Great American Beer Festival (p64) The nation's largest beer celebration brings craft beer fans to Denver to taste almost 9500 brews, competing in 109 different categories.

Food & Wine Classic (*classic.foodandwine. com*) An epic Aspen fest, filled with tastings, cooking demonstrations and panels with celebrity chefs and beverage connoisseurs.

Taste of Colorado (*atasteofcolorado.com*) Local food vendors fill Denver's Civic Center Park at this giant event (pictured), which also features live music and artisan booths.

Pueblo Chile & Frijoles Festival (*pueblochilefestival.com*) Live performances, a vibrant farmers market and roasted green chiles are hallmarks of this homegrown festival. Don't miss the chihuahua parade!

Colorado Mountain Wine Fest (*coloradowinefest.com*) Colorado's premier wine festival featuring 50+ local wineries, unlimited tastings, educational workshops and tours of Palisade vineyards.

ALEXANDRALAW1977/SHUTTERSTOCK

Colorado lamb chops

DENVER OMELET	COLORADO-STYLE PIZZA	COLORADO LAMB	GRILLED TROUT	BISON BURGERS
Egg dish stuffed with bell peppers, onions, ham and cheese.	Topping-heavy pizza with a thick, braided crust made with honey.	Known for its rich flavor, every cut is a delicacy.	Quintessential Colorado dish; the rainbow trout is often locally caught.	Leaner than beef burgers, though with similar taste.

Local Specialties

Street Food

Breakfast burritos Flour tortillas stuffed with scrambled eggs, country-style potatoes, bacon or chorizo, cheese and, often, green chile.

Street tacos Corn tortillas filled with sizzling meats, often carne asada (grilled steak), al pastor (rotisserie-style pork) or carnitas (braised pork). Topped with onions, cilantro and salsa.

Sliders Bite-sized beef or bison patties on mini buns, often topped with sauces like green chile aioli or chipotle mayo.

Gyros Pita sandwiches stuffed with thinly sliced rotisserie lamb, chicken or beef, topped with tomato, onion and tzatziki (yogurt sauce made with cucumber and garlic).

Churros Strips of fried dough, dusted with sugar, cinnamon or both. Typically paired with hot cocoa.

Favorite Hiking Treats

Homemade trail mix Combo of nuts, seeds, dried fruit and sometimes chocolate chunks, prepped from bulk food.

ANDY CROSS/THE DENVER POST/GETTY IMAGES

Breakfast burritos

Jerky Dried and flavored meat, typically beef, bison or turkey. Lightweight and easy to pack.

Dried fruit Dehydrated apricots, mangos or apples providing natural sugars and quick energy.

Organic energy bars Grab-and-go bars with loads of protein and minimal processing.

Seaweed snacks Crunchy and salty treat, often in thin sheets or strips.

Electrolyte packets Single serve powder added to water bottles to replenish lost minerals and decrease risk of dehydration.

MEALS OF A LIFETIME

Beckon (p88) Michelin-star restaurant in Denver with an evolving menu inspired by Scandinavian flavors and local ingredients.

Tennessee Pass Cookhouse (p216) Snowshoe, ski or hitch a snowmobile to this yurt turned gourmet restaurant in the forest near Leadville.

Bosq (p223) Aspen's only Michelin-starred restaurant offers a sumptuous and artful tasting menu integrating global flavors with Rocky Mountain flair.

James Ranch Grill (p262) Authentic farm-to-table dining on a working family ranch outside Durango; dishes are almost entirely sourced on-site.

Friar's Fork (p317) James Beard–semifinalist serving indulgent Italian fare in a repurposed adobe church. Enjoy cocktails in the Sanctuary beforehand.

THE YEAR IN FOOD

SPRING

Spring is marked by the appearance of leafy greens like spinach, arugula and lettuce. Asparagus, radishes and turnips are in season too. Though available year-round, Colorado lamb is especially popular for Easter and Passover meals.

SUMMER

Farmers markets are rife with local produce: Palisade peaches and Olathe corn, Pueblo green chiles and Rocky Ford cantaloupe plus zucchini, tomatoes and cucumbers from the Arkansas Valley. Fresh rainbow trout is a go-to.

AUTUMN

As fall arrives, expect heartier produce like pumpkins, squash, broccoli, brussels sprouts and beets. Apples and pears figure big in pies and cider. Farm-raised venison and elk also appear on menus.

WINTER

Winter brings a shift to root vegetables like potatoes, carrots and onions plus winter greens like kale and Swiss chard. Locally raised beef and bison are often the base of hearty dishes and stews.

FROM LEFT: VVOE/SHUTTERSTOCK, SERHII KHRYSTENKO/SHUTTERSTOCK, STUDIO BARCELONA/SHUTTERSTOCK, SERHII KHRYSTENKO/SHUTTERSTOCK

HOW TO...

Choose a Brewery

With over 400 breweries across the state, there's no doubt that Colorado is a craft beer haven. Whether you're a beer connoisseur or just enjoy the occasional pint, there's pretty much something for everyone. So what'll it be? A cozy mountain taproom or urban beer garden, a neighborhood watering hole or a lively brewery with food trucks? Here are some tips to help you choose the perfect spot.

Style

First, identify what you like to drink. While most breweries stock a range of beer styles, many specialize in particular brews. Perhaps you're in the mood for a bitter, hoppy IPA (a Colorado favorite) or a light, crisp lager. Or maybe you'd prefer a dark, full-bodied stout. Or is it a night for a sour beer or an experimental brew flavored with an unusual ingredient, say, jalapeño?

Whatever your preference, start by looking for breweries near you (or on the road!) that offer what you like to drink.

For tips on how (and what) to order, see p343.

Vibe

Next, consider the environment you'd like. Are you looking for a bustling spot with live music and trivia night or do you want a laid-back evening by a fire pit? Are mountain views or a cityscape important to you? Also, If you're traveling with kids or pets, make sure the brewery can accommodate them (often, they can!). Brewery websites have this info, so it's relatively easy to find out in advance.

Eats

Finally, decide whether you need a meal with your suds. Sure, you'll find light snacks in every Colorado taproom (hello, salty popcorn) but options for real meals vary dramatically. Food trucks are the most common, each night a different vendor pulling up to the brewery. Nightly options can range from Texas BBQ to Korean dumplings, which folks are welcome to bring into the taproom. Many breweries also have in-house kitchens, with menus that pair with their beers. And a handful of taprooms allow you to bring in food from nearby restaurants too.

RESOURCES

Honing in on a brewery often involves talking to locals and concierges plus checking out brewery websites. Here are some other avenues to consider.
Untappd An app allowing users to discover nearby breweries, real-time tap lists and daily events. Specific beers are rated too, so you can see what's popular in town.
Awards and Accolades The prestigious Great American Beer Festival (p64) and World Beer Cup (*worldbeercup.org*) post breweries and beers that have won awards. Many Colorado breweries are represented – see if there's one nearby!
Colorado Brewers Guild The CBG's website (*coloradobeer.org*) is a valuable tool for searching breweries by location and beer style.

41

FROM LEFT: MIRALEX/GETTY IMAGES, SEAN XU/SHUTTERSTOCK

Skier, Vail (p207)

THE OUTDOORS

Colorado's outdoors reign supreme and with so many options – terrain, elevation, season, sport – there's no doubt it was made for play.

Winter, spring, summer or fall, the Colorado outdoors will blow your mind. Spanning diverse geographic zones from the Great Plains to the Rocky Mountains to the desert canyons of the Colorado Plateau, there are boundless opportunities for outdoor adventure. It doesn't hurt that Colorado is home to four national parks, 11 national forests, 42 state parks and more…all totaling millions of acres of public lands. Pick your adventure – whether you're an experienced outdoor enthusiast or just starting out, you're sure to enjoy it!

Hiking

Colorado's far-reaching and diverse trail system beckons hikers of all levels and offers year-round access to the state's impossibly beautiful landscapes. Imagine trekking through the majestic Rocky Mountains surrounded by snowy peaks, shimmering alpine lakes and dense forests. Or the feeling of accomplishment as you summit a mountain, your heart pounding as you take in the panoramic views. Or the tranquility of hiking through meadows dotted in wildflowers or the quiet while walking through a red-rock canyon. Colorado's trails range from tidy loops through lovely landscapes to multiday backcountry routes that challenge even the most experienced trekkers. Every corner of the state has trails where you can immerse yourself in the natural beauty all around. So, grab your water bottle and some high energy snacks, lace up your hiking boots and prepare to take in Colorado.

Adventure Sports

ROCK CLIMBING
Join locals at Boulder's **Flatirons** (p117), one of the country's most extensive and varied rock climbing areas near a city.

ICE CLIMBING
Climb (or learn to climb) on 150 routes up frozen waterfalls at the world-class **Ouray Ice Park** (p268).

VIA FERRATA
Make your way, hand-over-hand, across a mountain face on Telluride's **via ferrata** (p274).

Skiing & Snowboarding

Colorado is one of the top destinations in the country for skiing and snowboarding. Known for its high-altitude peaks, blue skies and deep champagne powder, the conditions are ideal for both sports. From cruisers and tree runs to back bowls and terrain parks, this is one of the best and most varied places to ski and snowboard in the US. In fact, some of the world's best skiers and riders are from Colorado, or have lived and trained here, including Lindsey Vonn, Mikaela Shiffrin, Red Gerard and Shaun White. With over 30 resorts to choose from – including backcountry guid-ed skiing at Silverton and world-renowned Vail, Aspen and Breckenridge – there really is a mountain and ski town for every sort of vacationer. Most resorts and their respective ski towns also have robust activity offerings like snowshoeing, cross-country skiing, ice-skating, sledding and, of course, there's always après-ski.

Mountain Biking

The state's rugged terrain, diverse landscapes and endless trails offer something for all riders – from the rocky, technical trails in Fruita and Four Corners to the high-altitude singletrack in Crested Butte and Breckenridge. Many ski resorts also offer downhill riding with lift service, bermed-out mountain-bike trails and jumps included. In fact, mountain biking is so big that you can ride on dedicated bike paths from Glenwood Springs to Aspen, and from Vail to Breckenridge. Gondolas, buses and even Lake Dillon ferries are all outfitted to tote bikes. In cities like Denver, Boulder and Fort Collins, you'll find hundreds of miles of dedicated bike trails, plus a bike-friendly culture that includes shared bike programs, plenty of bike lanes and even the occasional cruiser ride. In Colorado, mountain biking is more than just exercise: it's a lifestyle.

Cyclist, Lakewood (p97)

SANDBOARDING
Sandboard down the tallest dunes in North America at **Great Sand Dunes National Park** (p313), an otherworldly sight.

RAFTING
Paddle the **Arkansas** (p238), with everything from mellow ripples in Bighorn Sheep Canyon to white water in the Royal Gorge.

SUPING
Stand-up paddle your way around the waters of **Blue Mesa Reservoir** (p282), Colorado's largest and most striking body of water.

FISHING
Cast for Colorado trout in the gold-medal waters surrounding Basalt, a true fly-fishing paradise in the **Roaring Fork Valley** (p233).

PETER AMEND/GETTY IMAGES

Rocky Mountain National Park (p146)

Camp

Camping in Colorado is an unforgettable way to experience the state's stunningly diverse natural beauty. With about 43% of the state designated as public land, there are lots of places and opportunities to sleep under the stars. Here are some planning tips.

Decide on a Camping Experience

Developed campgrounds A convenient option, these are tent sites with parking spots and amenities like fire pits, picnic tables, tent pads and, often, food storage lockers. There are public restrooms, from pit toilets to bathrooms with showers. Sites range in cost ($18 to $40 per night) and can get crowded.

Dispersed camping A more rugged experience, this means pitching your tent somewhere in a national forest or Bureau of Land Management (BLM) land. Typically, it's off a backroad so you've still got easy access to your vehicle. Plan on packing everything in and out; and burying your human waste appropriately (or in some areas, carrying it out!). Camping is free and often there are few or no people around.

Backcountry camping This is similar to dispersed camping but involves hiking deep into the wilderness, carrying all your gear and food. This is for campers who are in good physical condition and comfortable in remote locations.

Deal with the Red Tape

Developed campgrounds Make a reservation. Colorado's campgrounds fill up quickly, especially in summertime!

- National forests and parks: *recreation.gov*
- Colorado state parks: *cpw.state.co.us*
- Private campgrounds: *hipcamp.com*

Dispersed camping Public lands have designated dispersed camping areas. As you plan, look up the rules or call a ranger station to avoid getting fined or kicked out of your spot.

- National forests: *fs.usda.gov*
- BLM land: *blm.gov*

Backcountry camping Some areas require backcountry permits to prevent overcrowding and to protect the ecosystem. Check requirements, especially in popular destinations like Rocky Mountain National Park (p146).

Follow 'Leave No Trace' Principles

Once you're camping, be sure to:

- Store your food and scented items in bear-proof containers, food lockers or your car.
- Use designated fire rings or camping stoves for cooking.
- Extinguish fires completely at night and before leaving.
- Clean up your site, including packing out all trash and biodegradable waste.

And of course, have fun!

PACK SMART

Regardless of your camping spot, here are some must-haves.

Shelter & Bedding

- Tent suitable for potential high winds and rain
- Sleeping bag rated for the expected temperatures (note: nights can be cold, even in summer!)
- Insulated sleeping pad for comfort and warmth

Safety

- Headlamp or flashlight plus extra batteries
- First aid kit
- Multi-tool
- Hardcopy maps
- Hand sanitizer or soap

Food & Drink

- Water or water filtration system (even if a campground claims to have potable water)
- Easy-to-cook meals (eg oatmeal, pasta, freeze-dried food)
- Bear-proof container (especially for backcountry campers)
- Camping or lightweight cookware
- Matches or other fire starter

KYLE LEDEBOER/AURORA PHOTOS/GETTY IMAGES

Camping off the Million Dollar Highway (p271)

JEFFGOULDEN/GETTY IMAGES

Hiker, San Juan Mountains (p270)

TRIP PLANNER

COLORADO HIKING 101

Colorado hiking is an embarrassment of riches: over 22 million acres of gorgeous valleys, rugged peaks and high desert mesas, all connected by a vast network of well-maintained trails. It pays to plan ahead, and knowing the Colorado basics will put you one step closer to a hike of a lifetime.

When to Go

Colorado beckon hikers from late May to early October. At lower elevations – along the Front Range, the Great Sand Dunes National Park and Colorado National Monument – many trails are accessible year-round. Elsewhere, with the right gear and training, you can head out on snowshoes. If in doubt, contact the local ranger district!

Fourteeners

Colorado has 58 mountains that top 14,000ft, more than any other state in the nation. Locals call them 'fourteeners' (also '14ers'), and many try to bag 'em all. But not all fourteeners are created equal. Divided into four categories, they range from straightforward hikes on well-marked trails (Class 1) to steep treks that incorporate technical climbing (Class 4). There are even two you can drive up: Pikes Peak and Mt Evans. Whichever way you summit, check 14ers.com for up-to-date information, including routes, planning tools, peak conditions and more.

Crossing the State on Foot

Two well-maintained long-distance trails cross Colorado, offering singular opportunities to experience the state's epic alpine backcountry. Both are divided into numerous segments, making it easy to drop in for a section or to complete over several seasons.

HIKE SAFE

Altitude sickness is no joke – symptoms include headache, exhaustion, dizziness and nausea. Take time to acclimate and take it slow the first few days. If your symptoms worsen, descend to a lower elevation!

Start your hikes early and be off mountain peaks and passes by midday. In summer, afternoon rains are frequent and lightning above the timberline is a real danger. Don't hesitate to turn back if gray clouds appear – it could save your life.

Tell someone where you're going and when you expect to be back.
Make noise on the trail to avoid unexpected encounters with moose, bears and mountain lions.

COLORADO TRAIL

The Colorado Trail is the state's signature trail. Known as the 'CT,' it starts at Chatfield State Park (p82) in Denver's suburbs before winding some 567 miles to Durango. The trail passes through eight mountain ranges, six national forests, six wilderness areas and five river systems – all in all involving 90,000ft of vertical climb, making it a spectacular and serious hike. Generally, it takes thru-hikers four to six weeks to complete. The Colorado Trail Foundation *(coloradotrail.org)* is a great resource, offering maps and books that describe the trail in detail.

CONTINENTAL DIVIDE NATIONAL SCENIC TRAIL

The Continental Divide National Scenic Trail or 'CDT' is a 3100-mile US hiking trail that extends like a backbone along the Rockies between Canada and Mexico. An 800-mile section of the CDT passes through Colorado, most of it above 10,000ft, including the highest point of the entire trail, Grays Peak (14,270ft). It joins the CT for 314 miles, most of it running through Lake County. The Continental Divide Trail Coalition *(continentaldividetrail.org)* has detailed information about the CDT, including maps and tips by state.

Hiker, Colorado Trail

PATRICK POENDL/SHUTTERSTOCK

BE PREPARED

● Carry plenty of water or water purification equipment. Colorado's dry climate makes it easy to underestimate how much you need, especially on the trail. In general, adults need 1L of water per two hours of moderate exercise in moderate temperatures; adjust accordingly for the heat and intensity of the hike.
● Bring high-energy snacks packed with protein, carbs and electrolytes.
● Wear a billed hat, sunglasses and slather on sunscreen. Don't forget lip balm with SPF! The sun's rays are strong, even on overcast days.
● Bring layers, including a windbreaker, fleece, warm hat and gloves. Weather conditions can change quickly year-round.
● Some popular trails require permits – check ahead of time!
● Carry a trail map, compass and headlamp – don't depend on your cellphone.
● Don't forget wag bags! Most hikers know to pack out whatever they pack in. In Colorado that often includes your poop. Some areas offer free human waste bags or 'wag bags' at trailheads, and they are easily purchased online. If you must, bury your feces at least 6in underground and 200ft from any water source, and you should still pack out your toilet paper!

ACTION AREAS

Where to find Colorado's best outdoor activities.

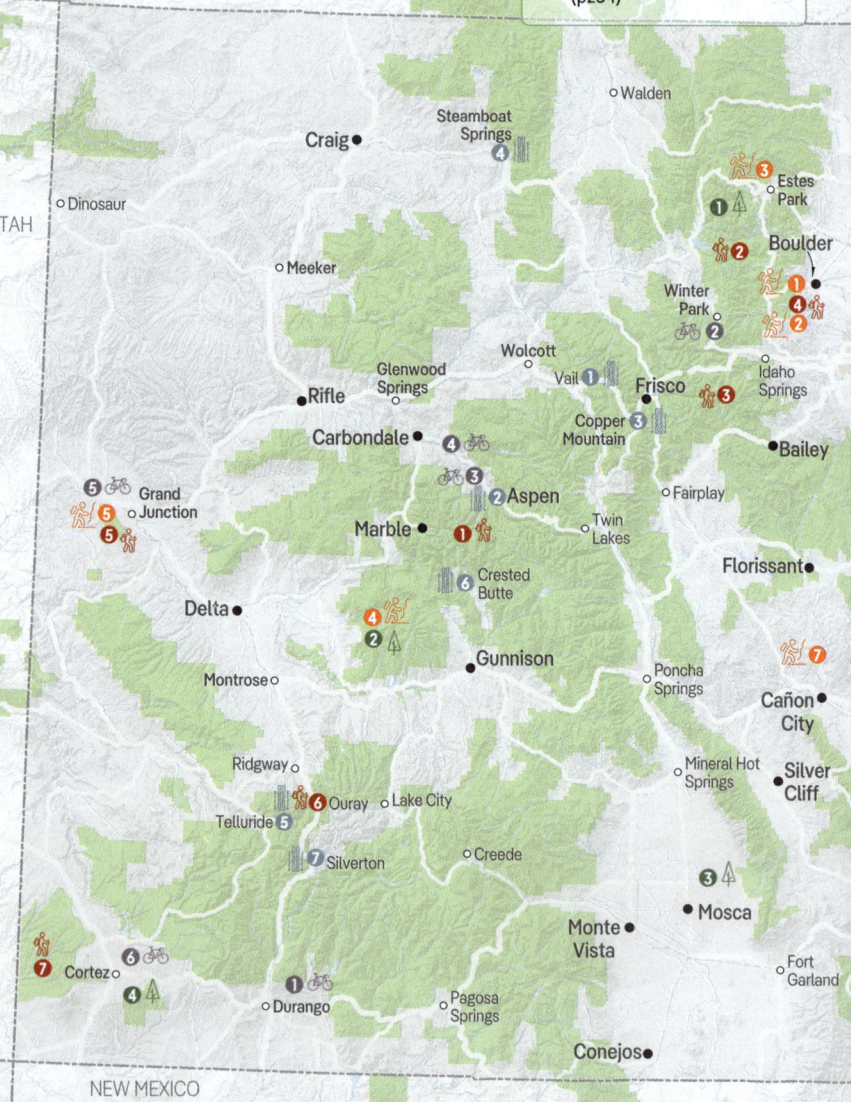

WYOMING

UTAH

NEW MEXICO

Walden

Steamboat Springs 4

Craig

Dinosaur

Meeker

Estes Park 3

Boulder 1

Winter Park 2

Glenwood Springs

Rifle

Wolcott

Vail 1

Frisco

Copper Mountain 3

Idaho Springs 3

Bailey

Carbondale 4

Grand Junction 5 5 5

Aspen 3 2

Marble 1

Twin Lakes

Fairplay

Florissant 7

Delta

Crested Butte 6

4 2

Montrose

Gunnison

Poncha Springs

Cañon City 7

Ridgway

Ouray 6 5

Lake City

Mineral Hot Springs

Silver Cliff

Telluride

Silverton 7

Creede

Mosca 3

Cortez 7 6 4

Durango 1

Pagosa Springs

Monte Vista

Fort Garland

Conejos

Hiking

1. Maroon Bells (p222)
2. Chasm Lake (p152)
3. Mt Bierstadt Trail (p190)
4. Bear Peak (p125)
5. Monument Canyon Trail (p291)
6. Perimeter Trail (p266)
7. McElmo Canyon Trail (p259)

Skiing & Snowboarding

1. Vail (p207)
2. Aspen (p218)
3. Copper Mountain (p204)
4. Steamboat Mountain Resort (p164)
5. Telluride Ski Resort (p273)
6. Crested Butte (p243)
7. Silverton Mountain Resort (p276)

Mountain Biking

1. Monarch Crest Trail (p239)
2. Trestle Bike Park (p194)
3. Rim Trail (p226)
4. Lupine Loop (p245)
5. Kokopelli's Trail (p289)
6. Phil's World (p260)
7. Red Rock Canyon Open Space (p304)

Climbing

1. The Flatirons (p117)
2. Eldorado Canyon State Park (p127)
3. Lumpy Ridge (p150)
4. North Rim (p281)
5. Otto's Route (p291)
6. Red Rock Canyon Open Space (p304)
7. Shelf Rd Recreation Area (p326)

Cheyenne

Julesburg

NEBRASKA

Fort Collins

Sterling

Greeley

Fort Morgan

Yuma

Fort Lupton

Denver

Castle Rock

Limon

Burlington

Colorado Springs

Kit Carson

Fountain

Pueblo

Lamar

La Junta

Walsenburg

KANSAS

Trinidad

0 — 100 km
0 — 50 miles

COLORADO

THE GUIDE

Rocky Mountain National Park & Northern Colorado p140
Boulder p100
DENVER p52
Vail, Aspen & Central Colorado p178
Mesa Verde & Western Colorado p249
Southeast Colorado & the San Luis Valley p299

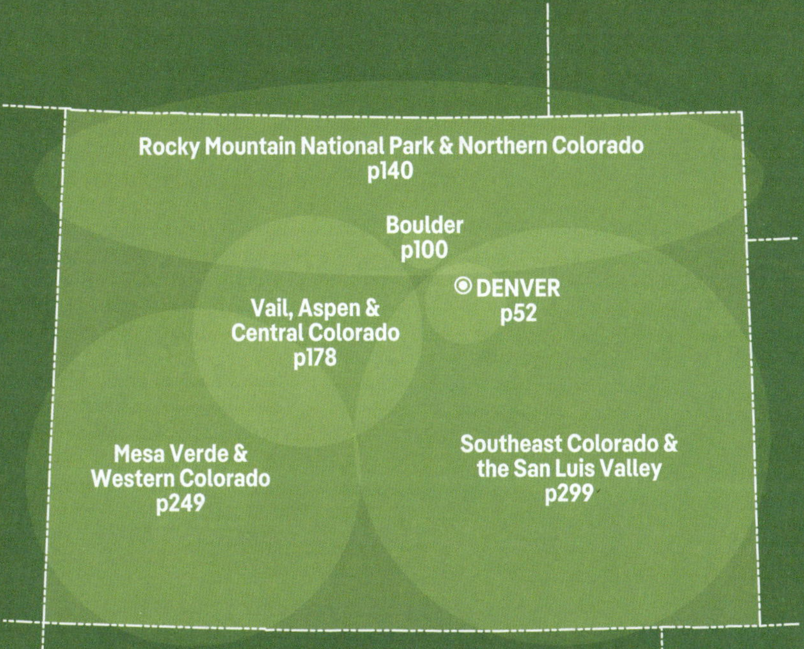

Chapters in this section are organised by hubs and their surrounding areas. We see the hub as your base in the destination, where you'll find unique experiences, local insights, insider tips and expert recommendations. It's also your gateway to the surrounding area, where you'll see what and how much you can do from there.

Emerald Lake trail (p149), Rocky Mountain National Park

SEANXU/GETTY IMAGES

Denver

URBAN, ARTSY AND SPORTY

Denver has hit its stride as one of
the treasures of the American West and a gateway to the Rockies.

The Mile High City has finally arrived. A cow town no more, Denver is an urban gem, with revitalized neighborhoods, rich cultural offerings and a booming craft brewery scene. It boasts big league sports (go Broncos!) and a lifestyle where the outdoors rules. Denver is one of the US' fastest growing cities, with a mix of locals and transplants transforming it from the inside out. Denverites enjoy (and nowadays expect) first-class arts and a hopping restaurant and bar scene; they take full advantage of the city's sunny days and city parks. And who wouldn't want easy access to the country's most impressive mountain range?

Denver has seen its ups and downs, of course, all the way back to its founding in 1858. An early gold rush petered out, but the city pivoted into a supply and transportation hub for mining communities. This brought wealth to Denver, some of which is still visible in its grand buildings and robust parks system.

But the balloon inevitably burst, and Denver experienced a century of boom-and-bust cycles. Gold. Silver. Plutonium.

Oil. The city's fortunes were pinned on commodities and their volatile prices. By the mid-1980s, Denver had an urban center dotted with half-empty skyscrapers, dilapidated buildings and vacant lots. But the 1990s sowed the seeds that changed it all: seeing potential where others saw blight, entrepreneurs invested in the downtown area. Artists followed. By the early 2000s, the city's core neighborhoods were being revitalized.

Today, each of these neighborhoods has a personality all its own. At the center, Downtown and LoHi have historic buildings and sights, performing arts venues and some of the best restaurants in town. Just south, Golden Triangle, Capitol Hill and Cheesman Park are home to museums and civic life, while further south and east Wash Park, SoBo and City Park have big green spaces and gritty edge. North of downtown, Five Points and RiNo are the heart of cool, with street art and hipster nightlife. Though individual and unique, Denver's neighborhoods remain connected through history and the thread of possibility winding its way through them all.

JSPANNHOFF/SHUTTERSTOCK

THE MAIN AREAS

DOWNTOWN, LOHI & PLATTE RIVER VALLEY
Revitalized city center. **p58**

GOLDEN TRIANGLE, CAPITOL HILL & CHEESMAN PARK
Museums and historic sights. **p70**

WASH PARK & SOBO
Vibrant park and urban edge. **p78**

RINO & FIVE POINTS
Street art and nightlife. **p83**

CITY PARK
Outdoor activities and kid-centered fun. **p89**

For places to stay in Denver, see p99

KRUCK20/GETTY IMAGES

Downtown Denver (p58)

Find Your Way

While known for its proximity to the Rocky Mountains, Denver itself is on the plains and mostly flat. From the downtown core, most of Denver's sights, nightlife and traveler services are located within a 4-mile radius. If you get turned around, look for the mountains, an ever-present beacon to the west.

△ City Park

City Park
p89

**RiNo &
Five Points**
p83

**Golden Triangle,
Capitol Hill &
Cheesman Park**
p70

American Museum
of Western Art

🏛 Denver Art Museum

Clyfford Still
Museum

🏛 History Colorado Center

🏛 Union
Station

**Downtown, LoHi &
Platte River Valley**
p58

Denver Performing
Arts Complex

Ⓝ

0   0
1 miles
0   2 km

54

Denver Botanic Gardens

WALK

Denver is a very walkable city, giving you flex to explore each neighborhood at your own pace. Low humidity, sun-filled days and mild weather year-round (even in winter) make for pleasant exploring. And it's flat! Bring good walking shoes and layers.

FROM THE AIRPORT

Denver International Airport (DIA) is one of the country's biggest and busiest airports. It's located 24 miles east of downtown Denver, about 30 minutes by car if there's no traffic. RTD trains also run to Union Station (p58) – a sure thing any time of day.

Washington Park

Wash Park & SoBo

p78

Meow Wolf

↑ *Dinosaur Ridge (9.3mi)*
Red Rocks Amphitheater (12.5mi)

BUS & LIGHT-RAIL

Denver's public transportation system, RTD, crisscrosses the city via bus and light-rail routes. It makes travel between neighborhoods easy and cheap. Single rides are $2.75, unlimited day passes are just $5.50. Discounts available for seniors; youth 19 and under travel free.

RIDESHARES

Lyft and Uber are popular ways to get around in Denver, especially at night or for destinations further afield like Red Rocks (p93) or the airport. You'll enjoy door-to-door service and avoid the hassle of driving and parking in Denver's increasingly congested streets.

Plan Your Days

Lace up your shoes and fill up your water bottle to explore this multilayered Western city where art, history and the outdoors intersect with craft beer and a love of sports.

Denver Botanic Gardens (p74)

Day 1

Morning

● Fuel up at **Denver Milk Market** (p60), a trendy food hall, before heading to **Union Station** (p58). Wander through the historic station, popping into the shops. Afterwards, join a tour of the **Museum of Contemporary Art** (p62) or catch a game at **Coors Field** (p62).

Afternoon

● Enjoy downtime among locals, even white-water kayaking, in **Confluence Park** (p60). Stroll through the adjoining **Commons Park** (p63), making your way across the river into the trendy LoHi neighborhood.

Evening

● Enjoy a plate of Michelin-star tacos at **Alma Fonda Fina** (p69). Afterwards, push past a false bookcase for post-dinner drinks at **Williams & Graham** (p67), a tony speakeasy.

YOU'LL ALSO WANT TO...

There are even more quintessential Denver spots to hit, including iconic venues, museums and sporting events, as well as lively events and parks.

HAVE A WORLD-CLASS LISTEN

Catch a concert at **Red Rocks** (p93), arguably the finest natural amphitheater in the country, even the world. Arrive early to hike through the red rocks or tailgate with locals.

SEE A LIFE'S WORK

Take in the **Clyfford Still Museum** (p72), home to nearly every work by the famed abstract expressionist. Check the website for special events while you're in town – concerts, lectures, even guided meditation.

SIP FROM THE SOURCE

Visit **Great Divide Brewing Company** (p66) to learn how the award-winning brews are made. Or join a guided tour of **Laws Whiskey House** (p80), lauded for its Four Grain Bourbon.

MO REIDY/SHUTTERSTOCK

Day 2

Morning
● Take an early-morning stroll past the large-scale and living art at **Denver Botanic Gardens** (p74). Afterwards, walk through the famed **Cheesman Park** (p75), scoping the rolling lawns for paranormal activity. Head to **Colfax** (p91) for a tasty meal at pay-what-you-can **SAME Café** (p91).

Afternoon
● Spend the afternoon learning all about the Centennial State in the excellent **History Colorado Center** (p73) or perusing the impressive collection at **Denver Art Museum** (p70).

Evening
● Have a vegan bite at **Bang Up to the Elephant** (p74) before beelining for a show at the **Denver Performing Arts Complex** (p60). Afterwards, snap pics with the iconic 40ft-tall **Blue Bear** (p69).

Day 3

Morning
● Spend the morning wandering through the psychedelic art installations in **Meow Wolf** (p63) or take in the laser light show at the **International Church of Cannabis** (p80). Afterwards, take the light-rail to RiNo, and have a leisurely lunch at **Stowaway** (p88).

Afternoon
● Once you've refueled, wander through the neighborhood, taking in the **murals** (p83) as you make your way to the **Blair-Caldwell African American Museum** (p84) to learn about the neighborhood's history.

Evening
● At sunset, head to **Nocturne** (p84) for live jazz or check out RiNo's breweries, making sure to taste the lagers at **Bierstadt** (p87) and the eclectic brews at **Our Mutual Friend** (p87).

CHEER ON CHAMPS
Sport burgundy and blue, the Avalanche team colors, and catch a hockey game at **Ball Arena** (p67). Or wear your Nuggets gear and take in a basketball game instead. They share the space!

STRETCH YOUR LEGS
Explore Denver's **City Park** (p89), 320 acres of trails, playgrounds, lakes, a zoo, science museum...even a golf course! Or try historic **Wash Park** (p78) instead for its gardens, lakes and vibrant community feel.

PARTY IN THE STREETS
Head to Denver's art districts – RiNo and Santa Fe – for **First Fridays** (p84), when galleries and studios stay open late and revelers fill the streets.

CELEBRATE COWBOY CULTURE
Cheer on cowboys every January at the **National Western Stock Show** (p87), with rodeos, horse shows and livestock exhibitions. Don't miss the 17th St kick-off parade, led by teams of long-horned cattle.

Downtown, LoHi & Platte River Valley

REVITALIZED CITY CENTER

GETTING AROUND

Union Station makes it easy to get to downtown Denver; buses and trains arrive here every few minutes.The downtown area is plagued with bumper-to-bumper traffic so avoid driving. Take the Mall Ride, a free shuttle along the length of 16th St Mall, a 1.25-mile pedestrian walkway to Civic Center Park (p73). Or walk; wide, well-maintained sidewalks make it easy to get around. Beyond Downtown, three short bridges connect it with the action in LoHi.

☑TOP TIP

Public restrooms can be hard to find in Downtown. Union Station is the most reliable option with restrooms open 5am to midnight. There's a bathroom near the Downtown Denver Rink (p65) and parks have porta potties (BYO paper).

Present-day Downtown – Confluence Park to be exact – is where Denver started. The Arapaho people had long wintered near the river junction but were pushed out by a surge of white settlers after gold was found in the South Platte River in 1858. The gold-seekers eventually moved into the mountains, but Denver remained an important supply town and railroad depot. Across the Platte River Valley, the Lower Highlands (LoHi) was historically an immigrant neighborhood, connected to Downtown by bridges and streetcar lines. Throughout the 20th century, both neighborhoods went through periods of boom and bust; like many urban centers, downtown Denver was rough during the 1980s and '90s, but slowly revived with an influx of youthful entrepreneurs (including a brewery owner named John Hickenlooper, who later served as mayor, governor and US senator). Today, both areas, including the micro-neighborhood LoDo (Lower Downtown), are vibrant and revitalized, populated with skyscrapers and historic sites, theaters and stadiums, hipster restaurants and breweries.

Tony Venues & Train Tickets

Much more than a station

An iconic landmark, the Beaux-Art style **Union Station** (*denverunionstation.com; free*) opened its doors in 1914, the third train station built on-site (the first burned down, the second was too small). It has served as Denver's main transportation hub ever since, today used by local and long-distance buses, light-rail and **Amtrak** (*amtrak.com*). But it's way more than that. Wander through the Great Hall, taking in a waiting area with soaring ceilings and chandeliers, filled with leather couches, hardwood tables and free wi-fi; lively bars and cocktail lounges line the walls alongside ice-cream shops and bookstores. Or stay for a meal at one of the swanky restaurants – including Mercantile (p60) and **Ultreia** (*ultreiadenver.com*), brainchildren of James Beard Award–winning chefs. Or stay

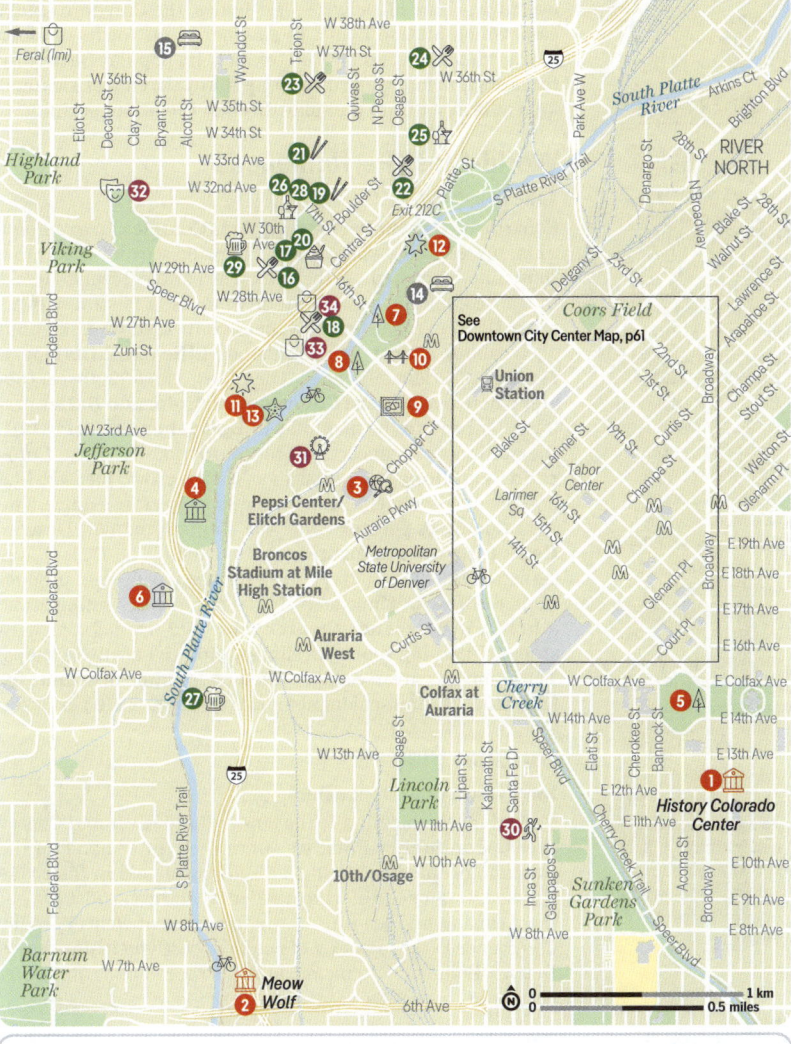

HIGHLIGHTS

1 History Colorado Center
2 Meow Wolf

SIGHTS

3 Ball Arena
4 Children's Museum of Denver
5 Civic Center Park
● Colorado Avalanche (see 3)
● Colorado Mammoth (see 3)

6 Colorado Sports Hall of Fame
7 Commons Park
8 Confluence Park
● Denver Broncos (see 6)
● Denver Nuggets (see 3)
● Empower Field at Mile High (see 6)
9 MCA Denver
10 Millenium Bridge

ACTIVITIES

11 Confluence Kayaks
12 Denver Skate Park
13 Downtown Aquarium

SLEEPING

14 Kasa Union Station
15 Lumber Baron Inn & Gardens

EATING

16 Alma Fonda Fina

17 El Five
18 Just BE Kitchen
19 Kawa Ni
20 Little Man Ice Cream
21 Nana's Dim Sum & Dumplings
22 Noisette
23 Tamales by La Casita
24 Wildflower

DRINKING

25 High Lonesome
26 Lady Jane

27 Raíces Brewing
28 Williams & Graham
29 Zuni St Brewing

ENTERTAINMENT

30 Colorado Ballet
31 Elitch Gardens
32 Holiday Theater

SHOPPING

33 REI
34 Wilderness Exchange

LARIMER SQUARE

Larimer St, between 14th and 15th Sts, is where Denver was born. Named after the city's founder, it was Denver's first city block, first commercial district, and home to its first bank, first bookstore, even the original City Hall. By the 1940s, Denver was expanding, the old City Hall was torn down, and Larimer fell into disrepair. But a handful of the original structures were rescued by a conservation-minded developer, who gave the block its current name, and in 1971 Larimer Sq (which is not a square at all) became Denver's first Historic District. Today it's known for its boutique shops and fine dining, many with lovely outdoor seating beneath lights strung across the street.

overnight – one of Denver's best hotels, the Crawford (p99), calls Union Station home. In summer, come for its outdoor plaza, where you can pick up treats at its popular **Saturday farmers market**, while its **pop-up fountain** entices kids (and kids at heart) to run and play through the urban sprinklers.

World-Class Performances

Take in a show

Come to the **Denver Performing Arts Complex** *(artscomplex .com; prices vary)*, where you can bank on scoring tickets to a show almost any night of the week. The nation's second-largest theater complex occupies four city blocks in bustling downtown Denver. You'll find 10 venues connected by a sky-high glass canopy, among them the historic **Ellie Caulkins Opera House** (affectionately called 'The Ellie'), a luxe 2200-seat theater where both **Opera Colorado** and **Colorado Ballet** perform. Or head to the magnificent **Boettcher Concert Hall**, the nation's first concert hall-in-the-round, where the **Colorado Symphony** plays classics as well as crowd pleasers like holiday movie screenings with the score performed live. The Arts Complex's theater wing, the similarly named **Denver Center for the Performing Arts** (called 'The DCPA'), has eight venues staging everything from experimental productions to Broadway musicals. If you're a theater junkie, take a **behind-the-scenes theater tour** *($12 per person)* with stops in dressing rooms, design studios and costume shops. The complex's diverse stages often offer online discounts for kids, students and seniors, some starting at just $10 per ticket.

Outdoor Play

Have fun in Confluence Park

Named for the meeting of the South Platte River and Cherry Creek, **Confluence Park** was once the winter home of the Arapaho people. But the 1858 discovery of gold in the rivers sparked a stampede of white settlers to the area, pushing out the Arapaho and leading to the founding of Denver. Today Confluence Park is a pocket of outdoorsy activity in downtown Denver. Come here to picnic on its terraced lawns, jog along

 EATING IN DOWNTOWN: OUR PICKS

Just BE Kitchen: Cheery, casual cafe serving keto and gluten-free dishes, plus no sugar, no egg and dairy-free options. Kids menu too! *9am-7pm* **$**

Biker Jim's Gourmet Dogs: Try hot dogs made of boar, reindeer, even rattlesnake with toppings to match. *11am-8pm Sun-Thu, to 9pm Fri & Sat* **$**

Gaia Masala Burger: American, Mediterranean and Indian dishes. Chicken tikka masala burger, anyone? *10am-3am* **$$**

La Diabla Pozole y Mezcal: Cantina-style restaurant serving Mexican faves, including posole, a hominy-based soup. *hours vary* **$**

Denver Milk Market: Artsy food hall with everything from gelato to poke bowls. Full bar too. *7am-9pm Sun-Thu, to 11pm Fri & Sat* **$$**

Stout Street Social: Bustling restaurant with an eclectic menu to tempt the pickiest diners. *11am-11pm Sun-Thu, to midnight Fri & Sat* **$$**

Mercantile: Half upscale market, half fancy favorite serving elevated comfort food. Served family-style. *11am-2pm & 5-9pm Mon-Sat* **$$$**

A5 Steakhouse: This steakhouse serves lesser-known cuts, eclectic sides and tiki-style drinks. *3:30-10pm Mon-Thu, to 11pm Fri & Sat, to 9pm Sun* **$$$**

DOWNTOWN CITY CENTER

See Union Station Enlargement

Union Station

HIGHLIGHTS
1 American Museum of Western Art
2 Union Station

SIGHTS
3 Boettcher Concert Hall
4 Colorado Rockies
5 Coors Field
● El Chapultepec 'El Pec' Piano Lounge (see 32)
6 I See What You Mean
7 Museum for Black Girls
8 Museum of Illusions
9 National Ballpark Museum

ACTIVITIES
10 Downtown Denver Rink

SLEEPING
11 Brown Palace Hotel & Spa
12 The Crawford
13 Hostel Fish
14 Oxford Hotel
15 Rally Hotel
16 Slate Hotel Denver Downtown

EATING
17 A5 Steakhouse
18 Biker Jim's Gourmet Dogs
19 Denver Milk Market
20 Gaia Masala Burger
21 La Diabla Pozole y Mezcal
22 Mercantile
23 Stout Street Social
24 Ultreia

DRINKING
25 54thirty
● Cruise Room (see 14)
26 Great Divide Brewing Company
27 Lincoln's

ENTERTAINMENT
28 Clocktower Cabaret
29 Colorado Convention Center
30 Comedy Works Downtown
● Dazzle (see 32)
31 Denver Center for the Performing Arts
32 Denver Performing Arts Complex
33 Ellie Caulkins Opera House
● Great American Beer Festival (see 29)
● Opera Colorado (see 33)

SHOPPING
34 5 Green Boxes
35 Colorado Artisan Center
36 Denver Pavilions
37 I Heart Denver
38 Rockmount Ranch Wear
39 Wild West of America

TRANSPORT
40 Amtrak

AURARIA CAMPUS

Across from Downtown sits **Auraria** *(ahec.edu)*, a vibrant college campus shared by three schools. It's also Denver's oldest neighborhood, older than the city itself. Founded in 1858, Auraria was a mining town on the banks of Cherry Creek. (Denver City was founded three weeks later, a few hundred feet away.) A rivalry grew between them but it was short lived, and the towns merged into 'Denver' in 1860. Successive waves of working-class immigrants called Auraria home until a devastating flood in 1965 displaced its then mostly Latinx residents. Seeing an opportunity, and despite protests, the city redeveloped Auraria into an urban campus. Today, the 1866 Tivoli Brewery is still visible from Downtown, doubling as the student union and a nod to the past.

PHILLIP RUBINO/SHUTTERSTOCK

Coors Field

the waterfront, even just to sun or splash on the park's small sandy beach. In the summer, you also can rent inner tubes and kayaks to take on a fun artificial stretch of white water. Rentals are available at **Confluence Kayaks** *(confluence kayaks.com; from $55 per day)*. **Cherry Creek Trail**, a popular cycling route, starts here too, meandering 40 miles through urban landscapes and green spaces, including past the swanky **Cherry Creek shopping district** *(cherrycreeknorth.com/ things-to-do/shop)*.

Catch a Ball (Game)

Watch major league baseball

Coors Field *(mlb.com/rockies/ballpark)* is one of the MLB's most home-run-friendly ballparks (apparently, it's the thin air), and catching a **Rockies game** *(mlb.com/rockies; adult/ child from $4/1)* is loads of fun...even if the home team isn't winning. It's easy with 80 home games and tickets starting at just $1 in centerfield (aka the Rockpile). Theme nights include freebies like trucker hats and commemorative cups; if you come around July 4, expect post-game fireworks. Tours *(adult/child $27/10)* of the stadium are offered year-round and include access to the field, club houses and mile-high seats; they run 70 to 80 minutes. If you're a die-hard fan, cross the street to the **National Ballpark Museum** *(ballparkmuseum .com; adult/child $20/free)*, which is jam-packed with ballpark memorabilia.

Art that Makes You Think

Contemporary art museum outing

Occupying a four-story glass box near the South Platte River, **MCA Denver** *(Museumn of Contemporary Art; mcaden ver.org; adult/child $14/free)* was built with interaction and engagement in mind – whether the art provokes, confuses or delights, it'll always make you think. Free guided tours on Friday and Saturday offer deep dives into showcased exhibits. Afterwards, the rooftop cafe is a great spot for an exhibition-inspired cocktail or mocktail with spectacular Downtown views. Don't miss the MCA's satellite – the **Holiday Theater**, which extends the museum's programming into the nearby LoHi neighborhood with concerts, film screenings, artist talks and more. A historic building decked out in Egyptian-inspired decor (a nod to the discovery of King Tut's tomb), the theater was the first in Colorado to screen Spanish-language films.

Tour the Old West
Admire American West masterpieces

It's easy to walk past the **American Museum of Western Art** (anschutzcollection.org; $5), thanks to the basement-level entrance and discreet signage. But this may be one of Denver's best-kept secrets (just keep it on the DL). Set in the historic Navarre Building, the museum holds over 600 masterpieces from the Anschutz Corporation's private collection. Together, the work tells the story of the western expansion of the US as seen by artists from the early 19th century to the present day. Take a guided tour (offered twice daily) or pick up a wand with a narrated self-guided tour. Children over eight years old only.

Psychedelic Art Installation
Step into art, literally

A mind-bending, interactive art exhibit, **Meow Wolf** (meow wolf.com; adult/child $50/45) leads you through a four-story building and art installations created by over 350 artists that examine a convergence of four worlds where memories are currency. Enter dark tunnels and tipping hallways, towering spaceships and psychedelic coral reefs, and keep your eyes peeled for the live performers who somehow creep onto the scene. It's another world (err, worlds). Tickets are timed. For an extra $3, tag on a QPASS, an ATM-like card that gives you digital access to hidden stories throughout the installation. Located near an I-25 underpass, plan on spending at least three to four hours inside.

Stroll Between Neighborhoods
Enjoy green space and art

Located next to Confluence Park (p60), **Commons Park** is a perfect place for a walk, with grassy knolls outlined in well-traveled paths and access to tiny beaches along the Platte River. Modern art installations dot the landscape; the undeniable centerpiece is **Common Ground**, a lyrical curving stairway to nowhere commissioned by the Gates Family Foundation to commemorate the millennium. The park also is a nexus of sorts: to the east, the picturesque **Millennium Bridge**, with its towering 200ft mast-like cable structure,

MICHELIN STARS ARRIVE

Denver's food scene has gone through as many changes as the city itself. The Buckhorn Exchange has been serving elk, bison and Rocky Mountain oysters for over a century, while, in the 1990s, Denver was dubbed the 'cradle of fast casual,' with Chipotle, Qdoba and Noodles & Company all launching here. But it was the Michelin Guide, in 2023, that let the world in on something locals have known for some time: there are some serious good eats in the Mile High City. Today, four of the six Colorado restaurants that have earned one-star designations are in Denver; some two dozen more were recognized for sustainability and value. For Denver's foodies and restaurateurs, the accolades were sweet confirmation, a long time coming.

16TH STREET MALL MAKEOVER

Designed by architect IM Pei, **16th Street Mall** has been the backbone of Downtown Denver since 1982. Running 1.25 miles from Union Station (p58) to Civic Center Park (p73), it's a pedestrian walkway with free shuttles down the middle. Lined in chain stores and restaurants (even an actual mall, **Denver Pavilions**), it's bustling during weekday work hours but mostly empty the rest of the time. Since 2022 the city has invested almost $175 million to make the thoroughfare more appealing. Scheduled for completion in 2025, it promises more trees, lounge areas and children's play structures. Don't miss the replacement diamond-patterned pavers, designed by Pei to resemble the scale pattern of the western diamondback rattlesnake.

connects the park to the **16th Street Mall**; to the west, **Highland Cable Bridge** leads over the river into LoHi and its trendy restaurants and bars. Pleasant waterfront trails also lead to the Platte River Valley neighborhood to the south; and if you're a skater, make your way north to **Denver Skate Park**, a 60,000-sq-ft cement gathering place for some of the best skateboarders in town. In the summer, join locals for a variety of **free concerts** *(riverfrontparkevents.com)* along the river; they're festive community events.

Throw Back Some Brews

Experience a giant beer fest

Colorado takes its beer seriously, raising craft brewing to a high art. And with over 150 breweries in metro Denver, you certainly won't go thirsty in this town. If you're visiting in autumn, try to score tickets to the **Great American Beer Festival** *(greatamericanbeerfestival.com; from $85)*, the largest beer festival of its kind in the US. Held in late September/early October at the **Colorado Convention Center** *(denver convention.com)*, the festival draws over 2000 master brewers from across the nation, with over 9000 beers vying for Best of Show medals in 263 categories ranging from American Style India Pale Lager and Classic Saison to Smoke Beer and Herb and Spice Beer. General admission tickets include unlimited one-ounce tastings; multiday admission as well as tickets that include pairings – small dishes created by lauded chefs – with a menu of beers are also offered. Best of all is the comradery of you and 40,000 beer buddies, all tasting outstanding brews once ounce at a time.

Small Stages, Big Performances

LoDo's jazz, comedy and burlesque clubs

Head to **Dazzle** *(dazzledenver.com; cover varies)* for jazz, the longtime Downtown go-to. Newly relocated to an intimate space in the Denver Performing Arts Complex (p60), it features nightly shows with touring musicians and top local talent. Buy tickets online for your choice of table seats ($10) or a spot at the bar (free). And plan on a drink or snack – there's a minimum two-item purchase. After the last show, a corner of Dazzle comes alive as **El Chapultepec 'El Pec' Piano Lounge** *(thepeclegacy.com/piano-bar; free)*, a nod to a long shuttered mom-and-pop blues bar. Today, it's a space for musical improv and surprise guests – perfect for a late set or nightcap.

DRINKING IN DOWNTOWN: OUR PICKS

Cruise Room: One of Denver's swankiest cocktail lounges, this art-deco gem opened the day after Prohibition. *5-10pm Sun-Thu, to midnight Fri & Sat*

54thirty: Sky-high open-air bar with spectacular mountain views; fire pits warm you up on chilly nights. *hours vary*

Raíces Brewing Co.: Community-oriented Latinx brewery offering award-winning beers, cultural events plus nibbles. *hours vary*

Lincoln's: Hidden underground bar with President Lincoln theme. Drinks $5; cash only. *4pm-midnight Mon-Thu, 2pm-2am Fri & Sat, 2pm-midnight Sun*

Larimer Square (p60)

If comedy is more your pace, head instead to nearby Larimer Square (p60), home to **Comedy Works Downtown** *(comedy works.com; prices vary)*. Though it's in a somewhat cramped basement-level theater, the club routinely brings in top comics. Consider New Talent Nights too – tickets are discounted, and renowned headliners sometimes crash it.

Or for a total change of LoDo pace, try the bawdy, sometimes naughty **Clocktower Cabaret** *(clocktowercabaret.com; prices vary)*. A table near the front will get you in the heart of the action, from drag queen theater and burlesque shows to aerialist performances. The theater is inside the historic D&F Tower, once the tallest building between the Mississippi River and California.

Ice-Skating among Skyscrapers

Glide on Downtown's ice rink

From Thanksgiving to Valentine's Day, take a spin on the free **Downtown Denver Rink** *(winterindenver.com/rink)*. Located on 16th Street Mall, the ice rink takes on a dance party-like vibe with DJs spinning tunes and ice-skaters moving to the beats. On holidays and for special events (say, a Rockies game), the tower is lit up. Ice-skate rentals (from $9) are available, as are skate aids (from $5) for those still learning to balance on blades. Free lockers too.

Victorian-Era Tastes

High tea at Brown Palace

Join in a Denver tradition by taking **Afternoon Tea** *(brown palace.com; adult/child $65/30)* at the Brown Palace (p99), Denver's most iconic hotel, dating to 1892. Guests get a sense of Denver's Victorian-era opulence seated in the luxurious central atrium under a sky-high stained-glass ceiling, live piano

BROTHELS IN DENVER

Fawn O'Breitzman, co-founder, Sexploratorium, *@sexploratorium denver*

When Denver was founded there were few, if any, laws. That led to opportunities for prostitution, alcohol and opium sales… Denver had it all. It was nicknamed 'The Wickedest City in America.'

Denver's first 'House of Prostitution' opened in 1858. Sex work grew exponentially. By its heyday (1870–1900), there were 600 sex workers. It paid well: $30–50 per customer (domestic servants earned $1 per week). The money gave them – and madams who ran the businesses – freedom and power in a time when women had few rights. By 1916 chastity laws led to the brothels' demise.

Today, a Red Light District plaque commemorates these sex workers. It sits on the corner of Market and 20th, the center of the action, long ago.

DENVER'S CHINATOWN

In the 1870s, Chinese immigrants began settling in Denver, mostly railroad workers and former miners. Together they created a small but vibrant Chinatown on Wazee St between 15th and 22nd Sts. But anti-Chinese sentiment was also on the rise, and on October 31, 1880, a mob of approximately 3000 white Denverites descended on Chinatown, destroying buildings, injuring hundreds and lynching a man named Look Young. Many Chinatown residents stayed to rebuild but the enclave never fully recovered and was eventually razed. Today, efforts are afoot – including at the History Colorado Center (p73) – to increase awareness not only of the dark events of 1880 but also of the many contributions of Colorado's Asian American community.

RAYMOND BOYD/GETTY IMAGES

Brown Palace (p65)

or harp playing in the background. Finger sandwiches, scones and pastries are served alongside fragrant pots of tea; bubbly and sparkling cider packages also offered. Prepare your pinkies.

Visit the OG

Tour an iconic brewery

Geek out over craft beer at **Great Divide Brewing Company** *(greatdivide.com)*. One of the country's most decorated breweries, Great Divide's exquisitely bold and balanced brews have won 19 Great American Beer Festival medals since its founding in 1994. **Tours** *($10 per person)* of its Downtown brewhouse give you a behind-the-scenes peek at how its magic sauces are made, from brewing to packaging. Reservations recommended (16 and over only).

Big Games, Big Shows

Pro football and concerts

The **Denver Broncos** *(denverbroncos.com)* play at **Empower Field at Mile High** *(empowerfieldatmilehigh.com; prices vary)*, a 76,000-seat behemoth just west of Downtown. It's a special place on game day, bathed in Colorado sunshine and pulsing with orange-clad fans. The Broncos have experienced glorious highs and heartbreaking lows – it's like the Colorado weather, you just never know (so always bring a jacket). Arrive early to check out the free **Colorado Sports Hall of Fame** near Gate 1, which showcases Coloradan athletic prowess with special exhibits on its inductees. Or come on an off-day for a 90-minute behind-the-scenes **tour** *(coloradosports.org; adult/child $40/35)* with stops at the visitors' locker room, the press booth and the stall of Thunder, the Bronco's live mascot. Or check-out the **concert schedule** – big-ticket performers like Taylor Swift and Metallica play here too.

Watch the Pros
Ball Arena's sports and shows
Denver loves its pro sports teams, and fans turn out in force whether the team is winning or getting clobbered. And few venues are more electric than **Ball Arena** *(ballarena.com; prices vary)*. Still called the Pepsi Center (its previous name) by locals, come here to cheer on the champion **Colorado Avalanche** *(nhl.com/avalanche)* hockey team, the **Denver Nuggets** *(nba.com/nuggets)* pro basketball team or the **Colorado Mammoth** *(coloradomammoth.com)*, the city's pro lacrosse team. The steep, tiered seating means there are no bad seats – even the nosebleeds have a good view and a great vibe. When there's not a game on, come to the area for big-ticket events like rock concerts, monster truck shows and Disney-themed ice-skating performances.

Engage Young Minds
Kiddie fun at the Children's Museum
At **Children's Museum of Denver** *(mychildsmuseum.org; $18.75)*, geared for kids eight and younger, you'll find there's something for just about every little one: cooking classes and maker spaces, bubble play and rocket experiments. Dress-up and imaginative play are woven throughout with a munchkin-size firehouse, vet office, grocery store and more. And there are loads of physical activities too: a three-story climbing structure (helmets provided) and an outdoor aerial course are favorites. If you've got an infant or toddler, there's a specially designed area reserved for them too, with padded floors, pint-sized play structures and cozy reading nooks. Come midweek for less of a crowd.

Underwater in the Mile High City
Admire sea life at the aquarium
Next to the Children's Museum, the **Downtown Aquarium** *(aquariumrestaurants.com; adult/child $27/21)* caters to all ages. Indoor walkways take you past dozens of tanks filled with over one million gallons of water, home to creatures from mountain rivers, coral reefs and rainforests. (Randomly, there's also a desert exhibit and tiger den and seafood restaurant.) Kids especially like the 'mermaid' shows; held on Friday evenings, they feature free divers decked out in sparkly tails and seashell bras, swimming alongside nurse sharks,

BEST OUTDOOR GEAR SHOPS & INFO

REI: Flagship store of this outdoor equipment super-supplier with top gear for sale and rent.

Outdoor Recreation Information Center (ORIC): Nonprofit offering free info on everything outdoors Colorado. Website is packed with details plus an REI outpost has knowledgeable staffers.

Wilderness Exchange: Downtown shop with an impressive collection of quality and well-priced gear; head to the basement for consignment and sample sales.

Outdoors Geek: Homegrown outfitter that creates packages of top gear for hiking, camping and glamping; delivery or pickup available.

Feral: Indie shop with a hipster vibe specializing in used outdoor gear, rentals and repairs. Lifetime satisfaction guarantee on all items.

 DRINKING IN LOHI: OUR PICKS

Williams & Graham:	Zuni Street Brewing:	Lady Jane:	High Lonesome:
Push past a wall of books to access artful cocktails, small plates and Old West luxe in this speakeasy. Reserve ahead. *5pm-1am*	Award-winning brewery with a laid-back neighborhood vibe. Live music Wednesdays and Saturdays. *hours vary*	Miami Beach–inspired cocktail lounge with tropical touches. Innovative drink menu. *4-11pm Mon-Thu, 4pm-midnight Fri, 2pm-midnight Sat*	Dimly lit bar with a cowboy saloon feel. Whiskey and a round of pool are musts. *4pm-2am Mon-Fri, 2pm-2am Sat & Sun*

BEST SOUVENIR SHOPS: DOWNTOWN DENVER

I Heart Denver: Small shop in Denver Pavilions selling well-made and quirky, I-must-have tees, hats, snacks and more; all created by locals.

Rockmount Ranch Wear: Historic LoDo shop selling authentic cowboy wear, including snap button shirts, boots and hats.

Colorado Artisan Center: 16th Street Mall boutique focused on handcrafted goods by Colorado artisans like jewelry, pottery, textiles and more.

5 Green Boxes: Union Station boutique with one-of-a-kind gifts and souvenirs, many with a vintage and whimsical feel.

Wild West of America: 16th Street Mall trinket shop filled with Colorado kitsch. Expect snow globes, magnets and cheap tees.

ARINA P HABICH/SHUTTERSTOCK

Elitch Gardens

sea turtles and barracuda. Uniquely, visitors also can get in the water for about 20 minutes – either **snorkeling with tropical fish** *($125 per person)* or in a cage **dunked into the shark tank** *($155 per person)*; both are guided experiences. Admission is a little pricey (skip the add-ons) but a visit here is a nice, if unusual, change of scenery.

Phenomenal Women

Inspiring African American cultural museum

A pop-up gallery turned 16th Street Mall (p64) fixture, the **Museum for Black Girls** *(themuseumforblackgirls.com; adult/child $25/18)* is all about celebrating African American women, their experiences and achievements. Exhibits are interactive, blending history, art and shared cultural memory (and loads of Black girl magic). Expect to read profiles of famous and forgotten historical figures, step into 'Grandma's Kitchen,' a common experience of African American women getting their hair done, and to write (and receive) an inspiring message for the 'Wall of Affirmations.' An empowering and educational experience, regardless of your race or gender. Check the website for after-hours events like poetry readings and paint and sip nights.

Trick of the Eye
Museum of Illusions' mind-bending fun

Good for a lighthearted afternoon of selfies, Denver's **Museum of Illusions** (*moidenver.com; adult/child $27/23*) is a labyrinthine spot that challenges your perceptions. Learn about tricks of the eye through simple hands-on examples and signage (how did that straight rod fit into the curved slot?) but also step into the exhibits themselves – a psychedelic tunnel that makes you feel like you're losing your balance, rooms created to make you appear drastically differently sized, or look like you're hanging upside down or like you've been cloned, or... Staff members are quick to answer questions and to take pics too (just ask!). Book online to save a bit on admission.

High-Octane Fun
Downtown's popular amusement park

If you're looking to shake things up (or your teens are driving you a little crazy), head to the impossible-to-miss amusement park, **Elitch Gardens** (*elitchgardens.com; $65*). Located along the riverfront, there are towering roller coasters and kiddie rides, water slides, tubing and a wave pool, even live entertainment. Open daily April to October, the park re-opens on December evenings for **Luminova Holidays** (*from $20*), the park glittering in four million lights and large-scale Christmas decorations, including 16ft-tall gift displays, a towering Christmas tree and visits with Santa. Best of all, several rides are open – a chilly but fun experience. Buy your tix online to save big on admission year-round.

BIG BLUE BEAR

Wandering through Downtown, it's almost impossible to miss **I See What You Mean**, Denver's iconic 40ft-tall blue bear, which stands peering into the Convention Center (p64). Commissioned by the city to create something for the site, the artist, Lawrence Argent, found himself inspired by a local newspaper photo of a bear peering into a Coloradan home – a surprising but not unfamiliar image in the state. Originally slated to be a sandstone color, a small prototype of the sculpture was created in bright blue, when the wrong color was left in the 3D printer. It was a happy mistake. Today, the giant bear epitomizes the friendly, playful and ever-curious spirit of the city. Its color, a nod to Colorado's big blue skies.

 EATING IN LOHI: OUR PICKS

Little Man Ice Cream: Handcrafted ice cream – even vegan varieties – served from an iconic 28ft-high dairy jug. *hours vary* $	**Tamales by La Casita:** Hands down, the best tamales in town. Choose between green chile or red pork. *7am-5pm Mon-Fri, from 8am Sat* $	**Kawa Ni:** Japanese-style pub; rice and noodle bowls, steamed buns, raw seafood dishes. *4-9pm Tue-Sun, 11:30am-2:30pm Sat & Sun* $$	**Nana's Dim Sum & Dumplings:** Casual restaurant with a seemingly endless variety of dumpling goodness. *hours vary* $$
Alma Fonda Fina: Modern Mexican fare by an award-winning chef. *2-10pm Mon-Thu, 2-11pm Fri, 4-11pm Sat, 4-10pm Sun* $$	**El Five:** Mediterranean-style tapas and city views. Summer nights brings patio seating. *5-10pm Sun-Thu, to 11pm Fri & Sat* $$	**Noisette:** French cuisine at the restaurant or melt-in-your-mouth croissants from its bakery. *8am-3pm & 5-9:30pm Wed-Sat, 8am-2pm Sun* $$$	**Wildflower:** Italian dishes integrating local flavors and influences in a plush art-deco dining room. *4:30-10pm Mon-Sat* $$$

Golden Triangle, Capitol Hill & Cheesman Park

MUSEUMS AND HISTORIC SIGHTS

GETTING AROUND

Getting to and moving between Golden Triangle, Capitol Hill and Cheesman Park is easiest by public transportation. RTD bus routes crisscross the area. Driving isn't bad – the most-traveled east–west streets (6th, 8th, 13th and 14th) and north–south streets (Broadway, Lincoln, Josephine and York) are one-way and typically move at a good clip. Parking is another issue. During the day, prepare to circle. Meters dominate Golden Triangle and the area around the Capitol building (there are also some parking lots). Further out, parking can be limited to a couple of hours or to residents only. Check the signage to avoid being ticketed or towed.

Truly the heart of Denver, Capitol Hill, Golden Triangle and Cheesman Park are home to many of Denver's top attractions, and combined, they embody the city's rich history and diversity. Where to start? Capitol Hill gets its name, of course, from the beautiful gold-domed state capitol; it was Denver's original Millionaire's Row, though most of the grand 19th-century mansions have been replaced by apartments and shops that lend the area its present-day energy and diversity. Golden Triangle and the nearby Art District on Santa Fe are home to art icons like the Denver Art Museum and Su Teatro, and were an important stage for Denver's historic Chicano Movement. Meanwhile Cheesman Park, and the adjoining Botanic Gardens, were Denver's original city cemetery and are now lovely green spaces and a hub for Denver's vibrant LGBTIQ+ community. Altogether, this is a vital, fascinating and must-see part of town.

Take in Masterpieces

Marvel at Denver Art Museum

The crown jewel of Denver's art scene, **DAM** *(Denver Art Museum; denverartmuseum.org; adult $27 Mon-Thu, $30 Fri-Sun, child free)* houses an eclectic collection, from the works of the Old Master painters to the greats of modern contemporary art. It is also home to a stunningly rich collection of

---

☑ TOP TIP

Though some sights are free (eg Colorado State Capitol and US Mint) and many places offer reduced admission for kids, you can save some cash by using a **City Pass** *(citypass.com/Denver; adult/child from $46/37)*, which bundles the cost of several sights around town.

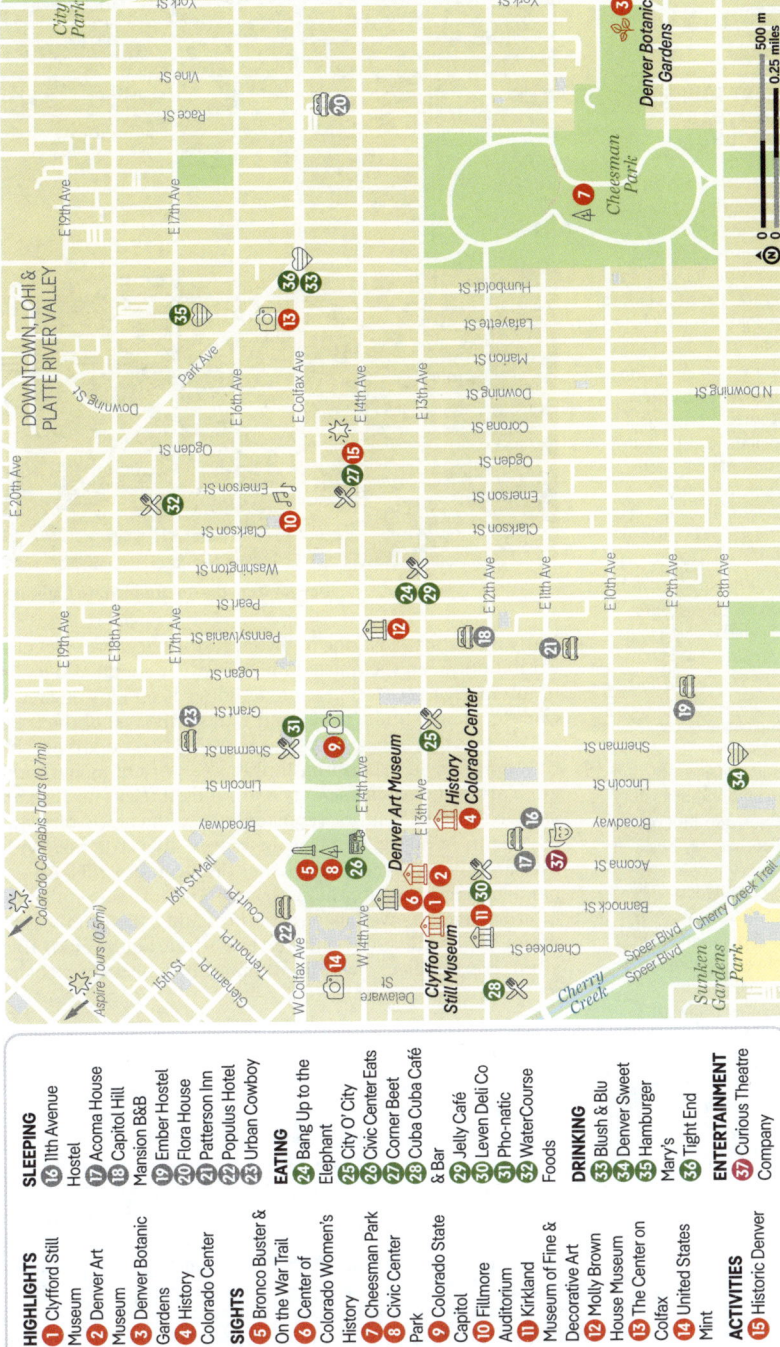

HIGHLIGHTS
1 Clyfford Still Museum
2 Denver Art Museum
3 Denver Botanic Gardens
4 History Colorado Center

SIGHTS
5 Bronco Buster & On the War Trail
6 Center of Colorado Women's History
7 Cheesman Park
8 Civic Center Park
9 Colorado State Capitol
10 Fillmore Auditorium
11 Kirkland Museum of Fine & Decorative Art
12 Molly Brown House Museum
13 The Center on Colfax
14 United States Mint

ACTIVITIES
15 Historic Denver

SLEEPING
16 11th Avenue Hostel
17 Acoma House
18 Capitol Hill Mansion B&B
19 Ember Hostel
20 Flora House
21 Patterson Inn
22 Populus Hotel
23 Urban Cowboy

EATING
24 Bang Up to the Elephant
25 City O' City
26 Civic Center Eats
27 Corner Beet
28 Cuba Cuba Café & Bar
29 Jelly Café
30 Leven Deli Co
31 Pho-natic
32 WaterCourse Foods

DRINKING
33 Blush & Blu
34 Denver Sweet
35 Hamburger Mary's
36 Tight End

ENTERTAINMENT
37 Curious Theatre Company

BEST TOURS: DENVER & AROUND

Historic Denver: Denver's preservation society offers 90-minute docent-led tours *(historicdenver. org)* of the city's oldest neighborhoods. Self-guided tours at *denverstorytrek.org*.

Denver Microbrew Tours: Knowledgeable guides lead 2½-hour tours *(denvermicro brewtour.com)* of award-winning breweries in LoDo and RiNo, tasting at least 10 brews.

Local Table Tours: Guided walking tours *(localtable tours.com)* cover some of Denver's top restaurants, integrating drink pairings and neighborhood history.

Colorado Cannabis Tours: Party-bus tours *(colorado cannabistours. com)* from two to 3½ hours, including grow operations and dispensaries.

Aspire Tours: Half- and full-day driving tours *(aspire-tours. com)* of Denver and surrounding areas, including sightseeing and hiking stops.

SANDRA FOYT/SHUTTERSTOCK

Denver from the Colorado State Capitol

Native American art, one of the largest in the world. Special exhibitions keep the museum buzzing year-round and loads of interactive art stations and activities keep kids engaged. Choose a few exhibits to see and wander the rest of the time – it's a massive museum spread between two buildings: the titanium-paneled Hamilton Building, a work of modern angular art that creates uncanny natural-light tricks inside (and vertigo for some visitors, reportedly), and the newly renovated Martin Building, a glittering fortress-like structure with over a million reflective glass tiles on its outer walls. An expanded welcome center holds art studios and community exhibition space as well as a restaurant and cafe for mid-visit treats. While kids under 18 are always free, adults enjoy free admission on select days almost monthly – check the website for the current schedule.

A Lifetime of Art

Take in modern art masterpieces

Dedicated exclusively to the work and legacy of 20th-century American abstract expressionist **Clyfford Still** *(clyffordstill museum.org; adult/child $15/free)*, this fascinating museum's collection includes more than 3100 of Still's bold and colorful pieces – some 93% of his lifetime production. In his will, Still insisted that his body of work be exhibited in a singular space; Denver beat out several cities for the prize of building a Still museum. The building, a beautifully stark structure, includes rooms of different heights and a unique waffled ceiling that specifically showcase Still's works. Special events – talks and concerts mostly – add a fascinating layer to a visit. A family-friendly place, a small maker's space helps keep kids busy while regular 'Art Crawls' invite toddlers to explore the collection.

Colorado State Capitol Tour

Guided architecture and history walk

With a gleaming gold-leaf dome, the impossible-to-miss **Colorado State Capitol** *(capitol.colorado.gov; free)* is a must for history and architecture buffs. It's home to the Governor's office as well as the Senate and House of Representatives, and a free one-hour tour takes visitors through the behemoth structure, with guides sharing fun tidbits about its design and history, plus time to wander within the dome. Be sure to make a pit stop at the small museum on the 3rd floor for videos and building memorabilia too. Afterwards, take selfies on the outer staircase, where the 13th step sits exactly 1 mile above sea level.

All about the Centennial State

Learn all about Colorado history

Learn all about the Centennial State's people and places, from ancient to modern times, at the state-of-the-art **History Colorado Center** *(historycolorado.org; adult/child $15/free)*. Thoughtful and ever-changing exhibits present the spectrum of Coloradan voices; displays are high-tech and interactive to keep visitors engaged. If time permits, fold some of the museum's excellent programming into your visit – a city walking tour, archaeological dig, a lecture and more. Or head to the nearby **Center of Colorado Women's History** *(historycolorado.org; adult/child $7/free)*, where the beautifully restored Byers-Evan House has exhibits on the lives of local turn-of-the-20th-century women. Guided **tours** *(45min, $3)* are offered daily.

Do Like Locals Do

Civic Center Park hangout

Stretching between Denver's City Hall and the State Capitol, **Civic Center Park** *(civiccenterpark.org)* was inspired by the 19th-century City Beautiful Movement with gardens, fountains and monuments, a library-turned-art gallery, even a Greek Amphitheater. Denver's largest cultural and civic events are typically hosted here, every month bringing a different line-up, from the Marade (p91) to Día de los Muertos, the Mexican celebration honoring the deceased through artful altars. In the warmer months **Civic Center Eats** *(11am-2pm Wed & Thu)* is a favorite, when food trucks roll into the park, live bands play and office workers picnic on the grass. Even if nothing is on deck, wander through the park, stopping to see iconic statues like **Bronco Buster** and **On the War Trail**, a cowboy and Native American warrior, created in the 1920s by sculptor Alexander Phimister Proctor to pay homage to Colorado's Wild West roots.

JOHN FIELDER: COLORADO ARTIST & ADVOCATE

John Fielder (1950–2023) was a renowned nature photographer and author, and a true Colorado treasure. Fielder created stunning photographs of nearly every square foot of Colorado, and his images have featured in countless publications around the world. His multivolume collection *Colorado 1870–2000* documents the state's changing landscapes through meticulous side-by-side photos. Fielder was a passionate and tireless advocate for wilderness preservation, especially in Colorado, and a crucial partner to numerous environmental initiatives, including the creation of Colorado's Scenic and Historic Byways program. Fielder bequeathed his life's work (over 200,000 images, plus personal items) to History Colorado Center, the state's main history museum; rotating exhibits of his work are often on display.

**DENVER'S
CHICANO
MOVEMENT**

Unbeknownst to many, Denver was a major hub of the Chicano Movement of the 1960s and '70s. 'El Movimiento' fought racism, labor abuses and police violence against Latinos in Colorado and beyond. Rodolfo 'Corky' Gonzalez, a poet and boxer who later worked with Dr King and Cesar Chavez, was born in Denver. The notorious West High School 'Blowout' – a three-day student walkout, violently broken up by police – happened here. Not surprisingly, Chicano roots run deep in Denver. La Alma/Lincoln Park, with its gorgeous murals, is a longtime gathering place for families and community organizers; in 2021 it was designated a Historic Cultural District. Nearby, the Santa Fe Art District is home to some of Denver's longest-standing Latinx institutions.

Join the Celebration
Celebrate LQBTIQ+ community and culture

Everyone is welcome at Denver's **PrideFest** (*denverpride.org; free*), one of the nation's largest LGBTIQ+ events. And arrive they do, from near and far – over 550,000 people typically attend the two-day celebration in June. Come for the kick-off Pride 5K (costumes encouraged) and stay for a weekend of free performances, drinks and eats, and general revelry in Civic Center Park (p73). Don't miss the signature PrideFest Parade, with bedazzled floats and rainbow-clad revelers congregating in Cheesman Park. Proceeds benefit the Center, the largest LGBTIQ+ community center in the Rockies.

Beauty in Function
Peruse a decorative art museum

The **Kirkland Museum** (*kirklandmuseum.org; adult $27 Mon-Thu, $30 Fri-Sun, child free*) showcases the beauty of functional art – furnishings and houseware – from every major design period from 1870 to the present. The art is displayed salon style, as if you'd walked into someone's home, with groupings of furniture set alongside fine art and period pieces like rotary phones and wall clocks; it allows you to appreciate the art in context, a surprisingly rare perspective. The museum also features paintings by Colorado artists, including the namesake artist, Vance Kirkland, whose studio is a centerpiece of the museum. Download the free audio tour on your phone for a self-guided visit. Children 13 and over only. Note that one admission ticket covers entrance into both the Kirkland Museum and Denver Art Museum (p70); keep your receipt handy as you walk between them (or better yet, buy your ticket online).

Stroll Through Urban Gardens
Find beauty in botanic gardens

A 24-acre oasis next to Cheesman Park, **Denver Botanic Gardens** (*botanicgardens.org; adult/child $15.75/11.50*) is a beautiful and soothing place to wander. Winding paths lead you through a spectacularly diverse collection of gardens with plants from around the world, water features and large-scale art by renowned artists like Calder and Chihuly. In summer, an **outdoor concert series** brings big-name acts to the gardens, with lawn seating surrounding the stage (buy tickets early and bring a picnic dinner). In fall, self-guided ghost

EATING IN CAP HILL: OUR VEGETARIAN PICKS

Corner Beet: Homey cafe with light eats, smoothies and extensive options of toast (really). *8am-8pm Tue-Fri, to 6pm Sat, to 4pm Sun, to 3pm* **$**

City O' City: Retro restaurant serving innovative vegan dishes running the gamut from kimchi to poutine. Happy hour offered twice daily. *9am-10pm* **$$**

Watercourse Foods: Longtime vegetarian favorite featuring comfort foods with Asian and Mexican influences. *11am-9pm Mon-Fri, 10am-9pm Sat & Sun* **$$**

Bang Up to the Elephant: A tropical-industrial hangout spot serving up vegan dishes with Caribbean twists and turns. *4-9pm Sun-Thu, to 10pm Fri & Sat* **$$**

tours lead visitors through the gardens on October evenings. In winter, come for the holiday light extravaganza. Younger kiddos also will enjoy the **Mordecai Children's Garden**, where hands-on play, including splashing and wading in Pipsqueak Pond, is encouraged. The on-site **Freyer-Newman Center** also features botany-related art exhibits and films.

Soak in City Life & Death

Chill out in Cheesman Park

Cheesman Park is a historic park located in its namesake neighborhood, one of the most LGBTIQ+ friendly in Denver. In June, join revelers here for the start of the PrideFest Parade, a sea of rainbow flags filling the park. The rest of the year, Cheesman is popular for its jogging paths and wide, grassy expanses, ideal for sunning, picnicking and epic volleyball games. Occupying what was once Denver's first cemetery, the park also is notorious for its paranormal activity – a botched effort in 1893 to relocate about 2000 bodies to another cemetery might be the cause. (Bones are still occasionally dug up while, say, repairing the sprinkler system.) Learn all the spooky details on an evening walkabout with **Denver Local Tours** *(denverlikealocaltours.com; $25 per person)*, with guides sharing tidbits of history and stories of ghostly sightings and experiences.

Celebrate Cannabis Culture

Partake in a marijuana fest

Denver's **420 Festival** *(milehigh420fest.com; free)* is the world's largest cannabis celebration. Held every April 20th in Civic Center Park (p73), it draws over 40,000 attendees and features hip-hop artists and an omnipresent blue haze (despite it being illegal to smoke pot in public). Cannabis isn't sold – you gotta go to a dispensary for that – but there's lots of pot paraphernalia and food trucks too. (You know, munchies and all.) Security is tight, so expect long lines while bags are searched.

Tour an Unsinkable Home

Learn all about Molly Brown

This beautifully restored house, designed by the noted architect William Lang, was built in 1889 and belonged to the most famous survivor of the *Titanic* disaster: the unsinkable **Molly Brown** *(mollybrown.org; adult/child with guide $22/18,*

THE CENTER

Established in 1976, the **Center on Colfax** *(lgbtqcolorado.org)*, called simply 'The Center,' is the largest LGBTIQ+ community center in the Rocky Mountain region. A vital hub for support, advocacy and education, its support services span from youth (Rainbow Alley) to elder (Sage of the Rockies) and transgender programming. It's a good resource for LGBTIQ+ travelers too! Health services (including HIV testing and prevention), counseling and legal referrals are freely given. Or come for a drop-in events – watch parties, cooking classes, yoga – that are regularly offered. The Center also hosts the must-experience annual PrideFest, one of the largest and most festive LGBTIQ+ pride events in the US.

 EATING IN CAPITOL HILL & GOLDEN TRIANGLE: OUR PICKS

Jelly Café: Retro diner serving creative all-day breakfasts. Cinnamon roll pancakes and made-to-order doughnut holes are faves. *7am-2pm Mon-Fri, to 3pm Sat & Sun* $

Leven Deli Co: Classic NYC deli meets Mediterranean restaurant with wine shop. Happy hour means charcuterie and cocktails on the patio. *8am-7pm* $$

Pho-natic: Cheery cafe serving traditional pho and other Vietnamese faves. Window seats mean views of the Capitol. *10am-8pm Mon-Fri, 11am-8pm Sat* $$

Cuba Cuba Café & Bar: Cuban classics pair perfectly with the restaurant's island vibe. *5-10pm Mon-Thu, to 10:30 Fri & Sat, to 9pm Sun* $$

TUNNELS UNDER DENVER

An important part of Denver's history is right beneath your feet. An extensive network of tunnels, some dating to the 1880s, crisscrosses downtown Denver beneath many historic buildings, including the State Capitol, Union Station and the Oxford Hotel. Rumors notwithstanding, most tunnels served practical purposes. Some carried warm air from coal-fired heating plants to hotels and offices. Others were used to transfer goods and construction materials, whether by light-rail or by mule-drawn carts. And, yes, some were used for Prohibition-era smuggling and to access underground speakeasies and brothels. Many tunnels have been destroyed or filled in out of safety concerns; those that remain are a little-known remnant of Denver's early days.

self-guided $17/13). Guides take you on a 45-minute tour of the house, sharing the life and history of this Colorado legend, including her activity in progressive politics and women's organizations, and as a keen theater performer. Brown died in 1932, a woman ahead of her time. If the tour is sold out, you can still visit the house on your own – download the self-guided tour from the website.

Learn about Your Dollars
Tour the US Mint

The single largest producer of coins in the world – about 7.5 billion per year – the **United States Mint** *(usmint.gov; free)* offers 75-minute guided tours of its facility (Monday through Thursday only). They're surprisingly interesting: you'll learn about the history of the mint and the manufacturing techniques behind the pennies in your pockets. Arrive at 7am to assure a spot; tickets can only be requested same-day and in person. Note: no cameras or bags – not even purses or fanny packs – are allowed on the tour; carry what you need in your pockets.

Listen to Live Tunes
Concerts on Colfax

Opened as a roller rink in 1906, the **Fillmore Auditorium** *(fillmoreauditorium.org; prices vary)* has had many lives: a car-manufacturing plant, a rec center, a nightclub, even a farmers market. Today, it's one of the most popular mid-size music venues in town, its big open space holding 3700 concert-goers, mostly standing (there are a few unreserved seats in the balcony and back). In a nod to its beginnings, you can even see the occasional roller derby match here too. Arrive early or pay an extra 10 bucks to skip the lines that often wrap around the block.

See a Show with Heart
Curious theater performances

'No guts, no story' is the tagline of the award-winning **Curious Theatre Company** *(curioustheatre.org; from $28)*. Plays pack a punch with thought-provoking stories that take on social justice issues; post-show talkbacks with actors allow audiences to dive deeper too. Set in a converted church, there's not a bad seat in the house.

 DRINKING IN CAP HILL, GOLDEN TRIANGLE & CHEESMAN PARK: LGBTIQ+ TOP SPOTS

Blush & Blu: Lesbian and transgender bar with loads of programming and cozy seating. *5-11pm Mon & Tue, 1-11pm Wed, 1pm-2am Thu-Sat, noon-11pm Sun*	**Tight End:** Queer sports bar with two patios, loads of big screens plus theme nights like trivia and karaoke. *3pm-2am Mon-Fri, noon-2am Sat & Sun*	**Denver Sweet:** Bear bar with a rooftop patio. Expect DJs and watch parties. *4-11pm Tue & Wed, 4pm-midnight Thu, 4pm-2am Fri, 2pm-2am Sat, 11am-11pm Sun*	**Hamburger Mary's:** Drag-themed bar and burger chain with karaoke, bingo and more. Reservations recommended. *3-11pm Wed-Fri, 10am-11pm Sat, 10am-10pm Sun*

EXPLORING SANTA FE ART DISTRICT

Wander the historically Chicano La Alma/Lincoln Park neighborhood, home to the Art District on Santa Fe, a bohemian, artsy area.

START	END	LENGTH
Armstrong Center for Dance	esp	0.9 miles; 4 hours

The heart of the Santa Fe district is four blocks long: start at the north end's ❶ **Armstrong Center for Dance**, which occasionally showcases new works by Colorado Ballet in its black box theater.

Heading south, stop at ❷ **Center for Visual Art**, Metro State's gallery, known for its bold, contemporary works by international artists. Afterwards, walk a block to ❸ **Museo de las Americas**, a small museum with ever-changing exhibits paying homage to Latinx diversity.

Keep heading south, popping into galleries like ❹ **BitFactory** or ❺ **RULE**, or do some window shopping at artsy boutiques like ❻ **Green Lady Gardens** or ❼ **Abstract**. You'll eventually run into ❽ **Denver Art Society**, a co-op with dozens of open artist studios plus a cavernous gallery, displaying the finished work.

Hunger will strike – hit up ❾ **El Taco de Mexico**, a no-frills, fluorescent-lit restaurant, known for its *chile relleno* burrito, a glorious disaster of stuffed peppers, refried beans and homemade salsa verde wrapped in a tortilla. Loosen your belt and cross the street to mural-covered ❿ **Su Teatro Cultural and Performing Arts Center**. Born from the Civil Rights Movement, the company stages performances focused on the Chicano experience.

Cap off your stroll heading back north to ⓫ **Room for Friends**, a cozy wine bar or, for something edgier, ⓬ **esp**, a trendy hi-fi lounge.

The dilapidated art-deco building is **Aztlán Theater**, a Spanish-language movie theater turned go-to venue for one-time underground bands like Red Hot Chili Peppers and Metallica.

While there are loads of **murals** on Santa Fe, check out the alleys too. The one between 8th and 9th is particularly inspired!

W 11th Ave
START
END ⓬
W 10th Ave
❷
Santa Fe Dr
W 9th Ave
❸
⓫
❹
❺
W 8th Ave
Lipan St
Kalamath St
Santa Fe Dr
Inca St
Galapagos St
Fox St
❻
❼
❽
❿
❾
W 7th Ave

Speer Blvd
Cherry Creek Trail
Speer Blvd

Sunken Gardens Park

0 — 200 m
0 — 0.1 miles

Wash Park & SoBo

VIBRANT PARK AND URBAN EDGE

GETTING AROUND

Public bus and light-rail make it easy to access the Wash Park and SoBo neighborhoods. The park itself is about 11 blocks east of SoBo, a short 1-mile stroll or bus ride. Driving is easy too. There's metered parking on Broadway but if you venture a couple of blocks (or near the park), there are free spots on residential streets. Walking is the most convenient way to explore. Cyclists can rent all manner of bikes, from cruisers to quirky quadracycles, at Wash Park's boathouse.

☑ TOP TIP

For a water refill, head to Fire Station 21 at the northeast corner of the park. There's a water fountain near the front door (plus one for pooches!). If it's dry, use the refill stations at the Washington Park Rec Center, just south of Smith Lake.

The adjoining neighborhoods of Washington Park and South Broadway are like two sides of the same coin. Wash Park, as it's called, dates to 1886, created as an escape from the 'unsavory elements' of the big city. Today, it's an upscale neighborhood lined in tall, leafy trees and dotted with historic brick homes and modern duplexes. Its namesake park, designed in the early 1900s, is beautifully landscaped with trails, lakes and the most extensive public garden in Denver. South Broadway, or SoBo, is Wash Park's edgy little sister. Originally a transportation corridor served by horse-drawn street cars, the city grew around it, bringing bustling commercial districts. Urban renewal efforts in the '60s pushed the seedier elements of downtown Denver – unsavory bars, adult bookstores, porn theaters – to the neighborhood, eventually making SoBo a hive of counterculture activity. Today, the porn is (mostly) gone but SoBo remains an uber-urban area known for its dive bars and cocktail lounges plus an eclectic mix of thrift, vintage and antique shops.

Outdoors in the City

Walk, paddle or pedal Wash Park

The calling card of its namesake neighborhood, **Washington Park** is a hub of activity and, arguably, Denver's most beautiful green space. Spanning over 160 acres, its tree-lined paths, lakes and gardens are a welcome place to spend an afternoon, especially if you're yearning for the outdoors or want to exercise (join the Denver club!). Ground zero is the **historic boathouse**, where from March to October you can have some fun **paddling** *(wheelfunrentals.com; $15-30 per hr)* around Smith Lake on a kayak, paddleboard or, best of all, a swan-shaped paddleboat. If you prefer wheels instead, rent a **cruiser or surrey bike** *($15-40 per hr)* to explore the park, making sure not to miss the replica **Mount Vernon garden**

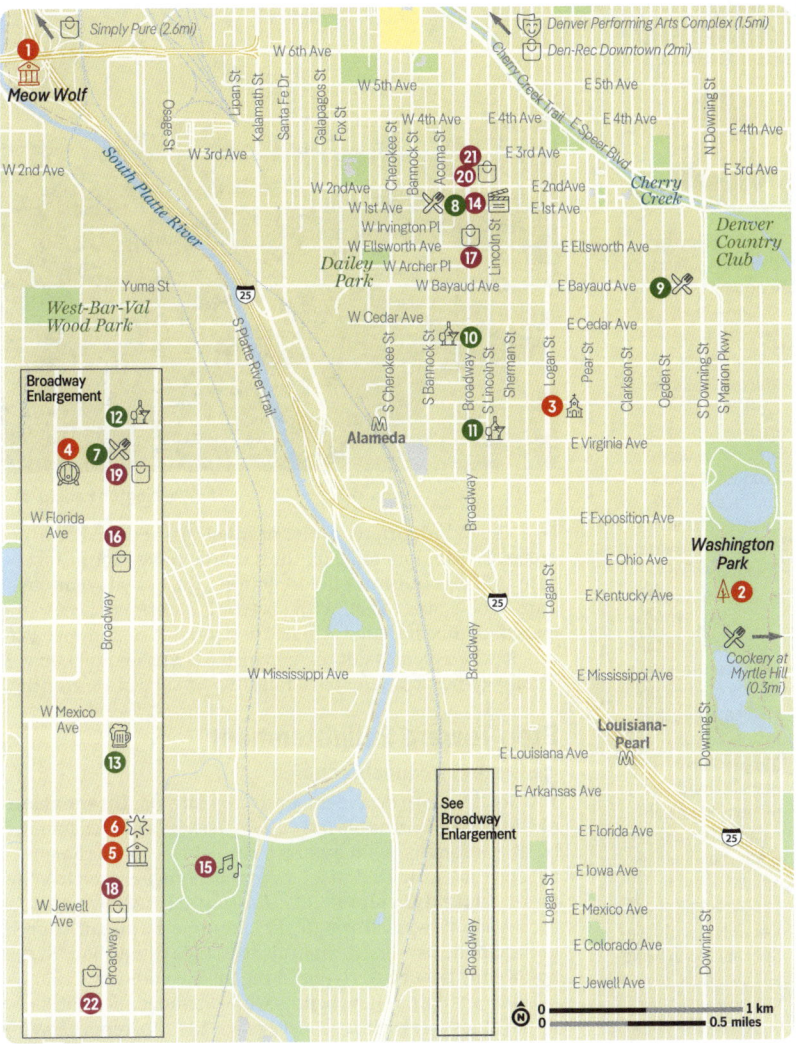

HIGHLIGHTS
1 Meow Wolf
2 Washington Park

SIGHTS
3 International Church of Cannabis
4 Laws Whiskey House
5 Spectra Art Space

ACTIVITIES
6 Sexploratorium

EATING
7 LaTinto Café
8 MAKFam
9 Mister Oso

DRINKING
10 Adrift

11 BurnDown
12 Dive Inn
13 Public Offering Brewing Co.

ENTERTAINMENT
14 Landmark Mayan Theatre
15 Levitt Pavilion

SHOPPING
16 Antique Exchange Co-op
17 Boss Vintage
18 Fifty Two 80's
19 Gallagher Books
20 Goldmine Vintage
21 Maikoh Holistics
22 Reefer Madness

DENVER'S BEST DISPENSARIES

Meghan Howes, industry expert and longtime Denverite, shares a few of her favorite marijuana dispensaries.

Maikoh Holistics
Go-to spot for the freshest, most affordable flower. Product is sold in jars or 'deli-style,' so clients can handle it before purchase. Located in SoBo.

Reefer Madness
SoBo shop offering a premier selection of concentrates at a variety of price points. Medical weed sold too.

Simply Pure
Black-owned dispensary in LoHi selling premium organic cannabis. Knowledgeable budtenders too.

Verde Natural
Specializing in living soil cannabis; most is grown vertically, in-house. Storefront is near City Park.

Den-Rec Downtown
LoDo institution carrying a great selection of flower at fair prices.

Wherever you go, don't forget to tip your budtender – remember, they're providing a service!

Washington Park (p78)

on Lake Windermere, a bloom-filled attraction. For a no-nonsense run, join folks on the 2.6-mile **paved loop**. Just be sure to look both ways before joining the crowd – you must cross a bike lane (often with speeding cyclists) to access the walking/running lane! Almost best of all are summer evenings, when picnics dot the expansive lawns and pickup volleyball games keep the park buzzing – a slice of Denver life.

Step Toward Enlightenment

Meditate in a cannabis church

You don't have to be a member to step into the **International Church of Cannabis** (*elevationists.org*), a church founded by 'Elevationists,' who embrace cannabis as a sacrament to aid spiritual growth. In fact, everyone is encouraged to come for the **laser light show** (*$25*). Lasting around 30 to 45 minutes, visitors walk through the one-time Lutheran church, taking in the psychedelic murals by artists Okuda San Miguel and Kenny Scharf. Arriving in the multicolored sanctuary, a 3D videomapping show begins while a guided meditation on mindfulness and self-discovery plays. Visitors report leaving at peace and happy (and nope, it's not the weed – partaking is not permitted on the property by nonmembers). Be sure to come early to take full advantage of the church's meeting room, complete with Ping-Pong, Galaga and Ms Pac-Man, all included in the price of admission. Munchies extra.

Sip Colorado Goodness

Tour a craft whiskey distillery

Even if you rarely drink whiskey, touring **Laws Whiskey House** (*lawswhiskeyhouse.com; $20*) is time well spent. Visitors start with a chalkboard lecture on the whiskey-making process, learning all about how the Colorado grains are cooked, fermented and distilled, followed by a guided tour of the distillery. Highlights include walking past seeing the open-air fermentation tanks and barrel rooms, where the goods are aged for a minimum of two years. The one-hour tour ends in a tasting, including sips of its award-winning Four Grain Bourbon and Rye. Age 21+ only.

Seeking Treasure

Thrift and vintage shopping

Thrifting and vintage shopping has become a sport on South Broadway, with everything from Denver's hottest **Goodwill** (*goodwillcolorado.org*) to designer consignment shops (and pretty much everything in between). Shops are sprinkled across the busy Broadway thoroughfare though most are clustered around two commercial areas. The one closest to downtown, between 3rd and Bayaud, is trendier with a decidedly hipster-grunge vibe (and higher prices). Bars and restaurants sit alongside shops like **Goldmine Vintage** (*goldmine vintage.com*), jam-packed with clothing and accessories from the Victorian era to the 1990s, and **Boss Vintage** (*bossvintage. com*), a curated spot often used to source clothing for movie sets. The other commercial zone, between Arkansas and Jewell streets, has less cachet and everyday buzz but includes **Antique Row** (*facebook.com/DenverAntiqueRow*), a collection of several dozen shops veering from **Gallagher Books** (*gcbooks.com*), with rare books and library-related antiques, and **Antique Exchange Co-op** (*303/777-7871*), a labyrinthine co-op of antique vendors to **Fifty Two 80's** (*the80sareawe some.com*), a shop with totally rad threads from the 1980s and '90s. Poke around, move between SoBo sections; wherever you land, you're sure to find a treasure.

Step into Another World

Immerse yourself in art exhibits

A dynamic, artist-run gallery, the immersive installations at **Spectra Art Space** (*spectraartspace.com; adult/child $20/12*) are a lighthearted and wow-inducing way to spend a couple of hours. Depending on the time of year, the multiroom art installations toggle between Nova Ita (dreamy, fantastical worlds) and Spookadelia (creepy, kitschy worlds); visitors walk through the surreal, psychedelic and ever-changing environments. Actors are occasionally integrated into the art too. Sure, it's kind of like a smaller, less-intricate Meow Wolf (p63)...though Spectra was here first!

PUBLIC ART FUND

Almost everywhere you turn, public art and cultural outlets are woven into Denver. The reason? State law directs a portion of sales taxes to cultural organizations large and small, resulting in an annual distribution of $60 million; additionally, a city ordinance requires that any public works project over $1 million dedicates 1% of its funding to the arts. Over 400 public artworks have been funded through these means, including the giant *Dancers* at the Denver Performing Arts Complex (p60) and *Signs of Life*, a collection of cheerful street signs in SoBo with messages like 'You're a Shining Star.' Even Denver's airport is widely known for its art collection, including the iconic blue mustang known as *Blucifer* because of its glowing red eyes.

 EATING IN WASH PARK & SOBO: OUR PICKS

LaTinto Café: Colorful cafe specializing in Colombian coffee drinks and breakfasts. Freshly baked traditional pastries and stuffed treats. *8am-2pm Tue-Sun* **$**

Cookery at Myrtle Hill: Local hot spot with a homey vibe. Hearty American fare served, from benedicts to pot pies. Cellphone use prohibited. *7am-3pm* **$$**

Mister Oso: Tacos rule here, stuffed with smoked pork, lamb and goat and topped with homemade salsas. *11am-10pm Sun-Thu, to 11pm Fri & Sat* **$$**

MAKFam: Serves a mix of traditional and inventive Cantonese dishes. Order at the counter and afterwards enjoy table service. *11am-8:45pm Wed-Mon* **$$**

**DENVER'S BEST
BIG PARKS**

**Rocky Mountain
Arsenal National
Wildlife Refuge:**
Enormous urban
refuge with over 330
species of wildlife,
including bison and
bald eagles. Ten
miles of trails, plus
ranger-guided tours.

**Cherry Creek State
Park:** Sprawling
forested park
with reservoir and
spectacular Rocky
Mountain views.
Expect multiuse trails
and sandy beaches.

**Bluff Lake Nature
Center:** Scenic
wildlife refuge known
for rich birdlife. Enjoy
wetlands, ponds and
a creek along a leafy
1.5-mile trail.

**Chatfield State
Park:** Go-to park
for water play
with a massive
reservoir perfect for
paddleboarding and
boating.

**Roxborough State
Park:** Dramatic
red-rock park with 14
miles of trails crossing
forests and prairies.
A photographer
favorite.

Our Bodies, Ourselves
Get real at the Sex Museum

The titillatingly named **Sex Museum** (*sexploratoriumden
ver.com; $15*) is the brainchild of two professors, one of whom
taught Human Sexuality to college students for over 20 years.
The museum is, effectively, that college course. A fascinating,
fun and educational examination of sexuality, the one-room
museum is packed with information on poster boards, pro-
jections and displays. There are even QR codes for deeper
dives. Expect exhibits as varied as fertility and sexual anat-
omy to prostitution and kink – prepare to see lots of geni-
tals! Also expect to walk through a giant vagina to access it.
The museum is located inside **Sexploratorium**, a center offering a wide range of lectures ('Sexuality as We Age'), classes (nude yoga) and events (burlesque); check the website for
the monthly calendar of events.

Movie Night
Art-house theater films and events

Landmark Mayan Theatre (*landmarktheatres.com; adult/
child $15/12*), typically called 'the Mayan,' is a historic art-
house theater in the heart of SoBo, and makes for a fun night
at the movies. Built in 1930, it's just one of three theaters in
the US built in the art deco Mayan Revival style, integrating
clean lines and geometric shapes with Mesoamerican influences like ornate sculptures and vibrant murals. All manner of independent and foreign films (plus classics too!) are
screened here; special events like film fests and theme nights,
even Q&As with filmmakers are often on deck too. Whatever
the screening or event, arrive a little early to enjoy a drink on
the balcony-level cocktail lounge. And no need to rush – you
can bring your drinks into the theater!

The Sound of (Free) Music
Free concerts at Levitt Pavilion

Just west of South Broadway is **Levitt Pavilion** (*levittden
ver.org*), a massive amphitheater set on the grassy slopes of
Ruby Hill Park. Each summer, it hosts over 50 concerts – a
mix of national, local and emerging artists from genres ranging from opera to rap. (Hello G Love & Special Sauce!) Spon-
sored by the Levitt Foundation, concerts are free, and always
all-ages. The reason? The belief that music has the power to
bring people together. Bring a blanket for the lawn seating
or if you plan to dance, beeline to the stage!

DRINKING IN WASH PARK & SOBO: OUR PICKS

Adrift: Tiki bar complete
with totem poles, tropical
decor and cocktails
served in coconuts.
Polynesian eats too.
*5-10pm Tue-Thu, 4pm-
midnight Fri & Sat*

BurnDown: Furniture
store turned sprawling bar
with rooftop views. Live
music on weekends. *11am-
10pm Mon, to 11pm Wed &
Thu, to 1am Fri, 10am-1am
Sat, 10am-10pm Sun*

**Public Offering Brewing
Co.:** Industrial-chic
brewery specializing in
gluten-free and -reduced
beers. *3-9pm Tue-Thu,
1-10pm Fri, noon-10pm Sat,
noon-8pm Sun*

Dive Inn: Popular dive
bar known for its cheap
drinks, lawn games and
speedboat-doubling-as-
bar seating. *11:30am-2am
Mon-Fri, 10am-2am Sat
& Sun*

RiNo & Five Points

STREET ART AND NIGHTLIFE

Denver's most dynamic neighborhood today, Five Points and RiNo has a long history. This was historically an African American enclave, the result of racial segregation and redlining, but a thriving community all the same – its jazz clubs earned it the nickname 'Harlem of the West.' As redlining was curtailed in the 1960s, Black residents decamped for other neighborhoods, the sudden exodus leaving Five Points gutted, as empty as the old railyards and warehouses on its western edge. It wasn't until the 1990s that artists appeared and began converting those same warehouses into studio spaces and homes. Eventually the River North or 'RiNo' Art District was born, home to galleries, bohemian cafes, breweries and lots and lots of murals. Today, Five Points and RiNo are ever evolving, the influence of developers and interests of longtime residents often at odds. Nevertheless, it remains complex and supremely engaging, a place to visit with eyes wide open.

Street Art Everywhere

Be wowed by RiNo's murals

Unexpected and totally fabulous, the trendy RiNo neighborhood is draped in hundreds of murals covering every sort of surface, from parking-lot walls and alleyways to power boxes and garage doors. Bright, opinionated and ever-changing, the artwork stops you in your tracks, speaking volumes about Denver's diversity, history and musings of day-to-day life. With well over 200 murals and more added each month, it's easy to just wander the neighborhood and take them in. If you want a bit more structure, check out any number of on-line maps that pinpoint faves (RiNo's website is a good start: *rinoartdistrict.org/art/murals*). For an even deeper dive, take a guided tour; they're offered by various local companies and typically run around two hours, strolling past notable pieces and including details about the artists and the historical and social context of each. If in doubt, try **Denver Graffiti**

GETTING AROUND

Just northeast of downtown, RiNo and Five Points are serviced by city buses and light-rail. You'll see people on lime green e-bike and e-scooter shares. There's isn't typically much traffic but the stop signs and pedestrians can make driving slow going. Parking is tough, especially in RiNo. Public lots are limited so most days. Parking enforcement is fierce; even returning a couple of minutes late can land you a ticket. Once here, travel by foot.

☑ TOP TIP

RiNo Art District's website *(rinoartdistrict.org)* is a valuable resource. It features detailed information about galleries, murals, monthly events and more. Interactive maps, organized by theme, make it especially easy to track down a favorite shop, restaurant or bar.

DENVER WALLS

Street art helped turn the run-down warehouses of RiNo into a vibrant art district, and big murals fests have had a major hand in the change. In 2009 CRUSH Walls started as a 'graffiti weekend' but quickly morphed into a week-long arts festival attended by tens of thousands. The extravaganza spurred rapid change (some say gentrification) of the RiNo neighborhood, which bustles with bars, galleries and more. A #MeToo scandal doomed CRUSH Walls in 2021, but it was quickly succeeded by **DENVER WALLS** *(denverwalls.com)*, a women- and immigrant-owned festival held annually in October, which focuses on supporting under-represented artists. Today, DENVER WALLS, along with RiNo Art District, is not only a festival but a powerful force for arts education, neighborhood beautification and connection to the art world.

Tour *(denvergraffititour.com; adult/child $30/15)* for its small groups and custom tours. Whichever way you see RiNo's murals, prepare to be wowed.

Hidden History
Learn local African American history

Tucked into the 3rd floor of its namesake library, the multimedia **Blair-Caldwell African American Research Library Museum** *(history.denverlibrary.org/blair; free)* provides a thoughtful overview of African Americans in the West – from their arrival as pioneers in the pre–Civil War era to their achievements in the face of deep-rooted discrimination. Be sure to check out the exhibits on Wellington Webb, Denver's first African American mayor, and on the development of the Five Points neighborhood. The library itself houses archives and rare documents focusing on the rich cultural heritage of African Americans in the West.

Art Walk/Street Party
First Fridays in RiNo

A long-standing tradition, First Friday is the day each month when Denverites head to the city's art districts after work to wander through art galleries, studios and co-ops that keep their doors till 9pm. **RiNo's First Friday** *(rinoartdistrict .org/visit/first-Fridays; free)* is among the liveliest of them all with show openings, live music and a general sense of revelry in- and outdoors. Start at the **Dry Ice Factory**, a collective of over 30 studios, and wander from there. Favorite stops include **Plinth Gallery** *(plinthgallery.com)* focused on ceramics, **fooLPRoof contemporary art gallery** *(foolproof contemporaryart.com)* for its range of mediums, and **Dateline** *(dateline.bigcartel.com)* for its emerging artists. Along the way, enjoy drinks and nibbles – RiNo's streets, especially Larimer St, are lined with options

Up Close & Personal
Live music in small venues

To add a layer of music to a night out in RiNo, check out **Nocturne Jazz & Supper Club** *(nocturnejazz.com; from $22)*, an art-deco-meets-industrial-chic spot. Nationally touring jazz musicians regularly perform here, but the real stars are the artists in residence who take the stage for four- to eight-week runs. Sit at the bar or enjoy a prix fixe meal with the show. If mosh pits are more your vibe, try the nearby **Larimer Lounge** *(larimerlounge.com; from $10)* instead. A gritty proving ground for indie rock acts, there's live music almost every night, a reliable bet if you want to take in a last-minute show. Escape to the patio when you need a break from the crowd. Or if you're looking for a hybrid, check out **Two Moons Music Hall** *(twomoonsmusic.com; free to $10)*, a cocktail lounge with a Southwestern vibe and a stage featuring everything from honky-tonk to hip-hop artists.

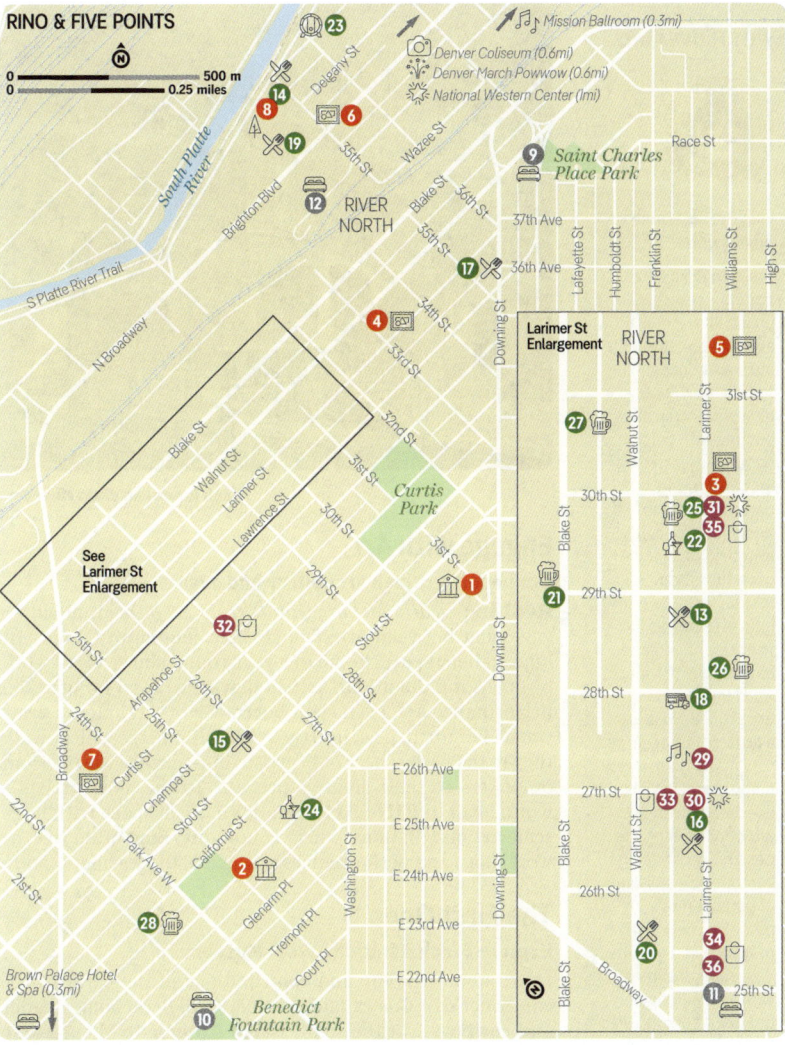

RINO & FIVE POINTS

Mission Ballroom (0.3mi)

Denver Coliseum (0.6mi)
Denver March Powwow (0.6mi)
National Western Center (1mi)

Saint Charles Place Park

RIVER NORTH

Curtis Park

See Larimer St Enlargement

Larimer St Enlargement   RIVER NORTH

Brown Palace Hotel & Spa (0.3mi)

Benedict Fountain Park

SIGHTS
1 Black American West Museum
2 Blair-Caldwell African American Research Library Museum
3 Dateline
4 Dry Ice Factory
5 fooLPRoof contemporary art gallery
6 Plinth Gallery
7 RedLine
8 RiNo Art Park

SLEEPING
9 Catbird
10 Queen Anne B&B
11 Ranbke Hotel
12 Source Hotel

EATING
13 Beckon
14 Comal
15 Curtis Park Deli
16 Denver Central Market
17 Hop Alley
18 Mile High Hibachi Food Truck
19 Safta
20 Stowaway

DRINKING
21 Bierstadt Lagerhouse
22 Finn's Manor
23 Ironton Distillery & Crafthouse
24 Monkey Bar at Welton Room
25 Odell Brewing Five Points
26 Our Mutual Friend
27 Stem Ciders
28 Woods Boss Brewing

ENTERTAINMENT
29 Larimer Lounge
30 Nocturne Jazz & Supper Club
31 Two Moons Music Hall

SHOPPING
32 Alchemy Ritual Goods
33 Be a Good Person
34 Old School Cool Vintage Markets
35 Three Arrows Gallery
36 Topo Designs

WHY I LOVE RINO

Liza Prado, Lonely Planet writer

Walking RiNo's streets, I see possibility everywhere: the old warehouses turned brewpubs, once-forgotten alleys busting with color, community-driven art centers and parks where empty lots once stood. It's my go-to for a night out – the vibrant restaurants and edgy bars offering, as if with extended hand, an outing with friends. And I love that each time I go, RiNo is just a little different…a new mural here, a new menu there. RiNo is like being given the gift of discovery, the possibility of seeing something inspiring, of considering a place in a new light, of witnessing growth. Yes, change comes with its challenges, but like a person, RiNo feels alive, worth knowing and watching where it'll go next.

Black American West Museum

Engage with Art

Community-driven art gallery and events

RedLine *(redlineart.org; adult/child $5/3)* is all about engagement between artists and their community. Enjoy the huge gallery space, home to a year-round showcase of works by emerging Coloradan artists that's also used for art talks, performance art, even slam poetry nights. Whatever draws you in, be sure to peek into the studios lining the gallery walls; they're the workspaces of 15 artists-in-residence who welcome onlookers to their creative process. To see more artists at work, head to **RiNo Art Park**. It's a green space with large-scale art installations, where community (and often free) art workshops and performances are held in the warmer months.

The First Ones

Explore Black American West Museum

Learn about the life and contributions of the earliest African American Coloradans – miners, soldiers, homesteaders and cowboys – at the small **Black American West Museum** *(bawmhc.org; adult/child $15/10)*. The exhibits are set in the former home-turned-clinic of Dr Justina Ford, the first licensed African American female physician in Colorado who,

DRINKING IN RINO & FIVE POINTS: THE HARD(ER) STUFF

Finn's Manor: Tiny bar featuring Denver's top tap and spirits list. Patio-bound food trucks are a hit. *5pm-midnight Tue-Thu, 2pm-1am Fri & Sat, 2-9pm Sun*

Ironton Distillery & Crafthouse: Distillery with cocktails on tap; ski lifts double as chairs on the patio. *4-8pm Mon-Wed, noon-10pm Thu-Sat, noon-8pm Sun*

Stem Ciders: Craft cidery with a country vibe; come for live music and trivia nights. *2-9pm Wed, noon-10pm Thu & Fri, 10:30am-10pm Sat, 10:30am-9pm Sun*

Monkey Bar at Welton Room: Lounge serving cocktails using extras like cotton candy and liquid nitrogen; gourmet bites pair beautifully. *3-10pm Tue-Sat*

barred from working in hospitals because of her race, set up a private practice in her home. Don't miss the fascinating display on Dearfield Colony, a long-abandoned African American settlement in northern Colorado that's listed on the National Register of Historic Places.

Hands-On Learning
Experience museum-like CSU Spur

Part of the National Western Center, **CSU Spur** *(csuspur.org; free)* is a state-of-the-art educational facility, with loads of hands-on experiences for the public. Thematic buildings allow visitors to observe equine therapy and veterinary surgeries, take cooking and gardening classes, and learn all about water conservation. An interesting way to spend an afternoon, especially for older kids.

Celebrate!
Attend Denver's annual powwow

Since 1984 Denver's Native American community has hosted an annual **Denver March Powwow** *(denvermarchpow wow.org; $7)* in the **Denver Coliseum** *(denvercoliseum.com)*. Over 100 tribes from across the US and Canada come together to celebrate their heritages through song, dance and storytelling. Held for three days each March, it's one of the largest powwows in the country. Join this impressive celebration, eat Native foods and buy Native art, all the while learning about the country's original inhabitants.

Sport Your Stetson
Check out the stock show

Saddle up for the **National Western Stock Show** *(nationalwestern.com; adult/child from $17/4),* one of the country's biggest stock shows and a Denver tradition since 1906. A 16-day event held every January in the **National Western Center** *(nationalwesterncenter. com)*, the event includes 20+

STEER AT THE BROWN
Since 1945, the stock show's Grand Prize Champion steer is paraded through the **Brown Palace** hotel during Afternoon Tea (p65), guests treated to tea sandwiches and selfies with the famous bull.

THE GREEN BOOK: ROSSONIAN HOTEL

For African American travelers in the mid-1900s, there was no more important resource than the Green Book. The annual travel guide listed hotels, restaurants and other businesses where African American travelers could safely visit, including Denver's Rossonian Hotel. Not only were they welcome there, the Rossonian Lounge was considered the best jazz club between St Louis and LA, hosting greats like Duke Ellington and Louis Armstrong. Ironically, as racial segregation laws faded, so did the Rossonian – African American travelers and entertainers had many more choices of where to stay and eat. Efforts to restore and reopen the Rossonian – as a hotel, halfway house, or office building – have mostly fizzled, but it remains standing, a monument to jazz history - and African American travel.

DRINKING IN RINO & FIVE POINTS: CRAFT BREWS

Odell Brewing Five Points: The OG of IPA, half the taps are experimental releases brewed here. *noon-10pm Mon-Thu, noon-midnight Fri & Sat, noon-9pm Sun*

Our Mutual Friend: Brewing Master of eclectic beers, artsy OMF makes award-winning brews from locally grown hops and barley. *11am-10pm*

Bierstadt Lagerhouse: Cheery warehouse serving Denver's best slow-pours. Yard games, live music. *2-10pm Mon-Thu, noon-midnight Fri & Sat, noon-9pm Sun*

Woods Boss Brewing: Sprawling brewery with award-winning brews and weekly events. *2-8pm Mon & Tue, 2-10pm Wed & Thu, noon-10pm Fri & Sat, noon-7pm Sun*

BEST SHOPPING IN RINO & FIVE POINTS

Topo Designs: High-quality, locally made outdoor gear, including clothing and bags. Located inside a converted shipping container.

Three Arrows Gallery: Collective of 60 local artisans, all women-owned businesses, selling everything from homegoods to accessories.

Old School Cool Vintage Markets: Pop-up vintage flea market with clothes, vinyl and furniture. Held first Fridays and last Saturdays, April to November only.

Alchemy Ritual Goods: Metaphysical items – crystals, herbs, handmade tools – for wellness and spiritual healing; tarot card readings and divinations too.

Be a Good Person: Trendy shop with the aspirational brand name boldly printed across every item, mostly hoodies and bags.

PHOTO-DENVER/SHUTTERSTOCK

Mission Ballroom

rodeos, 15,000 farm animals, dancing horses, even dog shows. Don't miss the iconic kick-off parade, when dozens of longhorn cattle are herded down 17th St in downtown Denver, high heels and power suits giving way to cowboy hats, chaps and impressive belt buckles.

Big Ticket Concert

Mission Ballroom extravaganzas

If big concerts are your jam, add the **Mission Ballroom** (*missionballroom.com; price varies*) to your short list. Voted Best Indoor Venue in 2023 by locals, the bowl-shaped auditorium is reminiscent of Red Rocks (p93): wide ledges for dancing and unobstructed views of the stage, high tech lighting and excellent acoustics are a given. Most concerts are general admission, the spots under the massive glittering disco ball filling first (arrive early for those!).

 EATING IN RINO & FIVE POINTS: OUR PICKS

Curtis Park Deli: Deli focused on freshly made and locally sourced eats – even the condiments! Eat curbside or take to go. *10am-4pm Mon-Sat* **$**

Mile High Hibachi Food Truck: Hibachi-style meals doled out from a truck on Larimer and 28th. *1-9pm Sun-Thu, to 10pm Fri & Sat* **$**

Comal: Training for migrant women aspiring to own restaurants; mostly Latin American dishes. *11am-2pm & 4-6pm Tue-Fri, noon-4pm Sat* **$$**

Denver Central Market: Warehouse turned gourmet marketplace; has meal options. *8am-9pm Sun-Thu, to 11pm Fri & Sat* **$$**

Stowaway: Sunny brekkie and lunch spot serving healthy world fare, coffee and hard stuff too. *8am-2pm Thu-Mon* **$$**

Hop Alley: Chinese restaurant with inventive dishes and cocktails; try the tasting menu at the chef's counter. *5-10pm Mon-Sat* **$$$**

Safta: Israeli comfort food in an industrial-chic dining room; weekend buffet brunch. *5-10pm daily, 10:30am-2pm Sat & Sun* **$$$**

Beckon: Intimate Michelin-starred restaurant with changing Scandi-inspired menu. Pre-payment required. *5-10pm Wed-Sat* **$$$**

City Park

OUTDOOR ACTIVITIES AND KID-CENTERED FUN

At the heart of City Park neighborhood is, of course, City Park itself – one of the oldest public spaces in Denver. Conceived in 1882, shortly after Denver's founding, many of the park's current features – the winding paths, the lakes, the zoo and spectacular city views – were modeled after NYC's Central Park. City Park neighborhood grew up around this verdant mile-long park, many of its so-called Denver Squares (boxy brick houses) popping up after the 1893 silver bust, as they were cheaper to build than Victorians. Today, some of these same houses serve as cafes, bars and shops. Colfax Ave, running along the southern edge of the park, is still growing up. From its Wild West roots to today's mix of homegrown restaurants and trendy venues, it's a transitioning place, highlighting City Park's fascinating cross-section of people and places.

Cornucopia of Activity

City Park goings-on

City Park is the largest of Denver's open spaces, a 320-acre megapark located just east of downtown. Come stretch your legs on its leafy trails, **paddle boat** *(wheelfunrentals.com; adult/child $12/7 per hour)* on its lakes or even to play a round of **golf** *(cityofdenvergolf.com; from $33*. Or bring the kids to run wild on its sprawling **playgrounds** and **splash pads** or to check out the creatures at Denver Zoo (p91). The Denver Museum of Nature & Science (p90) is another family fave, though adults will enjoy a quiet after-hours visit (including adult drinks) on most Friday nights. From spring to autumn, a weekly **farmers market** *(cityparkfarmersmarket.com)* brings a festival-like feel to the park too, with live music, food trucks and all manner of locally grown picnic fixins'. Summer brings thousands of locals to free jazz concerts too. In winter, City Park is the starting point of the historic Marade (p91) in honor of Dr Martin Luther King Jr. And oh, that view: Denver's skyscrapers with a snowcapped mountain background, it's the icing on City Park's multilayered cake.

GETTING AROUND

It's a breeze to get to City Park by bus or car. There's loads of parking in the park itself and on nearby streets. Once here, walking is a pleasant way to explore. That said, unless you're sticking to the zoo and DMNS (they're next door to each other), distances aren't short; within the park alone, it's about a mile from end to end. Consider using the Lime or Lyft app to find an e-bike or e-scooter share, especially inside the park. (Outside the park, the traffic can be tricky to navigate.)

☑️**TOP TIP**

Denver Museum of Nature & Science (p90) offers free days several times each year. Time your visit to save on admission, just arrive early to beat the crowds! Denver Zoo (p91) offers free days as well, but only by lottery – check the website for deets.

Marczyk Fine Foods (0.5mi)

Civic Center Park (1.2mi)
Ellie Caulkins Opera House (1.8mi)

HIGHLIGHTS
1 City Park

SIGHTS
2 Denver Museum of Nature & Science
3 Denver Zoo

EATING
4 Molotov Kitschen & Cocktails
5 SAME Café
6 Sapsua
7 Vine Street Pub & Brewery

DRINKING
8 Cerebral Brewing
9 Middleman
10 PS Cocktail Lounge
11 Thin Man

ENTERTAINMENT
12 City Park Jazz
13 Denver Film Festival
● Sie Film Center (see **13**)

SHOPPING
● Tattered Cover (see **6**)
● Twist & Shout (see **13**)

Concerts & Community
Live jazz in City Park

Every summer since 1986, **City Park Jazz** *(cityparkjazz.org; free)* has produced concerts on Ferril Lake in City Park. Held on Sunday evenings, well-known Colorado-based bands play everything from classic jazz and blues to R&B and salsa. The series typically attracts around 10,000 concert-goers each week – bring a picnic blanket, borrow a lawn chair or just join the dancing in front of the bandstand. If hunger strikes, food trucks offer lots of options or BYO eats from **Marczyk Fine Foods** *(marczykfinefoods.com)*, a small local market with good made-to-order sandwiches, snacks and drinks. Come early to stake out a good spot!

Fill Up on Science
Experience Denver's science museum

Denver Museum of Nature & Science *(DMNS; dmns.org; adult/child $26/21)* is a magnificent must-do, especially for kids. A massive three-story building, it's packed with exhibits that make science and the natural world interesting and fun. It takes on everything from dinosaurs to outer space,

DRINKING IN CITY PARK: OUR PICKS

Thin Man: Bathed in red lights and religious art, this neighborhood bar is all about infused vodka and a Saturday-night vibe. *3pm-2am*

PS Cocktail Lounge: Sixties-style dive doling out free shots. Cash only. *3pm-midnight Sun & Mon, to 1am Tue-Thu, to 2am Fri & Sat*

Cerebral Brewing: Award-winning brewery serving IPAs to sours. *2-9pm Mon & Tue, noon-10am Wed & Thu, 11am-11pm Fri & Sat, to 9pm Sun*

Middleman: Industrial-style cocktail bar known for unusual liquors and combinations. *4pm-midnight Mon-Thu, to 2am Fri & Sat, to 10pm Sun*

with loads of hands-on experiences, live shows and science demos (and a few old-school dioramas thrown in). Faves include Expedition Health, with state-of-the-art exhibits on the human body (on-site genetics lab anyone?), as well as a Discovery Zone for little ones with water play and even puppet shows. The **IMAX theater** and **planetarium** make for a welcome break. Don't miss the excellent temporary exhibits covering topics as varied as mythical creatures and the biomechanics of bugs. Timed tickets are required – save a bit by buying them online.

See & Feed Wild Animals

Stroll through the Denver Zoo

Next to DMNS, the **Denver Zoo** (*denverzoo.org; adult/child $25/19*) is a pleasant place to spend a morning, with expansive habitats and up-close views of over 3000 animals from around the world, even tigers and elephants passing on bridges overhead. Animal feedings are especially fun to watch, with staffers sharing interesting facts about the creatures and answering audience questions (signs are posted throughout the zoo with feeding schedules). For a nominal fee, you also can feed lorikeet parrots as you walk through their habitat or gentle cownose stingrays from the rim of their 15,000-gallon tank. If your budget can swing it, **face-to-face encounters** (*$150 up to six people*) are possible with giraffes, sloths, rhinos and more, or get a behind-the-scenes tour of the zoo's animal hospital.

Films, Books, Records, Oh My!

Sie Film Center offerings

After a day in the park, chill out at the **Sie Film Center** (*denverfilm.org; from $10*) an art-house theater screening independent and avant-garde films. Before the show, pop into the **Tattered Cover** (*tatteredcover.com*) next door, an outpost of Denver's most beloved indie bookstore, or peruse the vinyl at **Twist & Shout** (*twistandshout.com*). The Sie also is home to the **Denver Film Festival**, the Rocky Mountain region's largest film festival, which brings over 200 films from across cultures, identities and countries to Denver every November. The fest includes Q&As, panel discussions and soirees with filmmakers and actors. Opening night is typically held at the beloved Ellie Caulkins Opera House (p60).

THE MARADE

Denver's Marade – part march, part parade – is a huge, joyous, serious, welcoming, historic event. It's the largest Martin Luther King Jr Day celebration in the country, bringing together tens of thousands to celebrate the life of Dr King and continue his fight for social justice. It's a massive outpouring of local people – students, elders, politicians, artists, workers, families with strollers, and activists with bullhorns – joining and chanting to manifest a better world. Marchers gather at the Dr King statue in City Park (p89) and march down Colfax Ave to Civic Center Park (p73) for rousing speeches.

EATING IN CITY PARK: OUR PICKS

SAME Café: Pay-what-you-can, fair-exchange cafe serving ever-changing menu of healthy dishes, including vegetarian options. *11am-2:30pm Mon-Fri* **$**

Vine Street Pub & Brewery: Neighborhood fave with mouthwatering pub grub and hearty salads; patio seating is tops. *3-10pm Wed & Thu, noon-10pm Fri-Sun* **$$**

Sapsua: Lauded Vietnamese restaurant serving non-traditional dishes with flair; menu changes seasonally. *4:30-9pm Sun & Mon, Wed & Thu, to 10pm Fri & Sat* **$$**

Molotov Kitchen & Cocktails: Small restaurant with big Eastern European flavors. Dishes nod to the chef's Ukrainian heritage. *5-9:30pm Tue-Sat, 4-8pm Sun* **$$$**

Beyond
Denver

Golden · Denver

Red Rocks Park & · Lakewood
Amphitheater

· Morrison

Take a day (or two) to explore the region just west of Denver, filled with history, music and outdoors adventure.

Places

Morrison p92
Golden p96
Lakewood p97

Tucked between Denver and the great swathe of mountains to the west is an often overlooked grab bag of outdoorsy fun and iconic Colorado destinations. Sure, the low, rocky foothills don't pack the same punch as the snowy peaks rising in the distance, but Golden, Morrison and their surrounding areas are no less engaging: a land of dinosaur tracks and early mining days; forest hikes and white-water adventure; iconic breweries and Colorado kitsch. And, of course, there's the megastar of it all: Red Rocks Amphitheater, a red-rock wonderland with world-class music, sweeping views and more. All that, just minutes from downtown Denver.

GETTING AROUND

Having a car makes it easy to explore the sights just outside Denver. Sure, there's a city bus to downtown Golden and, on concert days, there's a shuttle to Red Rocks but beyond that you'll be stuck. Rentals are available from the airport but they are much cheaper in town (no pesky airport fees!). The roads are generally well maintained and easy to navigate. Just try to avoid rush hours, especially Friday afternoons, when bumper-to-bumper traffic will add precious time to your travel.

Morrison

TIME FROM DENVER: **30 MINS**

The footprints of giants

The discovery site of the first stegosaur, **Dinosaur Ridge** *(dinoridge.org; free)* is also home to some of the most well-preserved dinosaur tracks and fossils in the world. Located on public land sandwiched between Hwy 470 and Red Rocks Amphitheater, the exposed rock surfaces here reveal 250+ dinosaur footprints and sandstone-encased fossils dating to the Jurassic and Cretaceous periods. A steep, paved **interpretive**

Continued on p96

DANIELLE BEDER/SHUTTERSTOCK

Fossilized footprints, Dinosaur Ridge

TOP EXPERIENCE

Red Rocks Park & Amphitheater

Built between towering 300ft-high red sandstone fins, Red Rocks may well be the world's most iconic outdoor concert venue. Renowned for its natural acoustics and stunning beauty, it has become synonymous with big-ticket concerts. But even if you can't make a show (some sell out in minutes), the venue and its surrounding 816 acres are free to visit and well worth the 15-mile trek from Denver.

Listen to World-Class Musicians

There's something almost primal about attending a concert at Red Rocks – the sounds of instruments and song, the sight of people dancing, an umbrella of dark sky above, and the iconic 300ft-high red sandstone monoliths standing guard on either side. For many, it's reason enough for a trip to Colorado. Definitely try to score tickets to a show – from April to November big-name musicians, symphony orchestras and solo artists perform at the venue; some like U2 and the Grateful

DON'T MISS

Concerts

Hiking

Films on the Rocks

Yoga on the Rocks

The view

Wandering the venue

PRACTICALITIES
Scan this QR code for upcoming concerts, events and more.

Dead have even recorded live albums here. Tickets are sold through **AXS.com**, or save on service fees and buy directly from the on-site box office or at Denver's Coliseum. Seating is on wide, wooden terrace benches built into the amphitheater's steep natural incline; over 9500 seats spread across 70 rows. There are no bad seats! The lower the number, the closer to the stage; the higher the number, the better the views. Concerts typically start at sunset, with the rocks aglow and city lights twinkling beyond.

Catch a Film

If a concert isn't on the cards, **Films on the Rocks** *($20)* is a fun runner-up. On set summer evenings, **Denver Film Society** *(denverfilm.org)* projects classic and cult faves onto a huge screen, converting the venue into a large-scale outdoor movie theater. Packed with locals on blankets, noshing and chitchatting, there's a laid-back community vibe. Pre-show performances by up-and-coming comedians and bands kick off the evening. As the sunlight fades and the stars emerge, the movie begins. Popcorn and Sno-Caps sold separately.

Perfect Your Downward Dog

If morning is your jam, come at sunrise for **Yoga on the Rocks** *($20)*. A regularly scheduled summer weekend class, thousands of yogis set up their mats along the amphitheater's terraced seating. Led by some of Denver's top yoga instructors, the all-levels classes cost around the same as a drop-in class does in town but the peaceful outdoor setting is unmatched: the morning air and expansive views, the sun rising over the red rocks...all add to a sense of tranquility and connection. BYO mat.

Take in the (Free) Views

In addition to being a world-class concert venue, Red Rocks is also a Denver Mountain Park, one of a handful of parks located within 60 miles of Denver that is maintained by the city. Because of this, the amphitheater and the land surrounding it are free and open to the public from sunrise to sunset. Come during the day to wander through the theater, snap photos next to the stage (or on the stage if you're lucky!) and of the iconic redfin monoliths, **Ship Rock** and **Creation Rock**, that help make the remarkable acoustics. You can also join locals working out on the steep stairs – a common sight, year-round. For Red Rocks' famous 360-degree panoramic views, head to the landing above the highest row of seats. Note: on event nights, the amphitheater closes at 2pm.

Hit the Trails

Red Rocks has a handful of trails that wind through its 800-plus acres of hilly landscape. Each showcases the park's stunning geology along with those sweeping views extending to downtown Denver. Most have interpretive signs that detail the area's history, geology and plant life. For a moderately easy hike, try **Trading Post Trail**, a 1.4-mile loop weaving through the heart of the park, past meadows and between towering red rock formations. The trail starts at the namesake Trading Post, a historic building with a souvenir shop, snack bar and bathrooms – perfect for a pre- or post-hike pit stop. For a longer, more strenuous hike, hit **Red Rocks Trail** – a 6-mile out-and-back hike that begins near the lower north parking lot and connects to the **Morrison Slide Trail** in the neighboring Matthews Winters Park. The trail climbs through rocky terrain to higher elevations with views of the foothills and mountains beyond; sightings of prairie dogs, red foxes and mule deer are common in the early mornings and late afternoons. Alternatively, take Red Rocks Trail to the **Dakota Ridge Trail**, an out-and-back 4-mile route that follows the rocky spine of Dinosaur Ridge (p92). Whatever trail you choose, remember to stay hydrated. At 6450ft (and higher), Red Rocks' elevation is no joke. Look for fill stations at the visitor center and inside the venue. Note: Red Rocks Trail is the only multi-use trail in the park so you may encounter horseback riders and mountain bikers.

Check out Red Rocks Hall of Fame

Learn all about the artists and performances that have shaped the legacy of Red Rocks Amphitheatre at the **Red Rocks Hall of Fame** *(free)*. Located inside the visitor center, the exhibits provide context to the long list of artists that have given concerts at Red Rocks since 1947. See memorabilia like instruments, costumes and posters from past performances (here's looking at you John Denver and Jimi Hendrix); stop at listening stations to hear music by inductees; and learn all about the history of the locale. It's not the Smithsonian but it's worth a stop.

WHY RED ROCKS IS RED ROCKS

The red color of the rocks at Red Rocks Amphitheatre is the result of iron oxide, or rust, present in the sandstone. Over 300 million years ago, sedimentary rock containing iron formed, and exposure to oxygen turned it red. Geological forces later uplifted the rocks, creating the iconic formations seen today.

Continued from p92

BONE WARS

Dinosaur Ridge (p92) was the location of big dinosaur discoveries and a clash of even bigger egos. Renowned 19th-century paleontologists Edward Cope and Othniel Marsh feuded bitterly over the rich fossil deposits in the American West. They raced to excavate sites, seeking to identify, name and claim more new prehistoric species than the other. Dubbed the 'Bone Wars,' the men disparaged one another in scientific papers, made accusations of theft and plagiarism, bribed landowners and regulators to keep the other out of fossil beds, and even stole and vandalized one another's finds. Despite the hullaballoo, Marsh and Cope's work led to the discovery of famous dinosaurs like the stegosaurus and allosaurus on Dinosaur Ridge, securing it as one of the world's richest known deposits of Jurassic-era fossils.

trail (2.2 miles round trip) leads through the site, signage providing insight into the behavior, movement and tropical environment of the dinosaurs that once roamed here. For a deeper dive, a **self-guided audio tour** *($8)* can be downloaded at the visitor center. Or if hot weather makes hiking tough, take a 45-minute guided **bus tour** *(adult/child $20/14)*, which includes three stops and a cheery guide. Admission to a one-room **exhibit hall** *($4)* with loads of fossils is included with all tours. Located about 2 miles north of Morrison.

Deep dive into dinosaurs

Knowledgeable guides lead visitors through the small but excellent **Morrison Natural History Museum** *(morrisonco.us/ 335/Morrison-Natural-History-Museum; adult/child $18/12)*, where displays focus on the Jurassic and Cretaceous periods in the region. Expect dinosaurs skulls and skeletons, fossilized creatures, hands-on activities and the opportunity to watch – and even help - staffers clean fossils in the on-site Paleontology Lab. Tours last one hour; they aren't required but make the visit that much more interesting.

Golden

TIME FROM DENVER: **30 MINS** 🚗

Visit an iconic brewery

Coors has been brewing beer at the same location in Golden, Colorado, since 1873, when the honey-colored drink was a staple of miners' diet (it was safer and more filling to consume than water). Co-founded by its German namesake, Alfred Coors, the brewery survived Prohibition by producing malted milk and eventually went on to become one of the most iconic beer brands in the US. Today, over 250,000 people per year tour its facilities, a visit well worth the 15-mile trek from downtown Denver. Lasting 1½ hours, the **self-guided tour** *(coorsbrewery tour.com; adult/child $20/10)* meanders through the massive plant, integrating company history with its brewing, quality control and packaging processes. Knowledgeable staff are posted throughout to answer questions. The tour ends at the tasting room, where visitors (21+ only) happily sample freshly brewed beers. Reservations highly recommended.

Golden's treasures

Even if rocks and fossils aren't really your thing, **Colorado School of Mines' Museum of Earth Science** *(mines.edu/ museumofearthscience; free)* is fascinating: 15,000 sq ft of exhibits that reveal the earth's underground treasures (and a couple of the moon's too). Don't miss the recreated mine with

EATING NEAR RED ROCKS: OUR PICKS IN MORRISON

Red Rocks Beer Garden: Leafy patio pub serving thin-crust pizza, burritos and exclusively Colorado beers. *11:30am-10pm Mon-Thu, 11am-11pm Fri & Sat, 11am-9pm Sun $*

The Cow, An Eatery: Creekside diner with indoor/outdoor seating and an extensive menu of classic American fare. *7am-8pm $$*

Hungry Goat: Sweet little spot serving American comfort food; in summer, nab a seat on the garden patio. *11am-8pm Sun-Thu, to 8:30 Fri & Sat $$*

The Fort: Bent's Fort lookalike specializing in wild game and Rocky Mountain oysters. A Colorado institution. *5:30-9:30pm Mon-Thu, 5-10pm Fri & Sat 5-9:30pm Sun $$$*

sounds of dripping water, low lights and glowing ultraviolet minerals – a nod to the work that put Colorado on the map. If you have time, stroll along nearby **Mines Geology Trail**, an easy 1-mile loop featuring triceratops tracks and fossilized prehistoric leaves; download trail info from the museum's website.

Tubing on Clear Creek

On hot summer days, join locals by tubing on the refreshingly chilly Clear Creek. Snaking a mile through downtown Golden, the creek offers everything from Class III rapids to a lazy river current. For the former, put in at **Gateway Trailhead** near Rte 6; for a gentler experience, start down creek at **Lions Park**. The float takes 45 to 60 minutes but is easily repeated by walking a trail to another put-in or by taking a shuttle. Tube rentals (including lifejackets and helmets) and shuttles are available at the end point, Vanover Park, from **Adventure West** *(adventurewestco.com; tube from $21, tube plus shuttle from $36)* – look for the VW bus. Note: Tubing is permitted May to September only. Check conditions before jumping in – the water can be dangerously fast in the early season or after heavy rain.

Peek into the past

Explore the life of a homesteader by walking through **Golden History Park** *(goldenhistory.org; free)*, a re-created pioneer settlement on the banks of Clear Creek. An especially fun outing for families with younger kids, visitors take self-guided tours into original 19th-century buildings – a cabin, schoolhouse, blacksmith house, even a two-seat outhouse – getting a sense of what life was once like. Occasionally, experts in period dress work the homestead, teaching about life back in the Wild West; check the website for these special events.

Lakewood

TIME FROM DENVER: **20 MINS** 🚗

Iconic Colorado

Love it or hate it, **Casa Bonita** *(casabonitadenver.com; adult/ child from $30/20)* is a Colorado institution, fixed firmly in the hearts of locals and visitors alike. The Mexico-themed restaurant, located in a strip mall just west of Denver, is a maze of dining areas, souvenir shops and kooky entertainment. There's a 30ft artificial cliff from which divers flip and twist into a small pool below. There are magic shows, live music, a haunted tunnel and face painters. The Mexican food, once notoriously awful and overpriced, is passably OK now (including their famous sopapillas) thanks to a new chef hired by the new owners – South Park creators and Colorado natives Matt Stone and Trey Parker.

SOUTH PARK, THE SHOW

The hit Comedy Central show *South Park* was created by two CU Boulder students and is set in a fictional Colorado town of the same name. For Coloradans, the home state references are obvious: Colfax Ave, John Elway worship, and the real South Park (a region, not a town). Colorado doesn't feature in many TV shows or movies – *Dynasty* was set in Denver, *Dumb & Dumber* in Aspen – so South Park is arguably the state's most prominent pop-culture export. The show pokes plenty of fun at Colorado, including the kitschy restaurant, Casa Bonita. Yet when the restaurant faced pandemic-era closure, *South Park* creators Trey Parker and Matt Stone rescued and restored the iconic restaurant, which reopened with fanfare in 2024.

EATING IN GOLDEN: OUR PICKS

D'deli: Sandwiches stuffed with locally sourced ingredients, including corned buffalo and smoked elk. Bread made in-house too! *11am-5pm* **$$**

Woody's Wood Fired Pizza: Local haunt with wood-fired pies, monster burgers and sandwiches. Ask about the all-you-can-eat soup, salad and pizza deal. *11am-11pm* **$$**

Sherpa House: Beautifully presented Himalayan fare served in a recreated Nepali home. Patio seating is blanketed in prayer flags. *11am-2:30pm & 5-9pm* **$$**

Abejas: Rustic-chic bistro focused on seasonal (and indulgent) farm-to-table meals. Brunch brings global flavors. *5-9pm Tue-Sat, 9:30am-2pm Sat & Sun* **$$$**

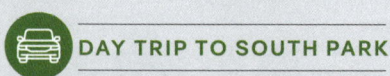

DAY TRIP TO SOUTH PARK

This scenic drive west of Denver avoids busy I-70 and includes small foothill towns and beautiful hiking areas.

START	END	LENGTH
Morrison	Fairplay	68 miles; 4 hours

Heading south from Morrison, take ❶ **Highway 285**, a one-lane road winding through the foothills, once a stagecoach trail used by settlers seeking their fortune in the mountains. As you drive, the rolling hills slowly transform into a dense pine forest, small communities dotting the road, and glimpses of snowcapped peaks in the distance.

Six miles south of Conifer, consider stopping for a hike in ❷ **Staunton State Park**. Known for its rich variety of landscapes – grassy meadows, dramatic granite cliffs, lakes, even waterfalls.

Continuing, cattle ranches begin to appear, the remnants of 1800s homesteads. Passing Bailey, and 19 miles of steady climbing, you'll come to ❸ **Kenosha Pass** (10,000ft), famous for its aspen

forests, which erupt in brilliant gold each fall. The view from the summit reveals ❹ **South Park Basin**, a 900 sq-mile high-altitude prairie where bison once roamed.

Descending, you'll pass about 20 miles of ranches before you hit ❺ **Fairplay**, South Park's main settlement. It was originally a mining site and supply town for Leadville (pack burros clopped over the 13,000ft Mosquito Pass to the west).

Visit ❻ **South Park City**, a re-created 19th-century Colorado boomtown, to get a taste of life back in the good-old, bad-old days of the gold rush. And yes, South Park fans, Fairplay does bear more than a passing resemblance to the hometown of Kyle, Cartman and the boys.

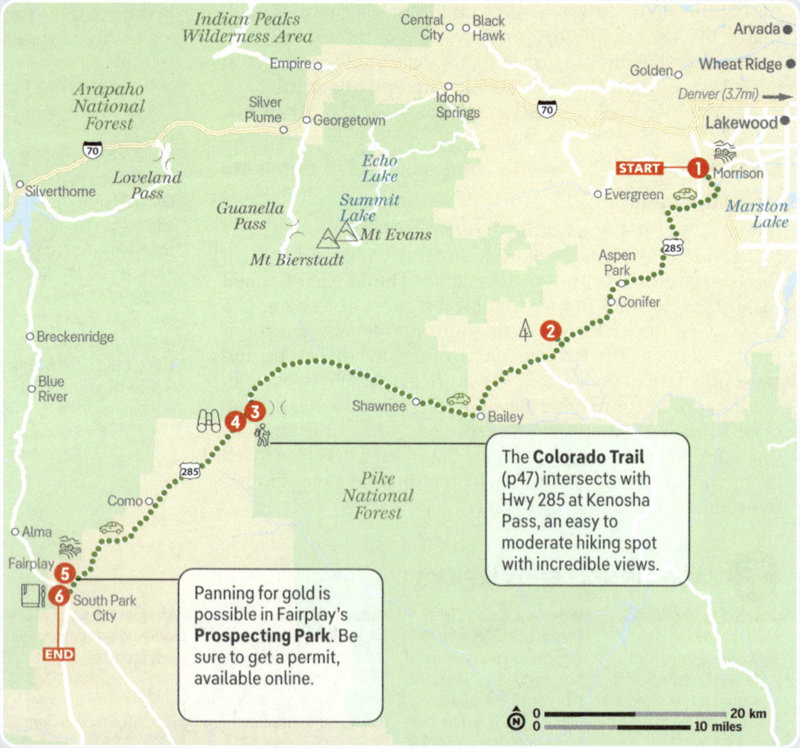

> The **Colorado Trail** (p47) intersects with Hwy 285 at Kenosha Pass, an easy to moderate hiking spot with incredible views.

> Panning for gold is possible in Fairplay's **Prospecting Park**. Be sure to get a permit, available online.

Places We Love to Stay

$ Budget $$ Midrange $$$ Top End

Downtown, LoHi & Platte River Valley p58

Hostel Fish $ Swanky hostel with plush dorms and cozy common areas. On-site bar plus neighborhood pub crawls bring a party vibe.

Lumber Baron Inn & Gardens $$ An 1890 bed-and-breakfast in LoHi. The five suites are decked out in period furnishings and wallpapered ceilings.

Kasa Union Station $$ Modern and stylish apartment-style hotel at Commons Park. Swimming pool and mountain views are cherries on top.

Slate Hotel Denver Downtown $$ Modern hotel in a historic school building. Rooms lack personality but common areas make up for it.

Crawford Hotel $$$ Luxurious and artful rooms inside Union Station, with restaurants, bars and the light-rail just steps away.

Rally Hotel $$$ Baseball-themed boutique hotel across from Coors Field. (Go Rockies!) Rooftop deck has pool plus gorgeous mountain views.

Oxford Hotel $$$ Historic hotel with a prized art collection. Luxe, modern rooms feature beautiful antiques.

Brown Palace Hotel & Spa (p65) **$$$** Denver's most famous hotel, hosting presidents and rock stars. Rooms are modern and plush.

Golden Triangle, Capitol Hill & Cheesman Park p70

11th Avenue Hostel $ Renovated hostel with squeaky-clean rooms, from dorms to private suites. All ages welcome. Community kitchen, lounge and on-site cafe too.

Ember Hostel $ Vintage-chic hostel with upscale amenities, social atmosphere and organized excursions (even group hikes!). The hot tub and fire pit are pluses.

Flora House Denver $$ Renovated 19th-century home with modern rooms, some with kitchenettes. Self-serve continental breakfast and bike rentals too.

Acoma House $$$ One-of-a-kind artist-designed rooms with deluxe amenities, including kitchenettes. Tucked away on a quiet side street near DAM.

Populus Hotel $$$ Luxurious carbon-forward hotel with nature-inspired features inside and out. Stunning city views. Rooms are a study in understated elegance.

Patterson Inn $$$ Victorian-era B&B with nine luxe rooms, made-to-order breakfast and a reputation for being haunted. Over 21s only.

Capitol Hill Mansion B&B $$$ Historic mansion with elegant and unique rooms. The gourmet breakfast is often vegetarian or vegan. LGBTIQ+ welcoming.

Urban Cowboy $$$ Rustic-luxe boutique hotel in an iconic 1880s mansion. Western-inspired decor is integrated into each unique suite, lounge area and bar.

RiNo & Five Points p83

Queen Anne B&B $$ Side-by-side Victorian-era homes double as one B&B with period antiques and artist-designed rooms, some with murals. Enjoy breakfast in the shared garden.

Catbird $$ Artsy hotel offering loft-style rooms with big windows and full kitchens. The rooftop has hammocks, hot tubs and live music.

Source Hotel $$$ Industrial-chic hotel above its namesake food hall. Head to the rooftop for mountain views and plunge pools that become hot tubs in winter.

The Ramble Hotel $$$ Sophisticated, vintage-inspired boutique hotel with a luxe cocktail lounge in the lobby.

Morrison & Golden p92

Dove Inn $ Immaculate 1866 home-turned-B&B in Golden. Rooms are stylish and homey, accented with period pieces. Hot tub and fully stocked guest kitchen too.

Origin Red Rocks $$ Contemporary hotel with a rock n' roll Western vibe. Set in the foothills near Red Rocks. Mountain bikes included.

Cliff House Lodge $$ Eight uniquely-themed cottages in Morrison, all with hot tubs. Free shuttle rides to Red Rocks concerts, one mile away. Cannabis-friendly.

Eddy Taproom and Hotel $$$ Upscale hotel in Golden's foothills with easy access to trails and tubing. Make time for brews by the fire pit.

Boulder

TWENTY-FIVE SQ MILES SURROUNDED BY REALITY

Welcome to the Boulder bubble: a world that is whimsical, wealthy, ecotopian-minded and uniquely gorgeous. And yes, they definitely tax soda here.

Driving up Hwy 36 from Denver, you eventually reach the spot: an overlook that peers down on Colorado's own Shangri-La, tucked up against the signature Flatirons. If this first glimpse of Boulder takes your breath away, well, you wouldn't be the first.

Over the past 135 years, the town has seen all sorts of idealistic dreamers come and go, from turn-of-the-20th-century health-food advocates to Buddhist hippie poets, and Nobel Prize–winning scientists to ultra-competitive athletes. As disparate as the groups may seem, there is a thread that ties them together: a love of the natural world.

And therein lies the pot of gold at the end of the rainbow. Talk to Coloradans from elsewhere in the state and you might not hear too many kind words about Boulder. It's pretentious. Sanctimonious. Full of rich, EV-driving, out-of-touch liberals. And yet, while it's easy to poke fun at the People's Republic, we dare any lover of the great outdoors not to fall for the city's 45,000 acres of trail-laced open space – that's 45 times the size of Golden Gate Park.

Sure, an unroped Alex Honnold might lap you while climbing the First Flatiron, or a former Tour de France cyclist might casually zip by on the Boulder Creek Path... riding a bike that costs more than your car. But if you can put aside your preconceived judgments for a day or two, how could you not have a great time?

Whatever your fancy – trail running, cycling, climbing, astrophysics, yoga or just plain picnicking in the park – you can bet that you'll find like-minded souls here. Some of them are Type A overachievers to be sure, but there are just as many oddballs as ever. For every Fastest Known Time record holder or founder of the latest health-food startup, there's someone else who spends their free time getting stoned and making stop-motion cartoons out of construction paper.

So hike the Mesa Trail, go thrifting off Pearl St and eat a guilt-free, farm-to-table, carbon-neutral meal. Because after a day like that, how could the world not be a better place?

KIT LEONG/SHUTTERSTOCK

THE MAIN AREAS

DOWNTOWN BOULDER
From Pearl St to Boulder Creek. **p106**

CU & CHAUTAUQUA PARK
Campus life and the Flatirons. **p115**

SOUTH BOULDER
The greatest variety of hiking trails in town. **p123**

NORTH & EAST BOULDER
Breweries, climbing gyms and the reservoir. **p128**

For places to stay in Boulder, see p139

ANDREW PEACOCK/GETTY IMAGES

Boulder from the Flatirons (p117)

Find Your Way

Boulder is a relatively small place, with most activities concentrated near Pearl St, the university and South Boulder. Most places can be easily reached via bike, bus or on foot. That said, if you are traveling elsewhere in Colorado, you will likely want your own wheels.

N

0   1 miles

0   2 km

North & East Boulder
p128

BUS
Boulder has decent public transportation, with several RTD bus routes crossing the city and connecting the Hill with downtown, North Boulder and East Boulder. Buses also run to Denver and Nederland; all buses have bike racks. Fares are $2.75 for three hours. Use the MyRide app.

CAR
Rush-hour traffic (including CU football games on Saturdays) is a headache, but otherwise Boulder is easy to navigate in a car. For parking, you'll want the Metropolis app for the city parking garages (free on weekends) and ParkMobile for street and trailhead parking.

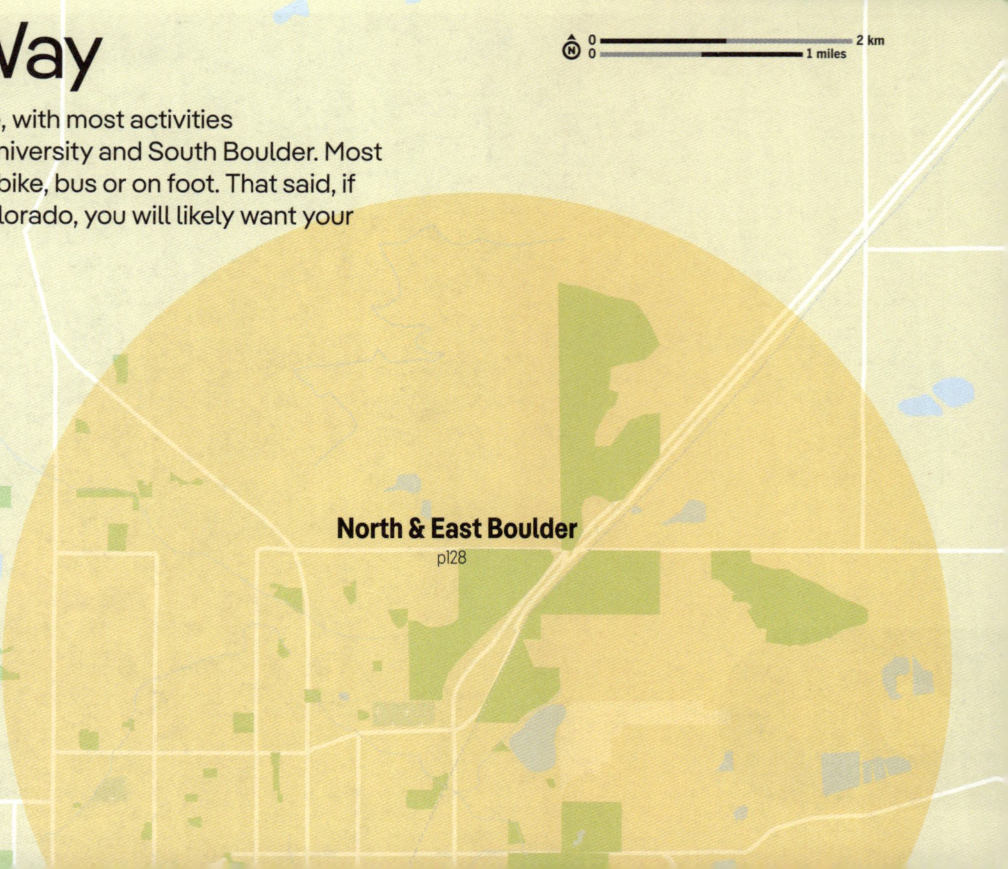

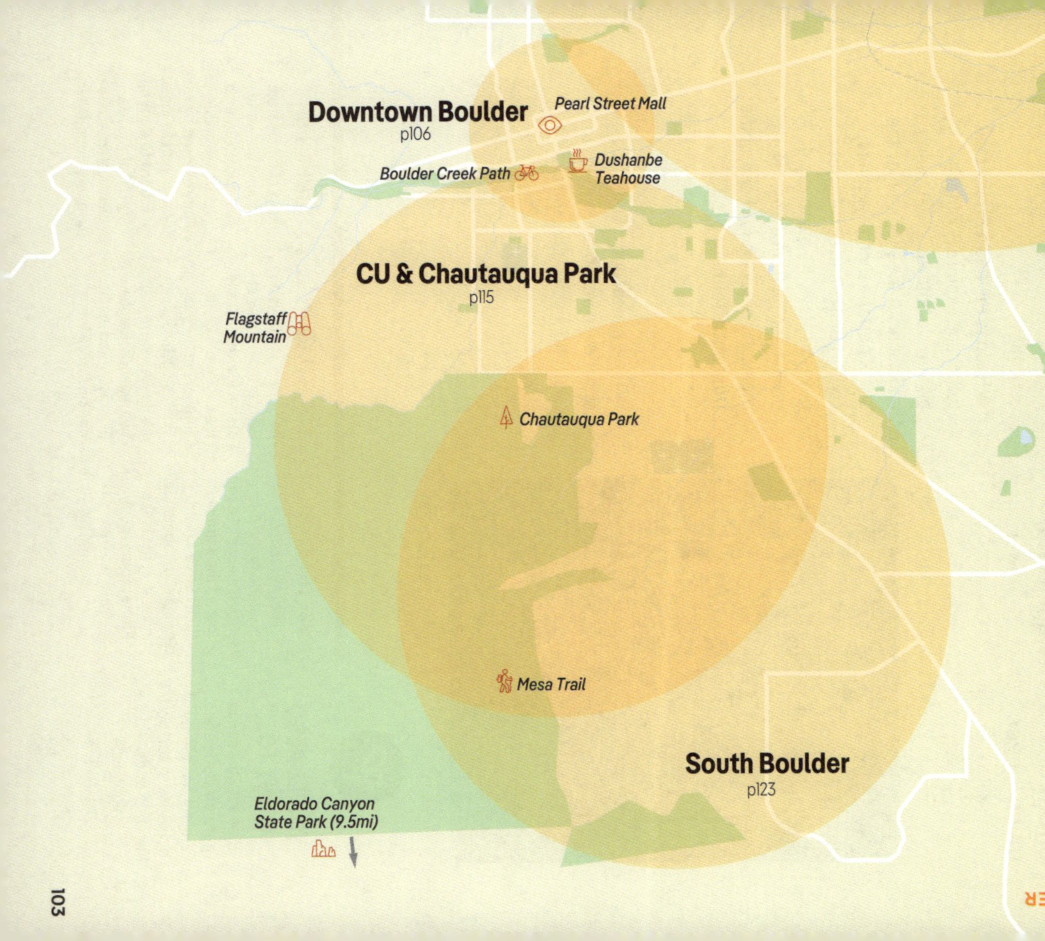

FROM THE AIRPORT

If driving, it's roughly 45 minutes from the Denver International Airport, depending on traffic. Although the toll road (E-470) is convenient, car-rental companies add an outrageous surcharge. Take I-70 instead. The AB airport bus ($10, one hour) is a great option, with multiple stops along Broadway in Boulder; the terminus is downtown.

BIKE

Bikes are a great way to get around, in particular if you're pedaling the traffic-free Boulder Creek Path. University Cycles has a convenient location downtown. The city does have a bike-share program, but unfortunately the cost is prohibitively expensive for visitors.

Downtown Boulder
p106

Pearl Street Mall

Dushanbe Teahouse

Boulder Creek Path

CU & Chautauqua Park
p115

Chautauqua Park

Flagstaff Mountain

South Boulder
p123

Mesa Trail

Eldorado Canyon State Park (9.5mi)

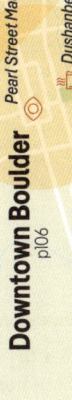

Plan Your Days

Picnic in the Flatirons above the city, watch fire-eaters on Pearl St or join a group run. And that's just on day one. You'll want to stay much longer.

Indian Peaks (p136)

D. SCOTT LARSON/SHUTTERSTOCK

Day 1

Morning

● First stop: **Chautauqua Park** (p118). Hike to the Flatirons, take photos in the meadow or bust your quads climbing to Royal Arch. Picnic beneath the ponderosas while you're at it.

Afternoon

● Head to the **Pearl Street Mall** (p106) and explore Boulder's historic downtown. In between checking out the shops, enjoy the street performances – jugglers, contortionists and sometimes a guy who plays the piano upside down hanging from a tree. Take a break and enjoy a cup of chai at the **Dushanbe Teahouse** (p113).

Evening

● Have a meal and a drink downtown: from beer gardens to gastronomic delights, the choice is yours.

YOU'LL ALSO WANT TO...

Rise with the sun or gaze up at the stars. Boulder has plenty of activities to suit both the early birds and the night owls.

SEE THE STARS

The University of Colorado is a NASA-research magnet. Learn about all the astronaut alum before a mind-blowing show about the universe at the **Fiske Planetarium** (p121).

CATCH THE BUFFS

The Buffs, CU's Division 1 sports teams, play at **Folsom Field** (p122) and the CU Events Center throughout the year. Football games give you the chance to spot two legends: Ralphie (the bison) and media darling Coach Prime.

CLIMB HIGH

Rock climbers from around the world descend on Boulder for its incredible variety of towering rock formations, like those at **Eldorado Canyon** (p127). If you're a beginner, start at one of the gyms around town.

Day 2

Morning
● Carpe diem, cyclists! Rent a bike at University Bicycles and pedal up canyon along the **Boulder Creek Path** (p111). If you're yearning for a real workout (or if you have an e-bike), keep riding up Chapman Dr – the secret way up **Flagstaff Mountain** (p115).

Afternoon
● Cruise downhill, following the Creek Path to the **CU campus** (p120). Follow lunch on the Hill with a visit to the **Art Museum** (p121) and the **Museum of Natural History** (p121).

Evening
● Bike over to the **Rayback Collective** (p131), Boulder's hoppin' food truck park and music venue. Grab a spot by the fire pit to enjoy a local beer.

Day 3

Morning
● Set off for the hills: go hiking or climbing at **Eldorado Canyon** (p127), explore the Indian Peaks outside **Nederland** (p136) or drive up **Flagstaff Mountain** (p115) for incredible views.

Afternoon
● Return to South Boulder for the interactive exhibits at the **National Center for Atmospheric Research** (p123), designed by IM Pei. Don't linger too long, though, as you don't want to be late for the 4:30pm brewery at **Avery Brewing** (p130) across town.

Evening
● Return to Pearl St for margaritas and a final gourmet dinner, then catch a concert at the **Chautauqua Auditorium** (p119), the **Dairy Arts Center** (p114) or the **Boulder Theater** (p114).

COOL OFF IN BOULDER CREEK
Go up canyon to **Eben G Fine Park** (p112), where sunseekers catch rays by the water. Wade into an eddy to get used to the glacial temps before hopping on an inner tube for a wild ride downstream.

FLY LIKE AN EAGLE
Take to the skies in an unforgettable ride above the Flatirons, in either a paraglider or a **sailplane** (p133), as the thermals lift you higher and higher for a bird's-eye view of town.

GEAR UP FOR A SNOW DAY
If you rent your skis in Boulder rather than at the resort, you'll save yourself a bundle. Or you can try out a pair of cross-country skis for the groomed backcountry at nearby **Eldora** (p136).

CELEBRATE OUTDOORS
Boulder has outdoor festivals throughout the year. The most famous is the costumed Memorial Day race, the **Bolder Boulder** (p133). Summer sees the acclaimed Shakespeare Festival at CU's amphitheater.

Downtown Boulder

FROM PEARL ST TO BOULDER CREEK

GETTING AROUND

Downtown is centered on Pearl St. One-way streets and large crowds make driving tricky in this area – ditch the car as soon as you can in a downtown garage (free on weekends) to explore the area on foot. The paved Boulder Creek Path runs right through the heart of downtown and is fabulous for both cyclists and walkers. The SKIP bus connects downtown with South Boulder, the Hill and North Boulder along Broadway. The bus depot is at Walnut and 14th St.

Downtown Boulder is all about Pearl St – the quirky, historic pedestrian mall that exemplifies the city's unique spirit. For as long as Boulder has existed, Pearl St has been the center of commerce. In the 19th century its sandstone buildings were home to banks and mining supply stores, while the streets bustled with horse-drawn carriages and mule-driven wagons loaded with goods.

Soon after, bell-ringing electric trolleys replaced the horses, and then came the chromed-up cars and university marching bands. Today, restaurants and bars cluster at either end of the redbrick pedestrian strip, while tarot readers, jazz trios and the occasional fire-breathing performer adds just the right touch of offbeat entertainment.

Not far from Pearl St is the city's other main lifeline: Boulder Creek. Cycle along its banks on the fabulous bike path or follow the college students upstream to hop in an inner tube and ride the rapids back into town.

Shopping along Pearl Street & Around

Buy local

The **Pearl Street Mall** is the heart of downtown Boulder. It's a vibrant, tree-shaded pedestrian zone filled with kids' climbing boulders and splash fountains, and lined with shops and galleries.

 EATING IN DOWNTOWN BOULDER: DIVINE DINNERS

Frasca: James Beard, Michelin and others have all named the northern Italian cuisine here as Boulder's finest. Prix-fixe menus only; reserve well ahead. *5-9pm* **$$$**

Oak: Zesty and innovative, Oak is great for those who love to share – its specialties are the dazzling small plates that pair perfectly with the sour cocktails. *5-9pm* **$$$**

Bramble & Hare: Farm-driven French cuisine with a modern American twist and a focus on sustainability. Three-course tasting menus only. *5-9pm Mon-Sat* **$$$**

Cozobi: Heirloom corn and regional Mexican cooking are the focus at chef Johnny Curiel's welcoming Boulder outpost. *2-9pm Mon-Fri, 4-9pm Sat & Sun* **$$$**

Pearl Street Mall

People-watching aside, shopping is Pearl's raison d'être, and the first thing you might notice is that it looks like the Champs-Elysées of outdoor wear. Everybody who is anybody has a retail outlet, from Italy's La Sportiva and Japan's Mont-Bell to North American brands like Patagonia, North Face and Black Diamond.

But it's not all ultralight puffies and dawn patrol ski jackets. Local vintage shops like **Apocalypse** and **Heady Bauer** (no relation to Eddie) are a fun browse and have a definite disco-hippie Boulder-esque vibe. **Umba** got its start selling clothing at music festivals while the **Ritz** is Boulder's best costume shop: both have a similar playful appeal.

If all that walking has tired out your feet, **Pedestrian Shops** is the place to head for great deals on Colorado-style comfortable footwear. Think Ecco, Dansko, Keen and Born.

East of 15th St (one end of the pedestrian strip) is home to boutiques including **Bliss** and **Jones + Company**, as well as the handmade cowboy boots at John Allen Woodward (p114).

At the other end of the strip, you'll find high-end boutiques, like **Classic Facets**, an antique jewelry shop that has carried famous pieces, like a diamond necklace that belonged to actress Mae West.

Whatever you do, don't miss **Piece, Love & Chocolate** at the far-western end of Pearl St: it's the perfect place to enjoy a velvety hot chocolate, slice of cake or decadent chocolate truffle.

BEST DOWNTOWN LOCAL SHOPS

Into the Wind: The local kite store is a favorite with kids of all ages, with a variety of delightful toys and games.

Jackalope & Co: Need a gift to bring back home? Stop at Jackalope for all your Colorado and CU-themed T-shirts, hats and other souvenirs.

Peppercorn: This whitewashed landmark stocks enough kitchen gizmos, locally produced foods and specialized cookbooks to delight every cooking geek.

Rebecca's Herbal Apothecary: Popular herbal apothecary where herbs are sold loose, in lotions and in oils. Aromatherapy cases of tinctures and expert herbalists to guide you through it all.

Ku Cha House of Tea: Imported loose-leaf teas, from oolong to create-your-own blends.

 EATING IN DOWNTOWN BOULDER: BUDGET EATS

Mountain Sun: The town's favorite brewery has great burgers, chili and brews, like Annapurna Amber. *noon-11pm Wed-Sun* $

Barchetta: Great selection of pizzas in an uber-casual space on 17th St. Pay-as-you-go beer and wine. *11am-9pm Wed-Mon* $

Avanti F&B: Food, drinks and panoramic views from the rooftop terrace in a multilevel food hall in the middle of Pearl St. *11am-11pm* $

Gelato Boy: Venetian-meets-Coloradan love story with a happy ending – perfect Italian gelato in a colorful palette of flavors. *noon-9pm* $

DOWNTOWN BOULDER

HIGHLIGHTS
1 Flagstaff Mountain
2 Pearl St Mall

SIGHTS
3 Boulder Museum of Contemporary Art
4 Eben G Fine Park
5 Museum of Boulder

ACTIVITIES
6 Alpine Base & Edge
7 Lions Lair Trailhead
8 Mt Sanitas Trailhead
9 University of Colorado at Boulder

SLEEPING
10 Bradley Boulder Inn
11 Foot of the Mountain
12 Hotel Boulderado
13 St Julien Hotel & Spa

EATING
14 Avanti F&B
15 Barchetta
16 Bohemian Biergarten
17 Boulder County Farmers Market
18 Bramble & Hare
19 Brasserie Ten Ten
20 Busaba
21 Centro
22 Cozobi
23 Frasca

24 Gelato Boy
25 Japango
26 Jax Fish House
27 Leaf
28 Lucile's
29 Mountain Sun
30 Oak
31 Pizza Alberico
32 Rosetta Hall
33 Sherpa's
34 Zoe Ma Ma

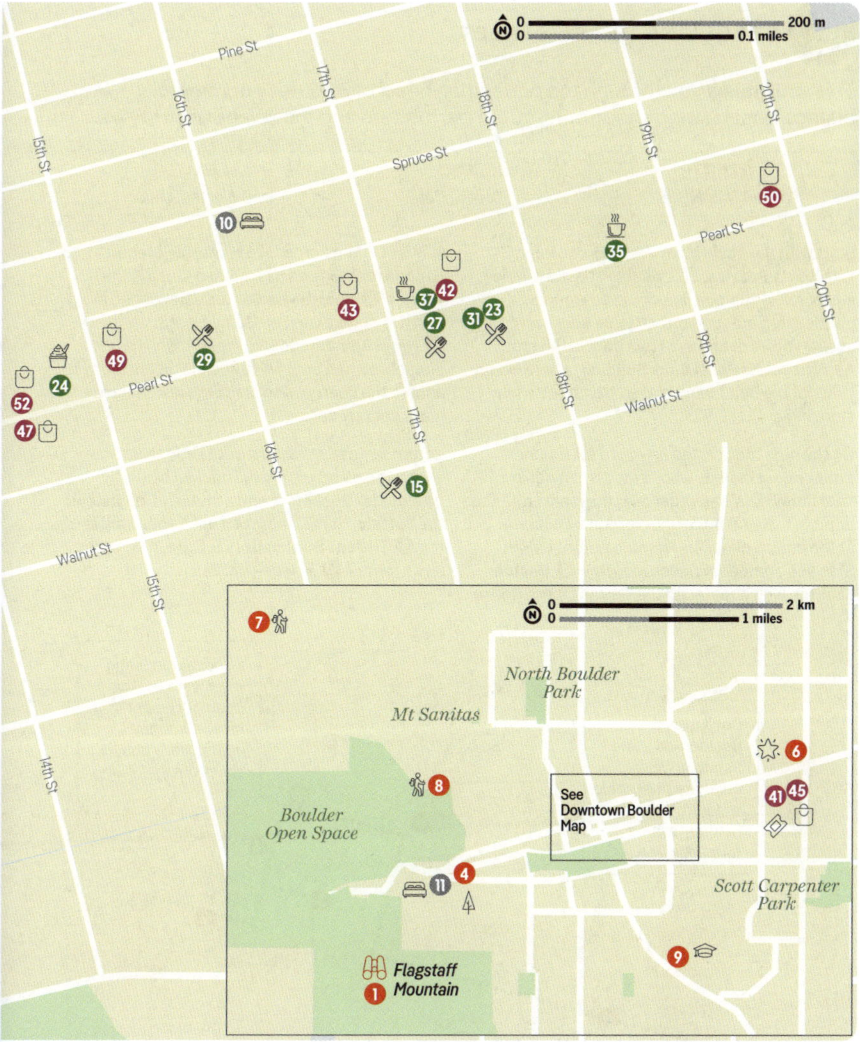

DRINKING
35 Boxcar Roasters
36 Dushanbe Teahouse
37 Laughing Goat
38 Ozo
39 Trident Cafe

ENTERTAINMENT
40 Boulder Theater

41 Dairy Arts Center

SHOPPING
42 Apocalypse
43 Bliss
44 Classic Facets
45 Crystal Ski Shop
46 Heady Bauer
47 Into the Wind

48 Jackalope & Co
49 John Allen Woodward
50 Jones + Company
51 Ku Cha House of Tea
52 Pedestrian Shops
53 Peppercorn
54 Piece, Love & Chocolate

55 Rebecca's Herbal Apothecary
56 Ritz
57 Umba

TRANSPORT
58 Boulder Creek Path
59 University Bicycles

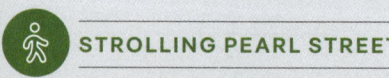

STROLLING PEARL STREET

This walk takes you through the pedestrian heart of Boulder's commercial district, past historic shopfronts, street performers and musicians of all styles.

START	END	LENGTH
Pearl & 15th Sts	Trident Cafe	0.5 miles; 1 hour

Start with the most whimsical shop on Pearl St, **1 Liberty Puzzles**. This Boulder-based puzzle-maker makes unique, handcrafted wooden puzzles that are guaranteed to be unlike any jigsaw you've ever tried. Next door is the old **2 Citizens National Bank Building**, where Glenn Miller of big band fame played trombone while studying at CU in 1923.

On the next block is the art-deco **3 Boulder County Courthouse**, whose modernist design dates to 1933. A bas-relief over the main entrance depicts the backbone of Colorado's economy at the time: a miner and farmer. Return to 14th St to see another art-deco icon, the **4 Boulder Theater**, which replaced the Curran Opera House in 1935. On the corner of Spruce, the green pagoda roof topped by a golden stupa is the Tibetan **5 Shambhala Center**, established in 1974. One block west on Spruce is the landmark **6 Hotel Boulderado** (1909; p139), which was publicly owned until 1940. Pop inside the lobby to admire the cherrywood staircase and stained-glass canopy ceiling.

Return to Pearl, continuing until you reach the end of the pedestrian strip, marked by the **7 Boulder Bookstore** and a statue of **8 Ralphie the Buffalo**, the CU mascot. Finish your walk at the **9 Trident Booksellers & Cafe**, next to the city's former **10 Armory** (1898).

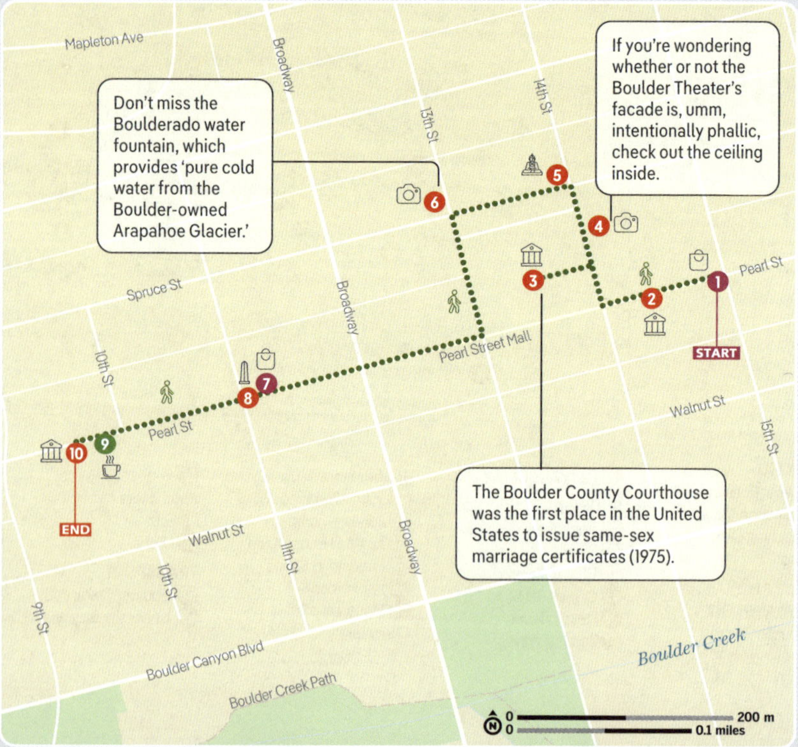

Don't miss the Boulderado water fountain, which provides 'pure cold water from the Boulder-owned Arapahoe Glacier.'

If you're wondering whether or not the Boulder Theater's facade is, umm, intentionally phallic, check out the ceiling inside.

The Boulder County Courthouse was the first place in the United States to issue same-sex marriage certificates (1975).

Mapleton Ave · Broadway · 15th St · 14th St · Spruce St · Broadway · Pearl St · Pearl Street Mall · 10th St · 11th St · Broadway · Walnut St · 15th St · 9th St · Walnut St · 10th St · Boulder Canyon Blvd · Boulder Creek Path · Boulder Creek

START · END · Pearl St

0 — 200 m
0 — 0.1 miles

Cycle Boulder Canyon
The city's best bike path

Boulder's reputation as an ecotopia is rooted in the collective call for outdoor adventure. Outside of Chautauqua Park and the Flatirons, the best place to experience this is the **Boulder Creek Path**, a gorgeous, car-free trail shooting directly through town to the mountains. Getting on the trail is easy as pie: rent a cruiser bike at the perfectly located **University Bicycles** (*ubikes.com; cruiser/e-bike $25/60*) at the west end of Pearl St, pedal two blocks south and you've arrived.

Cycling up the Creek Path and into Boulder Canyon is a great way to get a taste of the Front Range wilderness: the air is filled with the redolent scent of ponderosa pines, while all around are spectacular granite cliffs and forested hills.

The trail up the canyon is a reasonable 3.5 miles, passing Eben G Fine Park (p112) and plenty of opportunities to take a break and head down to the water and enjoy a picnic. The terminus is **Chapman Drive**, from where it's an easy coast downhill back into town. But if you've got the time and the stamina (or a class 1 or 2 e-bike), consider extending your ride to the summit of Flagstaff Mountain (p115).

From the Chapman Drive Trailhead, a a 2.5-mile gravel road climbs 1000ft. It's sweaty work, but it has a huge payoff: incredible views of the town and plains and a glorious downhill along the serpentine Flagstaff Rd. Do note that Flagstaff Rd is shared with cars, so retrace your path on Chapman Dr if you'd rather avoid vehicle traffic.

The Boulder Creek Path through the canyon is just as popular with walkers as it is with bikers, so be courteous and announce your presence when passing others.

Cycle Through Town
Follow the creek downstream

While Boulder Canyon is arguably more scenic, the Boulder Creek Path goes in the opposite direction too, following the creek for 4.5 miles as it crosses town along the riparian corridor and reaches a series of reservoirs beyond the Foothills Parkway. This ride is just as pleasant and is a great way to reach the CU campus (p120), accessed from a long ramp that climbs out of the trees to the backside of Folsom Field. With a bit of curiosity and determination you can bike to many other destinations in town, though not all bike paths are traffic free and the network can be confusing at first, so consult your phone as you go.

MARTHA MAXWELL

In the 1870s Eben G Fine Park was the location of Martha Maxwell's home. Maxwell was originally a schoolteacher from Wisconsin who moved to Colorado with her husband as part of the 1860s gold rush. During a dispute with a claim jumper, Martha occupied the squatter's cabin and made a shocking discovery – it was full of animals who had been frozen in time. It was at this point that Martha discovered her calling: taxidermy. She returned to Wisconsin, received training and then moved to Boulder where she gradually built up her collection. Soon after, she opened a museum consisting of some 100 species of Colorado wildlife. A Boulder original, Martha was an accomplished hunter...and a lifelong vegetarian.

 EATING IN DOWNTOWN BOULDER: BEST MIDRANGE

Centro: Lively Mexican restaurant has build-your-own taco boards, good veggie options and punchy cocktails. *11am-9pm* **$$**

Leaf: An ethical and elegant kitchen that serves meat-free gems, using ingredients grown at the restaurant's organic farm in nearby Lafayette. *11:30am-9pm* **$$**

Pizza Alberico: Beloved stepchild of upscale Frasca, come here for arancini, burrata pugliese and gourmet pizzas. *11:30am-9pm Thu-Sun, 4-9pm Mon-Wed* **$$**

Lucile's: This New Orleans–style diner has perfected breakfast, and the Creole egg dishes are the thing to order. *7am-2pm Mon-Fri, from 8pm Sat & Sun* **$$**

FARM FRESH

The twice-weekly **Boulder County Farmers Market**, a block-long sprawl in front of the Dushanbe Teahouse, is a massive spring and summer bazaar of colorful, mostly organic 100% local food. Find flowers and herbs, as well as brain-sized mushrooms, delicate squash blossoms, crusty pretzels, vegan dips, grass-fed beef, raw granola and yogurt. Live music is as standard as the family picnics in the park along Boulder Creek. The Saturday market is a real community event, and it feels like the whole city comes out to socialize in the morning (8am to 2pm). The Wednesday evening market (3:30 to 7:30pm) tends to be a little less busy, but it's still a notable midweek gathering place. In true Boulder style, all waste from the farmers market is recycled or composted. The market is closed in winter.

SUSAN LIEBOLD/ALAMY STOCK PHOTO

Boulder Creek

Tubing Boulder Creek

Summertime cool down

Head up Boulder Canyon on a hot summer day and you'll likely spot crowds of young people sunning themselves on the banks of the river and engaging in a favorite Boulder ritual: tubing Boulder Creek. Take note, however: this can be a fast, furious and freezing-cold ride, and is not suitable for everyone. At the very least, you must be able to swim, and you should definitely wear a life jacket and helmet. If you've never tubed the creek before, consider running short sections to get the hang of it before taking on the whole enchilada.

Any time the water is flowing over 200 cu ft per second can be a real rodeo; if it's above 300 cu don't go. Every year one or two people die in Boulder Creek during the spring run-off (May through June) – don't underestimate the power of the river. If you have young children, take them to a water park instead.

To be sure, this is generally a fun experience, so if you're comfortable in the water and the conditions are safe, head to **Crystal Ski Shop** (*crystalskishop.com; from $16*) or **Alpine Base & Edge** (*skiboulder.com; from $19*) to rent tubes.

The upper section around **Eben G Fine Park** tends to be the most popular put-in. It has the wildest rapids and chutes, but it's also above town, meaning the water is cleaner. By the

EATING IN DOWNTOWN BOULDER: LOCAL FAVORITES

Bohemian Biergarten: This perennially popular beer hall specializes in Central European brews and rib-sticking fare (brats, pretzels and schnitzel). *11am-10pm* **$$**

Rosetta Hall: A sophisticated food hall, serving everything from falafel to green papaya salad to empanadas. Rooftop bar too. *8am-11pm* **$$**

Jax Fish House: Running for two decades, this lively seafood shack is still an exquisite treat. Belly up to the circle bar for oysters and martinis. *3:30-9pm* **$$$**

Brasserie Ten Ten: Bust out the air kisses for the always sunny French bistro with an elegant atmosphere. *11:30am-9pm Tue-Fri, from 10am Sat & Sun, 4-9pm Mon* **$$$**

time you hit the public library at 9th St, the water is mellower but also less hygienic.

Find Peace at Dushanbe Teahouse

Sister city in the mountains

In 1983, near the tail end of the Cold War, three Boulder women decided to establish ties with a sister city in the USSR in the hopes of fostering more peaceful relations between the superpowers. Dushanbe, the capital of the Tajik Soviet Socialist Republic (now Tajikistan), was ultimately chosen due to its shared location along the 40th parallel and similar mountain landscape.

After the mayors of the two cities met for the first time in 1987, Tajikistan offered a traditional teahouse as a gift to Boulder. Over the next three years, over 40 artisans designed the essential components – carved cedar columns, painted ceramic panels, traditional stools and copper statuary – which were then shipped to Boulder piece by piece in 1990.

Eight years later the **Dushanbe Teahouse** was finally completed in its downtown location. Drop by to admire its ornate exterior and Tajik rose garden, or better yet step inside to relax by the central fountain with a pot of tea – there are over 70 varieties to choose from.

The dining menu is fittingly global, ranging from Tajik staples like *shashlik* (lamb kebabs) and *osh* (rice pilaf with grilled beef) to Persian chickpea *kufteh* (croquettes) and spiced chicken and pomegranate. The teahouse is open from 11am to 9pm Monday to Friday, and 8am to 9pm on weekends.

Summit Mt Sanitas

Hiking in the foothills

A contender for a top-five Boulder trail, **Mt Sanitas** is for the trail-running parents in the family who like to casually sprint up a peak or two while the kids are still asleep – or, at least, contently sitting in front of an iPad.

It's got all the hallmarks of a casual urban adventure: it's easy to access (end of Mapleton Ave, 1.25 miles from the Pearl St Mall), the trail is short (3.2 miles) and there are Instagrammable views from the summit (6483ft). To be sure, with 1250ft of elevation gain it is definitely steep, and the sandstone boulders make for some scrambly sections, but that's all part of its enduring appeal. Make it a loop by climbing the south ridge on the way up and descending the front side's tortuous switchbacks on the way down. The only catch is that parking is limited.

THE COLORADO SANITARIUM

Boulder has always been on a health kick. For proof, look no further than Mt Sanitas, which got its name from the Colorado Sanitarium, a health spa established in 1896 by none other than John Kellogg – the founder of Kellogg's cereal. *Sanitas* means 'health' in Latin, and the spa promised such amenities as the 'most healthful and equable of climates,' Swedish massage, 'baths of every description' and 'beautiful scenic surrounds.' Part of the program, which was run by the Seventh Day Adventist Church, was a natural diet rich in granola and (Kellogg's) corn flakes, combined with vigorous physical exercise that included hikes up the local mountain, dubbed Mt Sanitas. The sanitarium remained open until the 1950s.

DRINKING IN DOWNTOWN BOULDER: BEST CAFES

Trident Cafe: Brick walls, worn wood floors and red-vinyl booths steeped in the aromatic uplift of damn good espresso. *7am-9pm*

Boxcar Roasters: Asserting a PhD approach, this roaster offers single-pour beaker coffee that purists swear by. *7am-4pm*

Ozo: Boulder-based coffee roasters with a focus on sustainability and fair trade. They have two cafes on Pearl St; pastries too. *6am-6pm*

Laughing Goat: The ambience might be diminished by the glow of laptops, but the coffee is good and served in pint glasses. *6:30am-6pm*

JOHN ALLEN WOODWARD: A RARE ARTISAN

It's one part hidden gem, one part bucket list. **John Allen Woodward's** Pearl St shop is also the working studio of one of the last remaining American bootmakers. Woodward got his start as an apprentice in Nashville, opened up his first shop in San Diego, and then relocated to Boulder. He makes all of his boots, belts, wallets, handbags and leather accessories by hand on a 22ft bench in the store. He and his staff also make the silver accents and cut the gemstones themselves. Watch them working through the windows, stop in and ask questions and – if you have the means – order a custom pair of cowboy boots to fit. An unparalleled souvenir of Colorado's Old West.

An alternate way up is to approach from the west side on the **Lions Lair Trail**. This trail is slightly longer (4 miles out-and-back) but it has less elevation gain (820ft), making for a more moderate approach. Access the trailhead by continuing up Sunshine Canyon Dr (Mapleton) for 1.5 miles past the main trailhead.

Arts & Entertainment

Culture vultures

Boulder's cultural offerings may pale in comparison to Denver and Aspen, but as far as small cities go, it's not a complete philistine. A small collection of downtown entertainment venues and museums bring in a steady stream of art exhibits and films, and the city could get a much-needed shot of cultural juice if it's chosen to host the Sundance Film Festival beginning in 2027.

The top cultural hub in town is the **Dairy** *(thedairy.org)*, a historic milk-processing factory turned arts center. It's a state-of-the-art facility with three stages, four gallery spaces and a 60-seat cinema. There's always something going on, from film screenings and plays to modern dance and art exhibits. The exhibits are always free.

Another landmark entertainment venue is the colorful art-deco **Boulder Theater**, which brings in slightly under-the-radar acts like Aimee Mann and Richard Thompson. In a nod to its origins as a silent movie house, it also screens indie films and Warren Miller–type ski features.

Two small museums are good for the rare rainy day. The **Boulder Museum of Contemporary Art** *(bmoca.org; by donation)* hosts rotating exhibits in a historic brick house next to Dushanbe (p113). Mixed-media exhibits can include such whimsy as neon installations and life-sized cards, while provocative fashion concepts are displayed in the costume and wardrobe gallery upstairs.

The **Museum of Boulder** *(museumofboulder.org; adult/child $10/8)* presents a broad overview of Boulder history, with interactive exhibits that feel more geared to kids than adults.

 EATING IN DOWNTOWN BOULDER: BEST ASIAN

Zoe Ma Ma: From Beijing to Chengdu and Taipei to Mama's very own Boulder kitchen, this organic noodle shop knows its regional cooking. *11am-9pm* **$**

Sherpa's: Friendly Nepali cafe set in a converted home, with a great outdoor patio and simple home-style cuisine like tofu aloo. *11am-3pm & 5-10pm* **$**

Busaba: One of Boulder's best Thai restaurants is actually a Louisville transplant, but that doesn't make the Chiang Mai curries any less piquant. *11:30am-9pm* **$$**

Japango: Lobster potstickers, asparagus tempura maki rolls and premium sushi...chef Yukiji Iwasa has been delighting diners for over two decades. *11am-10pm* **$$$**

CU & Chautauqua Park

CAMPUS LIFE AND THE FLATIRONS

If Pearl St is the heart of Boulder, than the neighborhood surrounding the University of Colorado (CU) is the city's soul. Founded in 1876, before Colorado was even a state, the university's distinctive Tuscan-inspired architecture melds naturally into the landscape, and many a prospective student (and their parents) have fallen under the Boulder spell after a stroll through this gorgeous campus. And it's not just the architecture that woos visitors: from here, the matching sandstone Flatirons jut out of the mountains to the west, forming an eye-catching natural backdrop just beyond the terracotta roof tiles.

Campus life means plenty of lectures, cultural performances, sports events and youthful shenanigans. And CU's 37,000 students bring a healthy dose of youthful energy not just to campus, but the surrounding area west of Broadway, known as the Hill. This is where you'll find cheap eats, music concerts, late-night house parties and (thankfully out of earshot) the quintessential Boulder outdoor space, Chautauqua Park, where the spectacular Flatirons beckon visitors into the hills.

Follow the Sun on Flagstaff Mountain

Boulder's best drive

Hairpin turns, wild turkeys and giant sandstone boulders mark the breathtaking 4-mile drive up **Flagstaff Mountain** (7283ft), the easiest way to climb the peaks west of town. Flagstaff's secret is that it not only has views that open up over Boulder, but also looks west over the snowcapped Indian Peaks. A log cabin nature center is located at the summit, though actual wildlife sightings up here are better than the exhibits.

A number of trails traverse the summit area. We recommend the easy **Boy Scout** (1 mile), which provides stellar panoramas from west to north to east as it circles the peak. Be sure to take the short detour to **May's Point** for unimpeded views of Boulder's gorgeous backcountry. Another can't-miss stop

GETTING AROUND

CU has several visitor parking lots; fares are hourly and payable at the lot or with the ParkMobile app. The HOP bus runs in a loop through the main campus, the Hill, downtown and the 29th St Mall. The SKIP bus runs past the campus along Broadway, and links CU to South Boulder, downtown and North Boulder. Chautauqua Park is served by a free park-and-ride shuttle from Memorial Day to Labor Day; if you're not on a bike, this is the best way to get here. Parking spaces are limited.

☑**TOP TIP**

The oldest building on campus is Old Main, home to the Heritage Center. The most popular exhibit is a scale model of campus built entirely of Lego. Unfortunately, Old Main is closed for renovations through 2026.

CU & CHAUTAUQUA

CU Enlargement

HIGHLIGHTS	**ACTIVITIES**	**SLEEPING**
1 Chautauqua Park	**10** Chautauqua Trail	**18** Basecamp Boulder
2 Flagstaff Mountain	**11** Fiske Planetarium	**19** Boulder Guest House
SIGHTS	**12** Flatirons Trail	**20** Moxy
3 Chautauqua Auditorium	**13** Gregory Canyon Trailhead	**21** University Inn
4 Community House	**14** Mesa Trail	**EATING**
5 CU Art Museum	**15** Royal Arch Trail	**22** Cafe Aion
6 CU Events Center	**16** Sommers-Bausch Observatory	**23** Carelli's
7 CU Museum of Natural History	**17** University of Colorado at Boulder	**24** Chautauqua Dining Hall
8 Folsom Field		**25** Dark Horse
9 Third Flatiron		**26** Flagstaff House

EATING (cont.)
27 Gaia Masala Burger
28 Ginger Pig
29 Illegal Pete's
30 The Corner
31 University Kitchen

ENTERTAINMENT
32 Colorado Shakespeare Festival
33 Fox Theatre
34 Macky Auditorium Concert Hall

is the **Sunrise Amphitheater**, which has some of the best views of CU, Chautauqua and the First Flatiron's summit block jutting out of the side of Green Mountain. From here, geography geeks can try to pick out **Baseline Road**: it got its name because it was built atop the earth's 40th parallel, and you can see its faint trace as it extends eastward to the horizon, bisected in the middle by a reservoir.

Picnic tables, giant rocks and shady seats abound on Flagstaff. This is a great place to spend a half a day or to have a picnic. From May through October, you can drive all the way to the summit; once the snows start, you'll need to park at Realization Point and hike the Ute Trail (0.5 miles) the rest of the way. In winter, microspikes are a good idea. Purists can hike the entire way from either Chautauqua Park (p118) or Gregory Canyon; the trail is only 2.7 miles, but with 1500ft of elevation gain you'll be working those leg muscles.

On the way to the summit you'll pass **Flagstaff House**, an haute-cuisine restaurant with gorgeous views over the city, gourmet prix-fixe dinners (from $138) and a superb wine collection.

Finally, be aware that Flagstaff Rd is extremely popular with cyclists. Drive slowly and always use your blinkers when stopping at a pullout, as some cyclists race downhill at high speed. There have been several bad accidents on this road in the past.

Hike in Boulder's Backyard

Off the beaten track

Flagstaff Rd doesn't end on Flagstaff Mountain – keep driving west and you'll soon reach the breathtaking hills behind the Flatirons. Most people never get this far, pulling off immediately at Lost Gulch to take in the views (0.75 miles past Realization Point), but keep going for the easily missed Green Mountain West Ridge Trail (1.7 miles) and historic Walker Ranch (4.5 miles).

Green Mountain (8148ft) is Boulder's third-highest summit. The traditional way up is via the 5.4-mile trail (round trip) from **Gregory Canyon**, a shady but steep excursion that climbs roughly 2350ft. But what if we told you there was a much easier way to get to the top? That would be the **Green Mountain West Ridge Trail**, a fabulous short hike that starts close to the peak elevation. The trail is 3.8 miles (round trip), with only 680ft of elevation gain – expect to do some scrambling near the end. Parking near the trailhead is limited.

Further west is the gorgeous **Walker Ranch**, an 1880s homestead that has reverted to open space. The landscape here is quite different: it's mostly high grasses, scrub and cinema-worthy rock formations jutting out of the steep canyons. The full loop hike, which descends to South Boulder Creek and the back door of Eldorado Canyon (p127), is a tough 8 miles, but shorter variations are possible. It's quite exposed to the elements here, so don't go in the mi-day summer heat. This is also a popular mountain-biking area.

Climb the Flatirons

On belay!

If you've been thinking to yourself, 'I bet climbing a Flatiron sure would be fun,' you're not alone. While the First, Second and Third are the most famous formations, there are dozens of other giant sandstone slabs in the foothills above Boulder, and you can bet that every single one of them has at least one route to the top.

Many serious climbers regard these low-angle faces as no more than scrambles, but if you want to experience the thrill of multipitch climbing in a magnificent setting, look no further.
Continued on p120

Continued on p120

SKYLINE TRAVERSE

Boulder has five main peaks that form the backdrop to the city: South Boulder Peak (8549ft), Bear Peak (8461ft), Green Mountain (8148ft), Flagstaff (7283ft) and Mt Sanitas (6483ft). Link them together, and these five summits form the Skyline Traverse, a 16.7-mile hike or trail run across Boulder's highest ridgeline, with 6073ft of elevation gain along the way.

The roller-coaster journey is an epic to be sure: hikers typically take over 10 hours to complete the trip, while trail runners might take upwards of seven or eight hours. Of course, superhuman endurance athletes will generally do it much faster: the fastest-known time (FKT) is a blistering two hours and 42 minutes.

PAGE LIGHT STUDIOS/SHUTTERSTOCK

Third, Second and First Flatirons

TOP EXPERIENCE

Chautauqua Park

This historic park is the gateway to Boulder's most magnificent swathe of open space: where the massive 1000ft Flatirons rise up out of the plains, a majestic landmark that signals the beginning of the Rocky Mountains. The Flatirons are the symbol of the city, and no trip to Boulder is complete without a hike up to the foot of these sandstone monoliths.

History

Chautauqua gets its name from a movement that began in rural New York in 1875. It was basically an educational summer camp for adults, where participants could listen to guest lecturers, attend music concerts and plays, and become civically engaged – in addition to camping out in canvas tents and having fun in nature. The idea soon caught fire, and by 1915 some 12,000 communities across the US had hosted a Chautauqua. Boulder's Chautauqua was founded in 1898 through a partnership with Texas schoolteachers and the Gulf & Southern Railway. Much of the campus as you see it now – the dining hall, the auditorium, the general store – was built in a matter of weeks, just in time for the July 4 opening.

DON'T MISS

The Flatirons

The Royal Arch

The Mesa Trail

The Chautauqua Dining Hall

Concerts at the Auditorium

PRACTICALITIES
Scan this QR code for more on events, lodging and dining at Chautauqua.

Today, Boulder is home to the only remaining Chautauqua west of the Mississippi, and it continues to operate under the original premise, offering lodging, entertainment and outdoor fun.

Hiking

Chautauqua's wide-open prairie is the perfect foreground for the main attraction rising above: the dramatic red-rock Flatirons. This particular viewpoint, with the foothills' gentle swell extending away into the distance, will always be the Boulder's calling card.

From here, three Flatirons are visible: the First, Second and Third (right to left). You can hike up to their base, scramble up to their summits and even go far beyond. Or, if you just want a quick taste, a simple climb through the grassy meadow will suffice.

No matter your destination, most people start on the main **Chautauqua Trail**. While you can make this an out-and-back walk, connecting to Bluebell Rd makes for a relatively easy 1.5-mile loop. But take note: even these moderate hikes come with some significant elevation gain.

If you're itching to go higher, then the **Flatirons Loop Trail** (2.5 miles) is a fantastic choice. You can follow it to the base of the First, where climbers rope up for ascents, or do the full 700ft of elevation gain up to the top, following the trail as it zigzags up between the First and Second Flatirons.

Want to go further yet? The **Royal Arch Trail** (3.5 miles) has been a Boulder classic for over a century. This roughly 2½-hour trek leads you up to a natural arch past the Third Flatiron and has fantastic views. Expect to do some scrambling. The trails at Chautauqua – there are 15 in all – connect to the rest of the city's open space via the long-distance Mesa Trail (p126), giving you lots of options to customize your walk.

Concerts & Dining

The historic 1898 **Chautauqua Dining Hall**, which features a great wraparound porch, is a favorite with hikers. It's open for breakfast, lunch and dinner and is reasonably priced.

The barn-like **Chautauqua Auditorium**, another 1898 original, is definitely worth checking out – it seats 1300 and has seen the likes of Emmylou Harris, Gillian Welch and BB King on its stage. Concerts run from May through September. If you can't get tickets, some say that sitting outside on the lawn is almost as good.

In the winter months, the much smaller **Community House** (1918) hosts bluegrass acts in a much smaller and more intimate venue.

GEOLOGY PRIMER

Bonus points if you can guess how those 1000ft sandstone slabs came to be formed. If you answered 'uplift,' you're right! The red rock that comprises the Flatirons was deposited as eroded sand and rock roughly 280 million years ago. When the uplift that created the Rocky Mountains occurred 70 million years ago, the sedimentary layers in the foothills were tilted downward, creating the Flatirons we see today.

TOP TIPS

● Parking is limited. From Memorial Day to Labor Day, the cost is $2.50 per hour. On summer weekends and holidays, visitors are encouraged to take the free **Park to Park Shuttle** (bouldercolorado. gov), which runs from downtown parking garages to the lots at the New Vista High School and the CU campus.

● Chautauqua's historic Craftsman cottages are fantastic accommodations options, but you'll need to reserve well in advance. Book online at chautauqua.com.

● Bring plenty of water and sun protection – the Colorado sun is intense and dehydration is common.

● Dogs are welcome on the trails here; however, they must be leashed.

CLIMBING 101

At its most basic, climbing is a two-person game. One person climbs, the other belays. The first person climbs above the belayer and places protection (like a metal chockstone or cam) into cracks in the rock. If there are no cracks, then bolts may be drilled into the rock instead. The rope is then attached to the protection. If the climber were to fall, theoretically the protection and the belayer would catch them.

After the leader reaches a good place to set up an anchor, they stop climbing and belay the second person, or the follower, up the route. In this way, pitch by pitch, a pair of climbers can eventually reach the top of anything they can climb, and do so in relative safety.

Flatirons

Continued from p117

As Yvon Chouinard, the founder of Patagonia, allegedly said, the **Third Flatiron** is 'the finest beginner climb in the country,' and we couldn't agree more. The climbing is easy, the exposure is thrilling and the pitches up the 1000ft face simply go on and on and on. The trick, of course, is getting down. Beginners may find the series of three rappels more challenging than the climbing, particularly the nervy traverse to the last rappel station.

Unless you're an experienced climber with your own gear, you'll need to go with a guide. Try out the **Colorado Mountain School** *(coloradomountainschool.com; $549)* or **Colorado Wilderness Rides and Guides** *(coloradowilderness ridesandguides.com; $540)*. It's considerably cheaper if you're at least two people. Several formations, including the Third, are closed for raptor nesting from February through July, but your guide will be able to suggest a suitable alternate.

A final word of warning: plenty of people free solo the Flatirons without a rope, but we definitely don't recommend this. Rescues are more common than you might think, and every year at least one person falls to their death.

See the Stars at the University of Colorado

Journey into the universe

CU is known as a party school, and at first glance some of the celebrity dropouts – Robert Redford, Glenn Miller, Jonah Hill, Trey Parker and Matt Stone (wait, the last two *did* graduate!) – seems to corroborate the reputation.

But spend a little bit of time here, and you'll quickly realize that there's a whole other side to campus life. CU conducts plenty of Tier-1 STEM research, particularly in the fields of

ZACH J6497/SHUTTERSTOCK

physics (four Nobel laureates), chemistry (one Nobel laureate) and aerospace engineering. In fact, the university receives more NASA funding then any other university in the world. Among the list of badass eggheads who did graduate with a CU degree are 20 astronauts, including Scott Carpenter (the second American to orbit the earth), Kalpana Chawla (the first Indian woman in space) and Takao Doi (the first Japanese to walk in space). Steve Wozniak also went here, but he got kicked out for hacking the university's fledgling computer system.

Visitors can join the astronomers at the **Fiske Planetarium** *(colorado.edu/fiske; adult/child $12/8)*, where shows on the 65ft-diameter dome ceiling bridge the divide between hard science and pop culture, with evenings dedicated to Pink Floyd, Taylor Swift and Lucy, an ongoing NASA mission to the Jupiter Trojan asteroids. The sophisticated star machine here can project some 20 million celestial bodies.

Afterwards, pop over to the next-door **Sommers-Bausch Observatory** *(colorado.edu/sbo)* for the real thing. The observatory holds free public stargazing every Friday night at 8pm (weather permitting) when school's in session. Head up to the observation deck, where you'll have full use of various telescopes, binoculars and the world's largest starwheel to look at the stars. University professors and grad students are on hand to talk about the universe.

Drop in to Boulder's Best Museums

Expand your mind

Boulder's two best museums are on the CU campus: the CU Art Museum and the Museum of Natural History.

For some reason the **CU Art Museum** *(colorado.edu/cuartmuseum; free)* largely flies under the radar in Boulder, but the curators here are fantastic and the art is certainly worth an hour of your time. If we had to pick one museum to visit in town, this is the one. The four rooms mix up exhibits from the permanent collection (Greek coins, Chinese funerary figurines, illustrated medieval manuscript leafs from Europe and Persia) with temporary showings that run the gamut from illustrations by Chagall and Goya to modern installations that represent different interpretations of the uncertain, unresolved challenges that the world faces today.

The **Museum of Natural History** *(colorado.edu/cu museum; free)* has two main exhibits: paleontology and anthropology, both of which are also impressive for their size. If you're

SPACE WALK

Just outside the Fiske Planetarium is a model of our solar system, built exactly at a one-to-10-billion scale. A sobering look at the size of celestial bodies and the distance between them, it offers a fascinating window into space. It all starts with the sun, which is roughly the size of a grapefruit. The earth, meanwhile, is no more than a pinprick – lost in the vastness of the CU campus, unless you happen to know just where to look for it. While the first four planets are within eyesight of each other, traveling to the dwarf planet Pluto (near Colorado Ave) is a 10-minute walk. To reach Proxima Centauri, our nearest star, meanwhile, would require walking another 2500 miles.

EATING ON THE HILL: BUDGET FAVORITES

The Corner: Popular student hangout serving soups, quinoa bowls, paleo bowls, veggie burgers and all-day breakfast. *8am-10pm* $

Gaia Masala Burger: India meets America at this late-night munchies favorite, serving tikka masala everything. We like the fries. *7am-4am* $

Illegal Pete's: The Colorado burrito chain is one of the most popular cheap meals on the Hill. *11am-10pm Mon-Wed, to midnight Thu-Sat, to 9am Sun* $

University Kitchen: Dig in to bibimbap, pad Thai, Chinese noodles and bento boxes at this underground Asian food court. *11am-8pm Mon-Fri* $

COLORADO SHAKESPEARE FESTIVAL

For over half a century, summer in Boulder has meant the **Colorado Shakespeare Festival** (*cupresents. org*). CU's lovely outdoor amphitheater, the Mary Rippon Outdoor Theatre, is surrounded by Italianate buildings with red-tiled roofs and has a distinctly Mediterranean feel to it: the perfect setting for the Bard's tragedies and comedies as evening begins to fall. Free pre-show talks are often offered by the producing artistic director, to give historical background and context for the plays. Performances are staged from June through early August.

The theater gets its name from Mary Rippon, CU's first female professor (1878–1909) and possibly the first woman in the United States to teach at a public university.

into fossils, you'll love the ground floor, which has dinosaur tracks, petrified sequoia cross-sections, orb spiders that are millions of years old as well as all the requisite dinosaur skeletons, including a triceratops head. The entire collection originates in Colorado. The anthropology exhibit focuses on the Mahaffy Cache, stone tools found in Boulder that date from the Clovis era (c 11,000 BCE). These hunter-gatherer tools reveal the types of animals that used to roam around town: elephants, camels and ground sloths, among others.

Catch a Show or a Game

From the Fox to the Buffs

The university is the nexus for all sorts of events: music festivals, modern dance, lectures from luminaries like the Dalai Lama or Neil deGrasse Tyson, in addition to the usual array of Division 1 college sports.

The **Macky Auditorium** (*colorado.edu/macky*) on the Norlin Quad is the main venue on campus, with 2000 seats and a range of events, from opera to TEDx talks to country music.

On the Hill just off-campus is the intimate **Fox Theatre** (*z2ent.com*), the best place in town to catch up-and-coming acts. You'll be elbowing your way through students to get near the stage of this mid-sized venue (625-person capacity), so head upstairs for a perch near the sound board for better views and acoustics. Expect big acts, popular jam bands and indie rock.

If sports is more your thing, then you'll already know that CU is home of the Buffs – and, as of 2023, Deion Sanders (aka Coach Prime). Sanders' arrival electrified the otherwise mediocre football program. The Buffs play football at **Folsom Field** (*cubuffs.com*). Even if you're not a football fan, it's worth staying abreast of their fall schedule, as Boulder traffic on Saturday afternoons can come to a standstill during home games.

The men's and women's basketball teams generally fare better than the football team; their home games take place at the **CU Events Center** (*cubuffs.com*).

The best athletics team at CU is unsurprisingly the **ski team**, which has taken home 21 national championships, most recently in 2024.

EATING AROUND CU: OUR PICKS

Dark Horse: This labyrinthine student bar is a great place to get lost. Plenty of burgers, wings and events. *11am-midnight Sun-Wed, to 2am Thu-Sat* $

Carelli's: On the east side of CU, come here for upscale Italian American cuisine. Several notches up from the usual student haunts. *4-9pm Mon-Sat* $$

Ginger Pig: A literal hole in the wall at the end of 13th St, serving Asian favorites from Chinese dumplings to Korean cornflake dogs. *noon-8pm Tue-Sat* $$

Cafe Aion: If you're a grown-up on the Hill, this is your spot – paella, tapas and sangria make for a sophisticated meal, day or night. *11am-9pm Tue-Sun* $$$

South Boulder

THE GREATEST VARIETY OF HIKING TRAILS IN TOWN

At first glance, South Boulder (SoBo) looks like many other suburban developments in the West, dotted with single-story ranch homes and kids biking through the streets on their way to school. But layered within this residential world is another one, the domain of bears, mountain lions, coyotes and antlered deer. It's a wild side that emerges after the sun sets and the creatures from the hills descend into town. Indeed, this intersection of human and wilderness is South Boulder's primary attraction – there are at least half a dozen trailheads snaking into the hills in this part of town, providing access to miles of hiking trails, high summits and hundreds of rock-climbing routes.

The most prominent trail begins at the National Center for Atmospheric Research (NCAR), which provides another window into Boulder life. Scientific research is an important driver of the town's economy, and national labs like NIST, NOAA and many others are clustered in South Boulder.

Study the Atmosphere at NCAR

Chase storms at the tornado generator

South Boulder's main attraction is the **National Center for Atmospheric Research** *(NCAR; scied.ucar.edu; free)*, which sits atop a mesa west of town. The earth-hued Tetris-like building is one of the earliest designs of architect IM Pei (of Louvre Pyramid fame), and can be reached by a gorgeous spiraling road that's accessible to both vehicles and cyclists. Hikers can tromp right up the north side of the hill following a seldom-used trail.

So what, you might be wondering, does NCAR do? In short, the scientists here study everything about the atmosphere and then run planetary simulations on a supercomputer up in Cheyenne, Wyoming. Research topics range from extreme weather to solar disturbances in the magnetosphere to climate change, and NCAR data is used for satellite communications, air safety (the FAA), pollution alerts and, of course,

GETTING AROUND

Table Mesa, running perpendicular to Broadway, is the main thoroughfare in South Boulder, extending from NCAR down to the King Soopers shopping center. While the SKIP bus runs up Table Mesa and south along Lehigh – connecting South Boulder to CU, downtown and North Boulder – it is easiest to get around via car or bicycle. Eldorado Canyon State Park, the South Mesa Trailhead and Marshall Mesa are located 6 miles south of town, off of Hwy 93.

☑ TOP TIP

Winter along the Front Range is surprisingly sunny and warm, and it's not unusual for locals to enjoy their favorite outdoor activities even in the depths of February. If you join them, remember your microspikes: snow and ice on north-facing trails melts at a much slower rate.

WHAT TIME IS IT?

The unassuming **National Institute of Standards and Technology (NIST)**, off Broadway Ave, sets the pace for the rest of the United States – literally. This federal lab is home to a cesium fountain atomic clock, which accurately measures time according to the natural resonance frequency of cesium (Cs; atomic number 55). The time is then broadcast via longwave and shortwave radio signals across the country. Call 303-499-7111 to hear the tick-tock broadcast, which announces the hour in Coordinated Universal Time – the mother of all timekeepers, based in the UK.

Other types of precise measurements that are calibrated at NIST include molecular and submolecular technologies, such as electron microscopes and quantum sensors.

weather forecasts. Their weather model is the most widely used system in the world.

Open to the public, NCAR has two floors of excellent interactive exhibits, including sample instruments used for data collection, a cloud machine and some fabulous photos. Free guided tours are offered at noon every Monday, Wednesday and Friday.

Hike to the Bat Cave

A South Boulder classic

South Boulder is littered with trailheads that head out into the city's open space (Shanahan Ridge, Bear Canyon and Skunk Canyon), but one of our favorite ways to get the most out of an open space hike with minimal effort – big views, rock scrambling, giant sandstone formations and ponderosa-scented forest – is to strike out from the **NCAR Trailhead** and hike up to **Mallory Cave** (3 miles round trip; 1175ft of elevation gain).

The hike begins with an interpretative walk along NCAR's 0.4-mile weather trail, where panels introduce regional phenomena like cold fronts and the flying-saucer-shaped lenticular clouds. At the end of the mesa top, the trail dips into a grassy saddle, giving you a taste of the sweeping views to

HIGHLIGHTS
1 Chautauqua Park

SIGHTS
2 National Center for Atmospheric Research

ACTIVITIES
3 Mesa Trail
4 NCAR Trailhead
5 Shanahan Ridge Trailhead

EATING
6 Chautauqua Dining Hall
7 Southern Sun
8 Sweet Cow
9 Tandoori Grill
10 Walnut Cafe

come. After climbing past the water tower you'll then come to an intersection with the Mesa Trail (p126). But instead of turning north or south, keep going straight up the mountain.

Before too long, you'll start to come to some of the big sandstone formations like **Dinosaur Rock**. While the uninitiated might assume climbers are most interested in the slabs' moderate east faces, it's at Dinosaur Rock where you'll see more extreme sport-climbing taking place right off the trail. Some of these lichen-streaked north-facing routes are graded at 5.13: basically, they are very, very, very hard.

From here, the trail feels increasingly like a labyrinth as you weave between the giant rocks all around – you may lose your way at times, but keep following the gully up and right. At some point you'll need to do some low-grade rock scrambling, so consider this to be a good stopping place if you're starting to feel uncomfortable. The cave itself is gated shut to protect the bats that live here.

This a great hike to bring a picnic on.

Summit Bear Peak

Boulder's best climb

The ultimate Boulder summit hike is **Bear Peak**, a fantastic if challenging excursion up the city's second-highest mountain. There are a variety of ways to get to the 8458ft summit; we recommend leaving from the **Shanahan Ridge Trailhead**, which is a 5-mile round-trip Stairmaster of a climb with 2675ft of elevation gain. The true summit requires some low-key rock scrambling, so keep that in mind if you're squeamish about heights.

From the trailhead, you'll climb up through the ponderosa forest, passing the Mesa Trail on a gradual ascent – gradual, that is, until you hit the Slab: a 500ft-tall chunk of sandstone that is the widest rock face in the Flatirons. This is where you enter Fern Canyon, an elevator-like ascent up the steepest part of the hike. It's not long, but it will likely take a lot out of you, especially if you're coming from sea level. After the canyon, you'll finally emerge on the ridge line – from here, it's a straight shot to the summit. The last section requires navigating the airy rocky ridge. It's not hard, but it can be intimidating if you aren't used to scrambling. Take it slow and admire the inspiring views of Denver, the plains and the Indian Peaks to the west as you go.

While you're up here, consider bagging the tallest peak in Boulder too. It's an extra 0.5 miles (one way) to South Boulder

OPEN SPACE IS NO ACCIDENT

Boulder's unique and vast swathe of undeveloped land started back in 1898 when the city helped purchase the plot that became Chautauqua Park. In 1907 the government floated a public bond to buy Flagstaff Mountain, and in 1912 purchased 1200 more pristine mountain acres. Then, in 1967, Boulder voters legislated their love of the land by approving a sales tax specifically to buy, manage and maintain open space. This was historic. No other US city had ever voted to tax themselves specifically for open space and Boulder's **Open Space and Mountain Parks** *(osmp.org)* office was launched. In 1989 76% of voters increased the tax by nearly 100%; today the OSMP protects over 46,000 acres of land, crisscrossed with 155 miles of hiking trails.

 EATING IN SOUTH BOULDER: OUR PICKS

Walnut Cafe: South Boulder's ultimate breakfast spot has been going strong for over 40 years. Come for pancakes, scrambles and chai. *7am-2pm* **$**

Sweet Cow: The Front Range ice-cream specialists have a busy SoBo location, serving scoops and milkshakes. *11am-9pm Sun-Thu, to 10pm Fri & Sat* **$**

Southern Sun: Sister to the downtown Mountain Sun, the Southern Sun has similar friendly vibes plus good beer, good burgers and no-hassle parking. *noon-11pm* **$$**

Tandoori Grill: Run by Paul and Gurjeet Dhanoa, this North Indian restaurant uses organic greens and house-made paneer. *11:30am-2:30pm & 4:30-9pm Tue-Sun* **$$**

NOAA

You've heard of NASA, but what about the **National Oceanic and Atmospheric Administration (NOAA)**? In charge of everything from deep-sea exploration to weather forecasting, you may be surprised to learn that this maritime agency has a lab in...Boulder? Sure enough, NOAA is yet another federal research facility in the city, but the landlocked lab isn't as out of place as you might think. NOAA's Boulder facilities began as the Central Radio Propagation Laboratory (CRPL) in the 1950s, with a focus on communications, the upper atmosphere and solar activity. If that sounds similar to what NCAR studies, you're right. Turning the city into an international hub of atmospheric and environmental research was no accident. Today, 17 federal laboratories are based in town.

Climber, Eldorado Canyon State Park

Peak along the ridge. While not as spectacular as Bear Peak, it is marginally taller at 8549ft.

This is an extremely strenuous hike; don't be fooled by the distance. Bring enough food and water, and be prepared to turn around in the event of a thunderstorm.

Walk the Mesa Trail

Boulder's longest through hike

Much like the Grand Canyon Rim Trail, the **Mesa Trail** isn't a hike that many people walk in its entirety, yet anyone who ventures into Boulder's open space will be sure to tread along it at some point. This gorgeous north–south connector runs through the foothills for roughly 6.5 miles (one way), all the way from Chautauqua Park to South Mesa outside Eldorado Springs. It crosses a variety of terrain and has fewer ups and downs than other Boulder hikes.

One fun excursion is to park the car at NCAR (p124), then follow the trail north. After about 1.5 miles, you'll see an old stone cabin on your left; turn left here for a short detour up to **Woods Quarry** (in operation from 1890 to 1920). The old quarry is now home to some quirky sandstone couches and armchairs, the perfect spot to have a seat, rehydrate and admire the view. Return downhill to the Mesa Trail and continue north across Enchanted Mesa – in just 1 mile you'll be at Chautauqua Park (p118), where you can finish off your stroll with a meal at the Chautauqua Dining Hall (p119).

If you choose to go south instead, expect fewer people and wilder scenery; it's roughly 5 miles to the South Mesa Trailhead from NCAR.

Regardless of the direction that you choose, the easiest way to get back to NCAR is to take a rideshare – or turn around and retrace your steps!

Storm the Bastille in Eldorado Canyon

A rock climber's paradise

Boulder is no Yosemite, but the sheer amount and variety of rocks here has turned it into a hallowed destination for climbers around the world. Of the three principal areas – the Flatirons, Boulder Canyon and Eldorado Canyon – it's the latter that is the most revered. And as you drive into **Eldorado Canyon State Park** *(cpw.state.co.us; $10 per vehicle)*, it's hard not to catch your breath – towering fangs of polished quartzite rock erupt in all directions, their sheer red faces splashed with patches of psychedelic neon green lichen. Thrilling multipitch arete climbs like the Yellow Spur, Rewritten and the Naked Edge are among the best vertical adventures in the United States; however, they're definitely not for casual climbers.

The good news is you don't have to be a thrill-seeker to enjoy the park. In fact, Eldo was a vacation resort long before deranged climbers discovered the place, and the park's best hike, the **Rattlesnake Gulch Trail** (3.5 miles round trip), ascends 1000ft up to the site of the old Crags Hotel, opened in 1908 and originally accessible from Denver via the nearby railroad (still in use) for a mere $1. The Crags tenure was short lived, however, as a fire burned it down in 1912. Just past the Crags ruins is the Continental Divide overlook – an admirable destination if you don't want to hike the full loop.

A less strenuous hike is the **Fowler Trail** (1.5 miles round trip), which starts midway into the park and contours back to the canyon mouth for views over the plains. Along the way you'll pass the mighty Redgarden Wall across the creek; this is the tallest and most distinctive crag in the park, rising some 700ft high. See if you can pick out the climbers on its face to get an idea of its size. Closer to the entrance you'll see the backside of the famous Bastille, the prominent formation near the park entrance. The Bastille Crack, visible from the road as you drive in, is a park classic and was the first climbing route established here in the mid-1950s, by soldiers from the 10th Mountain Division. The **Eldorado Canyon Trail** (6.5 miles round trip), meanwhile, links up with Walker Ranch (p117).

Eldo is a popular destination; from May 15 to September 15 you'll need to reserve a timed entrance *(cpwshop.com)*. Alternatively, ride the free shuttle on summer weekends *(bouldercounty.gov)*, which runs down Broadway from CU.

If you're feeling bold and can't wait to test your mettle on the Bastille, check in with the **Colorado Mountain School** *(coloradomountainschool.com; $349)* or **Colorado Wilderness Rides and Guides** *(coloradowildernessridesandguides.com; $540)* for guided trips. These climbs are not suitable for beginners.

Eldo is located 6 miles south of town, off Hwy 93.

ELDORADO SPRINGS

Just outside the state park is the tiny burg of Eldorado Springs, which amazingly was once proclaimed to be the 'Coney Island of the West.' The natural springs and spectacular scenery attracted upwards of 60,000 summer visitors annually in the first half of the 20th century, and the resorts here offered a mix of dancing, swimming, carnival games and fishing. Perhaps the most unusual attraction was tightrope walker Ivy Baldwin, who strung a cable between the Bastille and the Wind Tower and would walk across the canyon floor (580ft down) on a regular basis from 1906 to 1948 – his last walk came at age 82! Eldorado Springs today is borderline off the grid (please drive slow), though the chilly spring-fed swimming pool is still open to visitors.

North & East Boulder

BREWERIES, CLIMBING GYMS AND THE RESERVOIR

GETTING AROUND

The SKIP bus runs the length of Broadway, from South Boulder to North Boulder. The JUMP bus runs from downtown, following Arapahoe Ave through East Boulder and onto Erie. The BOUND runs along 30th St, from Baseline to Iris, passing CU's east side and the 29th St Mall. All buses are $2.75. Even though the bus system is decent, you may want a car or bike to get around East Boulder as destinations are fairly spread out.

☑TOP TIP

If you are driving in the North Boulder foothills, remember to share the road with cyclists and be a patient driver. Above all, never attempt to overtake a cyclist on a blind curve as you will be putting yourself and oncoming traffic at risk.

Downtown has Pearl St, the Hill has Chautauqua, and South Boulder has Eldo and dozens of Flatirons formations. In comparison, North Boulder (NoBo) and East Boulder are less obvious destinations for visitors, but that doesn't mean they're devoid of charms. Residential North Boulder has a variety of restaurants strung out along Broadway – the shortest way to reach Hwy 36 and the road to Rocky Mountain National Park. There's also easy trail access at North Boulder Park and Wonderland Lake, as well as a quirky art district at the edge of town.

East Boulder is a haphazard collection of office parks, industrial zones and quiet walks through the plains and wetlands areas. This is where you'll find the lion's share of Boulder's breweries and climbing gyms. The largest shopping area in town is the 29th St Mall, which sprawls over several blocks in between Arapahoe and Walnut Sts.

First Friday Art Walk

Local artists open their doors

The small, grassroots effort known as the NoBo Art District has grown into a robust group of more than 200 professional artists and creative businesses, centered around a funky green-colored warehouse district located off Broadway Ave at the northern edge of town. Here, you'll find artist-friendly warehouses, galleries and studios as well as innovative community projects.

The First Friday Art Walk is the best time to visit. Download a map *(noboartdistrict.org)* and follow it through the streets and doors you might otherwise never enter. Some studios are up staircases or tucked above a garage. Some aren't labeled at all. It's adventurous – and inspiring. Best of all, you'll get to meet the artists face to face and talk about their work.

Good places to start at include the **Bus Stop Gallery** and the **NoBo Art Center**. During the day, the **Amazing Garage Sale** is the only place that's reliably open – you'll find every-

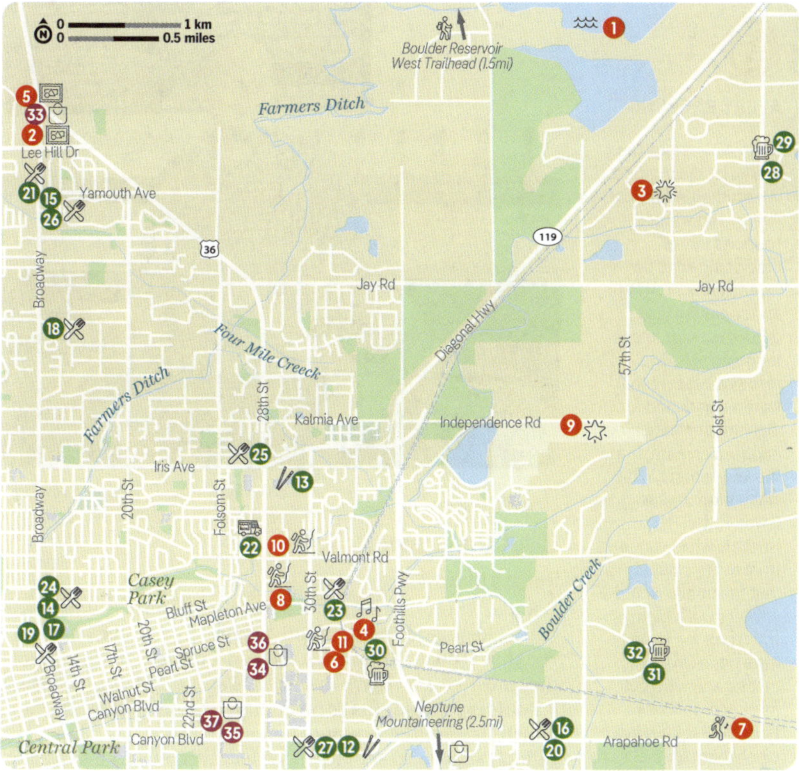

SIGHTS
1. Boulder Reservoir
2. Bus Stop Gallery
3. Celestial Seasonings
4. Junkyard Social
5. NoBo Art Center

ACTIVITIES
6. ABC Kids Climbing
7. Avalon Ballroom
8. Boulder Rock Club
9. Mile High Gliding
10. Movement
11. The Spot

EATING
12. A Cup of Peace
13. Aoi Sushi
14. Audrey Jane's Pizza Garage
15. Bacco
16. Blackbelly
17. Breadworks
18. Dagabi Cucina
19. Hungry Toad
20. Le Frigo
21. Moxie
22. Rayback Collective
23. Roadhouse Boulder Depot
24. Santo
25. Tangerine
26. Tierra Y Fuego
27. Voodoo Doughnut

DRINKING
28. Asher Brewing
29. Avery Brewing Company
30. Sanitas Brewing
31. Upslope Brewing
32. Wild Provisions

SHOPPING
33. Amazing Garage Sale
34. Crystal Ski Shop
35. Epic Mountain Gear
36. Fleet Feet Boulder
37. Larry's Boot Fitting

thing from Elvis cutouts to imported masks at this quirky consignment shop.

First Fridays are self-guided, so go at your own pace. Bright flags throughout North Boulder lead to the next surprise. Pop by the information tent for recommendations.

Expect to find revolving themed exhibits, food trucks, live music and plenty of local brews.

AVERY BREWING

Avery was established in 1993 by disgruntled law student Adam Avery, who wanted to spend more time doing what he loved: home brewing and spending time outdoors. A fondness for going off-piste resulted in beers that weren't marketed for mainstream tastes, and sure enough, the brewery's first big hit was a barley wine. It was called Hog Heaven, which came from Avery's belief that the public would only enjoy his beers when pigs fly. He may have been wrong on that account, but hard-won success wound up solidifying a penchant for the uncommon. Today, Avery's taproom in Gunbarrel has a whopping 30 beers on tap, ranging from pucker-up sours to potent rum-barrel-aged creations.

Sanitas Brewing

Boulder Brewery Tour

Raise a glass

Boulder's breweries are much like their hometown: idiosyncratic, idealistic and distinctly compelling. Today, there are roughly a dozen breweries located on the fringes of Boulder, most of which are excellent. Paving the way is **Avery**, a Boulder original that's been in in business since 1993 and which has led the way for the local brewery scene in Colorado. It's the largest of the Boulder taprooms by a long shot, but that just means more beer for you. At the upstairs restaurant, expect everything from soft pretzels to bowls of green chile, with an emphasis on products straight from nearby farms. Our favorite Avery brew will always be an unfiltered White Rascal: a zesty Belgian *witbier* with notes of cilantro and orange.

Within walking distance is **Asher Brewing** (2009), the first all-organic brewery in Colorado. All beer here is made from high-quality ingredients, with a close eye on environmentally sustainable and socially responsible practices. At the taproom, you can try the flagship ales or a seasonal brew on tap while relaxing on the patio.

The breweries in East Boulder, meanwhile, are closer to downtown. The award-winning **Upslope** (2008) leads the

EATING ON NORTH BROADWAY: OUR PICKS

Moxie: The best bakery in Boulder, selling heirloom flour, breads, pastries and espresso. Come early before it all sells out. *7:30am-4pm* **$**

Tierra Y Fuego: Homemade corn tortillas and *aguas frescas* make this taco restaurant a winner. *8am-2pm & 4-8pm Tue-Fri, 8am-8pm Sat, 8am-3pm Sun* **$**

Bacco: If you like specialty cheese and charcuterie plates, this mozzarella bar is the spot. Also serves pizzas and pasta dishes. *4-8pm Mon-Sat* **$$**

Dagabi Cucina: Spanish-Italian hybrid, hidden away on a tree-shaded square behind Lucky's Market. Tapas, paella, wood-fired pizzas. *5-9pm Tue-Sun* **$$**

way here, with its outdoor adventure emphasis. This is where climbing advocates like the Access Fund hold fundraisers, and Upslope does its part by donating a percentage of its craft lager can sales to Trout Unlimited to protect and restore fisheries and watersheds. Sustainability is a huge priority. A small burger stand serves food in a corner of the buzzy taproom.

Around the corner from Upslope is the new kid on the block, **Wild Provisions**. Part of the 4 Noses family (Broomfield), Wild Provisions focuses on Czech-style lagers and fermented farmhouse saisons. Definitely one for the beer nerds. A food truck serves pizza most days.

The warehouse complex where **Sanitas Brewing** is located doesn't exactly scream charm, but wait till you get inside. The low-key tap room has a hipster feel with cement floors and high, family-style tables, while patio seats have partial views of the Flatirons and great afternoon sun. A food shack serves tacos. Railroad tracks run right by the patio – don't miss the train deal special!

Learn to Rock Climb at the Gym

Crashpad not required

If you don't own a crashpad or a set of cams but are still itching to try out bouldering or rock climbing, the climbing gym is a great place to start. And for a relatively small town, Boulder has an incredible variety of gyms: everyone, from the littlest kid to the grumpiest piton-hammering legend, has a place to hang. All gyms rent shoes and harnesses.

Anyone with children should make for the **ABC Kids Climbing** (*abckidsboulder.com; per person $20*). Camps, birthday parties and open gym – all geared to younger climbers – make this an ideal place for kids to learn the basics. ABC is owned by the French-American Raboutou family, whose daughter Brooke has already competed in the Olympics (twice!). If you're a drop-in, open gym is 10am to 2pm on weekdays, and 12:30pm to 5pm on weekends.

If bouldering (unroped climbing) is your jam, **The Spot** (*the spotgym.com; adult/student $27/21*) is the go-to place. It has a large 15,000-sq-ft warehouse space with a variety of giant boulders and walls. There is a definite college-age vibe here, as gymnastic climbers crowd around the trickiest problems trying to figure out the sequence. They also have a slackline, beer on tap and a blacklight climbing competition.

Movement (*movementgyms.com; adult/child $28/18*) is arguably the hippest of the bunch. Bouldering here is a bit

BOULDER OLYMPIANS

It should come as no surprise that outdoor-crazed Boulder regularly sends a contingent of athletes to the Olympics. In the 2024 Summer Games, five Boulder County natives joined nine CU grads in Paris, and four of them took home medals. Climber Brooke Raboutou and swimmer Emma Weber both attended Fairview High; Brooke earned a silver while Emma won gold. Another Boulder climber, Colin Duffy, just missed out on a spot on the podium, finishing fourth in the men's competition. Morgan Pearson, a CU grad and Boulder resident, earned silver in the mixed triathlon. Another former CU Buff and Colorado native, Derrick White (now a Boston Celtic), played for the gold-medal basketball team.

EATING NEAR VALMONT RD: OUR PICKS

Rayback Collective: Huge outdoor space with fire pit, food trucks and bar, plus live music and Colorado brews. *8:30am-10pm Mon-Fri, from 10am Sat & Sun* **$**

Tangerine: Inventive breakfast spot; think puttanesca scramble, Amalfi Benedicts and endless pancake options. No reservations. *7:30am-1:30pm* **$$**

Roadhouse Boulder Depot: Feast on enchiladas, roadhouse burgers and poke bowls at the 1890 Boulder train station. *11am-10pm, from 9am Sat & Sun* **$$**

Aoi Sushi: Top-quality sushi and *izakaya* (small plates) from Keizo Aoi and Yuki. Don't miss the chef's lunch special. *11:30am-2pm & 5:30-9pm Tue-Fri, 5-9pm Sat* **$$$**

BEST OUTDOOR SHOPS

Neptune Mountaineering: Neptune's has a great collection of gear and apparel. They also rent AT skis, avalanche gear, ice axes and crashpads.

Fleet Feet Boulder: Everything you need for running track, street and trail. They also organize group runs.

Larry's Boot Fitting: This is where the national champion ski team at CU gets their boots fitted.

Crystal Ski Shop: Super-friendly rental store will get you sized up for demo skis, kids' skis and Nordic skis. Very affordable.

Epic Mountain Gear: Yes, they are part of Vail Resorts, but the Boulder store arguably has the best collection of skis and ski apparel in town.

Bolder Boulder 10K footrace

cramped, but for lead climbers the walls are tall (up to 40ft), the route-setting is clever and fun, and there is a good variety of grades over 22,000 sq ft of space. They have a good variety of classes (yoga, learn to lead, etc) and fitness equipment.

Finally, there's the OG **Boulder Rock Club** (*boulderrockclub.com; adult/child $28/18*). Like many of us as we age, the BRC is quietly good at a lot of different things without striving to be the center of attention. If you're looking for more of a low-key atmosphere, this 10,000-sq-ft gym is a good choice. It also has a dedicated kid's wall upstairs. Also note that the BRC has one thing Movement and The Spot do not: autobelay, which allows you to climb without a partner.

Paddle at the Reservoir

Summer in the city

When you're this far from the ocean, there aren't many choices for cooling off in the summer. Enter the 700-acre **Boulder Reservoir** (*bouldercolorado.gov; adult/child $12/7.25*) – from May through September, this is where folks come to suntan, swim, fish and play in the water. There's a big sandy beach, lifeguards and a well-maintained visitor center and

EATING ON ARAPAHOE AVE: OUR PICKS

Voodoo Doughnut: The best doughnuts on the planet come in every flavor imaginable. Vegan options too. *6am-10pm Sun-Wed, to midnight Thu-Sat* $

Le Frigo: A real French deli with an entire room dedicated to cheese. Best of all are *les sandwiches*. Patisseries too. *11am-7pm Mon-Sat, to 4pm Sun* $

A Cup of Peace: Sungmi's homestyle cafe serves healthy whole-grain Korean specials like *dubap* (BBQ bowl) and tofu-noodle soup. *11am-8pm Mon-Sat* $

Blackbelly: Gourmet restaurant-slash-butcher's Blackbelly has only the finest cuts, from Black Angus steak to braised short rib rigati. *7am-9pm* $$$

cafe. Kayak, paddleboard and canoe rentals are offered (from $30 per hour). Be sure to bring a hat and reapply sunscreen often – there's little shade. Dogs aren't allowed into the park between May 15 and Labor Day.

If you're more interested in the wetlands and wildlife than swimming, head to the **Boulder Reservoir West Trailhead** on 55th St, where a hiking trail follows the north shore. Birders have spotted bald eagles, ospreys, burrowing owls, bitterns and northern harriers in the tall grasses and reeds here.

Soar over the Flatirons

Take flight in a glider or paraglider

Maybe you've already hiked or climbed to the top of the Flatirons, but you haven't *really* seen them until you've gotten the bird's-eye view. Luckily, there are two ways to join the red-tailed hawks and golden eagles soaring on the thermals over town.

If you love the feel of wind whipping across your face, opt for an adventure with **Boulder Paragliding** (*boulderparagliding.com; flight $207*). Mauricio and Julian get guests airborne on seven- to 15-minute tandem flights over the Foothills. Meet up at Foothills Community Park in North Boulder, and figure on 90 minutes prep and hiking time to the launch area. The season runs from April to October.

If you'd rather fly at a higher altitude, with bigger views from inside a cockpit, then **Mile High Gliding** (*milehighgliding.com; $175 to $300*) might be for you. Trips are in a glider (like a small plane, but with no engine), with a soaring altitude of up to 10,600ft. There are three options, with flight times running between 15 and 35 minutes. You can fit two people in addition to the pilot inside the glider, and flights depart year-round. Flights depart from the Boulder Airport in North Boulder.

Dance the Night Away

From Latin to swing

If you love to dance, the **Avalon Ballroom** (*boulderdance.org; free to $15*) is the most happening spot in town. To be clear, we are not talking about clubbing or any sort of new-fangled electro nonsense. Avalon is decidedly old school. This is usually partner dancing, but across a wide breadth of styles: contra, swing, salsa, waltz, Lindy hop and even masquerade balls. Multiple dances are held daily, including classes.

BOLDER BOULDER

Boulder's biggest party is, unsurprisingly, a 10K footrace held every Memorial Day, snow or shine. With more than 50,000 runners and pros mingling with costumed racers, live bands and sideline merrymakers, **Bolder Boulder** (*bolderboulder.com*) may be the most fun 10km run in the US. Course-side antics range from slip and slides and Elvis impersonators to red, white and blue paragliders spiraling down to the race's end at Folsom Field. Participants are divided into 100 waves, with wheelchairs going first, followed by the pros. Then come the walkers, elementary school kids and the costumed – eventually everyone makes it to the finish line. The latest addition to the race calendar is Colder Boulder, a 5K race in early December.

EATING NORTH OF PEARL ST: OUR PICKS

Audrey Jane's Pizza Garage: Sister-and-brother duo sell naturally leavened pizza out of a decommissioned garage. Great topping combos. *11am-8pm* $

Breadworks: Nominally a bakery, Breadworks also has inexpensive soups and sandwiches in its airy cafe area, plus prepared entrees. *7:30am-4:30pm* $

Hungry Toad: For all things English, including Premier League matches on the telly, head to the local pub. *11am-9pm Mon-Fri, 8am-10pm Sat, 9am-9pm Sun* $$

Santo: Taos-inspired restaurant serving posole, *montadas* (smothered pork) and green-chile cheeseburgers. *7am-9pm* $$

ROAD CYCLING

Unlike many other Colorado cities, there are more options for road cycling in Boulder than mountain biking. In addition to the perpetually sunny climate, Boulder's location at the intersection of the foothills and the plains means there are multiple great climbs into the mountains, in addition to long scenic cross-country rides. Popular routes are mostly in North Boulder and include Olde Stage Rd, Left Hand Canyon, Lee Hill, Hwy 36 to Lyons and Flagstaff Mountain. They are all justifiably famous, but take care out there. Accidents are unfortunately all too common, do not always involve cars and more than once have happened to Tour de France veterans. Lee Hill is particularly dangerous. Nearly every year at least one road cyclist tragically dies in Boulder County in an auto-related crash.

BIG BLINK CREATIVE/SHUTTERSTOCK

Celestial Seasonings

Another popular East Boulder community hangout is **Junkyard Social** *(junkyardsocialclub.org; adult/child $5/12)*. By day it's a 6000-sq-ft kid's (junkyard) playground and cafe, but in the evenings it morphs into a bar with all sorts of events, from queer open mics, indie concerts and Latin salsa socials to game nights and drop-in mah-jongg.

Tour Celestial Seasonings

Tension tamer

If you like tea, you'll dig visiting **Celestial Seasonings** *(celestialseasonings.com; tour $5)*, one of the world's largest herbal tea producers. Join the 45-minute tour out in Gunbarrel, which includes a campy historical video and a walk through the milling, mixing and packaging areas. The Mint Room – packed with mint and peppermint bundles – leaves you feeling like you're inside a lozenge. It's open from 10am to 5pm, Tuesday to Saturday.

Beyond Boulder

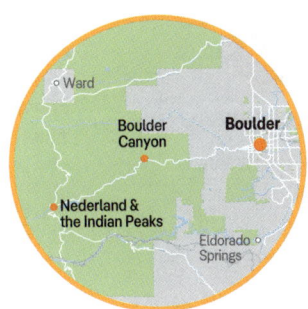

The nearby Indian Peaks Wilderness Area provides ample recreation opportunities in summer and winter, from high-altitude hiking to skiing.

Boulder is a perfectly situated base for all sorts of adventures, including Rocky Mountain National Park to the northwest, but it's the Indian Peaks that are the most convenient escape from town. Forming the impressive backdrop to Nederland, this national wilderness area is one of the most used in the country. With grand scenery on the scale of a national park, it offers many spectacular hiking and camping opportunities; be advised that Forest Service overnight permits, even for back-country campsites, are required from June to mid-September. And unlike national parks, dogs are allowed on almost all trails, but must be on a leash. In winter the area is popular with alpine skiers, backcountry skiers and snowshoers.

Boulder Canyon

TIME FROM BOULDER: **15 MINS**

Admire Boulder Falls

Punctuated with granite crags and sheer cliffs, the 15-mile Boulder Canyon is a devastatingly scenic route into the mountains. There are not a lot of places to get out of the car and explore (unless you're a climber) – the most obvious place is the 70ft **Boulder Falls**, which is a mere 15 minutes from town. The trail is a short 1 mile round trip, and ends at the falls, which alternate between trickling and gushing depending on the season. The hike itself is accessible to people of all ages and abilities, including dogs on leash. From the parking lot, there are several spots to climb down to the creek and dip your feet in while enjoying a picnic – be super careful in spring, however, when the water is raging fast.

Fly-fish on Boulder Creek

Matching wits with brown and rainbow trout in the waters above Boulder is a great way to slow down and disconnect from the modern world. Upper Boulder Canyon, past the falls, is a good place to cast, but be prepared for a challenge. The St Vrain above Lyons (north of Boulder) is another favorite destination, as is South Boulder Creek, which you can access by hiking down from Walker Ranch (p117). For alpine fishing, try **Brainard Lake**.

Places

Boulder Canyon p135

Nederland & the Indian Peaks p136

GETTING AROUND

Hwy 119 runs through Boulder Canyon for 16 miles from Boulder to Nederland. Having a car is easiest, but don't overlook RTD's NB bus ($5.50 day pass), which runs roughly every two hours in between Boulder and Nederland year-round. In summer it's equipped with bike racks; in winter skis and boards get stowed in the luggage bins. The bus stops at the Hessie Hiker Shuttle pickup on summer weekends, and at Eldora Ski Resort in winter.

GETTING TO BETASSO PRESERVE

If you're pedaling up from town, the easiest way to get to Betasso Preserve is to take the Boulder Creek Path to Fourmile Canyon Dr, follow Fourmile Canyon for 2.8 miles, then access the preserve via the Fourmile Link trail. If you are a hardcore biker with lots of experience and great cardio, the shortest way to go is to take the Boulder Creek Path to the 1.2-mile Betasso Link trail just before the tunnel. Be warned, this is very steep, and, in the words of one local mountain-biking mom, 'You will likely die on the Betasso Link if you don't know what you are doing.'

In town, stop by **Front Range Anglers** *(frontrangeanglers. com; class/guided trip from $150/295)* for gear, classes, info on daily conditions or to sign up for a guided tour.

Mountain bike at Betasso Preserve

The 1700-acre **Betasso Preserve**, with its rolling grasslands and ponderosa forest, is particularly popular with mountain bikers. It's not only a great place to ride, but you can even reach it by pedaling straight out of town on the bike path. The **Canyon Loop** and **Benjamin Loop** are two popular intermediate trails here, while the **Super Betasso** at 16.3 miles is the whole enchilada and best saved for experts.

Note that the preserve is closed to mountain bikers on Wednesdays and Saturdays. If you're a **hiker**, these are the two days to visit (otherwise you risk being run over). If driving here, access is via Sugarloaf Mountain Rd; it's 6 miles from Boulder.

Nederland & the Indian Peaks

TIME FROM BOULDER: **30 MINS**

Explore Nederland

Located at the western end of Boulder Canyon, the ramshackle little berg of **Nederland** (8235ft) is a mountain-town magnet for hippies looking to get off the grid. There's a sagging, happenstantial quality to its weather-beaten buildings, which are not without a certain rugged charm. The gateway to the Eldora Ski Resort and the Indian Peaks Wilderness, it's a good place to break for a meal and to let the little ones take a spin on the antique **Carousel of Happiness** *($3)*, which dates from 1910.

The **Wild Bear Nature Center** *(wildbear.org)*, which is slated to open in a new location in 2025 along the Peak to Peak Hwy west of town, educates visitors on local flora and fauna. It's aimed at families.

To learn about the town's history, visit the **Nederland Mining Museum** *(free)*. Heavy machinery, rusting tools and photos are displayed inside and out.

Ski Eldora

'Friends don't let friends drive I-70,' or so **Eldora** *(eldora.com; adult/child $180/150)* likes to say. At just 21 miles from Boulder (45 minutes on a good day) or 47 miles from Denver, this is the closest ski resort to the Front Range. When the wind is howling and the snow is thin, you may wonder why you

 EATING IN NEDERLAND: OUR PICKS

Crosscut Pizzeria & Taphouse: The thin-crust pizza here is tops, as is the patio seating alongside the creek. *3-8pm Mon & Wed-Fri, from 11:30am Sat & Sun* **$**

New Moon Bakery & Cafe: Bagels, quiche and breakfast burritos will get your day going right. *6:30am-1pm Mon-Fri, to 3pm Sat & Sun* **$**

Deli at 8236: Nothing fancy here – it's all about the top-quality subs and soups, which keep customers warm on snowy days. *10am-4pm* **$**

Salto Coffee Works: Start the day with egg sandwiches on brioche, then scarf down hefty salads and sandwiches for après. *7am-3pm Mon-Thu, to 6pm Fri-Sun* **$**

MATTHEW STAVER/BLOOMBERG/GETTY IMAGES

Eldora

GETTING TO ELDORA

Eldora's appeal is its convenience to the Front Range. Here's the catch, though. Parking is limited; if you want a spot on a powder day or weekend, you do need to be there early – 8:30am at the latest. The 5-mile road from Nederland up to Eldora is not bad, but all it takes is one 2WD Chevy Camaro spinning its wheels on the snowy hill to bring traffic to a standstill. Check their Snow and Operations page or Insta account for traffic and parking updates: when the lots are full, they will let everyone know. Alternatively, you can take the RTD bus to both Nederland and the resort from downtown Boulder (NB route); buses carry skis and boards. Under-19s ride free.

made the trip up here. But on a beautiful bluebird day after a foot of fresh powder overnight, the skiing here is as good as anywhere else in the state. This is a great place for newbies, with plenty of green and blue cruisers. It's also a good place to learn the ins and outs of terrain parks – **Woodward** runs half a dozen parks on Little Hawk Mountain, from the Start Park and Fun Zone for the littlest shredders to the full-sized Sundance and the Trick Ditch half-pipe for older daredevils.

For expert terrain, follow the long and winding Around the Horn run (blue) to get over to the Corona lift. Double black runs here are all about tree bashing, like the fun slaloming in Brian's Glades. Step it up a notch and head over West Ridge where extreme skiing awaits – Moose Glades, at the resort's boundaries, is an adventure, while Salto Glades is the steepest tree run at the resort.

Eldora also has a **Nordic ski area** *(eldora.com; adult/child $27/22)*, with 24 trails over 25 miles. It's gorgeous terrain back here and you're far enough removed from the downhill resort to make it a peaceful outing. There are snowshoe trails here as well. Little-known tip: the Colorado Mountain Club runs the **Årestua Hut** *(cmcboulder.org)*, a backcountry hut that's accessible via a 4.5-mile trail. It sleeps up to seven people, and is heated by a wood-burning stove. This is an easy and affordable way to spend the night in the snowy backcountry.

Hike the Indian Peaks

Nederland is the jumping-off point for gorgeous hikes into the Indian Peaks. Like the ski resort, the trails up here offer easy access to the high country, with minimal driving time. There are two main areas: Hessie Trailhead and Rainbow Lakes.

PLANE CRASHES IN THE PEAKS

Hikers summiting South Arapaho Peak (13,344ft) won't just skirt the shrinking Arapaho Glacier – which provides some 40% of Boulder's drinking water – they might also pass more macabre remains: a downed Air Force trainer aircraft that crashed into the mountainside during a 1960 snowstorm. Unsurprisingly, this is not the only plane wreckage in the Indian Peaks. According to the Boulder County Sheriff's Office, there are at least 20 crashes located above the tree line in Boulder County. Another prominent wreckage site near a summit route is that of a twin engine C-47, which went down on Navajo Peak during a storm in 1948. Most of the mangled aircraft is found at the top of Airplane Gully, just before the final push to the 13,409ft summit.

BRIAN WOLSKI/SHUTTERSTOCK

Arapaho Glacier

South of Nederland are the Hessie and Fourth of July trailheads. For **Hessie**, take the free hiker's shuttle from Friday to Sunday from Nederland High School. From the trailhead you can reach Lost Lake, a good 2.7-mile round trip with backcountry campsites, or head further for more alpine lakes and passes. **Fourth of July** is even more scenic, with access to Arapaho Glacier (7.9-mile round trip). Another recommended option from this point is the hike up to the 12,000ft Arapaho Pass (6.4-mile round trip). It's a gentle ascent but be prepared to spend the entire day – if the altitude doesn't slow you down, the scenery will. Note: the unpaved road to Fourth of July is best left to high-clearance or 4WD vehicles. Like the name suggests, it is snowbound until early July.

North of Nederland is the **Rainbow Lakes Campground**. Surrounded by lodgepole pines at an elevation of 10,000ft, it has access to brilliant hikes, including the Rainbow Lakes Trail (2.5 miles) and South Arapaho Peak (13 miles). The latter passes the Arapaho Glacier at the 6-mile mark. The campground is first-come, first serve, but extremely popular; access it via a 5-mile unpaved Forest Service road. Bring your own water.

INDIAN PEAKS

The best access point for the Indian Peaks wilderness is at **Brainard Lake** (p135), which is 17 miles north of Nederland on the Peak to Peak Hwy.

Places We Love to Stay

$ Budget $$ Midrange $$$ Top End

Downtown p106

Foot of the Mountain $
Nothing fancy here, just plenty of family-owned, wood-paneled charm near the entrance to Boulder Canyon.

Hotel Boulderado $$
With over a century of service, the charming Boulderado, full of Victorian elegance, is a National Register landmark and a romantic getaway.

St Julien Hotel & Spa $$$
In the heart of downtown, Boulder's finest hotel is modern and refined with Flatiron views and a full-service spa.

Bradley Boulder Inn $$$
A downtown Boulder mansion with polished wood, local art and stained glass salvaged from a nearby church makes this is a great upscale option.

CU & University Hill p115

University Inn $
Perks from this long-running motel include the central location, friendly staff and updated rooms. There's even a heated outdoor pool. Just off the Boulder Creek Bike Path.

Boulder Guest House $$
Gorgeous and comfy, this tranquil home has cozy rooms with a Buddhist influence. A tall fence and landscaped garden insulate it from busy Arapahoe Ave.

Moxy $$
Opened in 2024, this 189-room hotel has plenty of style, so-so service and a convenient location across from CU.

Basecamp Boulder $$
Great concept and central location. The mountaineering theme includes coolers as coffee tables and a climbing wall in the dining area.

Chautauqua Lodge & Cottages $$
Adjoining hiking trails to the Flatirons, this is a top Boulder pick. Cottages have one to three bedrooms with porches and patchwork-quilt beds.

Limelight Boulder $$$
Slated to open on the CU campus in 2025, the Aspen-based Limelight will offer Buffs fans easy access to the big games.

Rest of Boulder

Boulder Twin Lakes Inn $
Owned by a former Olympian, this budget choice out in Gunbarrel has large rooms, a communal kitchen and a year-round Jacuzzi.

Boulder Adventure Lodge $$$
You've come to Boulder to get outdoors, so why not stay nearer the action in Fourmile Canyon? Hiking, biking, climbing and fishing right from the property.

Hotel Boulderado

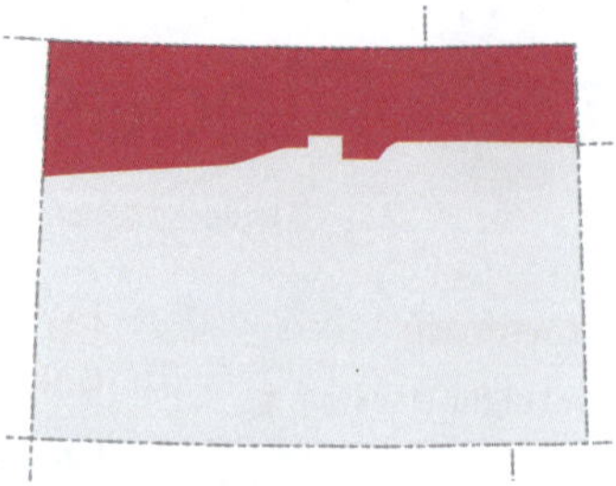

Rocky Mountain National Park & Northern Colorado

ACROSS THE GREAT DIVIDE

The wind whips wild and free through the northern reaches of Colorado.

With one foot on either side of the Continental Divide, Rocky Mountain National Park's vast expanse of wilderness leaves even repeat visitors in awe. Here you'll find the headwaters of the Colorado River – the principal architect of the Grand Canyon and the much-contested lifeline of seven Western states – as well as a handful of shrinking glaciers clinging high in the peaks, all that remain of the last ice age.

More recent history takes in the span of human habitation, from prehistoric mammoth hunters to the Ute and Arapaho, followed by surging waves of fur trappers, homesteaders, ranchers and other settlers from the 1800s on. The country's nascent conservation movement grew out of the increasing extraction, and destruction, of its natural resources, eventually leading to the creation of the National Park system. Rocky Mountain (RMNP) was the 10th such park to be created, and was signed into existence in 1915.

At times, the park may seem like a victim of its own popularity, but all you need is a few days in the rest of northern Colorado to realize that there are still vast swathes of wilderness here that few people ever step foot in. Keep driving west and you'll come to one of the state's most down-to-earth ski resorts, Steamboat Springs, nestled in a pristine landscape that invites adventure by foot, mountain bike, horse and kayak.

MICHAEL LIGGETT/SHUTTERSTOCK

THE MAIN AREAS

ROCKY MOUNTAIN NATIONAL PARK
Bugling elk, majestic peaks and gasp-worthy views. **p146**

STEAMBOAT SPRINGS
Ski. Soak. Repeat.
p164

FORT COLLINS
Bikes and beer.
p172

For places to stay in Rocky Mountain National Park, see p177

ROCKY MOUNTAIN NATIONAL PARK & NORTHERN COLORADO

DAWN WILSON PHOTOGRAPHY/ALAMY STOCK PHOTO

Bear Lake (p149)

Steamboat Springs, p164

Olympic skiing by day, hot-spring soaking by night, and two enormous wilderness areas for summer camping.

Rocky Mountain National Park, p146

A world of wildlife, the continent's highest continuous paved road and miles of aspen-laced hiking trails await at one of America's most popular national parks.

WYOMING

Steamboat Lake State Park

Routt National Forest

Indian Peaks Wilderness Area

Dinosaur National Monument

Rocky Mountains

● Craig

● **Steamboat Springs**

Rocky Mountain National Park

White River

○ Rangely

Flat Tops Wilderness

● Meeker

Granby ○

White River National Forest

Arapahoe National Forest

Winter Park

70

Colorado River

Glenwood ○ Springs

Holy Cross Wilderness

Vail

● Frisco

Grand Mesa National Forest

● Aspen

South Park

○ Grand Junction

Find Your Way

Stretching all the way to the border with Wyoming, northern Colorado is a massive and little-visited region. Outside of the national park, this is a place where off-the-beaten-path experiences reward the intrepid.

SAN LUIS VALLEY

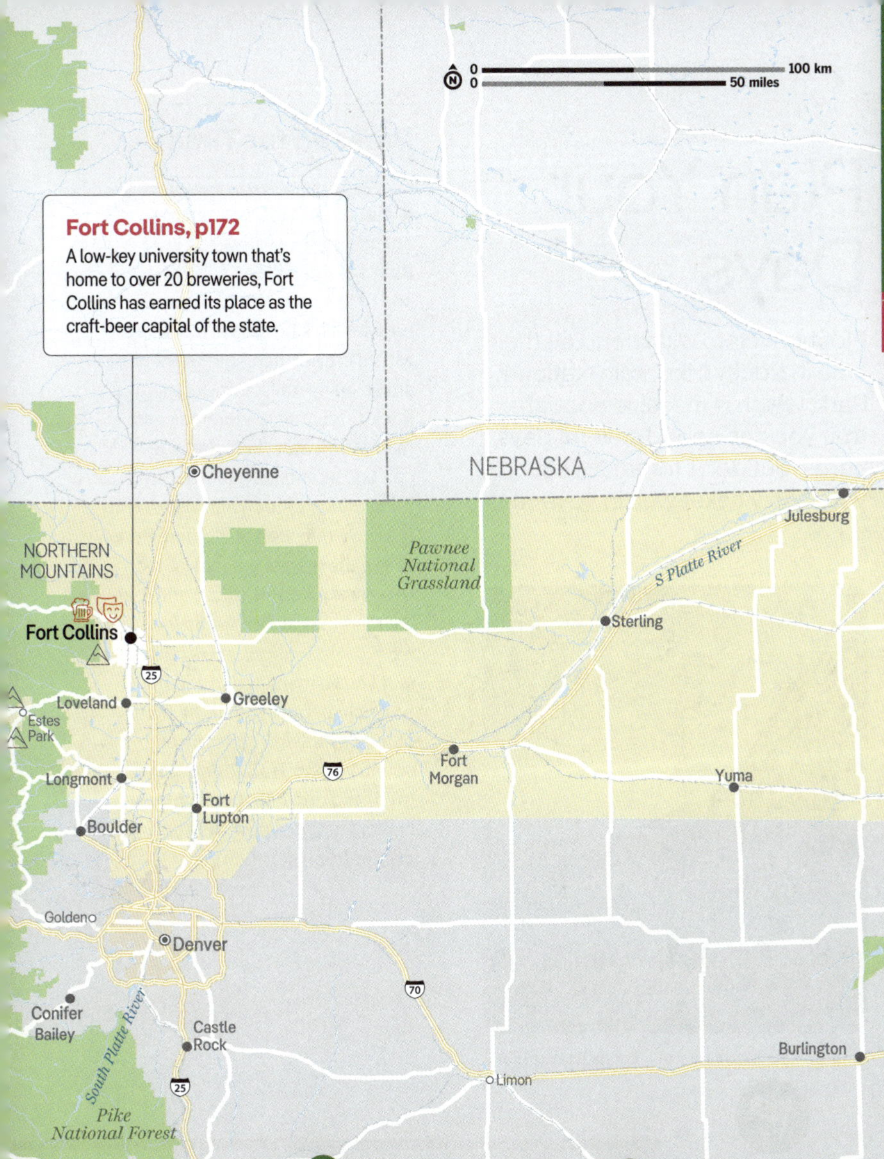

0   100 km
0   50 miles

Fort Collins, p172

A low-key university town that's home to over 20 breweries, Fort Collins has earned its place as the craft-beer capital of the state.

Cheyenne

NEBRASKA

Julesburg

NORTHERN
MOUNTAINS

Pawnee
National
Grassland

S Platte River

Fort Collins

Sterling

Loveland

Greeley

Estes
Park

Longmont

Fort
Morgan

Yuma

Fort
Lupton

Boulden

Golden

Denver

South Platte River

Conifer
Bailey

Castle
Rock

Limon

Burlington

Pike
National Forest

CAR

You definitely need your own wheels. In some areas, gas stations are few and far between; always fill up before setting out. Trail Ridge Rd in RMNP is generally closed from late October through late May.

PARK SHUTTLE

In summer and fall, hiker shuttles run to RMNP's Bear Lake corridor (but nowhere else). The park encourages visitors to take these shuttles when possible, as this helps reduce traffic and parking woes. Reservations must be made in advance.

BUS & AIRPORT SHUTTLE

The Estes Park Shuttle runs between Denver International Airport (DIA) and Estes Park, the gateway town to RMNP. Bustang runs public buses between downtown Denver and Fort Collins.

Plan Your Days

Most travelers will spend all their time in Rocky Mountain National Park, which is massive enough that you can spend several days here – but don't forget to reserve your entry ticket well in advance.

Longs Peak (p152)

DAVID SPATES/SHUTTERSTOCK

Pressed for Time

● Get up with the sun and hop on the shuttle or drive to the **Bear Lake trailhead** (p149), one of the most stunning – and popular – hiking areas. Yes, there will be crowds here, but there are so many trails, neck-craning Rocky Mountain panoramas and thundering waterfalls that you can't go wrong. Don't forget to bring plenty of food and water. On the drive out, stop at Moraine Park to see the glacier exhibits at the **Discovery Center** (p150) and real-life moraines in the meadow.

● If you've managed to secure a vehicle permit, spend the rest of the day driving up to the high country along **Trail Ridge Road** (p151) and pop into the country's highest national park **visitor center** (p151) at 11,796ft.

SEASONAL HIGHLIGHTS

July through mid-October is peak season in RMNP: the high country is (relatively) snow free and the wildlife is active. In winter and early spring, hit the slopes in Steamboat.

FEBRUARY
Ski conditions are near their peak: powder at Steamboat Springs is deep; day trips into RMNP are absolute magic. Presidents Day weekend is a big deal for ski resorts; try to avoid if you can.

MAY
Skiing is finally over and spring runoff – when all the snow turns into water and mud – is in full force. By late May, Trail Ridge Rd should be open. It's still too early to go hiking in the high country though.

JUNE
Wildflowers are blooming at lower elevations, school's out for the summer and paddling season is underway in Steamboat and Fort Collins. Believe it or not, however, much of the high country is still covered in snow.

Two Days to Explore

● With two days, you can explore the lesser-known **Wild Basin** or **Lumpy Ridge trailheads** (p152). The former is known for its waterfalls; the latter is peppered with fantastical granite domes. If you're acclimatized and in great shape, hike up to **Chasm Lake** (p152). If you've managed to snag a campsite at the Boulder Field, try to summit **Longs Peak** (p152) in a two-day trip. **Mt Ida** (p153) is an easier but no less stunning ascent along the Continental Divide. Outfitters in **Estes Park** (p146), meanwhile, can arrange fly-fishing excursions, via ferrata climbs and a host of other activities. Too much heart-pounding action for you? In that case, drive south along the **Peak to Peak Highway** (p162) to return to Boulder.

If You Have More Time

● If you have at least three days, then we recommend trying to snag a coveted wilderness camping permit so that you experience the park the way it's meant to be experienced – on a **backpacking trip** (p153) far from the crowds. Keep an eye out for bighorn sheep, elk, black bears and moose.

● Alternatively, consider a road trip that follows **Old Fall River Road** (p151) or **Trail Ridge Road** (p151) over the Continental Divide and down into **Kawuneeche Valley** (p159) and **Grand Lake** (p158). From here, continue on to **Steamboat Springs** (p164) where you can saddle up for a horseback ride, go white-water rafting or hike the remote Flat Tops. Afterward, circle back to the Front Range via Hwy 9 and I-70.

AUGUST
RMNP is as busy as it gets, mountain bikers are barreling down the trails at the Steamboat resort, and cooler temperatures at backcountry campsites and high elevations make for a great escape from summer heat.

SEPTEMBER
One of the best months: aspens shimmer gold, temperatures are cool but not cold and bugling elk are in action in Rocky Mountain National Park. This is a fabulous time to go camping.

OCTOBER
Last chance to visit before the snow arrives. Aspens are still turning early in the month and nighttime temperatures are crisp but not icy. Trail Ridge Rd closes for the season.

DECEMBER
The ski season kicks off in earnest with the holiday rush at Steamboat. Snow cover is still thin this time of year, but the festive atmosphere is sure to bring good vibes.

Rocky Mountain National Park

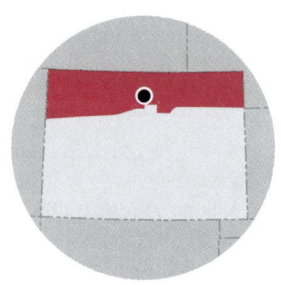

WILDLIFE | CAMPING | HIKING

GETTING AROUND

RMNP and Estes Park are roughly one hour from Boulder and 90 minutes from Denver on Hwy 36. Scenic Hwy 7 (Peak to Peak Hwy) also runs here from Nederland, passing the park's southern entrances. From Fort Collins and I-25, access the park via Hwy 34. Hwy 34 continues through the park and on to Grand Lake, which serves as the western entrance. A shuttle runs from Estes to the Bear Lake corridor, but for the rest of the park you'll need a car. The **Estes Park Shuttle** *(estesparkshuttle. com; $135 round trip)* runs to DIA.

☑TOP TIP

You must reserve entry between late May and mid-October. Reservations should be made on *recreation.gov* on the first day of the month prior to your entry. Last-minute reservations go on sale at 7pm for the following day.

Lace up those boots and step into the untrammeled wilderness of Rocky Mountain National Park, Colorado's crown jewel. A trip through the park will take you from riparian meadows, favored by herds of grazing elk and deer, up through the forests of ponderosa and spruce, before topping out on the windswept tundra. Here, where the earth meets the sky, the landscape contains galaxies of ephemeral summer wildflowers, and the silhouettes of sculpted peaks serve as a dramatic reminder of the last ice age.

Ford icy streams, huff up snow-dusted mountainsides and pass beneath groves of quaking aspen, fringed with gold beneath the sun. Like many national parks, it can be a zoo in the height of the summer season. But leave the main trailheads behind and you'll quickly find your own patch of solitude, so long as you're willing to share it with the wildlife that calls this place home.

Get Situated in Estes Park

Gateway to adventure

All roads lead to **Estes Park**: whether you're driving up Hwys 36, 34 or 7, over 90% of visitors on the way to Rocky Mountain National Park will pass through this crowded gateway town. And if you don't know a WhisperLite from a Jetboil, chances are you'll be spending the night here, too – or, at the very least, stopping for dinner.

Estes is a hodgepodge of T-shirt shops and ice-cream parlors, sidewalks crowded with tourists and streets jammed with RVs. But when the sun reflects just right off Lake Estes, or you spend an afternoon with a lazy coffee on the riverwalk, you might just find your own slice of Zen.

Although the strip malls pale in comparison to Rocky Mountain itself, Estes promises every convenience to travelers: gear rental, guided tours, upscale hotels, fine dining and even a kids' **adventure park** *(openairadventurepark.com; $35)* and

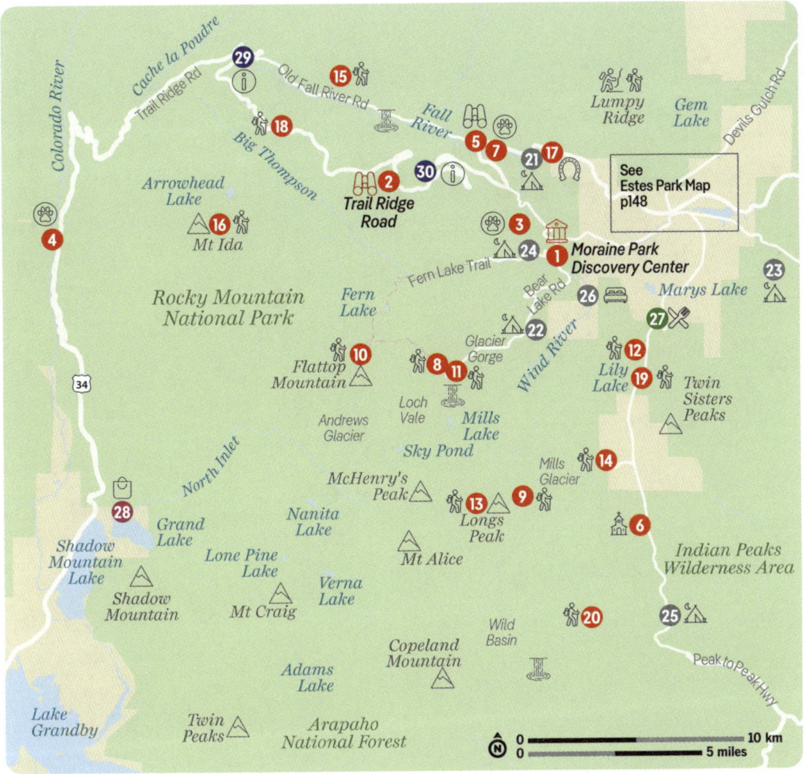

HIGHLIGHTS
1 Moraine Park Discovery Center
2 Trail Ridge Road

SIGHTS
3 Beaver Meadows
4 Kawuneeche Valley
5 Old Fall River Road
6 Saint Catherine's Chapel
7 Sheep Lakes

ACTIVITIES
8 Bear Lake Trailhead
9 Chasm Lake
10 Flattop Mountain
11 Glacier Gorge Junction Trailhead
12 Lily Mountain
13 Longs Peak
14 Longs Peak Trailhead
15 Mt Chapin
16 Mt Ida
17 National Park Gateway Stables
18 Tundra Communities Trail
19 Twin Sisters Peak
20 Wild Basin

SLEEPING
21 Aspenglen Campground
22 Glacier Basin Campground
23 Hermits Hollow Campground
● Longs Peak Campground (see 14)
24 Moraine Park Campground
25 Olive Ridge Campground
26 YMCA of the Rockies

EATING
27 Twin Owls Steakhouse

SHOPPING
28 Never Summer Mountain Products

INFORMATION
29 Alpine Visitor Center
30 Junior Ranger Headquarters

via ferrata routes (p155). There's also the **Estes Park Museum** *(free)*, which has a commendable rotation of exhibits on local culture and history.

In the grand scheme of things, however, you probably won't be spending much time here, outside of eating breakfast and dinner and catching some Zs.

ESTES PARK

SIGHTS
1 Estes Park Museum
2 MacGregor Ranch Museum

ACTIVITIES
3 Colorado Mountain School
4 Kent Mountain Adventure
5 Kirks Flyshop
6 Lumpy Ridge

SLEEPING
7 Black Canyon Inn
8 Deer Crest Resort
9 Estes Park Adventure Hostel
10 Murphy's Resort
11 Stanley Hotel
12 Stonebrook Resort
13 Trailborn Rocky Mountains

EATING
14 Antonio's Real New York Pizza
15 Bird & Jim
16 Claire's Restaurant & Bar

17 Ed's Cantina & Grill
18 Inkwell
19 Kissing Moose Cafe
20 Rock Inn Mountain Tavern
21 Scratch Deli
22 Seasoned Bistro
23 Smokin' Dave's BBQ
24 Village Bagels

DRINKING
25 Bull Pin
26 Rock Cut Brewing
27 The Barrel
28 Wheel Bar

ENTERTAINMENT
29 Adventure Park

SHOPPING
30 Estes Park Mountain Shop
31 Outdoor World
32 Scot's Sporting Goods

INFORMATION
33 Estes Park Visitor Center

THE GUIDE

Celebrate Frozen Dead Guy Days

Spring back to life

This macabre, bizarre and wonderful festival celebrates Grandpa Bredo Morstoel, a Norwegian transplant who is cryogenically frozen, surrounded by dry ice in a shed in the **Stanley Hotel**, awaiting reanimation. A three-day blowout event in mid-March, it brings live bands, coffin races and all the best zombie costumes out of the back of the closet. Can't make it? You can still see the body – ahem, storage container – on the **Stanley's Dead Guy tour** *(stanleyhotel.com; $20)*, where you'll learn all about cryonics. Or you could opt for the whiskey tasting instead.

Day Hikes at Bear Lake

Waterfalls and glacial lakes

The **Bear Lake** and **Glacier Gorge Junction trailheads** are the most popular destinations in the park, and for good reason. From here you'll have a front-row vantage point of the dramatic glacial valleys and hulking granite summits that make Rocky Mountain such a singular landscape.

Hikes range from easy jaunts to **Alberta Falls** (1.6 miles) or **Dream Lake** (2.2 miles) and **Emerald Lake** (3.6 miles) to more challenging excursions that follow the glacial valleys up to their origins. **Mills Lake** (5.6 miles) is a good choice, as is the **Loch** (6.2 miles), which can be extended to the exquisite **Lake of Glass** and **Sky Pond** (9.8 miles). And while **Flattop Mountain** (12,324ft; 8.8 miles) may not be the park's best summit, there's no denying its magnetic pull from down below.

The catch? The Bear Lake corridor requires a special entry reservation between 5am and 6pm, and these sell out faster than Taylor Swift concerts. However, there are a few workarounds. One possibility is to catch a shuttle from Estes Park to the Bear Lake Park and Ride (reservations required; p151) and then transfer to a free in-park shuttle. Another possibility is to reserve a campsite at Moraine Park, Glacier Basin or Aspenglen campgrounds. Finally, if you have a backcountry camping permit in the Bear Lake area, this will also grant you access. Remember: most high-country trails are snowbound through late June.

THE STANLEY HOTEL

The white Georgian Colonial Revival hotel in Estes Park stands in brilliant contrast to the towering peaks of Rocky Mountain National Park that frame the skyline. A favorite local retreat, this best-in-class hotel served as the inspiration for Stephen King's 1977 cult novel *The Shining*, in which recovering alcoholic and struggling writer Jack Torrance takes a job as the winter caretaker of the haunted Overlook Hotel, where things don't go *quite* according to plan...

If it's ghosts you're after, you should book room 401 to increase your chances of ghost-spotting – staff consider it the 'most haunted.' The hotel also offers spirited ghost tours, which nonguests can join to learn all about the spooky history.

EATING IN ESTES PARK: WORTH A SPLURGE

Bird & Jim: Foodie-driven kitchen serving local fare like pan-fried trout. On Hwy 36, just before the Beaver Meadows entrance. *11am-9pm* **$$$**

Twin Owls Steakhouse: Drive south on Hwy 7 and you'll reach this fabulous steakhouse in the Taharaa Mountain Lodge, near Lily Lake. *5-9pm Sun-Fri* **$$$**

Seasoned Bistro: Eclectic, seasonally driven menu from chef Rob Corey that draws inspiration from across the Americas. *5-9pm Wed-Sat, 10am-2pm Sun* **$$$**

Rock Inn Mountain Tavern: Landmark serving steaks, bison meatballs and a side of live bluegrass. Stick-to-the-ribs fare ideal for hungry hikers. *4-9pm* **$$$**

BEAR LAKE ALTERNATIVES

Couldn't score a coveted Bear Lake permit? Fret not, here are five destinations that are accessible with the regular entry permit.

Trail Ridge Road: Travel to the sky on this high-altitude drive that traverses the park.

Fall River Area: Hiking, bighorn-sheep spotting and the original high-altitude drive.

Lumpy Ridge Trailhead: Inspiring rambles among giant boulders and granite crags; Gem Lake (3.4 miles) is a favorite.

Wild Basin Trailhead: Often overlooked, the southern corner of the park is chock-full of waterfalls and fabulous backcountry campsites.

Longs Peak Trailhead: Variety of hikes from kid-friendly to the lung-busting peak itself.

YINGNA CAI/SHUTTERSTOCK

Trail Ridge Road

Wildlife-Watching

Here an elk, there an elk

Spend any amount of time in Rocky Mountain and you'll experience it: two dozen cars pulled over on the side of the road, the passenger doors flung open and one herd of people crowding into a meadow to snap pictures of another herd of elk or deer. At which point you might wonder, who's watching whom?

The park is home to some 800 elk, 350 bighorn sheep, 60 moose, 20 to 30 bears, an unknown number of mountain lions and countless mule deer – and those are just the big guys. Smaller critters include beavers, marmots, pikas, porcupines, otters, fox, coyotes and some 270 species of birds. While you probably won't spot the more elusive animals, if you pay attention, you'll likely see or hear traces of their passage.

Good places to look for wildlife include Moraine Park (start with the excellent **Discovery Center**), **Beaver Meadows**, **Sheep Lakes**, Trail Ridge Rd, and the marshy areas in the Kawuneeche Valley (p159).

Note, however, that accidents involving animals are more common than you might think, and almost always involve an overeager human encroaching on an animal's space. Don't want a 1000lb bull elk with a massive rack of antlers trampling you? Follow the rangers' guidelines and stay at least 75ft away

EATING IN ESTES PARK: QUICK MEALS

Kissing Moose Cafe: A godsend for hikers up early – quick affordable breakfast burritos from a food truck near the Beaver Meadows entrance. *5am-2pm* **$**

Scratch Deli: Another winner near the Beaver Meadows entrance is this tiny deli that packs sammies to go, from veggie wraps to pastrami. *8am-3pm Thu-Mon* **$**

Village Bagels: Homemade bagels, biscuits and cream cheese near the Estes Park Visitor Center, with veg options and quinoa tabbouleh on the side. *7am-3pm* **$**

Inkwell: The sweetest little cafe in Estes with baked goods, light sandwiches, stationery and great coffee. Overlooking the creek. *7am-7pm* **$**

from elk and sheep, and 120ft away from moose and bears. And please, don't feed anything, no matter how cute it looks.

Driving Trail Ridge Road

Drive to the sky

The highest continuous paved highway in North America, **Trail Ridge Road** is a remarkable 4000ft climb, offering visitors the chance to experience the Rockies' high alpine tundra, complete with bighorn sheep, whistling marmots and eye-squinting panoramas in all directions. You can start in the east or west entrances of the park, make it a through trip or an out-and-back adventure, use it as a springboard for high-altitude hikes, or simply content yourself with a dozen superlative-worthy vista points.

Eleven miles of the road are above tree line (the elevation above which trees can no longer survive) and you should be prepared for chilly temperatures (as much as 30°F cooler), intense sun, sudden thunderstorms and possible altitude sickness. Our number one recommendation is to stay hydrated (water, not beer).

Time your visit for July, and you'll be in the tundra for the 40-day growing season, when the hardy meadows and lichen-covered boulders briefly light up with a rainbow of wildflowers. Among the can't-miss sights are the **Alpine Visitor Center** (11,796ft), which looks out over a hazy expanse of 400 sq miles, and the info-packed **Tundra Communities Trail**. Further west is the Continental Divide.

Trail Ridge Rd is only open from June through mid-October, and, as one of the park's premier destinations, sees a lot of traffic. Expect to spend a half-day exploring.

Climb Old Fall River Road

Drive into the past

With a maximum speed limit of 15mph, **Old Fall River Rd** offers motorists a graveled, slow-paced drive into the park's high country. A 1920 original, this historic driving experience is narrow, one way (up) and without guardrails – it's also a bit hair-raising at times.

The road begins at Horseshoe Park, a short distance west of the Fall River Entrance, and winds 11 miles up to the Alpine Visitor Center at Fall River Pass. From there you can head southwest (right) on Trail Ridge Rd and follow it to Grand Lake (p158) on the west side of the park, or take a left and

ESTES PARK HIKER SHUTTLE

The **Estes Park hiker shuttle** *(9am-6pm daily late May–Sep, weekends only Sep–mid-Oct; $2)* is a great way to access trailheads in the Bear Lake and Moraine Park areas, no entry permit required. However, you will need to reserve your shuttle tickets on *recreation.gov*. These go on sale on the first day of the month prior to your entry date (so June 1 for all July dates); last-minute tickets are available at 7pm the night before. The shuttle runs from the Estes Park Visitor Center to the Park and Ride stop near Glacier Basin campground. From here, transfer to shuttles to Bear Lake or Moraine Park.

DRINKING IN ESTES PARK: OUR PICKS

Rock Cut Brewing: In business since 2015, Rock Cut went from homebrewing in a garage to the premier brewery in Estes Park. *11am-10pm*

The Barrel: Kick-back dog-friendly beer garden with 64 rotating taps of the good stuff and food trucks throughout summer. Or you can bring your own picnic. *11am-11pm*

Wheel Bar: Estes Park's favorite dive bar offers a rip-roaring good time, a killer porch on the riverwalk and plenty of foot-long beards. *11am-2pm*

Bull Pin: If you're looking for action, head to this bowling alley meets arcade meets sports bar. *11am-10pm Fri-Sun, from 3pm Mon-Thu*

UTE TRAIL

Trail Ridge Rd was not the first passage across this stretch of the Rockies. Before it opened in 1932, Fall River Rd was already in operation. But both of these roads, of course, were based on far older routes: the original trails that the Ute and Arapaho used to cross the mountains when traveling between their summer and winter hunting grounds. As you drive up Trail Ridge Rd, you'll intersect the park's Ute Trail – which follows the original path – in four spots: at Deer Ridge Junction, at an unmarked trailhead about 2 miles past Rainbow Curve, at Fall River Pass, and at Milner Pass along the Continental Divide.

loop back to Estes Park via Trail Ridge Rd. The views of the alpine tundra and the narrowness of the road make this an impressive drive. Count on 45 minutes going up.

Bagging Longs Peak

King of the Front Range

Iconic in every way, **Longs Peak** (14,259ft) is the pinnacle of Rocky Mountain National Park and one of Colorado's classic climbs. Longs is most often scaled via the exhilarating and exhausting Keyhole Route (15 miles round trip), which features on many visitors' to-do lists. The top of this route is the crux, consisting of narrow traverses, vertiginous cliff faces and heart-pounding scrambling up polished slabs of rock. Not only should you acclimatize before taking this on, it's imperative to keep an eye on the weather at all times. Statistically, this is the deadliest hike in the park, and the average profile for fatalities is a 32-year-old male.

The golden rule is to be off the summit by noon lest you be struck by lightning. For Longs this can be accomplished in two ways: either start the climb by 2am or 3am, or secure a wilderness permit to camp at the Boulder Field, just below the Keyhole.

The good news is that you don't actually have to reach the summit to experience Longs. **Chasm Lake**, located at the foot of the Diamond – the legendary east face where rock climbers rope up to scale the 1500ft wall – is one of the park's best hikes (11,760ft; 8.4 miles round trip), and features all the spectacular scenery of the peak without the risk and arduous ascent.

Wild Waterfalls

Discover Wild Basin

In the park's less-visited southeastern corner, **Wild Basin** offers several easy day hikes to cascading waterfalls, alpine lakes and swathes of wildflowers; all beneath some of the park's most stunning peaks.

Set out from the Wild Basin trailhead and you'll soon reach Copeland Falls (0.3 miles). Calypso Falls appears in less than 2 miles; and in another mile you reach **Ouzel Falls** and a nearby overlook of Longs Peak. Hikers can continue another mile to a junction with the Bluebird Lake Trail that follows Ouzel Creek, or take the northern branch to Thunder Lake in the upper St Vrain Creek. There are great backcountry campsites up here, including Sandbeach Lake (4.2 miles).

To reach the trailhead, drive 13 miles south of Estes Park on Hwy 7.

EATING IN ESTES PARK: CASUAL DINNERS

Smokin' Dave's BBQ: Loosen your belt and dig into buffalo ribs, fried pickles and chili verde at this northern Colorado institution. Beers on tap too. *11am-9pm* **$$**

Antonio's Real New York Pizza: Two outdoor patios and hand-tossed pies make this the best stop for a slice in Estes. *noon-8pm Tue-Sun* **$$**

Claire's Restaurant & Bar: Locally sourced ingredients in dishes like wild-game meatloaf. Great wraparound porch. *11am-8pm Mon-Fri, 8am-8pm Sat & Sun* **$$**

Ed's Cantina & Grill: Kick back on the outdoor patio with a margarita and bison tacos. Plantains and poblano cauliflower grilled cheese too. *11am-9:30pm* **$$**

DAVID SPATES/SHUTTERSTOCK

Ouzel Falls

Camping & Backpacking

Count the shooting stars

Let's be honest, you didn't come to one of the country's most beautiful wilderness areas to sleep in a hotel room, right? Under the big Colorado sky, camping opens up a world of possibilities.

The park's five drive-to campgrounds stage popular campfire programs and are reasonably comfy, with flush toilets, running water, picnic tables, fire rings and bear boxes for food storage (no showers or cell service, though). It is imperative that you make reservations six months in advance. Longs Peak is the outlier here: it does not take reservations, nor does it have drinking water. Moraine Park is the only campground to remain open from October through May; it was undergoing renovations at the time of writing.

Want to pitch your tent far from the crowds? We hear you. Feast your eyes on the map of the park's 120 backcountry campgrounds *(nps.gov/romo/planyourvisit)*, which are located in some spectacularly remote locations, from the Never Summer Range (p158) to jewel-like alpine lakes in the heart of Wild Basin. Distances from trailheads range from 1.2 to 10 miles, ensuring that everyone from the littlest toddler to seasoned climbers can find a site to suit their tastes.

In addition to the usual array of backpacking gear, all backcountry campers must have a wilderness permit (reserve online at *recreation.gov*, collect in person) and a bear canister. Reservations open March 1, and many dates sell out immediately.

BEST RMNP PEAKS

Lily Mountain (4 miles; 9786ft): A great choice for your first Colorado summit. The trailhead is just north of Lily Lake on Hwy 7.

Twin Sisters (7.4 miles; 11,428ft): An arduous climb that gains 2300ft in just 3.7 miles, but offers unequaled views of Longs Peak. Across the road from Lily Lake.

Mt Ida (10 miles; 12,880ft): Awesome views on the Continental Divide; easily accessed from Trail Ridge Rd at Milner Pass.

Flattop Mountain & Hallett Peak (8.8 miles; 12,324ft): Going up Flattop? Tack on an extra mile and bag Hallett too.

Chapin-Chiquita-Ypsilon (9 miles; 13,514ft): Invigorating three-peak traverse in the Mummy Range; access from Old Fall Creek Rd.

BEST BACKCOUNTRY CAMPSITES

Ypsilon Creek: Lawn Lake trailhead, 2.5 miles. Easy access makes this a good family choice.

Andrews Creek: Glacier Gorge trailhead, 3.6 miles. Great side trips to Andrews Glacier and Sky Pond.

Sandbeach Lake: Sandbeach Lake trailhead, 4.2 miles. Fantastic backcountry beach and lake.

Thunder Lake: Wild Basin trailhead, 6.8 miles. Basecamp for summiting the remote Mt Alice (13,310ft).

Pine Martin: North Inlet trailhead, 7.8 miles. Springboard for multiday trips on the west side.

LIGHTPHOTO/GETTY IMAGES

Lily Lake

Alpine Fishing

Cast for cutthroat

Casting for trout (crown, brook, rainbow and the native cutthroat) in the park lakes and streams is a popular activity. All you need is a current state license and your own rod, and you'll be good to go. Make sure to familiarize yourself with the regulations, and know when you are in catch-and-release waters.

The full-service **Kirks Flyshop** (*kirksflyshop.com; trips from $200*) offers a number of guided packages in the park and around. It also rents out equipment, guides overnight hikes and offers float fishing and group excursions. Get your feet wet with the introductory two-hour evening hatch.

Rocky Mountain for Kids

Bust out the s'mores

The park is an incredibly fun place for families to explore, though it may take some trial and error to find everyone's happy place. Budget time for special activities – horseback riding, a ropes course, ranger activities – to break up the monotony of driving around and posing for photos. Camping is a great way to keep the kids engaged with the outdoors: what could be more fun than setting up a tent or hammock? The added downtime in camp gives kids the unstructured space needed to chase after bugs, scramble over boulders and lead the way on their own mini adventures.

Junior ranger activity booklets are a sure-fire hit, with the promise of a special badge after completing the various nature checklists, games, puzzles and questions. Don't miss the **Junior Ranger Headquarters** in Hidden Valley, which runs kids-themed programs throughout the day. It's located near the beginning of Trail Ridge Rd. Evening campfire and stargazing programs, often staged at campgrounds, are also a good bet.

A few family-friendly destinations in or around the Park include Nymph and Dream Lakes (Bear Lake trailhead), Gem Lake (Lumpy Ridge Trailhead), MacGregor Ranch (adjacent to Lumpy Ridge), Eugenia Mine (Longs Peak Trailhead), Calypso Cascades (Wild Basin Trailhead), the Moraine Park Discovery Center (Bear Lake Rd), the Alpine Visitor Center (Trail Ridge Rd) and Lily Lake and Mountain (Hwy 7).

Horseback Riding & Llama Trips

Saddle up, pardner

Horses are synonymous with the American West, and a trail ride through Rocky Mountain can be a great way to relive that bygone era when they were an integral part of life. There are a handful of stables in the area, and tours generally range from two hours to a full day. **National Park Gateway Stables** (*skhorses.com; rides from $110*), at the Fall River Entrance, is a good choice. Pony rides for younger kids are also available.

If you're intrigued by the idea of a multiday pack trip through the backcountry, consider llamas. Sure-footed and accustomed to high elevations, llamas are considered to be lower impact than horses and mules. Several area outfitters run llama trips, including **Kirks** (*kirksmountainadventures.com; $450 per day*) in Estes Park.

Classic Climbs & Alpine Routes

From Lumpy with love

Climbing in the park is nothing short of amazing, but it's not for beginners – or even casual gym climbers. Still, we dare you to cast an eye on the granite protrusions of Lumpy Ridge and not feel the call of the wild stirring in the depths of your soul. So what to do?

The best advice is to sign up for a guided trip with **Colorado Mountain School** (*coloradomountainschool.com; from $230*). Simply put, there's no better resource for climbers in Colorado – this outfit is the largest climbing operator in the region and has expert guides, qualified to get you to the top of iconic alpine ascents, like Sharkstooth, the Petit Grepon and the Casual Route on the Diamond.

Another possibility is the **via ferrata** in Estes Park. More accessible than a full-on multipitch climb, a via ferrata can be a good way to experience the thrill of alpine exposure without needing to master all the technical know-how. Check out the routes run by **Kent Mountain Adventure** (*kmacguides.com; from $200*); Kent also runs guided climbing trips.

Cycling Circuits in RMNP

No pain, no gain

Cycling has continued to gain popularity despite the park's heavy traffic. It's a splendid way to travel, though it's restricted to paved roads and to one dirt road, Old Fall River Rd (p151).

Climbing the paved Trail Ridge Rd (p151) has one big advantage over Old Fall River Rd (a 9-mile one-way climb of more than 3000ft): you can turn around should problems arise.

PINE BEETLES

While mountain pine beetles have been around for a long time (there are 17 species native to the park), their impact on forests, particularly ponderosa and lodgepole pine, has reached unprecedented heights over the past two decades.

Drive up Trail Ridge Rd and you'll see lifeless stands of beetle-killed trees everywhere. Hotter, drier summers combined with warmer winters is at the root of the current epidemic. In addition to providing fuel for wildfires (p360), the dead trees present another hazard: eventually, they fall over. If you're camping, pay close attention to where you pitch your tent.

WHERE TO RENT GEAR IN ESTES PARK

From sleeping pads to tents and stoves to bear canisters, pick up everything you need for a camping adventure.

Estes Park Mountain Shop: One-stop outdoor shop and gear rental, carrying everything from standard gear to all-terrain wheelchairs and snowshoes.

Kirks Flyshop: Kid carriers, microspikes, sleds and more. They also run guided tours under the name Kirks Mountain Adventures.

Outdoor World: Come in for camping gear and leave with tips on the best hikes in the park.

Scot's Sporting Goods: Hiking poles, fishing rods, backpacks and sleeping bags.

Never Summer Mountain Products: In Grand Lake, renting bear canisters and cross-country skis and snowshoes.

Less daunting climbs and climes are available on the park's lower paved roads. A popular 16-mile circuit is the **Horseshoe Park/Estes Park Loop**. For a bit more of a climbing challenge you can continue to **Bear Lake Road**, an 8-mile-long route that rises 1500ft to the high mountain basin with a decent shoulder.

Discover Rocky Mountain History

Homesteads and chapels

It's not all mountains and marmots in RMNP – there are a handful of historical sites too. **MacGregor Ranch Museum** (*macgregorranch.org; adult/child $5/free*), near the Lumpy Ridge trailhead, is a living museum that features original housing and working quarters.

The gorgeous **Saint Catherine's Chapel**, near Wild Basin, is a century-old stone church dramatically situated at the foot of Mt Meeker.

The **Enos Mills Cabin** near the Longs Peak trailhead pays homage to naturalist Enos Mills (1870–1922), who helped establish Rocky Mountain National Park. Unfortunately, the site is closed to the public.

Snowshoe Safari

Winter wonderland

A silence so profound that it's deafening: if you've ever explored the Rockies on a winter day, you'll know the feeling. Whether you're wearing skis, snowshoes or just plain old snow boots, there's something particularly inspiring about fresh snowfall, transforming forest trails and jagged peaks into a picturesque tableau. The best part about visiting this time of year? Unlike Colorado's crowded ski resorts, you'll have Rocky Mountain's wilderness practically to yourself – during the winter, visitation drops by nearly 90%.

One of the easiest ways to get out into the snowy landscape is to strap on a pair of snowshoes. Snowshoes can get you across most trails in the national park, and the learning curve is practically nil – if you can walk, you can snowshoe. Look out for tours: national park rangers often lead walks on winter weekends.

Another popular winter activity is cross-country skiing. Its distinctive 'kick-glide' motion is harder to master, but once you've got it down, you can move faster than on snowshoes.

And if adventure is your calling, there's even more fun to be had. Learn how to use ice axes and crampons when you sign up for an ice climbing class or a guided trip through the Colorado Mountain School (p155). Climbing the park's dozens of dramatic ice curtains and pillars will be sure to keep your blood pumping even on the coldest of days.

Beyond Rocky Mountain National Park

From the far-flung gateway town of Grand Lake to the Indian Peaks, the Rocky Mountain has a foot on either side of the Divide.

Take the time to drive over Trail Ridge Rd in summer, and you'll be rewarded with a part of the park that few visitors ever set eyes on: the west side. The Never Summer Mountains form a remote and imposing backdrop to the wildlife-rich Kawuneeche Valley, while the meandering Colorado River flows into the historic gateway town of Grand Lake.

To the south of Rocky Mountain National Park, meanwhile, lies the gorgeous expanse of wilderness known as the Indian Peaks. Set out into the backcountry from Brainard Lake and hike to the Continental Divide, or follow the serpentine Peak to Peak Hwy as it wends its way back to the Front Range cities of Boulder and Denver.

Places

Kawuneeche Valley & Grand Lake p158
Brainard Lake p160

GETTING AROUND

The Grand Lake Entrance Station is the only entry to RMNP on the west side of the park. Winter closure of Hwy 34 (November to May), aka Trail Ridge Rd, makes access to this part of Park dependent on Hwy 40. Grand Lake is 45 minutes north of Winter Park.

South of Estes Park are the Indian Peaks, which are accessed via Hwys 7 and 72, the Peak to Peak Scenic Byway, which runs to Nederland.

Elks, Kawuneeche Valley (p158)

ROBERT O HULL/SHUTTERSTOCK

THE EAST TROUBLESOME FIRE

Colorado's second-largest wildfire started about 40 miles west of here near Kremmling, on October 14, 2020. At first, it was just another wildfire in one of the driest summers on record. But a week later, high winds led to a deadly explosion of flames: the fire's size increased 1000% in just 24 hours, enveloping stands of dead lodgepole pine (killed by beetles) and racing across the west side of RMNP at a rate of 6000 acres per hour. Then the unimaginable happened: high winds propelled embers across the barren alpine tundra of the Continental Divide and ignited forests on the park's eastern side, near Fern Lake. It was only thanks to an October 22 cold front that the fire was eventually contained, but not before destroying 555 buildings and killing two people.

Kawuneeche Valley & Grand Lake

TIME FROM ESTES PARK: 1½ HRS 🚗

Hiking on Rocky Mountain National Park's west side

Few travelers cross the Continental Divide to explore RMNP's western reaches, which makes for a distinctly quieter atmosphere. Even the Ute and Arapaho did not linger on this side of the pass outside of hunting season, as the higher elevation makes the winters harder to endure.

To be sure, this side of the park has none of the dramatic, glacier-carved cirques on the eastern side. Massive swathes of forest by the visitor center also burned during the East Troublesome Fire (2020), leaving an eerie landscape in places that is only now beginning to regenerate. But there are nonetheless some great trails to discover, as well as the headwaters of the fabled Colorado River – the same river that eventually flows into the Grand Canyon far downstream.

As you wind your way down Trail Ridge Rd from Medicine Bow Curve, you'll pass several trailheads, beginning with **Milner Pass** (10,759ft), from where you can set out for the summit of Mt Ida (p153). As far as RMNP peaks go, this 9.5-mile trail (round trip) is relatively tame, but don't underestimate the altitude or the weather up here – you'll be following the exposed Continental Divide most of the way. Views are otherworldly.

Another 6 miles down the road is the **Colorado River Trailhead**. There are a variety of hikes here, from the 7.3-mile round-trip trek to Lulu City ghost town and the river's headwaters to demanding excursions into the **Never Summer Mountains**, but perhaps the most enjoyable experience here is to simply walk down to the river and sit along its banks for a while. At this stage it's hard to believe that it will grow to become the most important waterway in the entire Southwest.

After this, the road follows the Kawuneeche (Arapaho for 'Valley of the Coyote'), where a lovely 1-mile hike brings you to the **Holzwarth Historic Site**. Incorporating both an abandoned homestead (1902) and the Holzwarth Trout Lodge (1917), this walk through the valley, crossing the meandering Colorado along the way, is extremely evocative. The Holzwarths were Denver saloonkeepers who left the big city during Prohibition to try out life as subsistence ranchers. Instead, what happened was their old friends from Denver kept coming to visit, which resulted in the property becoming one of Colorado's first dude ranches (cost: $2 a day for lodging and 'all the trout you can catch'). The original buildings are still standing, and rangers hold talks and historical reenactments here.

SOUTHBOUND TO THE SLOPES

Grand Lake is a mere 30 miles north of the **Winter Park Ski Resort** (p192) along Hwy 40. You'll pass Shadow Mountain Lake and Lake Granby on the way.

Mt Ida (p153)

Not long after this you'll enter the burn scar left by the 2020 wildfire, which extends to the park entrance.

Moose-spotting in the Kawuneeche Valley

The solitary, lumbering moose prefers marshlands and lakes; if luck is on your side, you may see them wading or trudging through wetlands in the **Kawuneeche Valley**, sometimes right off of Hwy 34. The moose's slightly goofy appearance belies just how ginormous they are: males can stand up to 7ft high and weigh as much as 1500lb. And while they are generally docile, don't be fooled: their behavior is unpredictable and they can gallop at 35 miles per hour (Olympic sprinters, in contrast, only run at 27mph). If you have a dog in your vehicle, be especially careful – nothing spooks a moose faster.

Explore Grand Lake

As the western gateway to Rocky Mountain National Park, Grand Lake is a foil to the bustling hub of Estes Park. The historic district has a number of friendly local cafes and art galleries, and the namesake lake – with a yacht club founded in 1901 – is blue and glorious. In summer, it offers a different

SULPHUR SPRINGS SHOOTOUT

In the late 1860s William Byers, founder of the *Rocky Mountain News*, acquired most of the land around Hot Sulphur Springs (25 miles southwest of Grand Lake) from itinerant Utes with a combination of legal maneuvering and the aid of the US Army. He immediately began promoting the local hot springs, and gradually the rivalry between 'Lake' and 'Springs' became tense. On July 4, 1883, the argument over which town would serve as Grand County seat came to a head with a fatal shootout between elected officials. In a strange twist, the sheriff of Hot Sulphur Springs was assigned to investigate the Grand Lake shooting – at which point it became known that he was one of the gunmen. In the end, the county seat was moved back to Hot Sulphur Springs.

EATING IN GRAND LAKE: OUR PICKS

Blue Water Bakery: Friendly bakery, cafe and breakfast-slash-lunch spot with water views from its sidewalk tables. *7am-3pm Thu-Tue* **$**

One Love Rum Kitchen: This colorful Caribbean joint dishes out curried sandwiches, fish tacos and plenty of cocktails. *noon-9pm Wed-Mon* **$$**

World's End Brewpub: It may not be the restaurant at the end of the universe, but why complain when you've got pizza and beer? *noon-9pm Thu-Sun* **$$**

Sagebrush BBQ & Grill: Bric-a-brac covers the walls of this barbecue joint, which serves steak and game dishes. Save room for the peach cobbler. *7am-9pm* **$$$**

ANCIENT ASPENS

Come late September, Colorado's roads fill with leap peepers, out in search of the glorious golden hues that wash across the mountainsides. Aspens, of course, are well known for their quaking leaves, but there's more to this tree than meets the eye. In fact, many aspen groves are not made up of individual trees, but are instead a single interconnected organism – the aspen's most common method of reproduction is cloning, where one plant sends out identical reproductions of itself via its root system. Because of this, aspens are not only considered the world's largest organism, but also the oldest: the Pando Grove in Utah (over 40,000 'stems' strong) is considered to be at least 10,000 years old.

ERICKPHOTOPRO/SHUTTERSTOCK

suite of recreational thrills: think stand-up paddleboarding, kayaking and other flavors of water-powered fun. Boat rentals are available along the waterfront ($30 per hour).

An amble along the boardwalk lining Grand Ave – aka Main St – is pleasant, with a hodgepodge of corny souvenir shops, decent restaurants, T-shirt shops and a few character-filled bars.

History buffs might want to pop in to the **Kauffman House Museum** *(grandlakehistory.org; $5)*, an 1892 log building that operated as a hotel until 1946. Now on the National Register of Historic Places, it contains period furniture, old skis, quilts and other dusty artifacts.

Several Rocky Mountain National Park trailheads are just outside the town limits, including those to the Tonahutu/ North Inlet Trail and the Adams Falls/East Inlet Trail. The **East Inlet Trail** is most popular – the falls are an easy quarter-mile from the trailhead. To get the most out of the hike, however, consider an overnight backpacking trip or a long day hike: the headwaters of Grand Lake are 4.5 miles away, where five alpine lakes are strung out like jewels in a necklace beneath 12,000ft peaks.

Brainard Lake

TIME FROM ESTES PARK: 1 HR

Hike to alpine lakes

South of Rocky Mountain National Park, the Indian Peaks – 35 in all – reign supreme. This is the home of six thirteeners (mountains taller than 13,000ft), 50 alpine lakes, six passes across the Continental Divide and the largest glacier in Colorado (Arapaho).

Brainard Lake

It's Boulder County's incredible backyard, but it comes with a catch: access points are few and far between. **Brainard Lake** is the largest of the bunch, with five main trailheads and half a dozen lakes that offer superb hiking, snowshoeing and trail-running experiences. Bear in mind that the elevation here begins at 10,000ft, so don't overdo it.

In summer, easy 1-mile hikes go to Long Lake and Mitchell Lake, but continue on for even better views at Blue Lake (Mitchell Lake Trailhead; 6 miles round trip) and Lake Isabelle (Long Lake Trailhead; 6.5 miles round trip). If you've got the stamina, next up is the gorgeous Isabelle Glacier (8.6 miles), which sits at the bottom of a cirque, once carved out by a much larger version of the glacier. Alternatively, Pawnee Pass and Shoshoni Peak (12,967ft; 10.7 miles round trip) are also both accessible from Lake Isabelle. Be forewarned that Lake Isabelle is drained at the end of August.

Winter is an even lovelier time to visit Brainard: the landscape is blanketed in snow, the lakes are frozen solid and day-trippers are far and few between. Cross-country skiing and snowshoeing trails begin at the Gateway Trailhead (2 miles before Brainard Lake).

In summer, you'll need a timed entry **reservation** *(recreation .gov; $14)*. In winter there is a $10 day use fee, though reservations are not required. Reach Brainard Lake via the Peak to Peak Hwy (p162).

Do note that while dogs are allowed on the trail, moose are common at Brainard Lake, and in 2023 one woman was trampled while walking her dog. For your safety, consider leaving your dog at home.

Driving the Peak to Peak Highway

This scenic 35-mile route weaves past granite outcrops, historic cabins, working ranches and high-altitude forest between Rocky Mountain National Park and the tiny town of Nederland. Known as the Peak to Peak Hwy, this was Colorado's first scenic byway, established in 1918. If you're headed back to Boulder or Denver, this drive gives you extra facetime with the gorgeous Indian Peaks Wilderness. There's no cell service here.

❶ Lily Lake

This highly photogenic lake is a great place to begin your drive. It has an unimpeded view of the king of the park, Longs Peak, which rises magnificently to the southwest with its twin, Mt Meeker (13,916ft). A relaxing trail (0.8 miles) loops around the shore; keep an eye out for wading moose and hardy tiger salamanders.

The Drive: Follow Hwy 7 for another 1.7 miles south to a dirt pullout on the right, marked 'Longs Peak View.'

❷ Longs Peak Overlook

From here you'll have a perfect view of the Diamond, Longs' sheer east face. Rock climbers dream of tackling the 'Casual Route' up the 1500ft granite wall here, but it's not for the faint of heart: it's psychologically intimidating, physically demanding and exposed to deadly storms.

The Drive: From here it's 2.5 miles south on Hwy 7 to Saint Catherine's Chapel.

Saint Catherine's Chapel

WIRESTOCK CREATORS/SHUTTERSTOCK

❸ Saint Catherine's Chapel

This gorgeous stone chapel, built atop a rocky outcrop and set against the magnificent backdrop of Mt Meeker, might cause some drivers to wonder if they're seeing some sort of heavenly vision. Nope, it's a real church, dating back to 1935, and was even blessed by Pope John Paul II.

The Drive: Continue south along Hwy 7 for two more miles to the turnoff for Wild Basin, on your right.

❹ Wild Basin

Wild Basin is the breathtaking and often overlooked southeastern corner of the park. Consider a quick jaunt up to the string of waterfalls along the main trail, like Copeland Falls (0.3 miles).

The Drive: Follow Hwy 7 for 6.5 miles southwest to the junction with Hwy 72. It's another 10 miles on Hwy 72 to the turnoff for Brainard Lake.

❺ Brainard Lake

Follow the sinuous blacktop past stands of aspen trees to reach Brainard Lake. This fabulous recreation area is the best place to access the Indian Peaks, and is known for its moose, lakes and rocky summits. You don't need to scale the heights for great views, however – plenty of short, easy trails like Mitchell Lake and Long Lake will have your camera working overtime. Advance reservations are required in summer (recreation.gov).

The Drive: Continue south on Hwy 72 for 12 serpentine miles. Make sure to slow down as you approach Nederland.

❻ Nederland

Quirky Nederland (p136) is a true mountain town, attracting ski bums, bluegrass musicians and elderly hippies. Break here for a meal or keep driving: from Nederland, it's 16 gorgeous miles downhill to Boulder.

Steamboat Springs

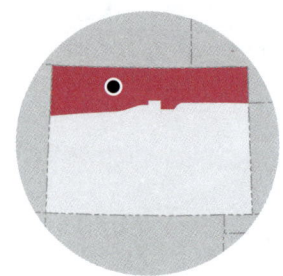

SKIING | HOT SPRINGS | HIKING

GETTING AROUND

Most people get into town by car from Denver via Rabbit Ears Pass on Hwy 40, though you can fly into Yampa Valley Regional Airport. **Go West Transportation** *(letsride.co; $130)* runs between Steamboat and Denver International Airport and the Yampa Valley Regional Airport ($60). The Bustang and Snowstang also serve Steamboat from Denver's Union Station *(ridebustang. com; $40 round trip).*

Steamboat Springs Transit runs a free bus service along Lincoln Ave, connecting to the ski resort. In summer, many locals cycle around; a fun bike path links the town with Steamboat Village.

Steamboat Springs is America's original ski town, with a history that dates back to 1915, when the modest Howelsen Hill – named after the Flying Norseman, Carl Howelsen – first opened to the public. And indeed, the jumps at Howelsen have sent more athletes to the Winter Olympics than anywhere else in the country.

Today's resort is considerably larger than the trailblazing ski hill (still in operation), and the combination of abundant winter storms, a down-to-earth, old-timey rancher's charm and one of the prettiest natural hot springs in the state keeps the regulars returning to this out-of-the-way corner. Shop for cowboy boots and Stetson hats in between powder-fueled days on the slopes, cozy up with a cup of coffee at the bookstore while planning an expedition into the little-known Flattops and Zirkel wilderness areas, or mellow out with a day fishing or floating on the Yampa River.

Skiing Steamboat

Ride with the Olympians

The Boat is known for two things: glades and snow. Yes, you're thinking, all the resorts in the Rockies have snow. But the famously light and fluffy powder of **Steamboat** (*steamboat.com; adult/child $285/230*), with storms blowing in from Wyoming and Utah, means the soft turns are virtually guaranteed. Throw in the cowboy-style charm and back-of-beyond location, and you have all the makings for a winter wonderland.

The stats speak for themselves: in total it's got 182 marked runs, 3668ft of vertical, and 3741 acres of terrain. While the summit only tops out at 10,568ft, Steamboat makes up for its dearth of high-altitude steeps with super-fun tree-slaloming runs: the gentle slopes and widely spaced aspens and spruce allow confident intermediate skiers to score first tracks in the glades with a touch less terror and a bit more grace than is generally possible.

HIGHLIGHTS
1 Tread of Pioneers Museum

SIGHTS
2 Bucking Rainbow Outfitters
3 Emerald Mountain
4 Howelsen Hill Ski Area
5 Howelsen Ice Arena
6 Old Town Hot Springs
7 Steamboat Flyfisher

SLEEPING
8 Rabbit Ears Motel

EATING
9 Back Door Grill
10 Bésame
11 Commons Food Hall
12 Creekside
13 Laundry
14 Salt & Lime
15 Seedz
16 Skull Creek Greek
17 Table 79
18 Winona's

19 Yampa Sandwich Company

DRINKING
20 Mountain Tap Brewery
21 Schmiggity's
22 The Press

SHOPPING
23 Boomerang Sports Exchange
24 FM Light & Sons
25 Off the Beaten Path
26 Steamboat Hatter

☑ **TOP TIP**

Steamboat Springs consists of two major areas: the relatively regular grid of central Old Town, which straddles Lincoln Ave (US 40), and the newer warren of winding streets at Steamboat Village, centered on the Steamboat Mountain Resort ski area on Mt Werner southeast of town.

THE FLYING NORSEMAN

Originally from Oslo, Carl Howelsen (1877–1955) was already a decorated Nordic ski racer when he emigrated to Chicago in 1905. In addition to working as a stonemason in his new home, he also picked up a side gig as the 'Sky Rocket' in the Barnum & Bailey Circus. His success in the 'perilous Scandinavian winter sport...of wondrous daring' attracted the attention of Steamboat resident Marjorie Perry, who convinced Howelsen to move to Colorado in 1913, where he promptly became one of the pioneers of the American ski industry. In addition to building a ski jump on what is now Howelsen Hill, he also founded a ski club and organized ski races and a Winter Carnival. He returned to Norway in 1922.

DAVID A LITMAN/SHUTTERSTOCK

Strawberry Park Hot Springs

Serious skiers will also dig a number of mogul runs on the hill, and although these trails are a virtual factory of Olympic skiers and snowboarders, you don't have to be world class to enjoy them. Wide, well-groomed runs are ideal cruising for intermediate skiers, making this mountain among Colorado's best all-rounders, particularly for families.

The **Ski Touring Center** *(nordicski.net; day pass $29)*, near the base of the resort, has excellent cross-country trails as well as home-cooked soups, chili and bread.

Want to nail some untracked lines? **Steamboat Powdercats** *(steamboatpowdercats.com; from $950)*, a tried-and-true cat-skiing operator, offers guided backcountry tours on Buffalo Pass.

Take Flight at Howelsen Hill
Fun for all ages

The continent's oldest ski area still in use and on the Colorado State Register of Historic Places, **Howelsen Hill** *(steamboatsprings.net; adult/child $47/34)* is worth a gander simply to check out the aspiring Olympians vaulting off the jumps.

 EATING IN STEAMBOAT: ON A BUDGET

Skull Creek Greek: From sheepherding to skiing – clever gyros and specialty pitas for hungry diners on a budget. *11am-8pm* $

Yampa Sandwich Company: This local sandwich chain is magic – fresh ingredients and an early open to sell boxed lunches to hikers. *7am-4pm* $

Winona's: Where gooey, monstrous cinnamon rolls and plump French toast are balanced by savory treats, such as crab eggs Benedict. *7am-3pm* $

Commons Food Hall: From Jamaican jerk chicken to Pacific poke bowls, all topped off with cocktails on the back patio. *11am-9pm* $$

And if you're a newbie on a budget, this is a great place to practice: not only are lift tickets affordable, they're even free on Sundays! Although there are only 14 runs, you can't beat the price.

There's also an indoor ice-skating facility, the **Howelsen Ice Arena** *($10)*, which operates from October until April, a tubing hill, a sledding hill and 13 miles of cross-country trails.

In summer, check out the **Howler Alpine Slide** *(steamboatalpineslide.com; $20)*, an adrenaline-pumped rip down a 2400ft track. The chairlift also provides access to mountain bikers.

Healing Waters

Steamboat's hot springs

Steamboat gets its name from the 150 natural springs in the area. One in particular was said to sound like a steamboat chugging up the Yampa River (civilization-starved French trappers clearly had fanciful imaginations). You can visit some of these mineral springs, collectively known to the Yampatika Ute as medicine waters, on a walk around town, but we recommend going straight to the good stuff: **Strawberry Park Hot Springs** *(strawberryhotsprings.com; $20)*.

Located 7 miles north of town, this is as idyllic as hot springs get, with a handful of natural outdoor pools set beside a cool mountain stream and nothing but acres of wilderness surrounding you. Evening visits are particularly magical: whether you're treated to a meteor shower overhead or the molten silver of a full moon rising through the pines, soaking in the steaming pools – with the occasional plunge into the river – is a marvelously restorative experience. Note that after dark, it's adults only. In winter, you'll need AWD and snow tires to get here; if your vehicle isn't equipped, or it's a busy weekend, take the shuttle instead. Alternatively, consider staying the night in the rustic lodging. Reservations are required.

If you're with kids or prefer a less rustic environment, the **Old Town Hot Springs** in the center of town *(oldtownhotsprings. org; adult/child $29/23)* is another option.

Summer Adventures

From singletrack trails to rapids

Come summertime, Steamboat Mountain Resort turns into the **Steamboat Bike Park** *(steamboat.com; day pass with bike rental $125)*, with 50 miles of bermed-out mountain bike

 EATING IN STEAMBOAT: MIDRANGE PICKS

Creekside: Fantastic location and patio on little Soda Creek. A great choice for a sunny-side-up breakfast. *7am-2pm* **$$**

Salt & Lime: Take your tacos and margs to the next level (shrimp BLT, perhaps?), or just swing by the outdoor burrito bar. *noon-8:30pm* **$$**

Back Door Grill: Ski-town grills can be decidedly mediocre, but the friendly Back Door gets the recipe right. *8am-10pm* **$$**

Seedz: International flavors rule here, from *yakisoba* noodles to chimichurri steak to bibimbap rice bowls. Smoothies too. *11am-8pm* **$$**

HAHNS PEAK

Twenty-seven miles north of Steamboat Springs is this quasi–ghost town. Built on the windswept plain at the base of a 10,774ft extinct volcano, it was originally a gold camp (the German founder Joseph Hahn was predictably betrayed by one of his partners, who absconded with all the gold – *right back with more supplies!* – and left him to starve to death during the first winter), and later the terminus of the Wyoming railroad. In 1898 two famous outlaws from the Wild Bunch were jailed here in the 'Bear Cage,' which was not as fearsome as it sounds. They easily escaped, were just as easily recaptured, and then proceeded to escape again using a whittled gun covered with tinfoil.

trails. Rent a bike at the bottom, pay for a gondola ride and lay waste from the top. Even if you're a first-timer, this is really, really fun.

Otherwise, Howelsen Hill and Spring Creek are just two of the trail networks that flow through the stands of aspens on the edge of town. Road riders can follow the **Yampa River bike trail** for 7 miles along the river from Old Town to Steamboat Village, or take to the road for trips over Rabbit Ears Pass.

For rentals, head to **Orange Peel Bikes** (*orangepeelbikes. com*) north of town, where a staff of serious riders and mechanics can offer tons of information about local trails, including maps.

The **Yampa River** is another popular summer draw. **Bucking Rainbow Outfitters** (*buckingrainbow.com; trips from $70*) runs a variety of half- and full-day raft trips, from Class II to Class IV, and also has the Blue Sky West tube shack right on the water if you're after a more mellow day. **Steamboat Flyfisher** (*steamboatflyfisher.com; trips from $350*) is the area's best fly shop, and organizes guided fishing excursions.

If you're interested in saddling up cowboy style, **Del's Triangle 3 Ranch** (*steamboathorses.com; rides from $115*) has both trail rides and pack trips in the Routt National Forest. It's located 20 miles north of town.

Afternoon Rambles

Hiking options around town

Most of the bike rides around town also make for good hiking. **Emerald Mountain** has great hikes, as does **Spring Creek**, accessed from 3rd St. This trail eventually takes you to Buffalo Pass and Routt national forests and can be backpacked. You can also have a shuttle drop you at the top of Rabbit Ears Pass and hike or bike your way back to town.

Fish Creek Falls is the obvious choice for a mellow walk with a big payoff. The 0.8-mile loop takes you to a scenic overlook with views across to the 283ft waterfall. From there, you can cut down past picnic areas, and hook up to a bridge that sits below the falls. The overlook section is wheelchair accessible.

Top hikes accessed easily from Steamboat include the **Mad Creek** (9 miles round trip) and **Red Dirt** trails (12.7 miles round trip); follow Elk River Rd north from Steamboat to the trailheads.

EATING IN STEAMBOAT: GASTRONOMIC

Table 79: Great happy-hour specials, from buffalo cauliflower and tuna poke to portobello fries. For mains, the Korean short rib is a winner. *4:30-9pm* **$$$**

Laundry: Small plates, craft cocktails and pickled everything – arguably the best choice in town, with a steampunk-meets-California chic. *4:30-9pm* **$$$**

Cafe Diva: This is the most exciting meal within walking distance of the gondola. Expect gastronomic creations like duck confit with fig and chèvre. *5:30-9pm* **$$$**

Bésame: Fantabulous tapas bar mixing Spanish and Latin American tastes with great happy-hour deals and late-night salsa dancing on Fridays. *4-9pm* **$$$**

AARON ROSEN/SHUTTERSTOCK

Fish Creek Falls

Follow the Tread of Pioneers

Local history

First opened in the Zimmerman House in 1959, the **Tread of Pioneers Museum** *(treadofpioneers.org; adult/child $6/2)* has a long history dedicated to the peoples and cultures of Routt County. Over the years, it has continued to expand, and is now situated in two turn-of-the-century Victorian homes. Home to an intriguing mix of permanent and temporary exhibits, expect even-handed displays of Native American weavings, pottery and basketry, the evolution of skiing, an introduction to Steamboat and Western heritage, and a hands-on exhibit for kids. Visitors can also take guided tours of the period-furnished ranch house. The museum is open from 11am to 5pm, Tuesdays through Saturdays.

BEST PLACES TO SHOP

FM Light & Sons: This cowboy shop has been hawking Stetson hats since 1905 and has a great collection of boots and other gear.

Off the Beaten Path: Among the crowded stacks and sharp fragrance of brewing coffee beans, patrons browse for books at this welcoming cafe.

Ski Haus: Rent top-quality brands, buy used demo skis and search for camping gear. They've been fitting skis for over 50 years.

Steamboat Hatter: Browse handmade cowboy hats or custom design your own at this Western wear gem.

Boomerang Sports Exchange: With all the athletes in town, this consignment shop could be your lucky day.

 DRINKING IN STEAMBOAT: OUR PICKS

The Press: Great live music weekend nights and a small dining area that's framed by timbers. *4pm-midnight Wed & Thu, to 2am Fri & Sat*

Schmiggity's: This place is perfect for boot stomping to bluegrass, taking shots or letting yourself go to local jam bands. *7pm-1:30am*

Mountain Tap Brewery: Head down to the Yampa for a dozen local beers on tap, ranging from sours to hoppy pilsners. *3-8pm Tue-Sun, 11:30am-9pm Sat*

Storm Peak Brewing: Northwest of town is this high-ceilinged warehouse space, with a great rooftop deck. *11am-10pm*

Beyond Steamboat Springs

Mt Zirkel Wilderness · Walden · Craig · Hayden · **Steamboat Springs** · Oak Creek · Yampa · Kremmling · **The Flat Tops Wilderness**

With wide-open skies and hills dappled with the shadows of passing clouds, Steamboat's surrounds are a slice of yesteryear Colorado.

Places

Mt Zirkel Wilderness p170
The Flat Tops Wilderness p171

GETTING AROUND

Many roads in this area are of the dirt and gravel variety, but still passable to 2WD cars. Mt Zirkel lies to the north of Steamboat along County Rd 129. The Forest Service road up to Slavonia Trailhead has several campgrounds; this is a fabulous place to pitch a tent. The Flat Tops are best accessed from Yampa, 30 miles south of Steamboat on Hwy 131.

Dotted with willow scrub and stands of bone-white aspens, their leaves blazing orange-gold in the autumn, this untouched swathe of northern Colorado invites exploration. To the north lies the far-flung alpine charms of the Mt Zirkel Wilderness, part of the Routt National Forest that extends south from Wyoming. Driving up here can feel like ascending into an untouched corner of paradise, where honest-to-goodness cowboys ride across a primeval landscape draped in morning mist.

To the southwest is the often-overlooked Flat Tops Wilderness: a massive area of high volcanic plateaus, glacier-carved cirques, and grazing elk and sheep. If you want to get off the grid, this is an excellent choice.

Mt Zirkel Wilderness

TIME FROM STEAMBOAT SPRINGS: 1 HR

Bobcats, bears and bald eagles

One of the five original wilderness areas in Colorado, **Mt Zirkel Wilderness** is an untamed, roadless expanse dotted with icy glacial lakes and granite faces, and is rife with opportunities for isolated backcountry hiking and camping. It's intersected by the Continental Divide and two major rivers, the Elk and the Encampment. Locals swear by the **Zirkel Circle hike**, which connects Gilpin and Gold Creek Lakes in a glorious alpine trek over roughly 10 miles. It starts at the Slavonia Trailhead, about 30 miles north of Steamboat.

Rising from the center of the area is the 12,180ft **Mt Zirkel**, named by mountaineer Clarence King to honor the German geologist with whom he reconnoitered the country in 1874. Zirkel is a fantastic summit, but a long excursion: at 18 miles with 4000ft of elevation gain, this is best done as a two-day trip.

Detailed maps and information on hiking, mountain biking, fishing and other activities in this beautiful area are available at the USFS Hahns Peak Ranger Office off Hwy 40 in Steamboat.

Fishing and boating at local lakes

Two little-known state parks are easy detours from the road to the Slavonia Trailhead. **Pearl Lake State Park** *(cpw.state.*

Devil's Causeway

THE MEEKER INCIDENT

Like much of the West, the Flat Tops has seen its share of bitter conflicts over resources. The most infamous moment took place in 1879, when Indian agent Nathan Meeker attempted to convert the White River Utes to Christianity. When Meeker plowed up pasture lands used for grazing and horse racing, it was the last straw: the Utes retaliated and killed Meeker and 23 men, and took a number of women and children as hostages.

The consequences were devastating: political pressure from miners and other settlers had already been mounting to expel the Utes from Colorado, and following this incident, earlier treaties were rescinded and the majority of Natives were forcibly relocated to Utah.

co.us; $10), centered around a small alpine reservoir, is a perfect spot for paddleboarding, canoeing and even ice fishing – though in winter you'll have to ski in. Lakeside campsites and yurts are glorious.

The larger **Steamboat Lake State Park** *(cpw.state.co.us; $10)*, meanwhile, has 35 miles of trails circling the lake, as well as campsites, cabins, paddleboards and plenty of fishing.

The Flat Tops Wilderness

TIME FROM STEAMBOAT: 1½–3 HRS

A geological tour de force

To check out a forgotten corner of Colorado, drive 30 miles south from Steamboat through the historic ranching and railroad towns of Oak Creek and Yampa, and then take a hard right. Those mighty mesas looming ahead are the **Flat Tops**, the remnants of 52-million-year-old volcanic uplift and glacial erosion.

Today, a drive down the unpaved 83-mile scenic byway between Yampa and Meeker leads to trout-filled lakes, backcountry campgrounds and herds of elk and sheep. Expect to spend a good three hours back here – more if you take the recommended detour to the otherworldly **Trappers Lake**, an excellent spot to pitch a tent and clamber up onto the surrounding plateaus. A popular backpacking trip that begins near Trappers is the **Chinese Wall** (#1803), which is often combined with other trails to form a 22½-mile loop.

A slightly easier day out is via Stillwater Reservoir, only 16 unpaved miles southwest of Yampa. Just past the Cold Water Springs campground is the start of the spine-tingling **Devil's Causeway** hike (#1119), which climbs to a razor's edge ridge. As you inch your way across the rocky outcrop, you'll be treated to stupendous views of the cirques on either side, with sheer 600ft drop-offs in both directions. Although it's only 6 miles roundtrip, at nearly 12,000ft, it'll feel like a lot more. Expect to spend the day. Forest Service trail numbers here will keep you on the right path.

Fort Collins

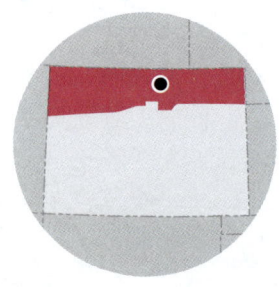

BEER | BIKES | WATER SPORTS

GETTING AROUND

Fort Collins is a very bike-friendly city, but short-term bike rentals are limited. Try Recycled Cycles or Pedago for e-bikes. Outside of the downtown area, it's best to have your own car, even for nearby excursions to the reservoir.

Fort Collins is 65 miles north of Denver, off I-25. It's 46 miles from Boulder, and 41 miles from Estes Park. The **Bustang** *(ridebustang.com; $10)* runs here from Denver's Union Station.

☑TOP TIP

Colorado State University (CSU) is the oldest public university in the state and a meander through the main campus in Fort Collins makes for a perfect afternoon stroll. It's particularly well known for its agricultural, forestry and science programs and has excellent gardens and an arboretum.

Fort Collins will never be the brightest star in the Colorado firmament – in a state that stretches from the granite-packed superlatives of Rocky Mountain National Park to the whispers of the past in the piñon scrub of Mesa Verde, there are simply too many other destinations vying for a visitor's attention. But 'overlooked' suits this university town just fine: this is a place that feels as unpretentious and honest as you can get.

For travelers, Fort Collins is most likely to wind up on the itinerary if you're headed north or south on I-25. The exception, of course, is if you're a serious beer drinker. If that's the case, you'll already know that the town is home to more breweries than anywhere else in the state.

Outdoor adventures await at the Horsetooth Reservoir, Lory State Park and along the undammed Cache La Poudre River.

Beers & Bikes

Two-wheeled, hop-powered fun

In 1988, a Fort Collins engineer named Jeff Lebesch lugged a mountain bike and a beer-lover's pocket guide over to Belgium, cycled across the lowlands, jotted down some local beer-making tips and piqued Flemish curiosity with his bike's 'fat tires.' Three years later, Jeff and Kim Jordan co-founded the New Belgium Brewery in their basement (first brews: Dubbel Abbey and Fat Tire), and the rest, as they say, is history.

In the decades since, Fort Collins has gone on to become a craft-beer powerhouse, today accounting for over 25 breweries and 70% of the beer produced in Colorado. Luckily for you, you don't have to get behind the wheel on your own personal Tour de Fat. Some 285 miles of bike lanes means that the town, and its outskirts, is a good spot for cyclists. Rent a cruiser at a bike shop like **Recycled Cycles** *(recycled-cycles. com; cruiser/e-bike $30/50)*, or try a four-hour Brew Cruise

SIGHTS
1. Avery House Museum
2. Fort Collins Museum of Discovery
3. Lory State Park

ACTIVITIES
4. Beer & Bike
5. Horsetooth Mountain Open Space
6. Horsetooth Reservoir
7. Mountain Whitewater
8. New Belgium Brewery
9. Rocky Mountain Adventures
10. What's SUP

SLEEPING
11. Armstrong Hotel
12. Elizabeth Hotel

EATING
13. Choice City
14. Colorado Room
15. Farmhouse at Jessup Farm
16. Ginger & Baker
17. Little on Mountain
18. Restaurant 415
19. The Regional
20. Young's Cafe

DRINKING
21. Crown Pub
22. Equinox
23. Funkwerks
24. Horse and Dragon
25. Odell Brewing Company
26. Prost

TRANSPORT
27. Recycled Cycles

with **Beer & Bike** (*beerandbiketours.com; $75*), and pedal your way from one vat of hops to the next.

East Lincoln Dr stretches from Odell (p174), Fort Collin's first craft start-up (1989), to the saisons and wild sours of Funkwerks (p174). College Ave, linking the delightful Old Town and university areas, packs in its own share of stops, from **Equinox** to **Prost**.

Or, if you'd like to see where it all began, then head over to the sustainable, employee-owned **New Belgium** (*newbelgium. com*). It runs two styles of tours: the free 45-minute version

PAWNEE NATIONAL GRASSLANDS

Grasslands in North America once covered a massive swathe of land, stretching from the Rocky Mountains in the west all the way to Indiana in the east: a veritable sea of windswept prairie. In Colorado, grasslands once covered half the state, but today the native habitat is only found in small oases like the patchwork Pawnee Grasslands, just 35 miles east of Fort Collins. Here, the semiarid shortgrass prairie dominates: this was the one-time home of thundering herds of bison and the Arapaho and Cheyenne who hunted them (the Pawnee homeland, in fact, is in Nebraska and Kansas). While the bison are nowhere near as numerous as they once were, much of the native wildlife remains, including antelope, deer, coyote, snakes, prairie dogs and hundreds of species of birds.

MAREKULIASZ/SHUTTERSTOCK

Horsetooth Reservoir

(first-come, first-served) and the longer 90-minute tour ($15, reservations recommended). Don't leave without sampling a malty Fat Tire, fresh from the tap.

Easy Outdoor Escapes

Water, rocks and trails

Located 4 miles west of Fort Collins is **Horsetooth Reservoir** *(larimer.gov; $10 per vehicle)*, created in 1949 to provide a reliable water source for the region's farms. You can't actually see the 6.5-mile-long reservoir from town, as it's hidden by a high ridge on its east side, which was plugged with four massive dams.

Horsetooth today is the city's favorite recreation area, welcoming roughly one million visitors annually. Swimming, motorboating, stand-up paddleboarding, kayaking, camping and fishing are all popular at designated beaches and coves along the shores. For paddleboard rentals, try out **What's SUP** *(nocosup.com; $25)*, which has three locations along the reservoir.

Rock climbing and bouldering sites can also be found along both the eastern and western banks of the reservoir.

DRINKING IN FORT COLLINS: OUR PICKS

Crown Pub: Friendly barkeeps and a dead-center location make this English-style pub a good place to sample all the local brews. *11am-midnight*

Horse and Dragon: Out-of-the-way brewery with convivial tasting room, a dozen beers on tap and patio. *2-7pm Mon-Thu, from noon Fri-Sun*

Odell Brewing Company: Some say Odell brews the best beer in Colorado. Twenty-one beers on tap; food trucks too. *11am-8pm Wed-Sun, noon-7pm Mon & Tue*

Funkwerks: If you're a fan of farmhouse saisons and funky sours, this is the spot. *11am-8pm Mon-Fri, to 9pm Sat & Sun*

On the southwest side of the reservoir is the **Horsetooth Mountain Open Space** *(larimer.gov; $10 per vehicle)*, criss-crossed with 29 miles of hiking and biking trails. Popular destinations include **Horsetooth Falls** (2.5 miles round trip) and the rocky outcrop of **Horsetooth Mountain** itself, which, according to legend, is the remains of a giant whose heart was cut twice by the Arapaho chief Maunamoku. The hike up to Horsetooth Mountain climbs 1300ft over 2.1 miles (one way).

At the northwestern side is **Lory State Park** *(cpw.state. co.us; $10 per vehicle)*, which has another 26 miles of trails, as well as a mountain-bike park. The most popular destination here is **Arthur's Rock** (3.4 miles round trip), a prominent feature of the landscape with superb views over the reservoir. Backcountry camping is possible in Lory if you're looking for an easy getaway.

Rafting the Cache La Poudre River

Wet and wild

Colorado's only nationally designated wild and scenic river, the Poudre (rhymes with neuter) allegedly gets its name from a band of French trappers who, caught in a raging blizzard in the early 1800s on their way to Wyoming, lightened their wagons by burying a cache of gunpowder near the mouth of the river canyon.

White-water rafting is an awesome way to experience the intense beauty of the Poudre, and outfitters in town, like **Mountain Whitewater** *(raftmw.com)* or **Rocky Mountain Adventures** *(shoprma.com)*, arrange for half-day trips on the lower section (Class 3, ages seven and up, $105) and all-day trips starting in the more technical Mishawaka Falls section (Class 4, ages 13 and up, $200).

Hwy 14 through the river canyon also qualifies as a scenic byway, and driving upstream reveals one bend after another filled with wild sights, from rock climbers ascending the cliffsides to bighorn sheep doing the same thing – but without ropes.

In addition to a handful of trailheads and superb campsites, the canyon also holds an awesome human-made attraction, the **Mishawaka Amphitheatre** *(themishawaka.com)*, roughly 24 miles from town. Walter Thompson first built his incredible venue in 1916, and the spirit of the place – restaurant, bar and music hall – remains over a century later.

THE GREAT DIVIDE

It's no secret that water is the West's most precious – and disputed – resource (p358). At the heart of the problem is where people have chosen to live over the decades. In Colorado, the majority of agriculture is in the semiarid eastern plains, while a whopping 85% of the state's population lives along the Front Range. But 80% of the state's water drains onto the Western Slope – that is, the other side of the Continental Divide. The 1890s Grand Ditch over La Poudre Pass was the first attempt to solve this inherent contradiction, but it wasn't until the 1930s that a more effective solution was devised: a 13-mile gravity-fed tunnel beneath Rocky Mountain National Park, which pipes in Colorado River water from Grand Lake (p158) directly to reservoirs in Fort Collins, Loveland and Boulder.

 EATING IN FORT COLLINS: CASUAL BITES

Colorado Room: A good pit stop on your bike tour, this bustling eatery serves sliders, Rocky Mountain oysters and poutine. *11am-10pm* **$**

Choice City: A Fort Collins icon, come to this old butcher shop for Reuben sandwiches and half-pound burgers. *11am-8pm Wed-Sat, to 3pm Sun-Tue* **$**

Restaurant 415: Old Town hot spot serving quinoa bowls, salads, pizzas and more. Vegan and gluten-free options. *11am-8pm Tue-Sun* **$$**

Young's Cafe: Going strong since 1987, Young's serves up steaming bowls of pho and other Vietnamese specialties. *11am-9:30pm* **$$**

ARAPAHO NATIONAL WILDLIFE REFUGE

Halfway between Fort Collins and Steamboat Springs is the Arapaho National Wildlife Refuge, founded in 1967 as a home for migratory birds that were being driven from their Midwestern habitat. The refuge is located in North Park, a high-elevation glacial basin similar to South Park near Denver. Today, nearly 200 species of birds frequent the summer sagebrush and wetlands, which were created by flooding the basin with water from the Illinois River. The star of the show is the sage grouse: its spring mating ritual – the lek – is an elaborate, territorial display of spiked tail feathers, puffy chests and nearly comical braggadocio. Other wildlife includes pronghorn antelope, coyote, moose and elk.

Cache La Poudre River (p175)

Visit Fort Collins' Museums

From science to history

The city's **Museum of Discovery** (*fcmod.org; adult/child $15/12.50*) focuses on hands-on, rotating science exhibits that are designed for children, mixing it up with permanent galleries on First Peoples, wildlife, agriculture and local history. The coolest thing on the grounds is an 1860s log cabin from the founding days of Fort Collins.

The **Avery House Museum** (*poudrelandmarks.com; tours adult/child $6/4*), meanwhile, is an 1879 home that belonged to Franklin Avery, the city surveyor of Fort Collins. Avery's foresight is evident in the tree-lined, wide boulevards that grace the city center. The Avery House is a stop along the self-guided historical walking tour, available from the Fort Collins Convention & Visitors Bureau, with guided tours Saturday and Sunday that take you through the historic building.

 EATING IN FORT COLLINS: FARMHOUSE GOURMET

Ginger & Baker: This cafe and bakery is based in an old mill, and hits the spot with flaky biscuits, pies and farm-to-fork fare. *7am-9pm Tue-Sun* **$$**

Farmhouse at Jessup Farm: A seasonal menu is the emphasis here, from pumpkin risotto to shepherd's pie. *11am-2pm & 4-9pm Tue-Fri, from 9am Sat & Sun* **$$**

Little on Mountain: Local farms and ranches are the secret to the simple but delectable creations at this upscale dinner destination. *4:30-8:30pm* **$$$**

The Regional: Comfort food meets sensational flavors, from short rib mole to Amish cheesecake with berry compote. *4-9pm Mon-Fri, 9:30am-2pm & 4-9pm Sat & Sun* **$$$**

Places We Love to Stay

$ Budget $$ Midrange $$$ Top End

Estes Park   p146

Estes Park Adventure Hostel
$ Climbers and backcountry skiers rejoice: affordable dorm-style accommodations with fellow mountaineers await.

Hermits Hollow Campground
$ Gorgeous spot in open space, minutes from Estes. Book through *larimercamping.com*.

YMCA of the Rockies $$ If you're on a family getaway, it's hard to beat the incredible array of activities at the Y.

Trailborn Rocky Mountains
$$ Stylish modern rooms combine with activities and great outdoor spaces; top pick for outdoorsy families and couples.

Murphy's Resort $$
Overlooking Lake Estes, this good-value motor lodge has plenty of family-friendly activities.

Stanley Hotel (p149) **$$$**
The iconic Estes Park hotel has a luxurious Old West feel, with stone fireplaces, leather couches and, of course, resident ghosts.

Black Canyon Inn $$$
Secluded 14-acre property has luxury suites and a 'rustic' log cabin with hot tub.

Stonebrook Resort $$$
Romantic retreats at these adults-only cabins, which look out over Fall River.

Deer Crest Resort $$$
Beckons guests with lots of green space for the kids to run around in, gas grills and the sound of the creek shushing guests to sleep.

Rocky Mountain National Park   p146

Glacier Basin Campground $
Ideally located in the Bear Lake corridor and surrounded by evergreens; 73 sites.

Aspenglen Campground $
With only 54 sites (some tent-only), this is the smallest and quietest option in the park.

Longs Peak Campground
$ Base camp for Longs Peak climbers; 26 tent-only sites. No water and no reservations; rangers recommend you show up before noon the day before your climb.

Moraine Park Campground
$ The biggest of the park's campgrounds near the Beaver Meadows Visitor Center; 244 sites.

Olive Ridge Campground $
One mile south of Wild Basin, this is a convenient spot with access to four nearby trailheads; no water.

Grand Lake   p158

Timber Creek Campground
$ The only campground on the west side of the park is 7 miles north of Grand Lake. There's little shade but moose sightings are common.

Sunset Point Campground $
Only 25 sites, but lovely views and a peaceful locale by Lake Granby, south of Grand Lake. First-come, first-served.

Shadowcliff Lodge $$ This ecofriendly mountain resort has gorgeous views of both the lake and the mountains, and is among the best-value accommodations in Colorado. Cabins, lodges and dorm beds.

Steamboat Springs   p164

Rabbit Ears Motel $ A diabolically chipper, pink-neon bunny welcomes guests at this simple roadside motel.

Seedhouse Campground
$ Twenty-four sites in the Mt Zirkel Wilderness, 25 miles north of Steamboat. Water available.

Gravity Haus $$ One of several Gravity locations in Colorado, with ski-in, ski-out access, yoga classes and stylish but affordable digs.

Vista Verde Guest Ranch
$$$ The most luxurious of Colorado's top-end guest ranches. If you have the means, this is it.

Fort Collins   p172

Armstrong Hotel $$$ Unique rooms in an elegantly renovated boutique hotel in the heart of Old Town.

Elizabeth Hotel $$$ Quirky luxury option, with in-room record players and an instrument lending library.

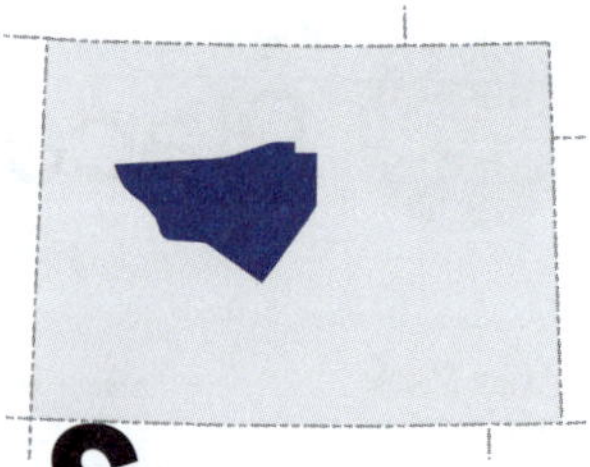

Vail, Aspen & Central Colorado

LIFE AT 110%

Brave the white-knuckle drive through a raging winter storm and you'll be blessed the morning after with a snow-kissed trip to heaven.

Spend enough time here, and eventually you'll hear it: that wild, uninhibited shriek of pure joy as someone, somewhere, launches themselves off the top of something insanely steep and into the void. They might be on a snowboard or a mountain bike, strapped into a paraglider or attached to a rope. But whatever it is that they're doing, you can be sure that primal scream – that momentary release from all of life's weight upon their shoulders – is the same cry that echoes in dozens of valleys across the Rockies. Ski bum or millionaire, Olympic athlete or unknown kid, moments like these are ones we all can share. Indeed, moments like these are the reason that so many people come here and, in some cases, never leave.

JOHN P KELLY/GETTY IMAGES

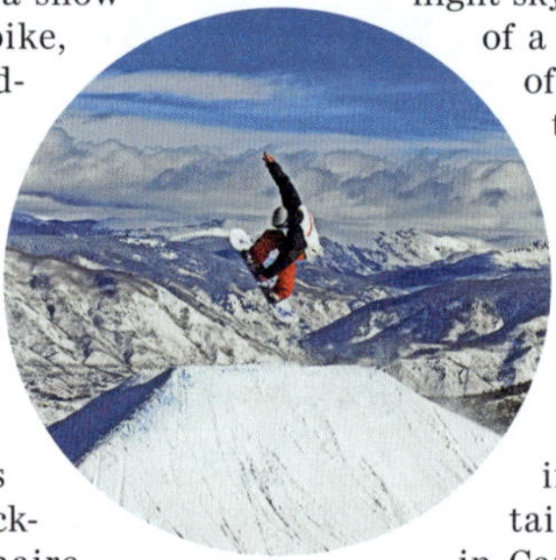

But there's more to it than supercharged fun. Back in camp, as evening falls and the fire flickers beneath the vastness of the night sky – when the sudden snap of a branch beyond the circle of light catches our full attention – these, too, are moments when we feel uniquely alive. It's in the ragged Elk Mountains outside Aspen and the mesmerizing swirl of the Arkansas River near Salida. The silence of falling snow atop Vail Mountain and a stranger's smile in Carbondale. If you're lucky enough to catch sight of it, don't forget to smile back.

Welcome to the mountains of Colorado.

THE MAIN AREAS

IDAHO SPRINGS
Denver day trips.
p186

WINTER PARK
Ski like a local.
p192

BRECKENRIDGE & SUMMIT COUNTY
Four unique resorts.
p196

VAIL
Big powder, big fun.
p207

For places to stay in Vail, Aspen & Central Colorado, see p246

TASSANEE RIEBPADITH/SHUTTERSTOCK

Maroon Bells (p222)

ASPEN
Beautiful landscapes, beautiful people.
p218

SALIDA & THE ARKANSAS RIVER VALLEY
River-running, bike-pedaling adventure.
p236

CRESTED BUTTE
Iconic Colorado ski town.
p243

Find Your Way

I-70 is Colorado's aorta, running straight through the center of the mountains. Unless you fly to Aspen or Vail, you can't avoid it – expect lots of traffic, especially on the weekends.

Wolcott

70

Glenwood Springs

Eagle River

Rifle

Sawatch Mountains

Aspen, p218

From Independence Pass to the Maroon Bells to the Hotel Jerome, this is Colorado at its most sublime and glamorous.

Carbondale

White River National Forest

Basalt

Roaring Fork River

Maroon Bells-Snowmass Wilderness

Crystal River

Aspen

Grand Mesa National Forest

Hunter-Fryingpan Wilderness

Marble

Raggeds Wilderness

Gunnison National Forest

CAR

If you're only here to ski, a car will be more hassle than it's worth. If you've got other plans, however – hiking, biking, ghost towns – an AWD vehicle is best. Parking, bad weather and traffic can be a headache.

Crested Butte

West Elk Wilderness

Fossil Ridge Wilderness

SHUTTLE

Private shuttles, like the Epic Mountain Express and Home James Transportation, run directly between Denver International Airport and most ski resorts.

BUS

The public Bustang runs from Denver's Union Station to Frisco, Vail and Glenwood Springs. Excellent bus networks (usually free) serve all the communities in the mountain counties, allowing you to get between the slopes, town and your accommodations with minimum hassle.

Crested Butte, p243

Legendary steeps in winter, wildflowers galore in summer, and golden aspens and endless miles of singletrack in autumn.

Vail, p207

It may be famed for its massive back bowls, but your pockets don't have to be flush with cash to enjoy the surrounding wilderness.

Winter Park, p192

Mountain fun that's easily accessed from Denver or, even better, the west side of Rocky Mountain National Park.

Idaho Springs, p186

Tour a gold mine, drive up a fourteener or hike to a glacier – and be back in Denver in time for dinner.

Breckenridge & Summit County, p196

Home to four ski resorts and historic Breckenridge, the aptly named Summit County is packed with sky-scraping alpine adventure, all year long.

Salida & the Arkansas River Valley, p236

The snowcapped Collegiate Peaks form the backdrop to one of the most popular stretches of white-water in the country.

Tabernash

○ Fraser

Indian Peaks Wilderness Area

Winter Park ●
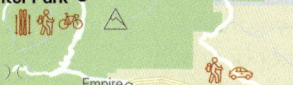

Green Mountain Reservoir

Byers Peak Wilderness

Eagles Nest Wilderness

Ptarmigan Peak Wilderness

Empire ○

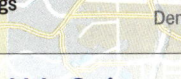 ● Idaho Springs

Denver ●

Silver Plume ○

Avon ○

 ● Vail

○ Dillon

Minturn ○

● Frisco   ○ Keystone

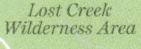 *Mt Evans Wilderness*

Holy Cross Wilderness

Copper ○ Mountain

● Breckenridge & Summit County

Arapahoe National Forest

Mt Massive Wilderness

San Isabel National Forest

Alma ○

● Bailey

Turquoise Lake

Lost Creek Wilderness Area

Twin Lakes Reservoir

Buffalo Peaks Wilderness

South Park

Pike National Forest

● Independence Pass

Collegiate Peaks Wilderness

Antero Reservoir

Arkansas River

Buena ○ Vista

Monument Park

San Isabel National Forest

Gunnison National Forest

 Salida & the Arkansas River

SAN LUIS VALLEY

0   50 km
0   25 miles

Plan Your Days

How you plan your time will largely depend on whether you're here in summer or winter. Regardless, leave yourself at least a day to get acclimatized – most towns are a minimum 8000ft above sea level.

DAVID SPATES/SHUTTERSTOCK

View from Mt Elbert (p216)

If You Only Do One Thing

● Skiing made Colorado the destination it is today, and if we had to pick how to spend one perfect blue-sky day, it would be on the slopes. While each resort has its own distinct personality, when push comes to shove, they all deliver the goods – that is, fresh powder and spectacular scenery. There's no need to complicate your life: eat a big breakfast, grab your skis or board, and hop on the nearest chairlift. Ride until you run out of steam. Have lunch in front of a big window or at a scenic picnic table in the sun. Hop back on your board or skis and ride some more. Then cruise down to town for dinner, margaritas and a soak in the hot tub.

SEASONAL HIGHLIGHTS

In winter and early spring, it's all about the snow. Summer in the high country comes later (late June–August), but cooler temps make this an ideal time to visit.

JANUARY

The **International Snow Sculpture Championship** brings temporal art to Breckenridge for two weeks. Winter storms are dumping powder across the Rockies, and the big resorts pack out for MLK weekend.

APRIL

The ski season is coming to a close – traditionally mid-April, but later on a good year – and festivals like Winter Park's **Spring Bash and Splash** herald outdoor concerts and wacky competitions.

JUNE

The rivers are raging and paddling season is underway, celebrated with **FIBArk** in Salida, the nation's oldest white-water festival. This is peak season for paddlers, but make sure you wear a wetsuit.

Three Days to Travel

● In summer, there's more reason to explore. Start with a day in **Breckenridge** (p196), hiking, biking or panning for gold, or head up to **A-Basin** (p206) to scramble up the continent's highest via ferrata (13,000ft). Have dinner in **Radicato** (p201) or catch a show at **Rocky Mountain Underground** (p200).

● The next day, cross Vail Pass on the way to historic **Leadville** (p215), via Minturn, Camp Hale National Monument and Tennessee Pass. In Leadville, rent a bike and pedal the **Mineral Belt** (p216) loop – or some wicked fast singletrack – while your body adjusts to life at 10,000ft. Enjoy a sundowner or dinner on the roof of **Treeline Kitchen** (p216).

● The next day, tackle the state's highest peak, **Mt Elbert** (p216), cross Independence Pass to **Aspen** (p229), or enjoy white-water thrills in **Salida** (p236).

Four Days in Aspen

● Day one: tour the **historic downtown** (p228) in the morning, followed by a hike beneath the **Maroon Bells** (p222) and a log-cabin dinner in **Ashcroft** (p224).

● Day two: spend an hour or two in one of the town's **museums** (p227) or the Aspen Institute, then a down-valley bike ride on the **Rio Grande Trail** (p226) or adrenaline-piqued mountain biking at **Snowmass** (p226). After a meal at **Matsuhisa** (p223) or **Meat & Cheese** (p223), catch a concert at **Silver City Aspen** (p224).

● Day three: drive to historic **Redstone** (p234) and the ghost town of **Crystal** (p234), capped off with a hot springs soak at **Avalanche Ranch** or **Glenwood Springs** (p230). Finish with a drive up **Independence Pass** (p229), stopping to hike at the Grottos or Lost Man trails, and then on to **Vail** (north) or **Salida** (south).

JULY	AUGUST	OCTOBER	DECEMBER
The high country is snow-free, wildflowers are blooming and the **Aspen Music Festival** kicks off eight weeks of classical music. Mountain bikers, meanwhile, are enjoying the blistering downhill trails at all the resorts.	High-altitude ultramarathons and 24-hour mountain-bike races in Leadville? Now that's vacation. This is also a great time to summit a fourteener or two, but make sure you're off the peak before the afternoon thunderstorms.	Aspens blaze gold across the state in early October. Make sure you book your hotel or campsite well in advance. This is a fabulous time for one last road trip before the snow begins.	**Ullr Fest** in Breck celebrates the god of snow while **Snow Days** brings live music to Vail. Ski season has begun! The Christmas and New Year holidays are busy times at the resorts.

HELP ME PICK:

Ski Resorts & Season Passes

Sticker shock is a big part of the Colorado ski experience, and it's not just limited to Vail and Aspen. That initial slack-jawed disbelief at the price of a lift ticket can quickly change to outright resentment, but with a bit of resourcefulness you can still make a ski trip work for your budget. The biggest resorts are all affiliated with one of two megapasses, Epic or Ikon, but don't overlook Colorado's indie mountains.

Where to ski if you love...

Family Vacations

Keystone, Breckenridge and Winter Park are all great destinations for kids, but they're not cheap for an out-of-state family of four: you can easily spend upwards of $10,000 for a week in high season. If you've got young kids who are still learning, consider a smaller resort like Ski Cooper, Monarc, or Sunlight where the prices for rental gear, lessons and accommodations are considerably cheaper. Howelsen Hill in Steamboat is free on Sundays, and Loveland and Eldora are easy day trips from the Front Range.

Great Skiing with Convenient Access

The resorts along I-70 are the largest in the state and are the easiest to access from Denver. You can't go wrong here: the peaks are high, the terrain is varied and the snow is feather light. Summit County alone has four big-name resorts:

Breckenridge, Keystone, Copper Mountain and A-Basin. Winter Park's turnoff is before the Eisenhower Tunnel, which sometimes translates into less traffic. Vail and Beaver Creek are the jewels in the interstate crown, but are located on the other side of Vail Pass.

Small Towns

If you want shorter lift lines and more throwback charm, consider basing yourself in an out-of-the-way mountain town. Crested Butte is a fabulous hideaway tucked behind Aspen. Steamboat is more upscale, but also has a remote enough location to keep away the crowds and preserve its Western charm. In the southwest, the steeps at Telluride and Silverton make experts go weak in the knees, but require flying into regional airports in Montrose or Durango. For more accessible terrain, head to Durango's offbeat Purgatory resort.

Aspen

And then there's Aspen. With its celebrity glitter, historic downtown and some of the best scenery in the state, Aspen is a terrific choice for those with an expense account. One lift ticket grants access to the Four Mountains: Aspen, Snowmass, Buttermilk and Aspen Highlands. There's plenty of upside-down-steep terrain here, X Games–level terrain parks, plus top-notch kids' amenities.

Backcountry & Cross-Country Skiing

If you love skiing but are less enthusiastic about the sport's corporate turn, then consider cross-country skiing. Groomed trails are found in most mountain towns, and day passes can cost as little as $30. Going into the backcountry, either on a day trip or via Colorado's backcountry hut system, is a magical opportunity, but training and proper gear are a must.

Keystone Resort (p205)

— **HOW TO** —

Don't overlook independent resorts like Telluride, Silverton, Wolf Creek, Monarch and Loveland, which also offer incredible skiing and deep powder.

Save money by packing a picnic. It sounds obvious, but the number of people who pay outrageous prices for cafeteria food is astounding.

Want first tracks in backcountry glades after a big storm? Go snowcat skiing at Purgatory, Steamboat, Shrine Pass, Jones Pass, Aspen, Monarch or Loveland.

Got the itch for steep lines and an 'I can't believe this is real' backdrop? Fork out for heli skiing in Silverton or Telluride.

Ikon Pass Versus Epic Pass

There has been a tremendous amount of corporate consolidation in the US ski industry, and the biggest names are now all affiliated with one of two season passes: Ikon or Epic. Don't get confused by the word 'season' – these passes are fully customizable, from one day to unlimited, and from a handful of local hills to the whole hog, including destinations scattered around the world. If you're headed to a big resort, getting a pass in advance – the best deals are offered in spring for the following year – will save you money and allow you the luxury of skiing in more than one place. Passes also come with perks, like discounted tickets for friends and family.

Ikon (*ikonpass.com; four-day/base/full $479/969/1359*) offers access to Winter Park, Copper, Steamboat, Eldora, A-Basin and Aspen in Colorado. Other destinations range from Big Sky (Montana) to Alta and Snowbird (Utah), and Jackson Hole (Wyoming) to Chamonix (France). The Winter Park local **passes** (*midweek/full $559/749*) are a cheaper option.

Epic (*epicpass.com; four-day/local/full $423/762/1025*) offers access to Vail, Breckenridge, Keystone, Beaver Creek and Crested Butte in Colorado. Other destinations include Whistler (Canada), Park City (Utah) and Heavenly, Northstar and Kirkwood at Lake Tahoe. If you're looking for a more targeted pass, consider the **Summit Value Pass** (*$615; Breckenridge and Keystone*) or **Keystone Plus** (*$408; Keystone, plus five days at Crested Butte*).

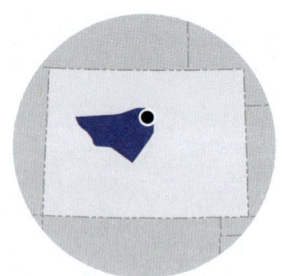

Idaho Springs

HIKING | FOURTEENERS | MINING LEGACY

GETTING AROUND

Almost halfway between Denver and several big ski resorts along I-70, Idaho Springs makes for a good pit stop. Take exit 240 for the main downtown area and Mt Blue Sky. St Mary's Glacier is just west of town at exit 238 (Fall River Rd). Georgetown is 13 miles west of Idaho Springs; access the Guanella Pass Byway from here.

☑TOP TIP

I-70's mountain stretch – particularly during ski season – often resembles more of a parking lot than a highway. On weekends, we strongly recommend avoiding peak times (6am to 9am westbound; 2pm to 6pm eastbound), but always check traffic conditions before setting out. Bad weather can be treacherous: drive slowly.

If you're only in Denver for a limited time, you can barrel up the road to Idaho Springs for a quick taste of Colorado's rough-and-tumble mining history. The rowdy gaggle of prospectors, gunslingers and rapscallions who dashed here to get rich in 1859 – all part of the larger Pike's Peak Gold Rush – have been (mostly) replaced by a notably more genteel crowd of day-tripping skiers, hikers and bikers on blindingly chromed-up Harleys, but the historic buildings along Miner St retain the creaking floors and antique character of the city's colorful past.

To the south of town rises Mt Blue Sky, one of the dominant landmarks of the Front Range and visible from Denver. Further up the road, Guanella Pass and Loveland Pass slingshot drivers into the high country, and in summer make for remarkably convenient trailheads for high-altitude hikes. Guanella Pass is accessed from historic Georgetown.

Gold Rush Legacy

Idaho Springs or bust

The year 1859 marked the beginning of the Pike's Peak Gold Rush, and while many early prospectors congregated along the South Platte River, the territory's first big find was made in Idaho Springs. On a cold January day, steam rising from nearby hot springs attracted one George Jackson, who proceeded to stumble upon placer gold in Clear Creek. Like many a miner, he hoped to keep his find a secret, but it wasn't long before the word was out and claims were filling the valley.

With the dozens of mines that sprung up in the area came the **Argo Mill** *(argomilltour.com; adult/child $30/20)* – that's the huge red building on the hill above town. Tours of the Argo explain how mills separate precious ore from waste rock, in addition to taking visitors inside the incredible 4.2-mile transport and drainage tunnel that connected to Central City. If you've ever wondered why the US Mint has a branch in Denver, the amount of ore that once came out of mills like the Argo is your answer.

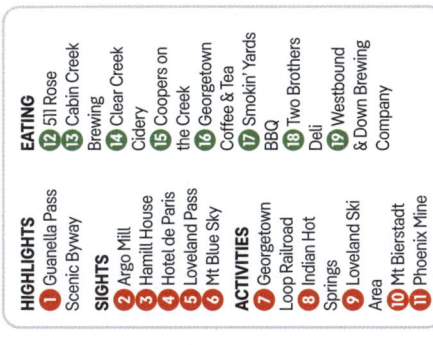

HIGHLIGHTS
1 Guanella Pass Scenic Byway

SIGHTS
2 Argo Mill
3 Hamill House
4 Hotel de Paris
5 Loveland Pass
6 Mt Blue Sky

ACTIVITIES
7 Georgetown Loop Railroad
8 Indian Hot Springs
9 Loveland Ski Area
10 Mt Bierstadt
11 Phoenix Mine

EATING
12 5II Rose
13 Cabin Creek Brewing
14 Clear Creek Cidery
15 Coopers on the Creek
16 Georgetown Coffee & Tea
17 Smokin' Yards BBQ
18 Two Brothers Deli
19 Westbound & Down Brewing Company

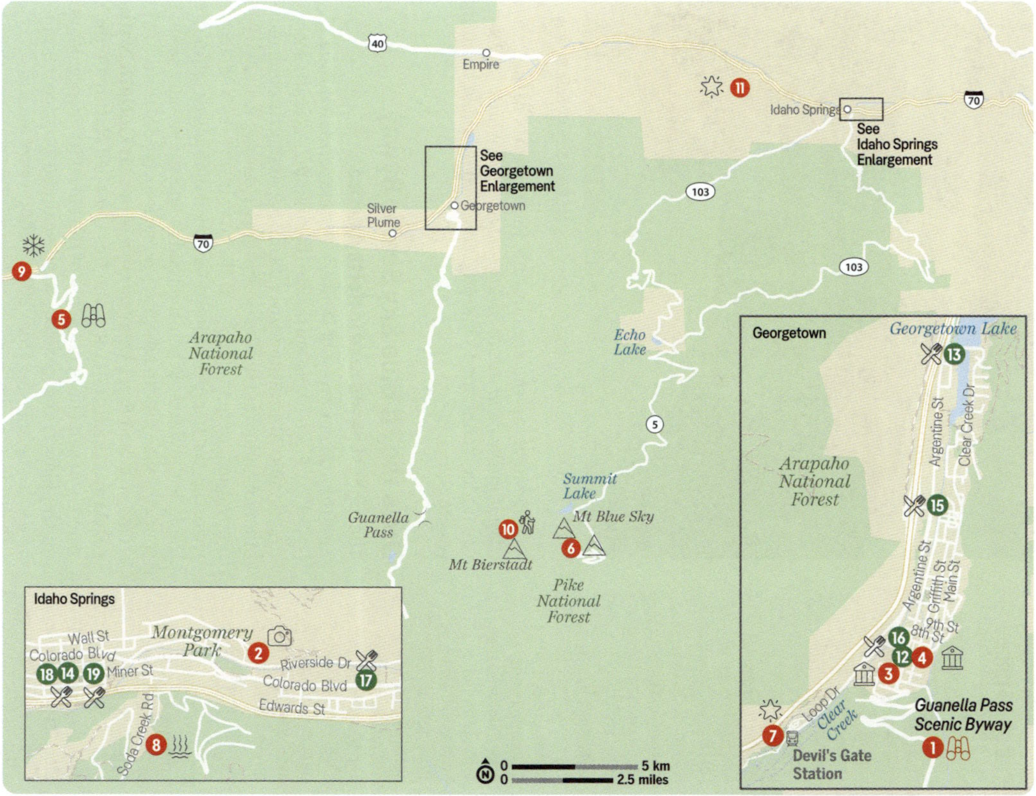

THE SAND CREEK MASSACRE

Mt Blue Sky was originally named Mt Evans, after the Colorado Territory's second governor, John Evans. Evans played a key role in the 1864 Sand Creek Massacre, a pivotal and tragic point in US–Native American relations. On the morning of November 29, an encampment of Arapaho and Cheyenne, flying the US flag at Big Sandy Creek in the Colorado plains, were killed and then brutally mutilated by the US Cavalry. The encampment consisted largely of women, children and the elderly, and it's estimated that between 165 and 230 lives were taken that day in a sickening fashion. Governor Evans was seen as a dishonest and contradictory figure in the failed peace negotiations months prior. In 2023 Mt Evans was renamed Blue Sky in honor of the state's Indigenous peoples.

SEAN XU/SHUTTERSTOCK

Mt Blue Sky Scenic Byway

Other sights in the area include the **Phoenix Mine** *(phoenixgoldmine.com; adult/child from $28/22)*, whose tour gets you underground for 45 minutes, followed by a gold-panning session.

Drive the Mt Blue Sky Scenic Byway

The highest paved road in North America

Less than an hour west of Denver's skyscrapers is **Mt Blue Sky** (14,265ft). From Idaho Springs to the summit, the road ascends roughly 6600ft in altitude over 28 miles, passing through montane, subalpine and tundra ecosystems. Note that massive road renovations were underway at the time of writing and access was expected to remain closed for over a year; check online for the latest updates. When the road is open, you must reserve your entrance time in advance *(recreation.gov; $15 per vehicle)*.

One stop you don't want to miss is the **Mt Goliath Natural Area** (11,540ft; park at the Dos Chappell Nature Center), where you can check out some of the oldest living organisms on the planet: the gnarled, wind-sculpted bristlecone pine. The trees here range from 900 to 2000 years old.

Continuing on the road past **Summit Lake**, you're likely to encounter Rocky Mountain goats and bighorn sheep. From the parking lot it's then a short but lung-busting scramble to the summit's transcendent views.

 ## EATING IN IDAHO SPRINGS: OUR PICKS

Smokin' Yards BBQ: Texas-style brisket and Carolina pulled pork ensure the parking lot is perpetually full. East of the historic district. *11am-8pm* $

Two Brothers Deli: The coziest cafe in town, this is an excellent option for refueling with a quick meal. *9am-4pm Mon-Fri, 8am-5pm Sat & Sun* $

Clear Creek Cidery: Cider flights and Sonoran-style grub, from chimichangas to Oh-My-Gawd green chile. *11am-9pm* $$

Westbound & Down Brewing Company: The Denver brewery joins forces with the Buffalo next door for malted barley and bison burgers. *11am-8pm* $$

The highway is only open from June to September. There's a campground at Echo Lake, just before the fee station.

Soak in Indian Hot Springs

Steamy relaxation

When gold was first discovered in Idaho Springs, it was thanks to **Indian Hot Springs** *(indianhotsprings.com; admission from $30)*, which must have seemed heaven-sent on a frigid winter day. Today, the mineral waters are the closest soak to Denver, and while they can't compare with other Colorado locales, few will argue with their convenience.

The main area is a family-style heated swimming pool that sits beneath a translucent dome and is surrounded by tropical plants. More serious hot springs aficionados may prefer the geothermal pools, which are located in underground steam caves. There's also a mud spa. Bring your own towels.

Hike to St Mary's Glacier

Summer snow

Wildflowers and windswept trails, boulders and snowfields – these are the disproportionately big rewards for the easy hike up to **St Mary's Glacier** *($20 per vehicle, cash only)*. The modest elevation gains, short distance (half-mile) and summer snow make it ideal even for the littlest hikers. Although the area gets fairly busy on summer weekends, the views are remarkable, and a scramble around the lake will bring you to the 'glacier' itself.

If you want to make a day of it, the gentle trail to **James Peak** (13,294ft) continues up another 3 miles past the base of the snowfield to the summit. It was named after the botanist Edwin James, who made the first recorded summit of Pikes Peak (Colorado's most famous landmark for pioneers and prospectors heading west) in 1820.

Tour Historic Homes in Georgetown

A silver miner's dreams

Smaller and more soulful than Idaho Springs, historic Georgetown's mix of Victorian architecture, secondhand bookshops and cafes make it a pleasant stopover on the way up or down I-70. At the end of 6th St (the main drag) is the 1875 **Hotel de Paris** *(hoteldeparismuseum.org; adult/child $10/5)*, opened by the mysterious Frenchman Louis Dupuy. Tours take visitors through 23 furnished rooms, filled with luxury furnishings.

BRISTLECONE PINE

Bristlecone pines are the world's oldest trees: Methuselah in the Great Basin Mountains of California is believed to be over 4800 years old. While Colorado's variety *(Pinus aristata)* isn't quite that ancient, it's still up there in terms of longevity. The oldest specimen in the Rockies is over 2500 years old, which means it began growing in the 5th century BCE. So roughly the same age as Socrates, Plato and Confucius.

Bristlecone pines can live at elevations of up to 11,700 ft, and you can see from their gnarled, stunted appearance that they are true survivors. One of their secrets to old age is likely the high elevation – the sparse vegetation in these subalpine environments has spared them from the ravages of wildfires.

EATING IN GEORGETOWN: OUR PICKS

Cabin Creek Brewing: Lakeside views, small-batch beers and the usual run of pub grub. North of town. *11am-8:30pm* **$$**	**Coopers on the Creek**: With a menu of duck poutine and bison ribs, this is the best choice for famished hikers and skiers. *11:30am-8pm Thu-Tue* **$$**	**511 Rose:** Country music vibes, veggie quinoa bowls and Colorado chile make the 511 Rose a Georgetown favorite. *11am-8pm Thu-Mon* **$$**	**Georgetown Coffee & Tea:** For a pastry and pick-me up, drop by this centrally located cafe. *10am-3pm Mon-Fri, 9am-4pm Sat & Sun* **$**

BIGHORN SHEEP & MOUNTAIN GOATS

If you spend time in the Front Range mountains, it's possible you'll spot both bighorn sheep and mountain goats. Both live in herds and are adept at navigating high-elevation rocky terrain. So how do you tell them apart?

The tawny-colored bighorn sheep are the natives. The males, which have large, spiraling horns and can weigh up to 500lb, are instantly recognizable. Ewes also have horns, but they are much shorter and only have a slight curve.

Mountain goats, meanwhile, were introduced from Montana and Canada in 1947. They're the cuter of the two, with fluffy white coats, straight horns and a knack for disappearing over cliff faces. They tend to live at slightly higher elevations as their dense wool can keep them warm in temperatures as low as -51°F (-46°C).

CARY L EPFERT/SHUTTERSTOCK

Silver Dollar Lake

The 1867 **Hamill House** (*historicgeorgetown.org; open by appointment only*) also offers tours of the one-time private residence of a silver-mine owner, providing a glimpse of up-scale tastes in 19th-century Colorado. The most distinctive landmark in Georgetown (not open to the public) is the all-important 1875 **Alpine Hose No 2 Firehouse**, with a white clapboard facade and distinctive square belltower, where hoses were once dried.

Drive to the Top of Guanella Pass

Fourteeners and alpine lakes

Built atop an old wagon road that once connected the silver-mining towns of Georgetown and Grant, the 22-mile **Guanella Pass Scenic Byway** (11 miles to the pass) climbs up to 11,669ft straight from Georgetown, and is an excellent staging point for fishing excursions and several alpine hikes. Sightings of bighorn sheep and mountain goats are common.

From the pass you can ascend **Mt Bierstadt** (14,060ft; 7 miles round trip), one of the most popular and accessible four-teeners along the Front Range. A shorter and less-crowded option is **Silver Dollar Lake** (3 miles round trip): this inspiring trail is mostly above the tree line and graced with thousands of tiny wildflowers in summer. The trailhead is located just past Guanella Pass Campground, at 11,000ft. The pass itself closes in winter, though the road is usually plowed past the Silver Dollar Lake trailhead.

Ride the Georgetown Loop Railroad

Narrow-gauge heritage

For the full silver-mining experience, hop on the **Georgetown Loop Railroad** (*georgetownlooprr.com; adult/child $35/29*), once part of a system that snaked through Clear Creek Canyon to connect Denver with rich mines in Silver Plume. Chugging along this loop is an entertaining way to leave the I-70 corridor and enjoy expansive views over Clear Creek Valley. The ride is 75 minutes each way, with a pause to tour a mine in between, and the scenery from one of the open passenger cars can make for a breathtaking, if chilly, afternoon. Themed events, seasonal packages and add-ons such as tours of the Lebanon Silver Mine also feature. Plan on spending about half a day. Book ahead.

Drive Loveland Pass

Rocky Mountain high

The alpine scenery in the Front Range is breathtaking enough, but it's not until you make it to **Loveland Pass** (11,990ft) that you really begin to feel that Rocky Mountain magic. The gateway to Summit County, the pass is flanked by a ski resort on either side – Loveland and Arapahoe Basin – and offers easy access to high-altitude hiking in the summer months.

The opening of the Eisenhower Tunnel in 1973 made the pass more of a scenic detour than a necessity, but if you're not in a rush, the hairpin turns bring inspiring views. It remains open year-round, though it can be treacherous in winter and will close in bad weather.

Accessible from the Loveland Pass parking lot, the steep, 4-mile out-and-back jaunt to **Mt Sniktau** (13,234ft) is a convenient way to experience the thrill of alpine hiking. If you barely broke a sweat on the way up, follow the ridge in the other direction for the more challenging **Grizzly Peak** (13,427ft; 5 miles round-trip).

Ski Loveland

High-elevation fun

Loveland Ski Area (*skiloveland.com; adult/child day pass $149/45*) may be smaller than its neighbors, but its old-school vibe, wide-open runs, cheaper lift tickets and proximity to Denver (53 miles) guarantee enduring popularity. With a base elevation of 10,800ft, much of the terrain is above the tree line, meaning gorgeous views when the sun shines but bitterly cold wind in bad weather.

To ski off the Continental Divide, take Chair 9 up to 12,700ft – from here you can then catch a ride on the free Ridge Cat (pick up your pass first at the base) along the ridge to Loveland's high point. Note there are two base areas: the Basin (main area) and the Valley (beginners).

FRONT RANGE 14ERS

Many people come to Colorado with the goal of summiting at least one fourteener: a mountain that's higher than 14,000ft. And because of the proximity to Denver, the four Front Range fourteeners that can be accessed from I-70 before the Eisenhower Tunnel tend to be the most popular. These include Mt Bierstadt, Mt Blue Sky (p188), and Grays and Torreys Peaks.

If you're thinking about attempting a summit, don't underestimate the challenge. Make sure to acclimatize, stay hydrated and get an early start: dawn is a good time to start hiking. Not only will this help you snag a parking spot, but it also ups your chances of getting off the peak by noon, at which point dangerous thunderstorms begin to roll in.

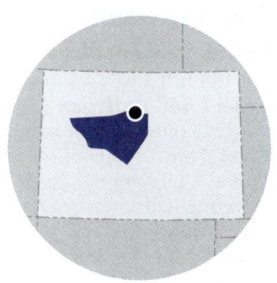

Winter Park

SKIING | HIKING | MOUNTAIN BIKING

GETTING AROUND

Winter Park is 70 miles west of Denver; turn onto Hwy 40 at the little town of Empire, off I-70. **Home James Transportation** *(ridehj.com; from $76)* runs a private shuttle from DIA, while Amtrak's *California Zephyr* stops in Fraser daily and the *Winter Park Express* (p194) stops at the resort. The Bustang's **Outrider** *(ridebustang.com; $11)* line runs once daily from Union Station in Denver to Winter Park. In town, the free shuttle system the Lift runs from the ski resort through Winter Park to Fraser.

☑TOP TIP

Winter Park gets kudos for being one of the few big ski resorts to offer free parking near the base of the mountain. The lots fill up fast, so be sure to arrive early. The Vintage Lot is the main paid parking area.

When everyone else is stuck in traffic on I-70, those in the know will veer off the interstate for Hwy 40, making the climb over Berthoud Pass and down into Winter Park. Located less than two hours from Denver, this unpretentious resort is a favorite with Front Rangers, who drive here to ski fresh tracks each weekend. Beginners can frolic on miles of heavily trafficked groomers, while experts test their skills on Mary Jane's SUV-sized bumps. For skiers with disabilities, the resort also offers one of the best adaptive skiing programs in the US.

The congenial, oh-so-slightly '70s town is a wonderful base for year-round romping. Most services are found either in the ski village, which is a mile before Winter Park proper, or strung along US 40 (the main drag). Follow Hwy 40 and you'll get to Fraser, Tabernash and the west side of Rocky Mountain National Park.

Ski the Bumps

When it hurts so good

Winter Park *(winterparkresort.com; adult/child day pass $249/154)* encompasses seven main territories and has a maximum vertical drop of more than 3000ft. It's most famous for the leg-crushing moguls on **Mary Jane**, though there's plenty more here to explore. Intermediate skiers can get above the tree line in the **Parsenn Bowl** (12,060ft), while experts will drop over the other side of the ridge to the glades of **Eagle Wind** or the off-piste chutes and cliffs in the **Vasquez Cirque**. Roughly a third of the main Winter Park mountain is groomed for greenies – and the addition of red wagons in which to tote the kids' skis is a nice touch as well.

Slopestyle fans will enjoy the seven terrain parks: you can learn to ride rails and pipes at **Starter**, kick it up a notch at **Ash Cat** or catch big air in the **Rail Yard**. Other winter activities include a tubing hill, a small skating rink, ski bikes, snowshoeing and sunset s'mores snowcat tours.

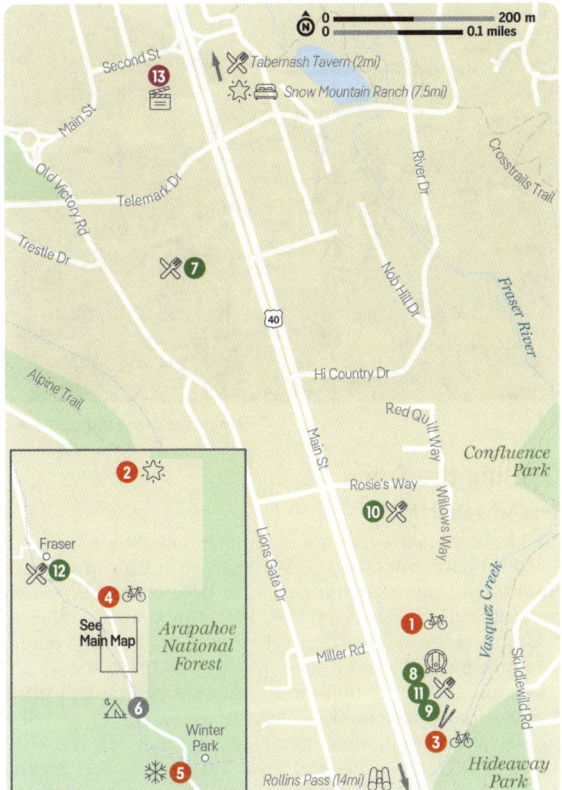

ACTIVITIES
1 Beaver Sports
2 Devil's Thumb Ranch
3 Epic Mountain Sports
4 Fraser River Trail
● Trestle Bike Park (see 5)
5 Winter Park Resort

SLEEPING
● Devil's Thumb Ranch (see 2)
6 Idlewild Campground

EATING
7 Fontenot's Seafood & Grill
8 Idlewild Spirits
9 Pepe Osaka's Fish Taco
10 Randi's Grill & Pub
11 Rudi's Deli
12 Shreddy's Tacos

ENTERTAINMENT
13 Foundry Cinema & Bowl

On the other side of Berthoud Pass and only 45 minutes from Denver, **Jones Pass Guides** (*jonespassguides.com; seat $700*) provides snowcat-accessed backcountry skiing off of Jones Pass. Avalanche gear, skis/boards, lunch and beer included.

Summer Hikes

From riverside to ridgetop

Once the temps begin to rise, hiking and biking rule. The place to start is the paved 6.5-mile **Fraser River Trail**, which follows the creekside from the ski resort all the way to Fraser. Popular with walkers, runners, cyclists, cross-country skiers and even skateboarders, this is a lovely way to get around.

While several trail systems leave from town, we recommend getting above tree line at Berthoud Pass, which is a convenient place to get on the Continental Divide Trail in summer. **Stanley Mountain** (12,521ft) is a 7.4-mile round-trip hike; from the Berthoud parking lot, cross the highway to access the trail.

Another good way to get up high is via the ski resort's gondola (single ride $29), which hauls you up to 10,700ft.

Finally, railroad and alpine lake enthusiasts can check out Rollins Pass (p195), though you'll need AWD to get there.

BERTHOUD PASS

The site of one of Colorado's first ski resorts, Berthoud Pass (11,307ft) is the gateway to Winter Park. In 1937 this was the site of one of the state's first-ever ski-related avalanche mortalities. While the ski area officially closed in 2003, the ease of access makes it a popular spot for backcountry skiers and snowshoers; it has over 50 lines and 25 miles of descent, spread evenly over blue and black runs. The avalanche danger remains, so don't think about going out without proper gear and training. **Friends of Berthoud Pass** (*berthoudpass.org*) offers free avalanche courses in winter.

THE SKI TRAIN

The Rockies may have better snow than the Alps, but they definitely can't compete with the romance of throwing your snowboard on a TGV in Paris and waking up a few hours later in snow-covered Bourg-St-Maurice. Voilà – no traffic-clogged highways necessary.

The sole exception is Winter Park, Colorado's only ski resort served by train. The *Winter Park Express* runs from Denver's Union Station direct to the slopes, passing through 31 tunnels on the way. The service operates Friday to Sunday, January through March. And if you're flying into DIA, the A-Line to Union Station guarantees a seamless rails-to-resort experience. It's roughly $80 per adult for a round-trip ticket.

FRANCISCO BLANCO/SHUTTERSTOCK

Alpine lake near Rollins Pass

Cycling the Trails
Two-wheeled thrills

For locals, the sport of choice in summer is mountain biking. If you don't have your own wheels, rent them at **Epic Mountain Sports** *(epicmountainsports.com)* or **Beaver Sports** *(winter parkskirental.com)* – they have everything from e-bikes to full-suspension carbon frames. Expect to pay $75 for a mountain bike for half a day.

Beginners should jump on the classic **Creekside/Flume Loop**, a 5-mile trail in Fraser that mixes easy green and blue singletrack, with minimal climbing.

The trail systems closer to town are considerably rockier and more technical (intermediate and up); a good choice to get acquainted is the **Vasquez Creek system**, which is accessed via a Forest Service road off of Vasquez Rd. Try out Leap Frog on your first go, then climb back up and finish with Razzmatazz, a smoother downhill ride with banked turns and jumps that dumps you off right in town.

If you don't want to sweat the uphills, however, the place to be is the **Trestle Bike Park** *(trestlebikepark.com; $174 for half-day, including bike rental)*. This is the ski resort's summer incarnation, and features three lifts and over 40 miles of free-ride trails and jumps for all levels.

Granby Ranch *(granbyranch.com; $134 for half-day, including bike rental)*, 20 miles north on Hwy 40, is another great bike park that's more affordable and less intimidating.

WHERE TO EAT IN WINTER PARK: OUR PICKS

Rudi's Deli: Great choice of paninis, subs, melts and soups, with veggie and gluten-free options too. Always busy, but service is quick. *10am-8pm* $

Fontenot's Seafood & Grill: Bringin' New Orleans' tasty brand of seafood love to the mountains. *11:30am-8:30pm Tue-Fri, from 9am Sat & Sun* $$$

Pepe Osaka's Fish Taco: You like sushi. You like fish tacos. And as it turns out, you love sushi tacos, because...why not? *4-9pm Wed-Fri, from noon Sat & Sun* $$$

Tabernash Tavern: Fresh local ingredients and a creative kitchen makes the Tavern tops. Six miles north of Winter Park. Reserve. *4-9pm Thu-Sun* $$$

Discover Rollins Pass

Hike, bike or drive to the Continental Divide

If you want a real workout, give **Rollins Pass** a go. This popular, rugged 14-mile 4WD road leads almost to the top of the 11,660ft pass (now closed to motorized vehicles). In the mid-1860s, JA Rollins established a toll wagon-road over the pass from Nederland and Rollinsville; early in the 20th century, David H Moffat's Denver, Northwestern & Pacific Railway crossed the Continental Divide here.

First known as Boulder Pass, then Rollins Pass, it also earned the appellation 'Corona' because railroad workers considered it the crown at the 'top of the world.' Remnants of the original line make it of particular interest to railroad buffs. Cyclists refer to this route as the **Indian Peaks Traverse** (take it all the way into Boulder), but there's plenty of hiking to do up here, too. The traverse to Rodgers Pass (5 miles round trip) from the trestle is both mellow and beautiful. From here, you can easily summit the west side of **James Peak** (13,294ft).

The turnoff for Rollins Pass is between the Winter Park resort and town; the road is very rocky and you definitely need AWD and high clearance. When you reach an intersection on the way up, keep going straight. Note: the last couple of miles probably won't open until July at the earliest because of snowpack.

Ranch Life

Ride the range

For an all-inclusive getaway, consider spending the night at a ranch. **Devil's Thumb Ranch** *(devilsthumbranch.com; day pass from $30)*, the classiest digs in the Winter Park area, offers an abundance of outdoor adventure, all of which is open to the public. In winter Nordic fiends descend for a scenic 65-mile network of groomed cross-country trails. Lessons and rentals are available, and they offer ice skating and fat biking, too. In the summer it's all about the horseback riding and mountain biking on 5000 acres of Colorado high country. Youngsters will enjoy the 1600ft zipline and hatchet throwing, while anglers are practically guaranteed a catch on a guided tour.

The nearby **Snow Mountain Ranch** *(ymcarockies.org; day pass from $29)*, run by the YMCA, is the cheaper version: 50 miles of cross-country trails in winter (rental equipment available), plus tubing, fat biking and even dogsledding. In summer, activities morph into horseback riding, mountain biking and climbing and challenge courses. Sleeping options range from yurts and campsites to fully furnished cabins and hotel rooms.

BIKING ETIQUETTE

Many mountain bike trails in Colorado are multiuse, so remember to always follow proper etiquette.

Yield to Others: Hikers and horses always have the right of way. Pull over when others are approaching.

Announce Your Presence: If you're about to overtake someone, clearly say 'on your left' or 'passing when there's a chance,' and give them enough time to react before you pass.

Yield to Uphill Riders: Downhill riders should always yield to uphill riders, unless they've pulled over for a breather.

Respect Trail Closures: If a trail is closed – whether because of trail work, wildlife or mud – please ride elsewhere.

 WHERE TO EAT & DRINK IN WINTER PARK: OUR PICKS

Shreddy's Tacos: Pair these beloved food-truck tacos with a beer and table at next-door Vicious Cycle Brewery. Just up the road in Fraser. *11am-9pm* **$$**

Randi's Grill & Pub: Field-to-fork ethos meets all your pub favorites – we're looking at you, Irish nachos. Oh yeah, there's beer too. *8am-10pm* **$$**

Idlewild Spirits: Excellent cocktails made from their own spirits, plus small plates (charred octopus with mole sauce). *5-9pm Wed-Sun* **$$**

Foundry Cinema & Bowl: Movies, bowling, wood-fired pizzas and beer guarantee fun for all ages. *4-9pm Mon-Fri, from 1pm Sat & Sun* **$$**

Breckenridge & Summit County

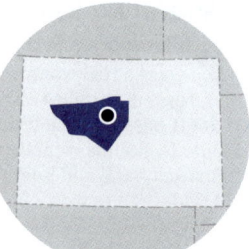

SKIING | HIKING | MINING HISTORY

GETTING AROUND

Breckenridge is 80 miles west of Denver via I-70 exit 203, then Hwy 9 south. On a traffic-free day (rare), it's only a 1½-hour drive. The most convenient parking lots are located at the base of the gondola, but they fill up quickly. A free lot on Airport Rd is a good alternative for day-trippers.

The **Summit Express** *(summit express.com; $95)* shuttle runs between DIA and Breckenridge. Free Ride buses serve the town and ski area and depart from next to the gondola. Free Summit Stage buses link Breckenridge with other Summit County ski resorts.

☑TOP TIP

Breck is not big, and you can easily walk to everything on Main St and Ridge St. Parking is limited and traffic is bad in winter; leave the car at your hotel or in one of the skier lots.

When it comes to ski towns with a soul, Breckenridge is near the top of the list. The colorful Victorian architecture recalls its origins as a rough-and-tumble mining outpost, and reminders of 19th-century fortune seekers are still scattered throughout the area. But while summer visitors may be eager to try out panning for gold, there's really no debating it. Wintertime rules.

That's when you'll see the real crowds: from ski bums to young families clomping down Main St, all eyes cast on the hulking Tenmile Range. And that's Breck for you – with a four-chairlift combo and a snap of your fingers, you'll be all the way at the top of Peak 8, where the turns are silky smooth and the views go on forever. And when the distant horizon fades from pink to blue to black, it's time to retreat to the hot tub and contemplate the Milky Way, arcing silently overhead.

Ski the Peaks

No friends on powder days

When Main St is at 9600ft and the peaks are so plentiful that the founders went with numbers over names, you know the skiing is going to be good. The **resort** *(breckenridge.com; adult/ child day pass $281/183)* spans Peaks 6 to 10, and thanks to the long and relatively flat green runs down low, Breck has always been known as a great family mountain. Beginners won't want to miss green runs like Silverthorne and Red Rover. But if you're ready to step it up a notch, don't fret – there are plenty of thrilling diversions higher up.

A favorite intermediate blue run is Cashier on Peak 9. Another great line on **Peak 7** is Wirepatch, featuring a series of 'rollers' – mini-hills, not moguls. **Peak 6** offers access to two intermediate bowls above tree line. Brave the gusting wind and take the creaking T-bar from Peak 7 or Peak 8, which pulls skiers to the single-black terrain of the North Bowl and the double-black bumps in the Horseshoe Bowl. And once

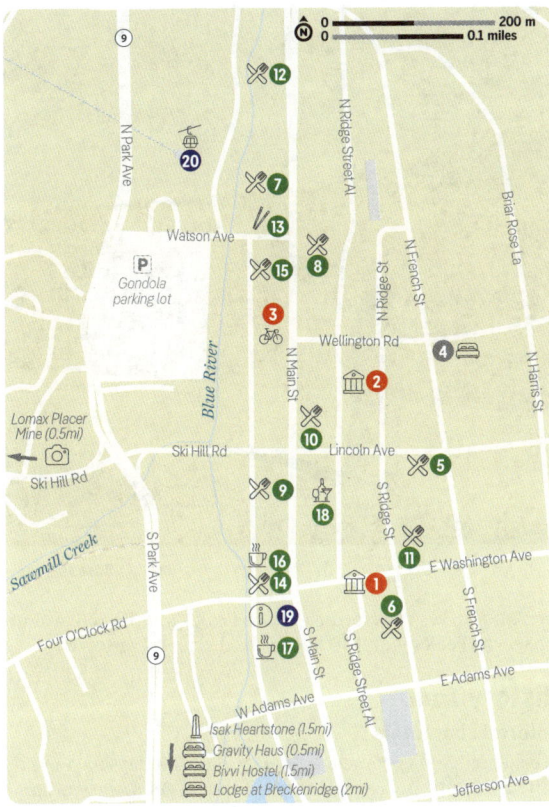

SIGHTS
1 Barney Ford Museum
2 Edwin Carter Discovery Center

ACTIVITIES
3 Carvers

SLEEPING
4 Fireside Inn

EATING
5 Amazing Grace
6 Aurum Food & Wine
7 Blue River Bistro
8 Canteen Tap House
9 Downstairs at Eric's
10 Giampietro
11 Hearthstone
12 Oaxacan Bites
13 Pho Real
14 Radicato
15 Semplice

DRINKING
16 Clint's Bakery & Coffee House
17 Crown
18 Rocky Mountain Underground

INFORMATION
19 Welcome Center

TRANSPORT
20 BreckConnect Gondola

you've got your snow legs under you, don't miss the highest chairlift in North America, the **Imperial Express** (12,840ft). This drops you off just below the summit of **Peak 8**, where you can traverse north along the ridge to Whale's Tail and Peak 7 Bowl, or steel yourself for the short, steep and lung-crushing hike to the true summit, where the views and terrain are simply spectacular.

From here you can cruise all the way down to Main St, picking up the 4 O'clock Trail on the way: a descent of 3400ft in elevation, over nearly 4 miles in length.

Access the mountain from the free **BreckConnect Gondola**, which runs from downtown Breckenridge Station (Watson

 EATING IN BRECKENRIDGE: BUDGET PICKS

Amazing Grace: This tiny house is Breck's premier pick to scoff hummus sandwiches, spicy tofu salads, smoothies and other vegetarian fare. *7am-3pm* $

Pho Real: The delicious aroma of star anise wafting down the sidewalk makes this Vietnamese pit stop impossible to pass by. *11am-9pm* $

Semplice: An only-in-Breckenridge miner's-style coffee shack serves breakfast burritos, bagel sandwiches and paninis to go. *7:30am-2pm* $

Oaxacan Bites: The closest thing to a food truck in town is this tiny yellow building near the gondola, dishing out Mexican street food. *9am-9pm* $

WHAT'S IN A NAME?

George Spencer officially founded the town of Breckenridge in November 1859 as a base camp for miners. Allegedly, he originally named the town 'Breckinridge' after the USA's sitting vice president, John C Breckinridge of Kentucky. It was sheer flattery, of course. Spencer wanted a post office; politicians being politicians, he was rewarded with the first post office between the Continental Divide and Salt Lake City, Utah. But when the Civil War broke out in 1861, and the vice president became a brigadier general in the Confederate army, the decidedly pro-Union citizens of Breckinridge decided to change the town's name. An 'i' turned into an 'e,' and it became Breckenridge forever after.

YAYA ERNST/SHUTTERSTOCK

Boreas Pass

Ave) and serves the Nordic Center, Peak 7 and Peak 8; a shuttle serves Peaks 9 and 10 at the southern end of town.

History Tour

Colorful characters

Breckenridge has come a long way since its days as a makeshift 1860s mining camp, but you can still get a sense of some of the characters who once lived here. When touring the town, the first stop should be the **Welcome Center** on Main St, which has a small but excellent free museum.

From here, head over to the **Barney Ford Museum** *(breck history.org; admission $5)*. Ford was an escaped slave who became a prominent entrepreneur and Colorado civil-rights pioneer, and made two stops in Breckenridge, where he ran a 24-hour chopstand serving delicacies such as oysters. He also owned a restaurant and hotel in Denver. The museum is set in his old home, where he lived from 1882 to 1890.

Next is the **Edwin Carter Discovery Center** *(breckhis tory.org; admission $5)*, which introduces the life of a Pike's Peak Gold Rush prospector who first arrived in Breck in 1860.

 EATING IN BRECKENRIDGE: APRÈS-SKI FARE

| **Canteen Tap House:** Why reinvent the wheel? All the ski-town staples are here, from burgers and flatbreads to bison chili. *11am-9:30pm* **$$** | **Giampietro:** NY-style pizza by the slice and other Italian American classics like baked ziti and chicken-parm subs. No reservations. *11am-9pm* **$$** | **Downstairs at Eric's:** Families flock to this basement joint for the brews, burgers and mashed potatoes. Arcade and ski ball too. *11am-11pm* **$$** | **Blue River Bistro:** Inventive selection of salads and sandwiches, from Thai steak to the grilled salmon BLT. Great cocktails. *11am-9:30pm* **$$** |

An original environmentalist, Carter noticed the impact of mining on wildlife early on, documenting genetic deformities that he suspected were linked to leaching toxins. He eventually became a taxidermist to preserve the wildlife he encountered in the area, and his collection grew to some 3300 pieces, which were displayed in his house (now the museum). After he died, the majority of his collection became the original foundation of the Denver Museum of Nature & Science. All museums are closed on Mondays.

Classic Hikes
Quad-busting fun

Summer in Breck brings invigorating hikes to high alpine lakes, waterfalls and a nearby fourteener. The sweat factor is up to you, but one thing's for sure: you won't run out of options. For a gentle introduction, try out **Boreas Pass**. Although you can drive all the way to the top of the pass (11,481ft), we recommend parking at the lot halfway and walking to **Baker's Tank** (6 miles round trip). This is a top spot for golden aspens in fall and an equally beautiful winter snowshoe excursion.

French Gulch, once the main mining area, has some great shorter rambles past old equipment and photogenic structures, like the B&B Mine and Sallie Barber Mine trails (both 3 miles round trip) – the autumn colors here are gorgeous.

Deep-green **Lower Mohawk Lake** (7 miles round trip) is tucked onto a tundra shelf with the ruins of a miner's cabin just below. Upper Lake views are an even more spectacular moonscape.

The 2.8-mile round-trip hike to **McCullough Gulch** is short enough for families, though huffing up the 1000ft of elevation gain will require some perseverance. Luckily you'll have plenty of scenery along the way, including thundering falls and a glacial lake.

Quandary Peak (14,265ft) is one of Colorado's easiest fourteeners. Though you'll see plenty of dogs and children, 'easiest' may be misleading – the summit remains three grueling miles from the trailhead. Note: for both Quandary and McCullough Gulch, you must reserve a parking spot or a shuttle seat in advance *(hikequandary.com; parking $10-55, shuttle $7)*.

Summer Adventures
From alpine slides to mountain biking

Epic Discovery *(breckenridge.com; $110)*, Breck's summer fun park, has a laundry list of made-for-thrills activities: big-air bungee trampoline, climbing walls, ropes course, a zipline tour, three alpine slides and the 2500ft forest coaster. A cheaper option, however, is to ride to the gondola (p197) from town to the base of Peak 8, which is always free.

Like elsewhere in Colorado, mountain biking is huge: while you can haul your bike up the SuperChair, trails on the mountain are limited; you're best off exploring the old gold mining trails or biking to Frisco on the bike path (p203). Bike rentals are easy to find: try **Carvers** *(breckenridgeskishop. com; from $60)*.

ISAK HEARTSTONE

Like every good mountain town, Breck has its own resident troll, though this one doesn't lurk beneath a bridge chomping up wayward children. No, *Isak Heartstone* is a 15ft wooden sculpture who seems to have emerged organically from the forest. Created by Danish artist Thomas Dambo out of recycled materials, this is one of 100 trolls found around the world, in locations as far flung as central China and Chile. It's only after visiting the first 99 that you're given the keys to finding the 100th troll, whose location remains a secret. So if you fancy yourself a troll hunter, be sure to read more on *trollmap.com*. Isak is located near the ice rink south of town.

WINTER FESTIVITIES

Two of Breckenridge's can't-miss festivals include the **Ullr Fest** (mid-December) and the **International Snow Sculpture Championship** (January). The Ullr Fest celebrates the Norse god of snow, with a wild parade and three-day festival featuring a ski and snowboard race, Viking helmet decorating, a bonfire and a ridiculous amount of drinking. The gods must be appeased!

The snow sculpture championship, meanwhile, is held over two weeks. During the first week, artists create their vision from 25-ton blocks of snow (no power tools allowed). During the second week, the sculptures are unveiled and judged by the public. Ephemeral by nature, they are then left to melt in the Colorado sun.

MARILYN D. LAMBERTZ/SHUTTERSTOCK

Panning for Gold

Strike it rich

Just how much work was it to pan for gold? Short answer: a lot. Don't believe us? Give it a try at one of two Breckenridge sites: the **Country Boy Mine** (*countryboymine.com; gold panning $20*) or the **Lomax Placer Mine** (*breckhistory. org; gold panning adult/child $20/10*). The Country Boy Mine puts together a full package of activities, from an actual tour of the mine and panning for gold to a treasure hunt and extreme sledding in winter. To get here, take the Purple Shuttle.

The Lomax Mine was a surface (placer) mine, so its operations were a bit different. In addition to panning for gold, you'll also learn how chemists assayed the valuable claims and check out the actual sluices and flumes used in such mines. This site, which was active in the 1860s, also gives visitors the chance to sniff around a miner's cabin, complete with wood-burning stove, musical instruments, snowshoes, pack saddles and other sundry items needed for survival. On Ski Hill Rd, you can walk here from town. And yes, if you find a gold nugget, it's yours to keep.

DRINKING IN BRECKENRIDGE: OUR PICKS

The Crown: The town's living room might as well be at the Crown, a buzzing cafe and social hub. *8am-6pm Mon-Fri, to 8pm Fri & Sat*	**Clint's Bakery & Coffee House:** Brainy baristas steam up a variety of specialty lattes and mochas. Downstairs bagelry if you're peckish. *7am-9pm*	**Rocky Mountain Underground:** If you're hankering to listen to some live music, then head for RMU's outdoor patio or subterranean bar. *noon-midnight*	**Broken Compass Brewing:** Order a pint of Coconut Porter or Ginger Pale Ale at this pooch-friendly warehouse space on Airport Rd. *11am-11pm*

Dog sledding

Go Dog Sledding

Mush!

Love dogs? Have we got an experience for you. **Good Times Adventures** (*goodtimesadventures.com; dog sledding $180 per person*) is a bona-fide dog-sledding operation, with a team of huskies pulling guests on a 6-mile trail through the Swan River Valley. Be sure to reserve far in advance and dress warmly – you'll be out for a good 1½ hours.

The fun isn't restricted to the winter season either. In summer, you can tour the dog kennels, meet lots of dogs and even help them train as they pull around golf carts to keep in shape.

Good Times also runs two-hour snowmobile tours over 40 miles of groomed trails, topping out on Georgia Pass and the Continental Divide.

BACKCOUNTRY HUT TRIPS

For some, backcountry skiing is what it's all about: pristine snow, all-pervading quiet and the magic of waking up in the wilderness on a winter's day. If you're keen, look into the **Summit Huts Association** (*summithuts.org*), which operates five huts that are accessible by ski and snowshoe, and usually sleep around 20 people. All have amenities such as wood-burning stoves, full kitchens and solar-powered lights; in addition, three have wood-burning saunas. The most popular hut is Francie's Cabin, a great choice for first-timers (though all groups should have at least one experienced, avalanche-trained member). Note that you need to enter a lottery by February 15 to book a hut for the following year.

EATING IN BRECKENRIDGE: DIVINE DINNERS

Radicato: Local chef Matt Vawter's five-course tasting menu takes its inspiration from the Italian Alps. Breck's best dining experience. *4-9:30pm* **$$$**

Breckenridge Distillery: Served in a big-city-cool dining space, the eclectic menu is perfect for pairing with the top-notch cocktails. *2-8pm* **$$$**

Aurum Food & Wine: Octopus carpaccio, curried cauliflower, gochujang fried chicken... dig in and enjoy the small-plate goodness. *4-9:30pm* **$$$**

Hearthstone: A restored 1886 Victorian that whips up creative mountain fare such as braised buffalo ribs and Colorado lamb in a rosemary-parmesan crust. *4-9pm* **$$$**

Beyond Breckenridge

Welcome to Summit County: home to three more ski resorts, a historic mining town and the Dillon Reservoir.

Places

Frisco p202
Dillon p203
Copper Mountain p204
Keystone Resort p205
Arapahoe Basin p206

GETTING AROUND

The Summit Stage, Summit County's handy free bus service, links Frisco, Dillon, Breckenridge, Keystone and Copper Mountain year-round. In winter, the Swan Mountain Flyer route runs from Breckenridge to A-Basin via Frisco and Keystone. Buses are equipped with bike racks in the summer months. **Fresh Tracks** *(freshtrackstransport ation.com; from $100)* and the **Summit Express** *(summit express.com; from $95)* run from DIA to various locations in Summit County.

The aptly named Summit County is close enough to Denver for a day trip but far enough away to feel like you've truly escaped the Front Range sprawl. In summer, cyclists enjoy the miles of paved bike paths that connect the major towns, while hikers scale the peaks in high country. Winter, of course, is all about the snow. Copper, A-Basin and Keystone each have their unique personalities, and a fantastic free shuttle system connects them all with Breckenridge. The historic town of Frisco, right off I-70, is at the center of it all, ringed by peaks and offering convenient access to many of Colorado's most famous resorts.

Frisco

TIME FROM BRECKENRIDGE: **20 MINS**

Geek out on cabin construction

Unusual for Summit County, the turn-of-the-century mining town of Frisco stands alone, with nary a ski run in sight. It makes for a great base, however, and the six-block stretch of historic Main St is where you'll find almost everything you could need. There are plenty of cute cafes and good restaurants, and it dead-ends at the scenic Dillon Reservoir, where you'll find a small **marina** *(townoffrisco.com; boat rentals from $50)*.

Frisco's top billing goes to the **Historic Park** *(free)*. Set on the site of the original town saloon erected 1889, which was later converted into the town's second school in 1901, this museum features a number of historical displays, including one on the Ute nation, a diorama of the original Ten Mile Canyon railroad that fed and connected the mining camps of Leadville and Frisco, and a historic map of Colorado (c 1873).

The main attractions, however, are the half-dozen old mining cabins scattered out back. Aficionados of log-construction techniques will appreciate the double-dovetail joints at the **Dills Ranch House** (c 1890) and the **Bailey House** (c 1895). Inside the **Trappers Cabin**, visitors will find the kind of pelts that once sustained the area's meager economy prior to mining. Other prize specimens include the Frisco jail and the town chapel, which screens a 15-minute documentary video. It's closed on Mondays.

Cycle Summit County

Frisco is Summit County's hub for over 50 miles of fabulous paved **bike paths** (*summitbiking.org*). From the Frisco Marina you can wrap most of the way around the reservoir to Dillon (7.5 miles), a great family trip with minimal elevation gain, and then on to Keystone (13.5 miles, 1200ft elevation gain) – or pedal around the other side and back to Breckenridge (9.5 miles, 500ft elevation gain).

Alternatively, you can head off in the other direction to climb Vail Pass (12 miles, 1550ft elevation gain) and roll all the way down to Vail. If you rent a bike from Frisco's **Pioneer Sports** (*pioneersportscolorado.com; half-day bike/e-bike $30/65*), they'll throw in a complimentary shuttle to the top of Vail Pass.

Remember that you can take bikes on Summit Stage buses if you run out of steam or only want to go one way.

Peak-bagging in the Tenmile Range

A **trail** runs straight out of Frisco, taking you right up to the beginning of the Tenmile Range. You can make this hike as short or long as you like, but either way get ready to sweat. It's 1.5 miles up to the ridge, where the trail forks; head right (north) to **Mt Royal** (10,052ft) for the easy summit.

Otherwise, opt for the tougher workout and turn left (south) to continue up the ridge to **Peak One** (12,805ft), which is 3.7 miles from the trailhead located at the west end of 2nd Ave. **Tenmile Peak** (12,933ft) is another 0.6 miles from here, but be prepared for some continuous class 3 scrambling along the ridge.

Dillon

 TIME FROM BRECKENRIDGE: **30 MINS**

Summit County sailing

In 1961 Denver finally made good on its turn-of-the-century plans to create a **reservoir** for the city. The old townsite of Dillon disappeared beneath the rising waters, and a new Summit County playground came into being. Driving down I-70, you can't miss it: a glittering expanse of blue backed by snowy peaks, with 27 miles of largely undeveloped shoreline.

In summer, anyone with a hankering to get out on the water can rent an SUP, kayak, sailboat or pontoon from one of two marinas: the main **Dillon marina** (*dillonmarina.com; boat rentals from $60*) or the smaller one in Frisco. An outdoor amphitheater is the setting for big-name concerts in the evenings, and a gorgeous paved bike path circles the water for superb Summit County views.

ACCLIMATIZATION

Denver may be a mile high, but Summit County is nearly 2 miles high. Even if you're not coming from sea level, let that sink in for a second. No matter how good a skier, hiker or cyclist you are, and no matter how much you work out, nothing really prepares your body for the shock of oxygen-thin air.

There are a few things you can do to minimize the impact, however. Drink plenty of water so that your body adapts to Colorado's low humidity. Give yourself time to acclimatize before hiking a fourteener or launching yourself down a double-black run. Finally, remember that the ultraviolet rays are much stronger up here: bring sunscreen, sunglasses and brimmed hat.

EATING IN FRISCO: ON MAIN ST

Butterhorn Bakery & Cafe: Bright pastel-brushed diner, always packed for breakfast and lunch. Vegan options and fresh-baked pastries. *7:30am-2:30pm* $$

Lost Cajun: A festive Louisiana soundtrack greets diners here. Tasty offerings include jambalaya, gumbo and seriously good lobster bisque. *11am-8pm* $$

Ein Prosit: It's bottoms up at Frisco's welcoming Bavarian beer hall, serving elk and bison bratwurst and pretzels. *11am-10pm* $

Greco's: Build your own pizzas and classic pasta dishes, plus cannoli and cheesecake to top off the night. *4-9pm Mon-Fri, from noon Sat & Sun* $$

OUTLETS AT SILVERTHORNE

Located just off I-70 at exit 205 are three **shopping villages** of designer-brand stores with discount prices. Brands include Calvin Klein, Levi's, Gap, Le Creuset and dozens of others. Not only is there a shuttle that runs between the villages (free), there are also shuttles here from Vail (Summit Express), Copper Mountain and Breckenridge (Summit Stage). The Blue River runs right next to the outlets, so if your group is of a divided mind when it comes to shopping, note that fly-fishing is always a possibility.

And if you left some essential piece of outdoor gear at home, REI is right on the other side of the interstate.

And if you're looking to pitch a tent? There are several campgrounds tucked between the forest and the shoreline, all connected to a network of hiking and mountain bike trails. Winter brings ice fishing and cross-country skiing. The **Frisco Nordic Center** *(townoffrisco.com; $30)* has 25 miles of cross-country ski trails on the Dillon Reservoir peninsula, on the south side of the reservoir. A **tubing hill** ($40 per hour) is also located here and is a good diversion for kids.

Note that swimming is prohibited – the water is too cold.

Copper Mountain   TIME FROM BRECKENRIDGE: 30 MINS 🚗

Ski like a local

The base village may be a bit too planned for some, but even the staunchest critics wouldn't thumb their noses at **Copper Mountain** *(coppercolorado.com; adult/child day pass $224/134)* itself. Rising 2738ft up to the 12,441ft summit, Copper has 2538 acres of terrain, carved with 157 trails equally divided for beginner, intermediate, advanced and expert skiers. No chichi Vail attitude here – Copper takes you back to skiing's play-hard roots, and indeed, perks like free parking make it a favorite with locals. Bonus: lift tickets are $99 on Thursdays.

It's an easy mountain to navigate – all levels have their own slice of paradise served by separate lifts, meaning beginners are unlikely to be run over by experts at the bottom of the mountain (and vice versa). Shredders won't want to miss the famous Woodward terrain parks: there are 10 in all, running from beginner to the pro-level Central Park. Several of the parks were developed in partnership with Olympic gold medalists.

There are plenty of other activities here as well, including 15 miles of free cross-country and snowshoe trails, a tubing hill, and, in summer, a bike park, golf course and adventure zone.

Freestyling at the Barn

Freestylers who want to learn their way around a terrain park should head straight to the **Woodward Barn** *(drop-in session $59)*, a way-cool 19,400-sq-ft playground. It's a year-round snowboard, ski, skate and BMX training camp complete with trampolines, skate parks, jumps and, thankfully, foam pits. It serves all levels of athlete, from beginners to the young and sponsored. The mandatory intro class grants you access to drop-in sessions.

During summer the Barn offers week-long day and overnight training camps, while on the mountain are two terrain parks made with leftover snow.

EATING IN FRISCO: OFF HWY 9

Pure Kitchen: Eclectic global offerings, from cauliflower hummus and zoodles to bahn mi sandwiches and flatbreads. *11am-9pm* **$$**

Bird Craft: Asian-inspired fried chicken, poke bowls and papaya salad from the folks at Outer Range Brewing. *11am-8pm* **$$**

China Szechuan: It's definitely not Chengdu, but you can still get your Sichuan peppercorn fix at this popular Chinese eatery. *11:30am-9pm* **$$**

Cielo Oaxaca: Mole enchiladas, street tacos and *quesabirria* (fried taco with stewed meat) are favorites at this Summit County Mexican. *10am-10pm* **$$**

Copper Mountain

Keystone Resort
TIME FROM BRECKENRIDGE: **25 MINS**

Summit's best family resort

Keystone (*keystoneresort.com; adult/child day pass $275/179*) is known as a kid-friendly ski destination: it's got plenty of groomed greenies and blues, plus an enormous snow fort, ice rink and off-slope cookie decorating. Because, let's admit it: most kids don't want to ski all day, every day. When they are on the slopes, however, be sure to hit Schoolmarm, an awesome 3-mile cruise that drops 2339ft, but keeps it wide open so there's plenty of space to practice those turns.

If you're not a newbie, don't be fooled into thinking that all the terrain here is tame – with 3149 skiable acres and a 3128ft vertical drop, it's unlikely you'll get bored, regardless of your ability. There are three main mountains: **Dercum** (front side), the **Outpost** and the **Outback**; it's also the only Summit County resort to offer night skiing. A new lift-served alpine area, the **Bergman Bowl**, offers beginner and intermediate skiers the opportunity to get above tree line. The lift also gives experts access to more remote hike-to terrain.

CLIMAX, COLORADO

The one-time site of the nation's highest post office and railway station is the now defunct town of Climax, sitting atop Fremont Pass (Hwy 91) at 11,342ft. Unlike the other mining towns in the area, it was neither gold nor silver that ushered Climax into existence – no, it was element 42, otherwise known as molybdenum. Used to strengthen steel, exports of molybdenum took off during WWI (German tanks) and then again in the 1930s, when Germany, Japan and the Soviet Union were Climax's three biggest customers. Unsurprisingly, the US government subsequently designated Climax Mine the nation's most important mine in the following decade. Although the town is long gone, the mine still operates today, but is off-limits to visitors.

EATING IN DILLON & SILVERTHORNE: OUR PICKS

Dillon Dam Brewery: One of Summit County's best, with dishes like duck confit over wild mushroom risotto and onion-aioli lamb burger. *11:30am-9pm* **$$**

Sauce on the Blue: Sophisticated, industrial-chic Italian backing onto the Blue River. Dishes come in individual and family sizes. *11:30am-9pm* **$$$**

Bluebird Market: Great new food hall with choices that range from crepes to pizza to empanadas. *7am-8pm Mon-Fri, to 10pm Sat & Sun* **$$**

Mint: Built in 1862, this still-dark, still-dusty saloon has tons of life and character, and is known for its grill-your-own steaks. *5-9pm* **$$$**

AVALANCHE

For serious skiers and snowboarders, the lure of fresh powder and untracked backcountry terrain is a powerful temptation, a chance to experience that heady rush of dopamine that momentarily overrides the brain's circuitry. Unfortunately, the risks associated with backcountry skiing are hardly inconsequential – every year in Colorado, roughly 20 people are caught in avalanches and seven of them die.

While it's convenient to believe that most avalanche victims are naive and unprepared, Colorado's unstable snowpack does not discriminate. If you're going out of bounds, you need to know how to minimize risk: get trained, carry the necessary equipment and check the daily avalanche forecasts from the **Colorado Avalanche Information Center** *(avalanche.state. co.us)*.

JEFFREY WERTHEIM/SHUTTERSTOCK

Arapahoe Basin

Arapahoe Basin

TIME FROM BRECKENRIDGE: **30 MINS**

Extreme skiing

You won't catch any Texans in ten-gallon hats or fur-clad ladies from the Upper West Side at **Arapahoe Basin** *(arapahoe basin.com; adult/teen $200/120)*. Offering up some of North America's highest (13,050ft) and most extreme in-bounds terrain, this is a resort (we use the term loosely) that caters to hardcore riders only. Chutes, cliffs and heart-in-your-throat steeps are the draw, but A-Basin is also beloved for its goofy, no-frills vibe. Want to ski dressed up like a giant banana? Want to ski naked? This is your spot.

The back bowl, known as **Montezuma**, is where you'll find two dozen or so hair-raising intermediate-to-expert runs. The Jump is the biggest, baddest run on Montezuma, beginning with a 10ft drop off the mountain's ledge onto a steep 35-degree slope. The **East Wall** (summit 13,050ft), which includes the hike-to Shit for Brains, is A-Basin's other legendary backcountry-style area. Or just keep it simple and do laps on one of Colorado's most famous lifts, the **Pallavicini** (or Pali), which accesses some of the steepest inbounds terrain in the state.

Superlative chasers lunch at **Il Rifugio** – located at 12,456ft, this is the highest restaurant in North America. When temps warm up enough, large tailgate cookouts and parties take over the Beach (the front-row of the parking lot). It's the last resort standing in spring, often staying open into June.

A **via ferrata** *(from $150)* offers in-shape hikers the chance to experience alpine exposure once the snow melts. Alternatively, give the high-altitude disc golf course a whirl.

Vail

SKIING | DINING | HORSEBACK RIDING

Standing on the edge of the Sun Up Bowl on a brisk February morning, the sun glinting off icy peaks in the distance and miles of untracked powder spread out beneath you – and knowing that it goes on and on and on, all the way to Outer Mongolia – this is the stuff that Colorado dreams are made of. Long easy groomers, kids' adventure playgrounds, glades, cliffs, chutes, terrain parks, wide-open bowls and backcountry-esque delights – whatever type of riding you do, you're bound to find it here.

Factor in Vail's gourmet offerings, well-coiffed clientele and powder-fueled staff and you have an adrenaline-addled yuppie utopia. Indeed, stress does not cling to the bones long here...until you get the bill. And even then you'll have had such a good time that the memories will last far longer than that icy splash of buyer's remorse.

Ski the Back Bowls

Blue-sky bliss

Vail Mountain (*vail.com; adult/child day pass $319/220*) is hands-down one of the best ski resorts in the world, with 5317 skiable acres, 278 trails and, ahem, some of the highest lift-ticket prices on the continent.

You can subdivide the mountain into three main zones: the front side, the back bowls and Blue Sky Basin. Distances are vast, and you will spend a lot of time getting from one place to another, so if you have a specific destination in mind, plan carefully.

GETTING AROUND

The base areas are traffic-free; drivers must park at the Vail Village or Lionshead parking garages (*$30 to $40 in winter*).

The Eagle County Regional Airport is 35 miles west of Vail. The **Epic Mountain Express** (*epicmountainexpress. com*) shuttle runs from Denver airport (up to $169) and Eagle County Airport ($49). **Summit Express** (*summitexpress.com*) runs a shuttle between Summit County and Vail ($50).

Vail Transit loops through all the Vail resort areas. Most buses have bike and ski racks; all are free. Eagle County buses offer transport to Beaver Creek, Minturn and Leadville.

EATING IN VAIL: UPMARKET CASUAL

Mountain Standard: A lovely riverside setting. Raw bar, salads and entrees from the grill or rotisserie. *11:30am-9pm* **$$$**

Up the Creek: Creekside patio with good lunchtime deals (turkey and brie sandwich) and hearty farm-to-plate dinners. *11am-10pm* **$$$**

Chasing Rabbits: *Alice in Wonderland*–themed entertainment venue has it all, from upscale meals to concerts to dance club. *5-10pm Tue-Sat* **$$$**

La Nonna: Italian chef Simone Reatti brings the Dolomites to Colorado, from house-made gnocchetti to wild boar ragu. *5-9pm Mon-Sat* **$$$**

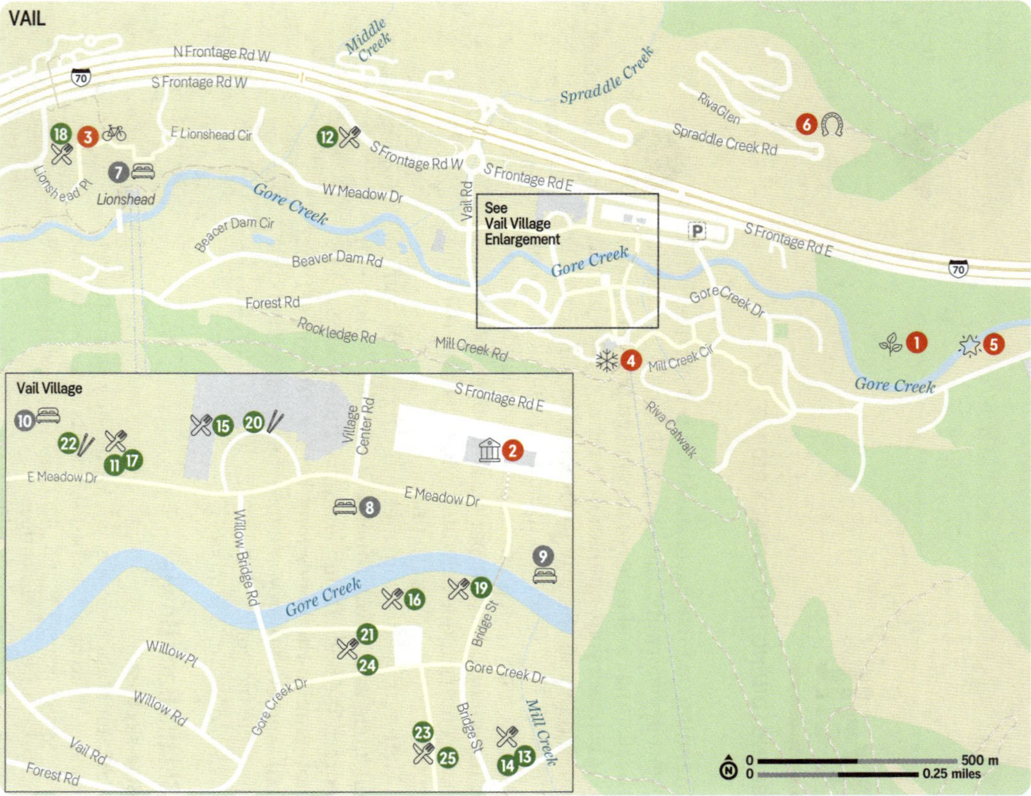
VAIL
N Frontage Rd W
S Frontage Rd W
Middle Creek
Spraddle Creek
RivaGlen
Spraddle Creek Rd
E Lionshead Cir
S Frontage Rd W
S Frontage Rd E
Lionshead Pl
Lionshead
Gore Creek
W Meadow Dr
Vail Rd
See Vail Village Enlargement
Beaver Dam Cir
Beaver Dam Rd
Forest Rd
Rockledge Rd
Mill Creek Rd
Mill Creek Cir
Gore Creek Dr
Riva Catwalk
70
P
Vail Village
S Frontage Rd E
Village Center Rd
E Meadow Dr
Willow Bridge Rd
Willow Pl
Willow Rd
Vail Rd
Forest Rd
Gore Creek Dr
Bridge St
Mill Creek
500 m
0.25 miles

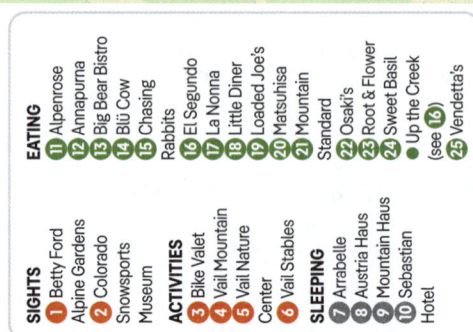

SIGHTS
1 Betty Ford Alpine Gardens
2 Colorado Snowsports Museum

ACTIVITIES
3 Bike Valet
4 Vail Mountain
5 Vail Nature Center
6 Vail Stables

SLEEPING
7 Arrabelle
8 Austria Haus
9 Mountain Haus
10 Sebastian Hotel

EATING
11 Alpenrose
12 Annapurna
13 Big Bear Bistro
14 Blü Cow
15 Chasing Rabbits
16 El Segundo
17 La Nonna
18 Little Diner
19 Loaded Joe's
20 Matsuhisa
21 Mountain Standard
22 Osaki's
23 Root & Flower
24 Sweet Basil
● Up the Creek (see 16)
25 Vendetta's

TOP TIP

With 32 lifts in operation it can be tough to find your way around, so spend some time studying the trail map. The two high-speed gondolas will get you out of the base areas: Gondola One (heated and wi-fi-enabled) serves Vail Village; Eagle Bahn serves Lionshead.

Beginners should stick to the front side, where most of the runs are groomed and the north-facing slopes offer good snow cover (particularly up top), even on sunny spring days.

Intermediate skiers have plenty of options, including the Northwoods and the Game Creek Bowl on the front side. But if you're itching to experience the massive back bowls, try out Poppyfields in the China Bowl – it's groomed and will get you down to the bottom safely.

For experts, meanwhile, there is simply no limit to where you can go back here. The seven legendary bowls are Sun Down, Sun Up, China, Siberia, Teacup and Inner and Outer Mongolia. The wide-open, spruce-dotted slopes here include favorites like Over Yonder (Sun Up), Forever (Sun Down) and Bolshoi Ballroom (Siberia).

Blue Sky Basin is the furthest-flung destination: this is an all-day trip (pack a lunch). Although there are a few blue runs here, because of the distance and the lack of amenities, this is an area best saved for the experts. In bad weather and flat light, skiing the back bowls can verge on impossible – stick to the tree runs on the front side.

Ride the Minturn Mile

Don't get lost

If you're itching to head off-piste, consider the **Minturn Mile**. One of the most famous out-of-bounds ski runs in the US, it's accessible from the top of chair 7 in the Game Creek Bowl.

At the top of the turn on Lost Boy, stay left and hike about 15 minutes up to Ptarmigan Ridge. Here you can take the access gate and begin a descent of 3 miles (roughly one hour) to the town of Minturn. Advanced skills are a must as you'll encounter a wide range of terrain, from deep powder to ice, slush, dirt, logs and rocks. Around midway you'll find the Beaver Ponds, which may require removing your skis or board, before hitting the Luge, a twisty old fire road that races the rest of the way.

Remember you'll be skiing beyond the resort boundaries – it is *not* patrolled. If you get lost or injured, you'll be on your own, and if you require rescue it will come at considerable expense. It's imperative that you ski with someone who has prior knowledge of the terrain and route, and be sure to have proper gear, equipment and an updated report on conditions. It is, by all accounts, a magnificent experience and requires a toast at the Minturn Saloon (p214) upon arrival.

THE VAIL DREAM

Tenth Mountain Division veteran Peter Seibert and his friend Earl Eaton climbed Vail Mountain in the winter of 1957. After one long look at those luscious back bowls, the pair knew they'd struck gold. At the time, the mountain was owned by the Forest Service and local ranchers. Seibert and Eaton recruited a series of investors and lawyers, eventually got a permit from the Forest Service and convinced nearly all of the local ranchers to sell. Much of the construction budget was raised by convincing investors to chip in $10,000 for a condo unit and a lifetime season pass. Finally, on December 15, 1962, the dream came alive. The cost of a lift ticket? $5 for nine runs.

EATING IN VAIL: ON A BUDGET

Big Bear Bistro: An affordable fave in Vail Village. Gourmet coffee, breakfast burritos and some damn good sandwiches at lunch. *8am-3pm* $

Blü Cow: Get the famous Swiss hot dog here – one pork brat and one veal brat, served with curry mustard on a baguette. *11am-11pm Mon-Sat, to 6pm Sun* $

Loaded Joe's: This low-key cafe serves pulled-pork breakfast burritos and espressos, sandwiches and smoothies, and beer and wine too. *7am-2am* $

Vendetta's: Throwback pizza joint with a great hidden terrace. It does pasta dishes too, but it's the pizza by the slice that keeps it affordable. *11am-midnight* $

THE 10TH MOUNTAIN DIVISION

Spend any amount of time in Vail or Aspen, and you'll be sure to hear about the 10th Mountain Division. You might even glimpse a photo of a WWII soldier, dressed in his trademark white parka and sunglasses, with skis slung over a shoulder, marching through Camp Hale (p215). But where did the idea of training soldiers on skis – which seems like a fanciful way to combat German tanks – come from? In fact the idea caught on in 1939, when small deployments of fast-moving Finnish skiers, dressed in white, were able to thwart the armored Soviet invasion of Finland using guerilla tactics. When the 10th Mountain Division was finally deployed in WWII, they fought primarily in Italy's Apennine mountains, helping Allied forces push through Germany's Gothic Line.

ROSEMARY WOLLER/SHUTTERSTOCK

Hiking outside Vail

For Free

Save a buck

Vail will always be an expensive destination, but you don't *have* to max out your credit card. The **Nature Center** *(walk ingmountains.org)* offers guided tours all summer long, from full-day backcountry hikes to more family-oriented activities. Free creekside nature tours run on Sundays; other popular kids activities include wildflower walks and evening trips to the beaver pond or stargazing with s'mores. There are also four short interpretive trails open to the public.

Another hiking option is the 2-mile walk to the 60ft **Booth Falls**, which follows USFS Trail 1885 into the Eagles Nest Wilderness Area. Continue beyond the falls to encounter meadows filled with wildflowers and views of the Gore Range. If you've got the energy, keep going to Booth Lake, 4.1 miles from the trailhead, with an elevation gain of about 3000ft.

 EATING IN VAIL: BEST MIDRANGE

The Little Diner: The most popular place for a made-from-scratch breakfast is in Lionshead. No reservations. *7am-2pm* **$$**

Root & Flower: Celebrate in style with wine and cocktails, paired with cheese and salumi plates at Vail's most elegant happy hour. *4pm-midnight* **$$**

Annapurna: Need a change from the usual ski resort suspects? This Nepalese restaurant in Lionshead is a winner. *noon-2:30pm & 4:30-9pm Wed-Mon* **$$**

El Segundo: Damn, it feels good to be enjoying margaritas, fish tacos and a lovely patio overlooking Gore Creek. *11:30am-9pm* **$$**

Betty Ford Alpine Gardens *(bettyfordalpinegardens.org)* is the highest botanical gardens in the US. Stop by for a soothing stroll past rock gardens, native alpine plants and collected species from as far as the Himalayas. Look out for activities, like yoga, butterfly launches and plant sales.

Humble but informative, the **Colorado Snowsports Museum** *(snowsportsmuseum.org)* unveils the connection between Vail's history and the 10th Mountain Division, as well as hilarious fashions from the past.

Summer Adventures

Climb to the Eagle's Nest

All the usual suspects set up shop in the summer, including cycling, horseback riding, climbing and ziplining.

Bearcat Stables *(bearcatstables.com; from $80)* and **Vail Stables** *(vailstables.com; from $165)* run one- to three-hour horseback rides, as well as longer trips like a four-day ride to Aspen. **Gore Creek Fly Fisherman** *(gorecreekflyfisherman. com; from $345)* runs both wading and float trips.

Zip Adventures *(zipadventures.com; $170)* runs six zipline tours over Alkali Canyon – followed by a cliff jump – with plenty of time to work on your primal scream. Easy and exhilarating, the 2½-hour romp is worth the splurge.

Apex Mountain School *(apexmountainschool.com; $200-450)* and **Paragon Guides** *(paragonguides.com; $200-450)* run guided climbing and mountaineering trips in both summer and winter, while **Bike Valet***(bikevalet.com; rentals from $40)* rents cycles and runs a shuttle up to Vail Pass for the easy, scenic cruise back down.

Vail's summer amusement park, **Epic Discovery** *(vail.com; from $119)*, gets so-so reviews, though the **gondola ride** *(adult/ child $59/39)* into the high country will always be impressive. But better still is a tandem flight with **Vail Valley Paragliding** *(vailvalleyparagliding.com; from $235)*.

HOMETOWN HEROES

Vail's status as a top ski resort is more than just marketing hype: it has the athletes to back up the claims. Two of the most famous hometown skiers to take home the gold include **Lindsey Vonn** (four-time World Cup champion, downhill gold medal in the 2010 Olympics) and **Mikaela Shiffrin** (five-time World Cup Champion, slalom and giant slalom gold medals in the 2014 and 2018 Olympics). Both women trained at the Ski and Snowboard Club, an elite racing program that has been based on Vail Mountain since 1962. If you'd like to see where the stars of tomorrow ski, head over to the Riva Bahn lift on the Front Side, which will take you up to Golden Peak, with 1700 vertical feet of racing terrain.

 EATING IN VAIL: RESORT ICONS

Sweet Basil: Vail's most celebrated restaurant serves excellent seasonal, eclectic new American fare. *noon-3pm & 5-9pm Wed-Sun, 5-9pm Mon & Tue* **$$$**	**Alpenrose:** For the full Alpine experience, get your pretzels, rösti and fondue at this Swiss German–themed restaurant. *11:30am-10pm* **$$$**	**Osaki's:** It might look like a hole in the wall, but this is Vail's most intimate and highly lauded sushi temple, with fresh fish from Japan. *5:30-9pm Tue-Sun* **$$$**	**Matsuhisa:** Legendary chef Nobu Matsuhisa has upped Vail's culinary standards with this modern, airy space in the Solaris complex. *5-9:30pm* **$$$**

DRIVE THE TOP OF THE ROCKIES SCENIC BYWAY

Drive from Vail to Aspen on this gorgeous high-alpine drive, passing the state's highest peaks and the dizzying Independence Pass.

START	END	LENGTH
Vail	Aspen	95 miles; 2½ hours

Vail's tumbling ski slopes are just a few miles east of Hwy 24, the principal ribbon of asphalt on this road trip. After exiting I-70, head south through **①** **Minturn**, a charming 1887 railroad town in the Eagle River Valley. Wind through groves of aspens and pines, with high rocky bluffs above, as the first glimpse of **Notch Mountain** (13,243ft) appears on the right. Passing the Holy Cross Wilderness on your right takes you to the single-span picturesque **②** **Red Cliff Bridge**, arching magnificently over the Eagle River. Pay homage to the 10th Mountain Division at **③** **Camp Hale National Monument**, pausing to see where the soldiers on skis used to train.

In another 6 miles you'll cross **④** **Tennessee Pass** (10,424ft) and the Continental Divide; once on the other side, Mt Massive, the state's second-highest peak, looms supreme. As you approach the former mining town of **⑤** **Leadville**, you'll see the state's highest peak, Mt Elbert, dominating the horizon south of Mt Massive. Gawp at the dilapidated cabins and abandoned mining shafts and stop for a coffee or meal in this quirky high-altitude town. South of Leadville, hang a right on Hwy 82 and head to **⑥** **Twin Lakes**, the largest glacial lakes in the state. From here, begin the serpentine climb up **⑦** **Independence Pass** (12,095ft; open June through October) and then begin the slow descent into Aspen.

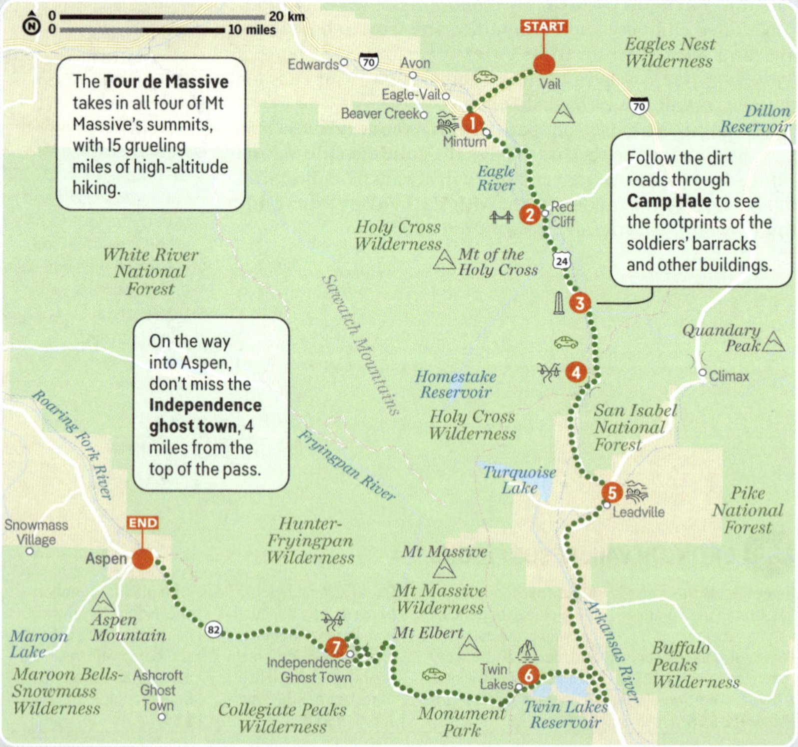

Map:

0 — 20 km
0 — 10 miles

START — Vail

Eagles Nest Wilderness

Edwards · Avon
Eagle-Vail
Beaver Creek · Minturn ①

The **Tour de Massive** takes in all four of Mt Massive's summits, with 15 grueling miles of high-altitude hiking.

Eagle River

Dillon Reservoir

Follow the dirt roads through **Camp Hale** to see the footprints of the soldiers' barracks and other buildings.

Holy Cross Wilderness
Mt of the Holy Cross
Red Cliff ②

24

③

White River National Forest

Quandary Peak
Climax

④
Homestake Reservoir
Holy Cross Wilderness

San Isabel National Forest

On the way into Aspen, don't miss the **Independence ghost town**, 4 miles from the top of the pass.

Sawatch Mountains

Turquoise Lake

Pike National Forest

⑤ Leadville

Roaring Fork River

END
Snowmass Village
Aspen

Hunter-Fryingpan Wilderness

Fryingpan River

Mt Massive

Mt Massive Wilderness

Arkansas River

Buffalo Peaks Wilderness

Maroon Lake
Aspen Mountain

82

Independence Ghost Town ⑦

Maroon Bells-Snowmass Wilderness
Ashcroft Ghost Town

Collegiate Peaks Wilderness

Mt Elbert

Twin Lakes ⑥

Monument Park

Twin Lakes Reservoir

Beyond Vail

Backcountry ski runs, 19th-century railroad towns, CIA training grounds and Colorado's highest summits await in the mountains beyond Vail.

It's refreshing how many quirky little mountain towns surround a resort that does its best to cater to the 1%. Follow the Top of the Rockies Scenic Byway south along Hwy 24 and you'll pass Minturn and Red Cliff, the gateways to the Holy Cross Wilderness Area, where you'll find some of the most spectacular hiking in the area.

Further along is Leadville, a creaky old mining town known for adventure in the surrounding hills. You can climb the two tallest peaks in Colorado, run a 100-mile race, mountain bike for 24 hours straight, cross-country ski to a gourmet meal or simply continue driving on to Aspen. Well, what are you waiting for?

Shrine Pass

TIME FROM VAIL: **30 MINS** 🚗

Backcountry fun, all year round

Halfway between Copper Mountain and Vail is **Shrine Pass** (11,178ft), accessed via an 11.5-mile dirt road/ski trail off of I-70. In summer, this is a very popular multiuse trail: you can drive it, bike it (three to four hours), use an ATV and, of course, go hiking – Shrine Mountain Trail is 4.2 miles round trip; the trailhead is 2.25 miles up the road. From Julia's Deck (Mile 3.75) you have good views of Mt of the Holy Cross. Biking is the most interesting option because once you hump the pass (2.5 miles in), it's all downhill to Red Cliff on the other side. If you have two cars you can set up a shuttle; otherwise sign up for a bike tour with Bike Valet (p211) in Vail.

In winter this area is known as the **Vail Pass Recreation Area**. It's used by both snowmobilers and backcountry skiers and boarders (often teaming together for the uphills), but with 55,000 acres of wilderness you should be able to find some seclusion. The Forest Service grooms 50 miles of trails back here, allowing you to get between Shrine Pass, Red Cliff and Camp Hale. Additionally, there are four huts in the area (Shrine Mountain, Fowler, Jackal and Janet's Cabin) for overnight trips. Avalanche gear and training are a must. If you've got the cash, **Vail Powder Guides** (*vailpowderguides.com; $950*) runs a full day of snowcat skiing.

GETTING AROUND

Hwy 24 runs 37 miles south from Vail to Leadville. From Leadville it's another 15 miles south to Hwy 82 and Independence Pass.

Eagle County Regional Transportation Authority offers affordable transport to Eagle County Airport, Beaver Creek, Minturn and even Leadville. Buses depart from the Vail Transportation Center.

MT OF THE HOLY CROSS

Mount of the Holy Cross (14,011ft) first caught the nation's attention in 1873, when William Henry Jackson photographed the mountain on the Hayden Expedition. A prominent 1400ft snowfield on the mountain's northeast face forms a giant cross in spring, which eventually melts into the Bowl of Tears Lake beneath.

Jackson's photography, along with Thomas Moran's paintings of the snow cross, came to symbolize the Colorado wilderness for millions of 19th-century Americans. Pilgrimages to view the cross led to the construction of a shelter at the summit of Notch Mountain in 1924. Although easier than Mt of the Holy Cross, Notch Mountain is still a strenuous climb, especially considering the clothing and footwear of the day.

To get here, take the Vail Pass exit (190) off I-70. The Minturn ranger office has maps and trail descriptions for the area – pick up a map before you go, as it's quite likely you'll get lost without one.

Beaver Creek

TIME FROM VAIL: **20 MINS**

Ski with the VIPs

Breach the regal gates in Avon and you'll emerge onto a private mountain road skirting a picturesque golf course as it climbs to the foot of a truly spectacular ski mountain. **Beaver Creek** *(beavercreek.com; adult/child day pass $319/220)* feels like one of those delicious secrets shared among the rich kids, and it is indeed a privilege to ski here.

Today, the perfectly maintained grounds and neo-Tyrolean buildings lend a certain looming grandeur, as do names like the Park Hyatt, set in the main village, and Ritz Carlton, in nearby Bachelor Gulch. Beaver Creek is a mellower, more conservative place than Vail and typically an older scene. It's the kind of destination where grandparents bring the whole family to enjoy a slew of all-natural adventures.

It's no secret: winter rules. The mountain offers a 4040ft vertical rise serviced by 24 lifts, with 167 trails through aspen forest and a wide variety of ski terrain.

Beginners like it in Beaver Creek because the mountain's easy runs are at the top, so they can enjoy the same spectacular views as the more advanced folks. Intermediate skiers have less choice, but the Coyote Glades and blue-cruiser Arrowhead Mountain are both good choices, as are Redtail and Harrier on the main mountain.

Experts should head to the double black diamonds at Royal Elk Glades and Bald Eagle off the Grouse Mountain Express lift: the runs are every bit as challenging as anything at Vail. Golden Eagle – the site of the Birds of Prey Men's World Cup Downhill course – gives you the chance to try out a competition-class downhill run, while the Stone Creek Chutes spike the adrenaline.

The posh reputation keeps away many, but that just means more powder for you.

Tennessee Pass

TIME FROM VAIL: **45 MINS**

Nordic skiing and winter glamping

Tennessee Pass (10,424ft) is just one pass among many in central Colorado, and while it may not be as glamorous as its

EATING IN MINTURN & RED CLIFF: OUR PICKS

Kirby Cosmo's: Carolina BBQ, located at the south end of town. Stalwarts include pulled-pork sandwiches, jalapeño poppers and short ribs. *11:30am-8:30pm* **$**

Rocky Mountain Taco: It's all about the tortillas here – dig into Yo Soy Hippy, White Chick and carne asada goodness at this ultra-popular locale. *11-9pm* **$**

Minturn Saloon: Sit by the crackling fireplace and knock back margaritas and bowls of green chile at this historic après-ski hangout. *5-9pm Tue-Sat* **$$$**

Mango's: Hidden in off-the-grid Red Cliff, 9 miles south of Minturn, is this three-story mountain pub famous for its fish tacos. *11am-8pm Wed-Sun* **$$**

ADAM LORBER/SHUTTERSTOCK

Beaver Creek

brethren, it actually has loads more to do. You'll know you've arrived when you spot the entrance to the ski areas: the down-hill resort is the small but affordable **Ski Cooper** (*skicooper.com; adult/child day pass $110/35*), which is a great place to learn the basics.

The **Nordic Center** (*tennesseepass.com; adult/child $25/18*), meanwhile, has 15 miles of groomed trails that leave from the base of Ski Cooper, and which are open to cross-country skiers and snowshoers. The highlight is the 1-mile haul to everyone's favorite gourmet yurt: the Tennessee Pass Cookhouse (p216).

And if you've always dreamt of nestling up in a snowy won-derland, check out the **Tennessee Pass Sleep Yurts**. With a woodburning stove, kitchenette and even luggage delivery and room service, this is a great way to enjoy all the magic of a quiet winter night without having to wake up in a snow cave with frostbitten toes. In summer, this is an easy place to hop on the Continental Divide Trail for some hiking.

Leadville

TIME FROM VAIL: **45 MINS** 🚗

Mining tour

Originally known as Cloud City, **Leadville** (elevation 10,152ft) was once Colorado's second-largest city and a quintessential Wild West town, where fortunes were made and lost over-night, swindlers ruled the roost and Doc Holliday got into a shootout with the law and won.

CAMP HALE NATIONAL MONUMENT

Established in 1942, **Camp Hale** was created specifically for the purpose of training the 10th Mountain Division, the Army's only battalion on skis. At its height during WWII, there were over 1000 buildings and some 15,000 soldiers housed in the meadow here, 6 miles north of Tennessee Pass.

After the war Camp Hale was decommissioned, only to be brought back to life in 1958, this time by the CIA. Over the next six years, CIA agents trained foreign freedom fighters in guerrilla warfare. In 1965 Camp Hale was officially dismantled, and the land returned to the US Forest Service. Today, it's a popular spot for mountain biking, hiking and cross-country skiing.

EATING IN BEAVER CREEK & AVON: OUR PICKS

Craftsman Brew: Down the road in Edwards are gourmet sandwiches, salads, poke bowls and, of course, beer. *11:30am-9pm Tue-Sun* **$$**

Vin 48: Pair small plates like bison tartare and scallops with Hollandaise sauce with thoughtfully curated wines at this Avon-based bar. *5-9:30pm* **$$$**

Mirabelle: Daniel Joly's modern French cuisine (sole meunière, lamb panaché) in a 100-year-old home at the entrance to Beaver Creek. *5:30-9pm Mon-Sat* **$$$**

Beano's Cabin: This destination restaurant involves a 20-minute open-air sleigh ride to a cabin on the slopes, warm from a crackling fire. *5-8:30pm Tue-Sat* **$$$**

MELANZANA

This unique outdoor clothing brand began in Leadville as Eggplant Mountain Gear in 1994 and never looked back. Patagonia may be more famous, and Black Diamond may have revolutionized the gear, but only **Melanzana** can claim to be 100% made in the USA. Using only Polartec fabric (made in Tennessee), every single item in this store is produced behind the counter, using solar power to boot.

This is definitely not fast fashion: shopping for Melanzana's iconic hoodies is a personalized experience, and requires a pre-booked appointment. On average, the store is booked out months in advance, but same-day appointments do open up in the event you didn't plan ahead.

It was silver, not gold, that brought riches to the lucky few here, but after the bottom dropped out of the market in 1893, the city took a serious nosedive. You'll find the remnants of the past all over town: start with the surprisingly good **National Mining Hall of Fame** *(mininghalloffame.org; $15)*, before sauntering over to the **Healy House Museum and Dexter Cabin** *(historycolorado.org; $10)*, two of the oldest homes in Leadville. The **Tabor Opera House** *(taboroperahouse.net; summer tours $15)* was once one of the premier entertainment venues in all of Colorado, if not the West, and hosted the likes of Houdini, Oscar Wilde and Anna Held.

Final stop is the **Matchless Mine** *(mininghalloffame.org; summer tours from $10)*, where silver magnate and Colorado senator Horace Tabor made and then lost millions in the 1880s, and where his glamorous and sensational wife, Baby Doe, eventually froze to death after spending the last three decades of her life in poverty.

Bike the Mineral Belt

The best way to explore Leadville is the paved 12-mile **Mineral Belt Trail**, which loops around the outskirts of the city, passing abandoned mine shafts and flumes, history panels and thick stands of aspen trees and pines – keep your eyes peeled and you might spot Sasquatch too.

Built atop former railroad grades, this would be a leisurely bike ride anywhere else, though at over 10,000ft above sea level you should expect some wheezing along the way. Clockwise is the way to go, with glorious downhill coasting for the final 6 miles.

Cycles of Life *(colbikes.com; bike rentals from $40)* has everything you need to hit the trail in all seasons, including fat-tire bikes and cross-country skis in winter.

Climb to the top of Colorado

Colorado's tallest peak and the second-highest in the continental US, **Mt Elbert** (14,433ft) is a relatively gentle giant. There are three established routes to the top, none of which are technical. The most common approach is via the northeast ridge; it's a 9-mile round-trip hike with 4700ft of elevation gain, so expect to spend most of the day. The turnoff for the main trailhead is just south of Leadville on Rte 300. If you have 4WD, the South Mt Elbert Trailhead is accessed via Hwy 82, just east of Twin Lakes. It's a slightly shorter hike with only 4100ft of elevation gain.

Just next door and dominating the western horizon is **Mt Massive** (14,421ft), the state's second-tallest peak. It has four summits and a 3-mile-long ridge, giving it more total area

EATING IN LEADVILLE: OUR PICKS

High Mountain Pies: Ultra-popular pizza joint with great toppings, though seating is limited, so be sure to arrive early. *11am-10pm* **$**

City on a Hill: Cozy cafe, serving sandwiches, soups, pastries and freshly baked quiches, plus great espresso drinks. *6am-4pm* **$**

Treeline Kitchen: The finest meal in Leadville, focusing on simple but delectable small plates, mains and desserts. *3:30-9pm Wed-Sun* **$$**

Tennessee Pass Cookhouse: Ski through the woods to an elegant four-course meal in a yurt. Reserve. *lunch Sat & Sun, dinner daily* **$$$**

CATRINA GENOVESE/SHUTTERSTOCK

Mineral Belt Trail

above 14,000ft than any other peak in the state. From Hwy 24, it dominates the western horizon. The classic route up the east slope is a real bruiser: you'll put in a grueling 13.6 miles of hiking round trip. The southwest slope is much shorter at 8 miles, but you'll need 4WD and high clearance to reach the trailhead. Both trailheads are accessed via Rte 300, south of Leadville.

Ride the LC&S

The **Leadville, Colorado & Southern Railroad** (*lead villerailroad.com; adult/child $57/34*) follows the old Denver, South Park & Pacific and Colorado & Southern lines to the Continental Divide. Time it right and you'll see fields of wildflowers give way to panoramas across the Arkansas River Valley, or stands of aspens shimmering gold on a crisp autumn day. Your tour guide will fill you in on Leadville's bawdy past along the way. Trips are 2½ hours and run throughout the year. Dress warmly.

Twin Lakes

TIME FROM VAIL: 1¼ HR

Hike or paddle to a ghost resort

Set on the shores of the largest glacial lakes in Colorado, at the base of Independence Pass, **Twin Lakes** was once a convenient rest stop on the Aspen–Leadville stagecoach line. First called Dayton during the 1860s gold rush, it was renamed Twin Lakes in 1879 when the silver rush revived the village.

Several historic structures still stand on the north lake shore, including the Red Rooster Tavern (aka the town brothel), now the visitor center. Canoe and SUP rentals are available in town; boat tours also run daily.

On the south shore of the main lake is **Interlaken**, the vestiges of what was once an exclusive resort, built in 1879. The ruins are a lovely 5-mile hike (round trip) along the lake; this is as easy as walking gets at 9400ft. There's good signage and you can even go inside millionaire James Dexter's 'cabin.' The turnoff for the Interlaken trailhead is 0.6 miles after you turn onto Hwy 82.

THE LEADVILLE 100

The Leadville 100 (p362), held in August, is one of the most famous and longest mountain-bike races in the world: 100 miles of lung-crushing, adrenaline-fueled riding on the old silver-mining roads that go from 9200ft to 12,424ft and back again. But the Leadville 100 is not just about the mountain bikers. The whole thing started in 1983 as a 100-mile ultramarathon along the Colorado Trail (45 racers started, only 10 finished) and the legendary run continues to attract ultramarathoners from around the world. The entire event includes four other races, spread out over the year: a 10K run, a marathon, a 50-mile run and a 50-mile mountain-bike race. Finish five of the six events to complete the ultimate endurance award: the Lead Challenge.

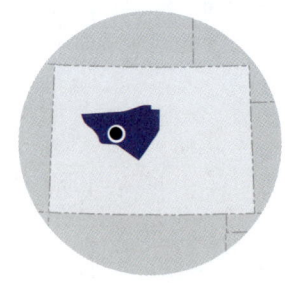

Aspen

NATURE | SKIING | ART

GETTING AROUND

Aspen is 41 miles south of Glenwood Springs on Hwy 82, and roughly four hours from Denver. In summer you can also get here over Independence Pass, which connects Aspen with the Arkansas River Valley and Hwy 24. The Aspen-Pitkin County Airport has flights from Denver and several other US cities.

Aspen's downtown is best navigated on foot, while free RFTA buses run to the surrounding towns and ski areas. VelociRFTA buses, equipped with ski/bike racks, serve the down-valley towns of Basalt (25 minutes), Carbondale (45 minutes) and Glenwood Springs (one hour).

What if the world was full of beautiful people, who were all kind, environmentally minded and well intentioned? Well, that's Aspen for you: when you drive into town, it's like entering the alternate John Denver dimension. But don't run off screaming just yet.

Aspen is unique in that it attracts intellectuals and world leaders, artists and activists, Hollywood celebs on the down-low and eccentric ski bums. This particular mix wasn't an accident: the mind-body-spirit ethos goes back to the 1940s, with the founding of the town's triumvirate: the Aspen Institute, a think tank that brings together top scientists, economists and artists; the Aspen Music Festival; and, of course, the Aspen Skiing Company.

Aspen may be wealthier than ever, but the unparalleled natural beauty and collision of ideas that brought all these people here is still freely accessible – as long as you know where to look.

Skiing the Four Mountains

In powder we trust

Aspen, for all its money, taste and eccentricity, owes its current status to the surrounding slopes. Above all, this is a ski town and one of the best in America, with four mountains accessible from a single **lift ticket** *(aspensnowmass.com; adult/child day pass $244/164)* – each offering a different adventurous twist.

Aspen Mountain offers more than 3000ft of steep vertical right from the front door of the Little Nell. There's no beginner

☑ **TOP TIP**

If your hotel doesn't have parking or you're just visiting for the day, save yourself the hassle and head straight for the town parking garage on Rio Grande Pl, which has the best daily rates around. RFTA buses connect Aspen with the Highlands (Maroon Bells), Snowmass and Buttermilk.

Snowmass

ELEMENT 47

In the late 19th century, an economic battle pitted the interests of farmers and the working class against the industrial elite of the Northeast. Workers and farmers wanted the US currency to be bimetallic – backed by silver and gold – while bankers and industrialists supported the gold standard. The argument for silver was that it would make currency easier to obtain and drive up inflation, which was seen as a way to counter the economic depression of the time (farmers in particular were in danger of losing their land to bankers due to deflated crop prices). Beginning in 1878, the government did briefly support the Free Silver faction, leading to silver mining boomtowns like Aspen and Leadville. This came to an end in 1893, with the repeal of the Sherman Silver Act.

terrain here, just 800 acres of bumps, trees and World Cup–worthy runs served by the Silver Queen Gondola (in 1946 it was the single-seat Lift 1, the longest chairlift in the world). Intermediate skiers and riders will dig Ruthie's, a wide-open groomed run with sweeping views. Local tip: stay skier's right at the top of Ruthie's and you'll head into the Jerry Garcia Shrine, accessed from the FIS and Ruthie's lifts.

Snowmass is the biggest of the four, with over 3300 acres of ridable terrain and 150 miles of trails – this is the best all-around choice. Sneaky's is a wide-open cruiser and the perfect blue groomer, with sweeping views of the Roaring Fork Valley, while those looking for a challenge can ski into powder and trees on either side of the run. Any run in the Cirque or the Hanging Valley Headwall will suit the adrenaline set. At some point make your way to the Elk Camp chairlift, which has awesome views of the Maroon Bells from the top.

Buttermilk has lots of beginner-friendly cruisers and great instructors, but it also has some gnarly terrain parks: this is where you can ride the same hits and 22ft superpipe as Chloe Kim, Shaun White and all your favorite X Games athletes.

Last but not least is **Aspen Highlands**. You know all those promo shots of beautiful people joyfully hiking atop an exposed snow-covered ridge with skis flung over a shoulder?

WHERE TO EAT IN ASPEN: ON A BUDGET

Big Wrap: These vaguely healthy and definitely affordable wraps have won over legions of fans. Downstairs from the main sidewalk. *10am-6pm Mon-Sat* $

Jüs: Tucked away among art galleries is this healthy outpost that prepares cleansing juices, wraps, quesadillas and smoothie bowls. *8am-5pm* $

Butcher's Block: Deli serving soups, salads, Belgian brownies, and gourmet sandwiches like the Gentlemen's Turkey with cranberry chutney. *9am-3pm* $

Silverpeak Grill: An on-site cannabis dispensary keeps hungry customers coming back for tacos, burgers and protein bowls. *10:30am-8pm* $

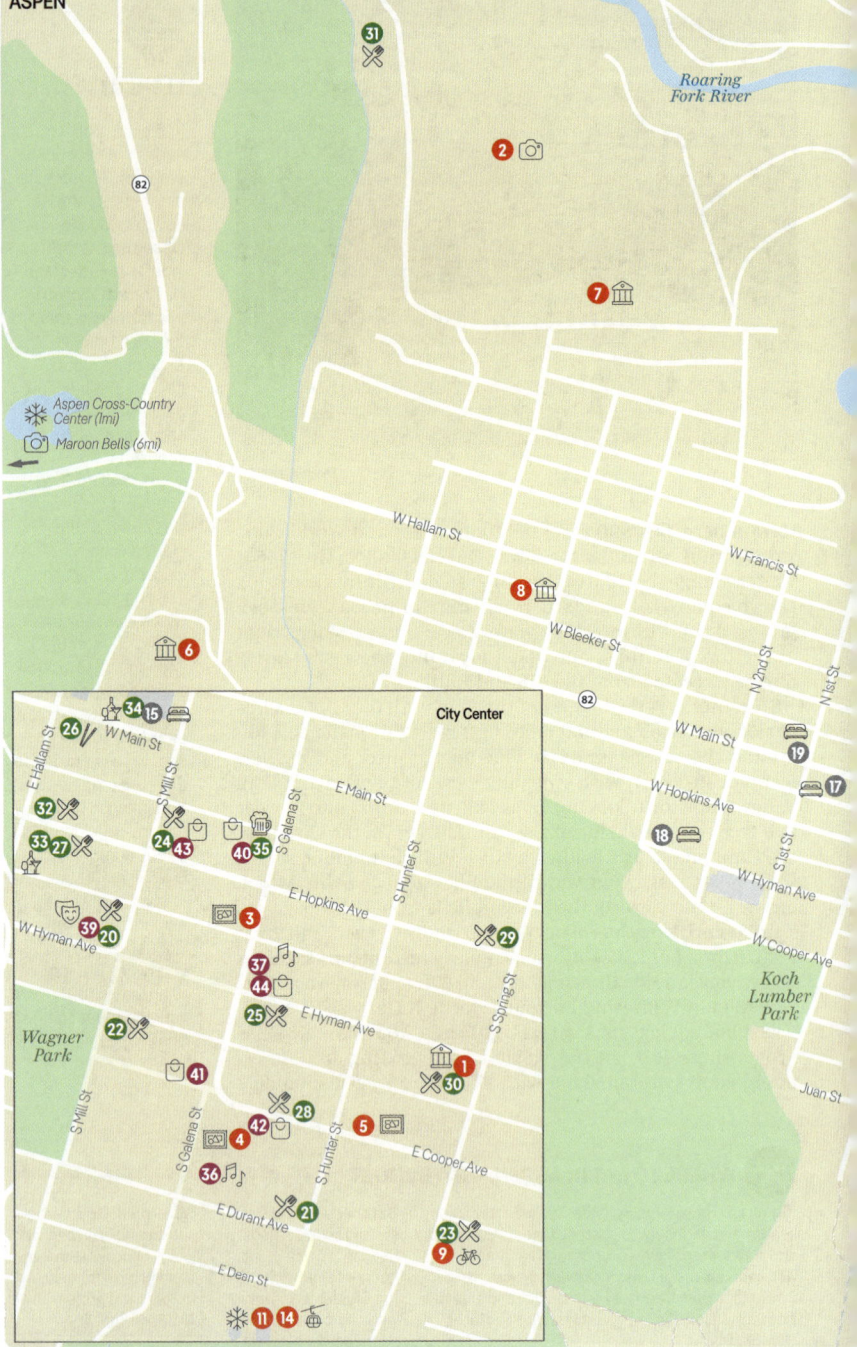

ASPEN

Roaring Fork River

Aspen Cross-Country Center (1mi)

Maroon Bells (6mi)

City Center

W Hallam St

W Francis St

W Bleeker St

W Main St

W Hopkins Ave

W Hyman Ave

W Cooper Ave

Koch Lumber Park

Juan St

E Hallam St

W Main St

E Main St

E Hopkins Ave

E Hyman Ave

E Cooper Ave

E Durant Ave

E Dean St

Wagner Park

S Mill St

S Galena St

S Hunter St

S Spring St

N 2nd St

N 1st St

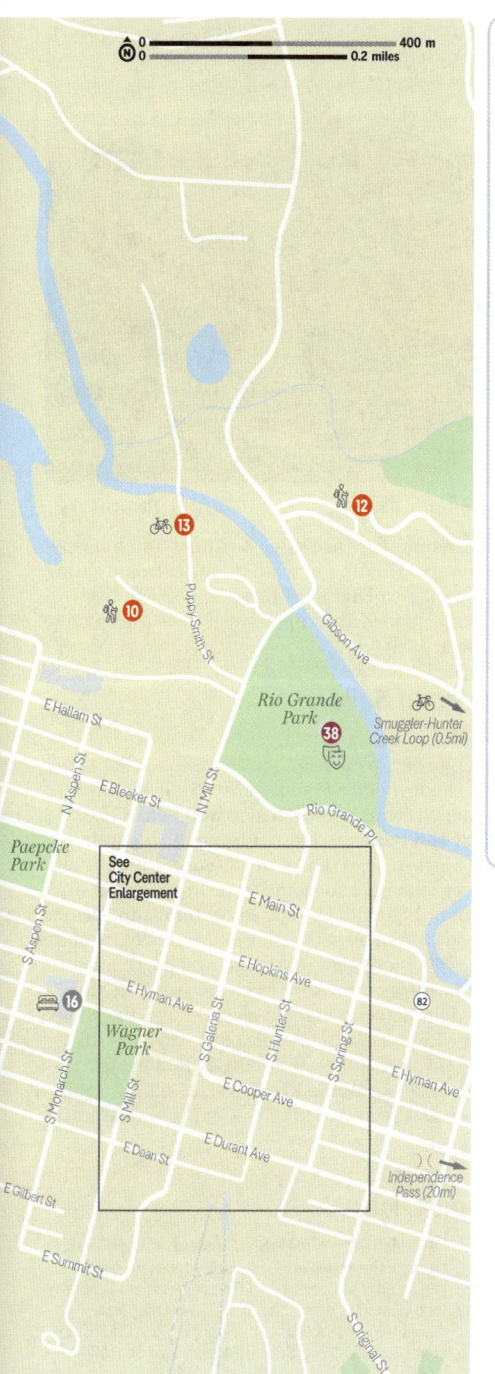

SIGHTS
1. Aspen Art Museum
2. Aspen Institute
3. Baldwin Gallery
4. Christopher Martin Gallery
5. Galerie Maximillian
6. Holden Marolt Mining & Ranching Museum
7. Resnick Center for Herbert Bayer Studies
8. Wheeler/Stallard Museum

ACTIVITIES, COURSES & TOURS
9. Aspen Bikes
10. Aspen Center for Environmental Studies
11. Aspen Mountain
12. Hunter Creek Trail
13. Rio Grande Trail
14. Silver Queen Gondola

SLEEPING
15. Hotel Jerome
16. Limelight Hotel
17. Mollie Aspen
18. St Moritz Lodge
19. Tyrolean Lodge

EATING
20. Aspen Public House
21. Big Wrap
22. Bosq
23. Butcher's Block
24. French Alpine Bistro
25. Jüs
26. Matsuhisa
27. Meat & Cheese
28. Silverpeak Grill
29. Spring Cafe
30. Swedish Hill
31. West End Social
32. White House Tavern

DRINKING & NIGHTLIFE
33. Hooch
34. J-Bar
35. Westy's Tap & Tavern

ENTERTAINMENT
36. Belly Up
37. Theatre Aspen
38. Silver City Aspen
39. Wheeler Opera House

SHOPPING
40. Aspen Thrift Shop
41. Kemo Sabe
42. Little Bird
43. Radio Boardshop
44. Ute Mountaineer

THE MAROON BELLS SHUTTLE

The most important thing to know when visiting the Maroon Bells is that you can't just drive there and park wherever you want – this area sees some 300,000 visitors each summer, so access is strictly controlled. Most visitors will need to park at the Aspen Highlands – it's very pricey, so we recommend taking the free RFTA bus from Rubey Park in Aspen – and then take a half-hour **shuttle ride** *(aspenchamber. org; adult/child $16/10; late May through October).* You must reserve shuttle tickets in advance. Alternatively, there are limited parking spots available at the trailhead, which are also available by reservation only ($10 per car; 5pm to 8am only). The access road is not plowed in winter, when you can cross-country ski to Maroon Bells Lake.

SEAN XU/SHUTTERSTOCK

Maroon Lake

That's here. Although there are some beginner and intermediate runs here, the Highlands is all about extreme skiing in the stunning hike-to Highland Bowl: expect chutes, vertiginous drop-offs, glades and super-steep lines that plunge 3600 vertical feet.

Hike the Maroon Bells

Explore the Elks

If you have but one day to enjoy a slice of pristine wilderness, spend it in the shadow of Colorado's most iconic mountains: the pyramid-shaped twins of **North Maroon Peak** (14,014ft) and **South Maroon Peak** (14,156ft). Eleven miles southwest of Aspen, it all starts on the shores of **Maroon Lake**, an absolutely stunning spot backed by the towering, striated summits. The surrounding wilderness area contains nine passes over 12,000ft and six fourteeners. Some jut into jagged granite towers, others are a more generous slope and curve, nurturing a series of meadows that seem to gleam from the slopes.

You can spend an hour up here or several days: the choice is yours. **Crater Lake** is only 1.8 miles one way, making for a nice day hike. If you're hungry for a little bit more altitude, we suggest pressing on to **Buckskin Pass** (12,462ft; 4.8 miles one-way) – from the narrow ledge you can see mountains

WHERE TO EAT IN ASPEN: MIDRANGE PICKS

Aspen Public House: Part of the historic opera house, this is one of the best options in town for a chill gastropub meal. *noon-10pm* **$$**

Spring Cafe: Vegetarian juice bar and cafe, with tofu scrambles, tempeh burgers, seitan fajitas and plenty of greens. *7am-5pm Mon-Fri, from 8pm Sat & Sun* **$$**

Swedish Hill: On the top floor of the Aspen Art Museum, it's all about the inspiring views of the mountains at this chic cafe. *8am-5pm Tue-Sun* **$$**

Sundeck: It may be a ski lodge cafeteria, but the food here is actually pretty tasty. And the views? Sublime. Atop the Silver Queen. *11am-3pm* **$$**

erupt in all directions. This is the start of one of the most popular hikes in Aspen: the **Four Pass Loop** (28 miles), a stunning multiday backpacking trip that crosses three other 12,000ft passes.

Another popular hike goes to Crested Butte (p243), roughly 11 miles away but 100 miles by car. From Crater Lake continue to West Maroon Pass (12,480ft), then descend to the Schofield Pass Trailhead on the Crested Butte side, where you'll need to arrange for a shuttle to take you the additional 14 miles into town. **Maroon Bells Shuttles** (*maroonbellsshuttles.com; $400*) will actually drive your car to either trailhead so that it's waiting for you upon arrival. The minimum hiking time is six hours, but plan on 10.

Ghost Towns

From boom to bust

Interested in learning more about Aspen's unique history? Check out one of the tours from the **Aspen Historical Society** (*aspenhistory.org; tours $25*), which take visitors behind the scenes at landmarks like the famous 1889 Jerome Hotel and Wheeler Opera House. They also manage two excellent museums: the **Wheeler/Stallard Museum** (*free*), set in an 1888 Victorian house, and the **Holden Marolt Mining & Ranching Museum** (*free*), which incorporates a mining mill and historic homestead.

Further out on Castle Creek Rd but absolutely worth visiting is **Ashcroft Ghost Town** (*$5 donation*), a silver-mining town founded in 1880. What remains are mostly miners cottages (log cabins with tin roofs), a couple of broken-down wagons stranded in the waist-high grass, a post office and a saloon. At its height in 1893 about 2500 people worked here, but the silver veins were quickly exhausted and by 1895 the town's population plummeted to 100 residents.

High up on Independence Pass at an elevation of 10,900ft is another boomtown gone bust, **Independence** (*$5 donation*). This one-time tent camp exploded in the summer of 1879, when a lucky miner struck gold on the 4th of July. The site offers the chance to see the remains of the old livery, the general store and a miner's cabin or three. After its population peaked at 1500, the town fell away during the harsh winter of 1899, when supply routes were severed. In typical Aspen fashion, residents made light of the situation by fashioning skis from spare timber and turning their escape into a downhill race.

THE ASPEN MUSIC FESTIVAL

Every summer since 1949, some of the world's best classical musicians have come to the Aspen Institute to play and learn from the masters of their craft. Founded by philanthropists Walter and Elizabeth Paepcke to celebrate the 200th birthday of German writer Johann Wolfgang von Goethe, the **Aspen Music Festival** (*aspen musicfestival.com*) was star-studded from the get-go, with luminaries like composer Igor Stravinsky and pianist Arthur Rubinstein attending in the early years. And while Aspen is best known for its skiing, the music festival has brought the town artistic credibility. Concerts are held at four principal venues for eight weeks, from late June to mid-August, and are performed by four orchestras, made up of 500 students and 100 faculty members.

WHERE TO EAT IN ASPEN: ICONIC VENUES

Bosq: Chef Barclay Dodge's playful, locally sourced menu (eg bison tartare and nasturtium) earned him Aspen's first Michelin star. Prix-fixe only. *5:30-10pm* **$$$**

Meat & Cheese: While the produce at this farm-to-table deli may be local, their culinary expertise spans the globe. *11am-9pm* **$$$**

Matsuhisa: This converted house is the original Colorado link in Matsuhisa Nobu's sushi empire. Lovely and intimate space. *5:30-10pm* **$$$**

White House Tavern: As American as a crispy chicken sandwich and kale salad, this is Aspen's premier lunch stop. No reservations, so arrive early. *11am-9pm* **$$$**

BEST ENTERTAINMENT IN ASPEN

Belly Up: The top nightspot in town, showcasing performers from John Legend to the Chainsmokers in intimate surrounds.

Silver City Aspen: This cowpoke-themed saloon in the basement of the historic Elks Building hosts live music performances as well as a weekly karaoke night.

Wheeler Opera House: A working theater since 1889, the Wheeler still stages opera, stand-up comedy, concerts and musicals.

Theatre Aspen: The gorgeous garden complex in Rio Grande Park is the summer home of the local theater, which puts on award-winning musicals and plays.

KRIS WIKTOR/SHUTTERSTOCK

Conundrum Hot Springs

A new museum celebrating Lift One is slated to begin construction at the foot of the ski resort.

Hiking in Aspen

Lace up your boots

The Maroon Bells trailhead (p222) is the starting point for some of Aspen's most famous hikes (the Four Pass Loop, Crested Butte), but if you want to avoid the crowds and shuttle logistics, there are plenty of other trails to explore.

The fantastic **Hunter Creek Trail** leaves right from town (N Mill St to Lone Pine Rd), following the creek northeast for about 4 miles, after which it links up with a plethora of other trails, including the popular network at nearby Smuggler Mountain (10,700ft).

Another easy adventure is to ride the **Silver Queen** or the **Elk Camp Gondola** *(single ride $37)* and strike out on any of the high-altitude trails. Yoga practitioners, take note: high-altitude outdoor classes ($25) are held on summer mornings at the summit of the Silver Queen.

If you're after backcountry hiking, Castle Creek Valley is a great spot to explore. Here you'll find the steaming **Conundrum Hot Springs**, west of Castle Peak (14,265ft), which are the reward for 8.5 miles and over 3000ft of climbing on the

WHERE TO EAT IN ASPEN: WORTH A SPLURGE

Mawa's Kitchen: Beloved French- and African-inspired cuisine near Aspen airport. *11am-3pm & 5-9pm Tue-Thu, 8am-3pm & 5-9pm Fri & Sat, 8am-3pm Sun* **$$$**

Pine Creek Cookhouse: This log-cabin restaurant is past Ashcroft's ghost town and is accessible via sleigh, skis or horseback. *lunch & dinner Dec-Mar & mid-Jun–Sep* **$$$**

West End Social: The setting at this gorgeous Aspen Institute restaurant pairs perfectly with the produce-driven menu. *7am-9pm* **$$$**

French Alpine Bistro: Every mountain town has to have one – a tip of the toque to cheese fondue and hearty boeuf bourguignon. *11:30am-11pm* **$$$**

Conundrum Creek Trail (USFS Trail 1981). The pools here have outrageous alpine views, but it's hugely popular, and you must make reservations on *recreation.gov*. Bear canisters are required.

Further up the valley is the **Cathedral Lake Trail**, which is particularly stunning in autumn when the aspens shimmer gold. With 2000ft of elevation gain over 3 miles, however, it's definitely no walk in the park. The trailhead is located near the Ashcroft ghost town; if you don't have AWD, park at the lot near the road.

Hike & Snowshoe with Naturalists

ACES high

The **Aspen Center for Environmental Studies** *(ACES; aspennature.org; free)* manages the 25-acre Hallam Lake wildlife sanctuary that hugs the Roaring Fork River and miles of hiking trails in the Hunter Creek Valley. With a mission to advance environmental conservation, the center's naturalists provide free guided hikes and snowshoe tours, raptor demonstrations (eagles and owls are among the residents) and special programs for families.

Popular guided tours include the Ice Age walk in Snowmass, hikes to Crater Lake in the Maroon Bells and year-round birding excursions.

There are two other locations in the region: Rock Bottom Ranch near Basalt, which offers farm tours, and the Catto Center at Toklat, across from the Ashcroft ghost town and where you'll find an artist in residence.

Nordic Bliss

Ski touring in style

Local outdoor outfitter Ute Mountaineer has operated the **Aspen Cross-Country Center** *(utemountaineer.com; ski rental adult/child $42.50/22.50)*, set on Aspen's public golf course, for four decades. Located near the Aspen-Snowmass Nordic Trail System (a 60-mile web of village-to-village trails linking Aspen with Snowmass, Ashcroft and Basalt), the center is a convenient spot to rent gear, take a lesson or head out on a guided tour.

Ashcroft Ski Touring *(pinecreekcookhouse.com; adult/child $25/15)*, meanwhile, serves 20 miles of groomed trails through 600 acres of backcountry – it's a bit more wild than your typical Nordic center. The mountain backdrop is

BEST SHOPPING

Kemo Sabe: Sister to Vail's cowboy apparel depot, Kemo Sabe vends the same handmade boots and Stetson hats – steam-shaped to please.

Little Bird: A gem of a consignment store with new and vintage designer scarves, dresses, handbags, shoes and more.

Aspen Thrift Shop: You just might find some genuine treasures in Aspen's cast-offs; going strong since 1949.

Radio Boardshop: Top-of-the-line skateboards and snowboards, plus beanies, tees and boots to match.

Ute Mountaineer: While you could shop for Hermès and Dior here, is that fancy French stuff going to keep you warm on the slopes? What you really need is top-of-the-line outdoor gear.

DRINKING IN ASPEN: OUR PICKS

Westy's Tap & Tavern: The local brewery has joined forces with Denver's Westbound & Down. Pizza too. *noon–9pm Mon-Fri, to 10pm Sat & Sun*

Hooch: Fun speakeasy mixing signature cocktails like the Wolf of Wall Street and the Notorious FIG. *5pm-1am Tue-Sun*

J-Bar: Once Aspen's premier saloon, this 1889 bar in the Hotel Jerome remains one of the classiest places in town for a drink. *11:30am-11pm*

Woody Creek Tavern: Enjoying a margarita at Hunter S Thompson's favorite watering hole is well worth the 8-mile bike ride. *11am-9pm*

spectacular, and the nearby ghost town of Ashcroft is equally eerie. They also rent classic cross-country ski equipment and snowshoes and run guided tours.

Cycling & Mountain Biking
Pedal power

There's no shortage of two-wheeled fun in the Aspen area. Road cyclists and e-bikers can pedal the paved **Rio Grande Trail** down valley (8.5 miles to Woody Creek Tavern, 42 miles to Glenwood Springs), the harder Maroon Bells Rd (11 miles) or the masochistic Independence Pass. If you're eager for blistering downhill and jumps, head for the **Snowmass Bike Park** *(aspensnowmass.com; half-day including bike rental $130)*, though there are also plenty of free singletrack classics to choose from too: the 10.5-mile **Rim Trail** is a top Snowmass ride that leaves from the Rodeo Lot.

Linking Snowmass with Aspen is the much-loved **Sky Mountain Park**, with a variety of terrain, while in Aspen itself you can head straight out into the open space on the **Smuggler-Hunter Creek Loop** – extending it all the way to Sunnyside if you're up for a challenge. In Aspen, rent mountain bikes and e-bikes at **Aspen Bikes**.

Hut-to-Hut Ski Trips
Say goodbye to lift lines

Imagine the thrill of gliding through the backcountry on skis: just you, your friends and quiet snowfall blanketing the mountainside. Well, thanks to the **10th Mountain Division Hut Association** *(huts.org)*, which manages a system of over 30 huts (some with wood-burning saunas), it can be done – without having to spend the night in a snow cave.

The huts are connected by a 350-mile trail network ideal for cross-country skiing and snowshoeing in winter, and mountain biking and hiking in the summer. You'll be out in the wilderness, so at least one person in your group should be an experienced backcountry skier familiar with avalanche safety. Better yet, go with a guide like **Aspen Expeditions** *(aspenexpeditions.com)*.

So how do you sign up for all this winter fun? The catch, of course, is securing reservations: these huts are incredibly popular and space is limited. Winter reservations for the following year begin with a member-only lottery on February 14. Call-in reservations for nonmembers open up on June 3.

WHERE TO EAT IN SNOWMASS: OUR PICKS

Fuel: The hard-rocking Snowmass cafe does two things exceptionally well – jet-fueled espresso and world-class breakfast burritos. *7:30am-3:30pm* $

New Belgium Ranger Station: Pretzel rolls and chili cheese dogs to go with Fat Tire and Voodoo Ranger on tap. Ski-in, ski-out. Yes! *noon-8pm* $$

Stew Pot: Stews, soups and chili are the reasons to come here, made all the more enticing by comedy nights on Tuesdays. *11am-9pm* $$

Il Poggio: If you want to up your game in Snowmass, head up the stairs to this Italian gem. Pizza, pasta and tantalizing tiramisu. *5:30-10pm* $$$

Ski hut

In other words, you have to plan your trip six to 12 months in advance and be somewhat flexible with your dates (avoiding weekends is key).

Art Galleries & Museums

Culture vulture

Aspen, like most towns in the Rocky Mountains, is less about seeing and more about experiencing. But with a handful of outstanding art venues downtown, this is the most culturally happening spot west of Denver. Start with the **Aspen Art Museum** *(aspenartmuseum.org; free)*, with three floors of gallery space enveloped in a striking exterior designed by Pritzker Prize–winner Shigeru Ban.

Less well known is the Aspen Institute's **Resnick Center for Herbert Bayer Studies** *(thebayercenter.org; free)*, which has rotating exhibits related to the Austrian artist and long-time Aspen resident. This is a treat for those interested in the Bauhaus movement.

Smaller galleries, meanwhile, are everywhere – follow your curiosity, and you'll be sure to turn up something unique. Longstanding studios include **Galerie Maximillian**, the **Christopher Martin Gallery** (a specialist in reverse glass painting) and the **Baldwin Gallery**.

HERBERT BAYER

You've probably heard of Paul Klee and Wassily Kandinsky. But what about fellow Bauhaus alum Herbert Bayer (1900–85)? While not nearly as famous, the Austrian artist played a singularly important role in shaping Aspen's artistic vision in the post-WWII years. Although his specialty was graphic design, his legacy is most evident in his adopted hometown's public spaces. He had a hand in designing the original Sundeck atop Aspen mountain, the outdoor tent used for the Music Festival and, most importantly, the layout of the **Aspen Institute**. The outdoor sculptures, the buildings' simple design and their seamless integration into the natural landscape are a tribute to Bayer's Bauhaus ethos. The campus is freely accessible to the public, as is the new Resnick Center for Herbert Bayer Studies.

ASPEN ON FOOT

Explore Aspen's historic landmarks and artistic legacy on this stroll through the center of town.

START	END	LENGTH
Jerome Hotel	John Denver Sanctuary	2km; 1½ hours

Begin at the landmark **1 Hotel Jerome** (1889), built during the town's short-lived silver boom – the bottom would fall out of the market just four years later in 1893. Pass the sidewalk judge statue outside the J-Bar to check out the old Underwood typewriters in the window of the adjacent **2 Aspen Times** (1881).

Return to Mill St and continue south to the **3 Wheeler Opera House** (1889), which, like the Hotel Jerome, was financed by Jerome Wheeler. Continue down Mill St for another block and turn left onto the pedestrian Cooper Ave, where you'll see the **4 Red Onion**, one of the town's original saloons.

Continue down Cooper Ave, then turn right to reach the base of Aspen Mountain, where the **5 Silver Queen Gondola** stands on the site of what was once the world's longest and highest ski lift (1946).

Backtrack on Hunter St, passing the **6 Galerie Maximillian** and the **7 Eden Gallery** at the intersection with CooperAve. Turn right on E Hyman Ave to admire the gorgeous lattice exterior of the **8 Aspen Art Museum**. Follow the sign for the Hunter St Trail down a ramp across from the church to reach the park. Cross the wooden Bridge to reach the peaceful **9 John Denver Sanctuary** and Theatre Aspen.

Jerome Wheeler was married to Harriet Macy Valentine, whose uncle founded Macy's Department Store in New York. He served as a partner in the 1880s.

The **Red Onion** allegedly had a brothel on the upper floor and a tunnel connecting to a nearby bank in the basement.

Peek through the windows of the **Galerie Maximillian** and you might see works by 20th-century artists like Chagall and Lichtenstein.

Rio Grande Park

Roaring Fork River

Paepcke Park

Wagner Park

W Main St
W Hopkins Ave
W Hyman Ave
W Cooper Ave
Juan St
S Aspen St
S Monarch St
S Mill St
N Mill St
S Galena St
E Hyman Ave
E Cooper Ave
S Hunter St
E Main St
E Hopkins Ave
E Hyman Ave
S Spring St
Rio Grande Pl
E Gilbert St
Juan St

0 200 m
0 0.1 miles

Beyond Aspen

Aspen's allure isn't the town but its surrounds: a snowball's throw in any direction and you're sure to hit Elk Mountain bliss.

Dominated by the magnificent, twin-peaked Mt Sopris (12,965ft), the rural Roaring Fork Valley is the gateway to Aspen. While you may be tempted to zip on through, we'd advise that you take the time to make a few detours and soak in some hot springs. At Carbondale is the junction for the romantic Crystal River valley, which cuts through a vivid and often-overlooked swathe of wilderness beneath Chair Mountain. Near Basalt, Fryingpan River and Ruedi Reservoir make up the breadcrumb trail that leads to another stretch of pristine landscapes and forested campsites. And exiting through Aspen's back door takes you to the top-of-the-world wonderland of Independence Pass.

Independence Pass

TIME FROM ASPEN: **45 MINS** 🚗

Driving the pass

Looming at 12,095ft, **Independence Pass** is one of the most high-profile mountain passes along the Continental Divide. Perhaps it's the proximity to Aspen (just 20 miles away on Hwy 82), or maybe it's the celeb quotient (Kevin Costner has a ranch on the western slope – rent it for $36,000 per night). But we think it's the drive itself.

Views range from pretty to stunning to downright cinematic, and by the time you glimpse swathes of snow on the ridges below, you'll be living in your own IMAX film. Late season you'll see everyone from guys dressed in camo to – no kidding – unicyclists attempting the unthinkable.

Along the way you'll pass hiking trails, fourteeners, serene campgrounds and even the ghost town of Independence (p223). The pass is only open from late May to late October.

Hiking the pass

The **Grottos**, roughly 9 miles from downtown Aspen, is a popular summer playground and great family hike. Access it via a web of short trails (most about half a mile) that sprout from old Weller Station on the original Independence Pass wagon road, leading to cascades and the unique water-carved slots known as the **Ice Caves**.

Places

Independence Pass p229
Glenwood Springs p230
Roaring Fork Valley p233
Redstone p234
Marble p234

GETTING AROUND

The Roaring Fork Valley is served by RFTA buses, with stops in Glenwood Springs, Carbondale, Basalt and Snowmass. Hwy 82 runs 41 miles (one hour) from Glenwood to Aspen, continuing up over Independence Pass and down into Twin Lakes. Hwy 133 begins in Carbondale, heading south to Paonia.

THE ROARING FORK RAILROAD RACE

The 1880s were a boom time in the United States: industry and mining were expanding like never before, and the Fed had committed to purchasing $2 million worth of silver annually from states like Colorado. The huge silver strike in Aspen meant certain riches, if only the mines could get the ore to the federal mints. Enter the railroad. Like many places out West, it was simply a matter of who would get there first. In Aspen, it came down to a race between the Colorado Midland and the Denver & Rio Grande, both of which were laying track furiously up the valley. In October of 1887, the Colorado Midland line ran out of steel girders 2 miles outside of Aspen; soon after, D&RGR clanged home its final spike to claim the prize.

TWIN LAKES

On the east side of Independence Pass are the **Twin Lakes** (p217) and Hwy 24, which connects Leadville with Salida.

Further up the pass is **Lost Man**, a classic high-alpine excursion past peaks and lakes. There are two trailheads; start at the upper one (past mile marker 59, last switchback before the pass; also known as Independence Lake), and you'll already be at 11,500ft. From here, hiking to Lost Man Lake is 4.7 miles round trip, with only 1100ft of elevation gain.

If you're after bigger fish, consider climbing **La Plata Peak** (14,336ft), the state's fifth highest. The trail leaves from South Fork Lake Trailhead on the eastern side of the pass. There are two routes to the top: the mellower Northwest Ridge and the more challenging class-III Ellingwood Ridge. Both routes are roughly 9.5 miles round trip with over 4000ft of elevation gain. Start early and remember: it's not a climb for beginners.

Glenwood Springs

TIME FROM ASPEN: **1 HR**

Soak in the hot springs

Let's start with the fun stuff. Doc Holliday – gunfighter, gambler, Wild West legend and, uh, dentist – died in Glenwood Springs. Why he came here is the first clue to the town's long-standing appeal: thermal hot springs. In Holliday's day they were thought to have restorative powers; he hoped they'd ease his chronic respiratory ailments.

Today, the main **Glenwood Hot Springs Resort** (*hotspringspool.com; day pass adult/child from $46/30*) pumps out 3.5 million gallons of mineral water a day, flowing through two main pools: the 400ft-long big pool at 90°F (32°C) and the 100ft-long therapy pool at 104°F (40°C). Kids have access to a splash zone and water slides, while adults can rejuvenate at the hotel and spa.

If you want a more intimate soak, **Iron Mountain Hot Springs** (*ironmountainhotsprings.com; day pass from $44*) offers a relaxing setting with 16 small pools. The **Yampah Spa** (*yampahspa.com; day pass from $25*), meanwhile, is something else entirely: at 110°F (43°C), entering these caves feels like descending into one of Dante's layers of hell. First developed by the Ute hundreds of years earlier for therapeu-

EATING IN GLENWOOD SPRINGS: OUR PICKS

The Pullman: This casual industrial space is Glenwood Springs' hippest hangout, where the open kitchen whips up modern American dishes. *4:30-9pm* **$$**

Co Ranch House: Sustainably raised local ranch ethos, with an emphasis on steaks and pan-fried trout. *noon-9pm Thu-Mon* **$$$**

Masala & Curry: Get your Nepali fix here with *momos* (dumplings) and *chau chau* (fried noodles) plus a good selection of Indian curries. *11am-9pm Tue-Sun* **$$**

Riviera Scratch Kitchen: For some, Riviera is Glenwood's best dinner experience. Duck confit, wild mushroom lasagna, gourmet burgers. *4:30-8:30pm Wed-Sun* **$$$**

Glenwood Hot Springs Resort

DOC HOLLIDAY

It's appropriate that the hike to Doc Holliday's memorial at Linwood Cemetery in Glenwood Springs might leave you breathless: the life of the legendary man was shaped by labored breathing. Seeking relief for tuberculosis, John Henry Holliday (1851–87) moved west from his native Georgia. He set up a dental practice in Texas, but the wheezing scared away patients. Turning to gambling and hanging out in saloons, Holliday met Wyatt Earp, with whom he participated in the most famous shoot-out of Western lore at the OK Corral. Despite the memorial, Holliday's exact place of burial is unknown: the records were lost when the cemetery was moved from an earlier location down the hill.

tic purposes, the steam-filled natural caves have been a commercial facility since the 1880s.

Explore Glenwood Canyon

Gorgeous Glenwood Canyon offers all sorts of diversions. Cycling over the smoothly paved **Glenwood Canyon Recreation Trail**, under the canyon walls, makes an excellent afternoon for riders of all abilities. The path follows the Colorado River upstream below the cantilevered I-70, and the river often drowns out the roar of traffic. It's about 16 miles from the Yampah Vapor Caves to Dotsero at the other end of the canyon; a good midway destination is Hanging Lake, roughly 10 miles up the canyon. Rent a bike at the **Hanging Lake Adventure Co-op** (go.theflybook.com; from $50 per hour).

The 1.2-mile **Hanging Lake Trail** leads to a waterfall-fed pond perched in a rock bowl on the canyon wall. It's a strenuous 1½- to three-hour round trip with a 1020ft elevation gain, but well worth the huffing and puffing. You must reserve a permit in advance (visitglenwood.com/hanginglake; from $12).

EATING IN GLENWOOD SPRINGS: OUR PICKS

Slope & Hatch: Cajun andouille fries alongside mouthwatering taco selection, plus natural hot dogs, craft beer and cocktails. Yum. *11am-8pm* $

Sweet Coloradough: Bakery south of town (look for the old police car out front), with cronuts, eclairs, doughnuts and bagel sandwiches. *6am-2pm Wed-Mon* $

Glenwood Canyon Brewpub: In the Hotel Maxwell Anderson, where the beers are hoppy and the night scene lively. Nachos, wings and other pub faves. *11am-9pm* $$

Tequila's: It may be a Colorado chain, but you can't beat the massive menu selection at Glenwood's most popular Mexican restaurant. *11am-10pm* $$$

WHY I LOVE GLENWOOD SPRINGS

Christopher Pitts,
Lonely Planet writer

Everyone *oohs* and *ahhs* over Aspen, but let's take a moment to spread some love to Glenwood too. While I never pictured my ideal hot springs experience as a gargantuan swimming pool, there's something about the location that keeps me coming back. Usually, I'm on the way home from some dust-covered fun in the Utah desert, muscles sore and in need of a break after hours of driving. Glenwood Springs lies at the perfect spot on I-70, and an hour or two spent floating in the warm mineral waters, amidst all the playing kids, chilling parents and day-tripping tourists, is the perfect way to reenter civilization after a week in the wilderness.

JAMILYA KHALILULINA/SHUTTERSTOCK

Glenwood Caverns Adventure Park

The trail was closed for renovations at the time of writing, but when open, it can only be accessed from I-70 East. The 3.5-mile **Grizzly Creek Trail** is another popular hike that gets out of the main canyon, though it's a tougher workout.

Beginning in May, the roaring **Colorado River** holds everything from beginner float trips to extreme white-water rafting. Most trips depart from east of town, on the stretch below the Shoshone Dam. Outfitters such as **Colorado Whitewater Rafting** (*coloradowhitewaterrafting.com*) and **Hanging Lake Adventure Co-op** (*hanginglake.com*) run trips from $75/130 for a half/full day.

From spelunking to scream machines

The family-oriented **Glenwood Caverns Adventure Park** (*glenwoodcaverns.com; admission caves & gondola/plus adventure park $55/84*) lumps together several attractions at once: the Fairy Caves (once billed as the eighth wonder of the world), a full-on amusement park, and a gondola ride 1300ft up to the top of Iron Mountain. The regular cave tour is the

 EATING IN BASALT: OUR PICKS

Free Range Kitchen & Wine Bar: Steve and Robin Humble work uniquely with local farmers and ranchers; worth a trip from Aspen. *5:30-9pm* **$$$**

Cafe Bernard: The place to indulge in escargots and other French bistro delicacies; breakfast too. *9am-2pm & 5:30-8pm Tue-Sat, 10am-2pm Sun* **$$$**

Heather's Savory Pies: Chicken pot pie, shepherd's pie and an array of small plates in fabulous garden seating. *11am-9pm* **$$$**

Estilo Salvadoreño: This Salvadoran food truck brings *pupusas* (stuffed tortillas), tamales and loaded potatoes to hungry diners. *10am-4pm Mon-Fri* **$**

main attraction here: this is the largest cave in Colorado open to the public. The Wild Tour of the caves, meanwhile, is a heart-racing experience for would-be spelunkers, allowing guests to crawl through narrow passages, though we like the Giant Canyon Swing, which sends folks squealing 1300ft in the air above the Colorado River at 50mph.

Down-valley skiing

Serious skiers head up-valley to Aspen or east on I-70 to Vail. But **Sunlight Mountain Resort** *(sunlightmtn.com; lift ticket adult/child day pass $90/45)*, 12 miles south of Glenwood Springs on Garfield County Rd 117, survives by offering good deals to families and intermediate skiers. The downhill area has 72 runs over 730 acres, with 2000ft of vertical. The cross-country ski area features 18 miles of groomed track and snow-skating trails, plus snowshoeing and ice-skating areas. A shuttle serves Glenwood Springs.

Roaring Fork Valley

TIME FROM ASPEN: **30-45 MINS** 🚗

Small-town charm

The **Roaring Fork Valley** runs from Glenwood Springs (down valley) to Aspen (up valley), connected by Hwy 82 and the paved Rio Grande Bike Trail (p226). In the shadow of twin-peaked Mt Sopris (12,965ft), artsy **Carbondale** – 30 miles from Aspen – is one of the most charismatic spots to cool your engine and grab a bite to eat when traveling up or down valley. Check out **Steve's Guitars** *(stevesguitars.net)*, an unassuming guitar shop that turns into an intimate one-room acoustic music venue on select nights. Shows at this community favorite start around 8pm, but it's best to turn up earlier if you want a seat. The cover charge varies, so bring cash.

A further 10 miles up valley is **Basalt**, Aspen's once-humble neighbor. Set at the confluence of the Fryingpan and Roaring Fork Rivers, it's framed by gold-medal trout waters, making this cute town something of a fly-fishing paradise. **Taylor Creek Fly Shop** *(taylorcreek.com; from $525)* rents rods and runs guided tours. Also on the river is a white-water park for kayakers and stand-up paddlers to play in. **Shaboomee** *(shaboomee.com; $54)* rents SUPs and kayaks.

The tiny town has a historic main street strip where you'll find plenty of dining options and cute boutiques. Stock up on groceries and outdoor gear at the newer Willits Town Center, 4 miles northwest on Hwy 82. Basalt is also the gateway to little-visited **Hunter-Fryingpan Wilderness area**.

FROM COAL TO STEEL

In the late 19th century, Colorado had an enormous appetite for steel, initially used to make the train-track rails laid across the West. Local production was carried out in the Colorado Fuel and Iron factory in Pueblo, but a key component in steel production came from places like Redstone: coke. Creating coke, basically refined coal with all impurities burned out, is an ancient technology and an essential component for blacksmithing. In the industrial age, massive amounts of the fuel were needed to power the blast furnaces in steel factories across the nation, giving rise to a proliferation of beehive kilns outside mining towns, like those in Redstone. The 250 ovens were eventually abandoned, and the first thing you'll see today are their remains, lined up across from the town entrance.

 EATING & DRINKING IN CARBONDALE: OUR PICKS

Village Smithy: For the best breakfast in town make for the historic blacksmith shop that locals adore. Breakfast burritos to go. *7am-2pm $*

Phat Thai: It may not look like Chiang Mai, but you won't find any naysayers here. Thai, Vietnamese and Malaysian classics. *5-9pm Mon-Sat $$*

Tiny Pine: Carbondale's top restaurant doesn't do fancy – think tiny tiki bar in the backyard – but it sure is good. *5-9pm Tue-Sun $$$*

Black Nugget: The local dive has it all – pool, rodeo nights, karaoke, DJ dance parties and plenty of live music. *noon-2am*

Redstone

TIME FROM ASPEN: 1 HR 🚙

History and hot springs

Seventeen miles south of Carbondale on Hwy 133, Redstone was a true company town, quite unlike the 'every man for himself' spirit of the gold rush era. Today it offers a chance for off-the-grid accommodations – no cell service back here – in an unheralded swathe of Rocky Mountain paradise.

Several of the original buildings are still standing, including the original chalet-style workers' cottages and founder John Osgood's personal residence, the 42-room **Redstone Castle** (*theredstonecastle.com*). Located 1 mile south of town on a private road, it was bought by a wellness company in 2022; renovations to turn it into a luxury spa were ongoing at the time of research. Check online for information on tours of the property.

Also in Redstone is the imposing neo-Tudor **Redstone Inn** (*redstoneinn.com*). Tucked away behind massive red cliffs, this hotel occupies a little slice of Rocky Mountain heaven. Opened in 1902 as bachelor housing for miners, the historic inn occupies 22 acres of pristine, secluded land surrounded by national forest. Paying homage to the American arts-and-crafts movement, the red-roofed lodge features more than 60 pieces of authentic Gustav Stickley furniture. Also look out for locally quarried and hand-cut marble, and gorgeous, handcrafted wrought-iron light fixtures in the rooms and lobby.

However, the best lodging in the area may be **Avalanche Ranch**, along Avalanche Creek. In addition to the 15 cabins and five covered wagons are lovely geothermal pools to soak in – open to nonguests if you reserve (*avalancheranch.com; day pass $32*). Insider tip: the **Penny Hot Springs** are right off Hwy 133 at MM 55 and free to access, though they can get flooded when the water is high.

Marble

TIME FROM ASPEN: 1½ HR 🚙

Off-road adventure to Crystal ghost town

One of Colorado's most famous ghost towns, **Crystal** is also one of the most photogenic, though it is smack in the middle of nowhere – which is certainly a good thing, as long as you're up for the detour.

The first mining in the area took place in the 1860s, but access was so poor it wasn't until the 1880s that it really picked up. By 1893 there were a half-dozen mines producing silver, lead and zinc, and the population spiked at several hundred. Despite having been virtually abandoned by 1915, there are several fairly intact structures still standing, including the iconic **Crystal Mill**, a turn-of-the-century power generator.

To get here, you'll need to pass through tiny **Marble**, whose quarry (still in operation) has supplied stone to some of the most famous monuments in the US. One of the more interesting experiences back here is following a flatbed truck haul-

Crystal Mill

ing a massive block of marble up the road – pray that those chains hold! The town has a great BBQ smoker and a small cafe should you discover you're short on picnic supplies.

Marble is located 28 miles south of Carbondale, about 6 miles up County Rd 3. After Marble the dirt road to Crystal is another 6 miles, but you'll need a serious off-road vehicle to make the trip; don't underestimate the driving back here. If your car isn't up to the task, contact **Crystal River Jeep Tours** *(smithfamilycolorado.com; $500 for up to five people)* or consider hiking instead. Budget three or four hours for a visit to Crystal. It's only accessible from June through November. **Out West Guides** *(outwestguides.com; horseback rides $110)* also runs a variety of horseback-riding and fishing trips from town.

THE YULE MARBLE QUARRY

It's fair to say that 19th-century miners were more interested in minerals than marble, and when they did find this deposit in 1882, shipping logistics kept the site from being developed for the next two decades. Unlike elsewhere, there was no race to Marble, and it took until 1906 for the Crystal River Railroad spur to finally link the town to the outside world. Italian stoneworkers were recruited, the town's population grew tenfold, and two – *two!* – newspapers opened on Main St. For a time, this was allegedly the largest marble quarry on earth. Some of the most famous monuments of their day used this stone: an estimated 500 railroad cars' worth of marble was shipped out in 1926 for the Lincoln Memorial and the Tomb of the Unknown Soldier.

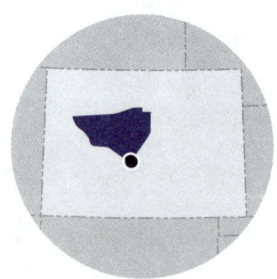

Salida & the Arkansas River Valley

RAFTING | HOT SPRINGS | HIKING

GETTING AROUND

Hwy 24/285 is the main thoroughfare here, running north–south alongside the Arkansas River. Located at the 'exit' of the Arkansas River Valley, Salida occupies a prime location at the crossroads of Hwys 285 and 50. South is the San Luis Valley, east is the Royal Gorge, west is Crested Butte, and north is Leadville and multiple high mountain passes. Hwy 285 North will take you to Denver in roughly 2½ hours. **Bustang** *(bustang. com; $29)* runs from Denver to Salida once daily, taking 3½ hours. Both Salida and Buena Vista are small and easily navigated on foot.

When a town of 5500 people has four microbreweries and just as many mountain bike shops, you know something's up. A former railroad hub turned ranching community turned outdoor hub, Salida is quintessential Colorado: where mud-spattered pickup trucks cruise the streets alongside battered Subarus adorned with rooftop kayaks, and mighty peaks form distant postcard panoramas everywhere you look.

Blessed with a historic redbrick downtown and backed by the massive Collegiate range, Salida is not only an inviting spot to explore, it also has an unbeatable location along the Arkansas River and Browns Canyon National Monument, one of the most popular stretches of white water in the US.

The plan of attack is to raft, bike or hike during the day, then come back to town to refuel with grilled buffalo ribs and a cold IPA at night.

And did we mention that the sun always shines?

Refuel in Buena Vista

Stroll down Main St

Salida isn't the only rafting town along the Arkansas – be sure to check out Buena Vista (that's pronounced 'byoona vista,' pardner) to the north, which makes for an excellent pre- or post-trip pit stop to your river or mountain adventure. With Mt Princeton (14,197ft) and the rest of the Collegiate Peaks providing a dramatic backdrop to the west, Buena Vista certainly lives up to its name. Grab a coffee or ice cream on Main St and check out the funky rock formations east of the river.

The **Barbara Whipple Trail** (2 miles) is accessed from the end of E Main St (turn north), where it follows an old railroad grade through the arid hills and funky rock formations east of the Arkansas River, with stupendous views back toward the Collegiates. Mountain bikers can combine this with other trails in the area.

SALIDA & THE ARKANSAS RIVER VALLEY VAIL, ASPEN & CENTRAL COLORADO

THE GUIDE

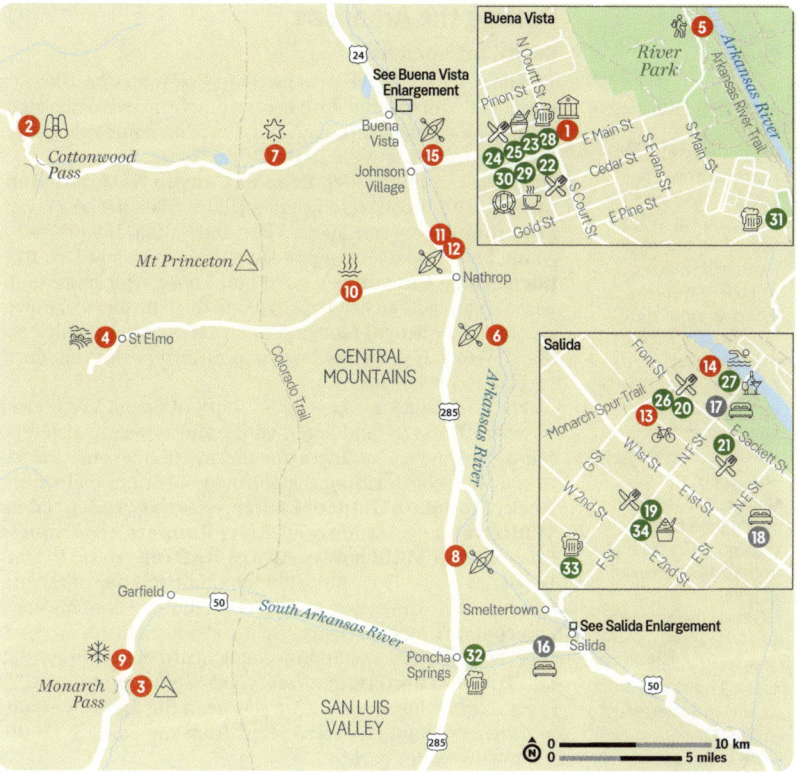

SIGHTS
1 Buena Vista Heritage Museum
2 Cottonwood Pass
3 Monarch Pass
4 St Elmo

ACTIVITIES
5 Barbara Whipple Trail
6 Browns Canyon National Monument
7 Cottonwood Hot Springs
8 Independent Whitewater
● Monarch Crest Trail (see 3)
9 Monarch Mountain
10 Mt Princeton Hot Springs Resort

11 River Runners
12 Rocky Mountain Outdoor Center
13 Sub-Culture Cyclery
14 Totally Tubular
15 Wilderness Aware Rafting

SLEEPING
16 Amigo Motor Lodge
● Ghost Town Guest House (see 4)
17 Palace Hotel
18 Simple Lodge & Hostel

EATING
19 Amicas
20 Biker & the Baker

21 Fritz
22 House Rock Kitchen
23 Louie's
24 The Olive
25 Simple Eatery
26 Sweetie's

DRINKING
27 Boathouse Cantina
28 Buena Viking
29 Buena Vista Roastery
30 Deerhammer
31 Eddyline Restaurant & Brewery
32 Elevation
33 Moonlight Pizza & Brewpub
34 Salida Pharmacy & Fountain

☑ TOP TIP

Campgrounds along the river here are picturesque, especially if you're on a boating trip, but not all have running water or shade. Go to *cpwshop.com*, click on Reserve a Campsite, and search for 'Arkansas Headwaters Recreation Area' to learn more about individual sites.

Rafting the Arkansas

Ready, set...paddle!

The headwaters of the Arkansas are Colorado's best-known stretch of white water, with everything from extreme rapids to mellow ripples. Although most rafting companies cover the river from Leadville to the Royal Gorge, the most popular trips descend through **Browns Canyon National Monument**, a 16-mile stretch that includes Class III to IV rapids, running between Buena Vista and Salida. If you're with young kids or just looking for something more low key, **Bighorn Sheep Canyon** is a good bet. Those after more of an adrenaline rush can head upstream to the **Numbers** or downstream to the **Royal Gorge** (Cañon City), both of which are Class IV to V. If you'd like to go solo, outfitters also rent duckies (inflatable kayaks).

Most companies are based just south of Buena Vista, close to where Hwys 24 and 285 diverge, and typically also offer full-day adventure packages that include zipline tours, via ferrata or horseback riding. Established outfitters include the **Rocky Mountain Outdoor Center** (*rmoc.com*), **Independent Whitewater** (*raftsalida.com*), **River Runners** (*riverrunners ltd.com*) and **Wilderness Aware Rafting** (*inaraft.com*). Expect to spend from $100/160 for a half/full day of rafting.

If you want to get out on the water but are looking for a less committing experience, then consider renting an inner tube, boogie board or stand-up paddleboard in downtown Salida. **Totally Tubular** (*totallytubularsalida.com; tubes/SUPs from $20/35*) has all the gear you need (including wetsuits and helmets) and is located steps from the Salida's 1200ft-long white-water park.

Biking S Mountain

No pain, no gain

First impressions of mountain biking may leave you wondering what sort of sick masochist came up with this sport. You spend an hour gasping for breath as you climb up a steep hill. Pedaling over roots and skull-sized boulders on a way-too-narrow path. If you fall, you'll tumble back down the hill, roll over a carpet of prickly pears, and break multiple bones. How is this enjoyable?

But trust us, once you reach the summit and start slaloming through the pines and zipping around banked turns, you will definitely be having fun. So much fun that you might decide you want to pedal up that damn hill a second time.

WHERE TO EAT IN SALIDA: OUR PICKS

Sweetie's: Uber-popular and superfriendly, with an incredible selection of over 60 hot and cold sandwiches, like the Flaming Goat. *10am-4pm* **$$**

Amicas: This pizza parlor is the perfect spot to replenish all those calories you burned off during the day. Microbrews too. *11am-9pm* **$$**

The Fritz: This fun parkside joint whips up clever American-style tapas, from elk sausage to fried green tomatoes. *4-9pm Thu-Mon* **$$**

The Biker & the Baker: Upstairs from Sweeties, B&B combines the winning combo of brunch, wine and dessert. *8am-noon Sun-Wed, 8am-noon & 4-10pm Thu-Sat* **$$**

Salida's excellent trail system starts just across the river beneath the giant S: rent a bike from **Sub-Culture Cyclery** *(subculturecyclery.com; half-day rental $70)*, pedal down F St and across the bridge (stopping to check out the old caboose) and start exploring. We recommend sticking to the green trails at first, especially if you're coming from sea level.

If you've done this before, then you know: the **Monarch Crest Trail** awaits. One of the most famous rides in Colorado, this is an extreme 35-mile adventure, with fabulous high-altitude views. It starts off at Monarch Pass (11,312ft), follows the exposed ridge 12 miles to Marshall Pass and then either cuts down to Poncha Springs on an old railroad grade or hooks onto the Rainbow Trail. The **High Valley Bike Shuttle** *(monarchcrest.com; $42)* picks up cyclists in Poncha Springs and brings them up to the trailhead twice daily, at 8am and 10am. **Absolute Bikes** *(absolutebikes.com; $39)* also runs shuttles on Fridays through Sundays at 8am.

Hiking & Skiing at Monarch Pass

Float like a butterfly

Twenty-three miles west of Salida is **Monarch Pass** (11,312ft), where a vintage tramway ($18) hauls visitors an additional 1000ft up to the top of the Continental Divide, and a gift shop and cafe warms the hands and hearts of the skimpily dressed. For those who are adequately prepared, however, the pass is a good launchpad for hikes (the Continental Divide and Colorado Trails) and bike rides (Monarch Crest).

Just downhill from the pass is **Monarch Mountain** *(ski monarch.com; adult/child day pass from $134/104)*, the local ski resort that has plenty of powder without the attitude. Although the 800-acre resort is on the small side, you'll still find excellent varied terrain and, most importantly, affordable lift tickets. For a real treat, sign up for their backcountry snowcat ski tours (from $500), which open up an additional 1600 acres of terrain.

Soak in Hot Springs

Unwind in style

It doesn't have to be 10 below with thick snowflakes falling from the sky to enjoy a soak in an outdoor hot spring, but it doesn't hurt. There are two springs within an easy drive of both Salida and Buena Vista, and whether you're relaxing

FIBARK

For days every mid-June, Salida hosts the nation's oldest white-water festival, FIBArk – aka **First in Boating the Arkansas** *(fibark. com)*. The festival got its start in 1949, when a few local river rats decided to race each other 57 miles down the river, from Salida to Cañon City. Of the six boats that entered, only one made it to the finish line, so the following year it was decided to exclude the Royal Gorge from the contest so that contestants wouldn't have to flirt so closely with death. Fast forward to the 21st century, and FIBArk is still going strong, drawing 10,000 spectators and a huge variety of boating, biking and trail running races in and along the Arkansas. There's live music too.

DRINKING IN SALIDA: OUR PICKS

Boathouse Cantina: Snag a table by the river and watch the kayakers float by. The buffalo chili and beer ain't bad either. *11am-9pm*

Moonlight Pizza & Brewpub: Homemade dough, beer brewed on site...is it any wonder that Moonlight has been going strong since 1994? *11am-9pm*

Salida Pharmacy & Fountain: It's back to the future at this 1950s style soda fountain, with root beer floats, sundaes and pop. *11am-9pm Sun-Thu*

Elevation: Out in Poncha Springs, this is a top pick for beer geeks, with 16 beers on tap, including four barrel-aged brews. Food truck too. *11am-9pm*

SALIDA'S HISTORIC DISTRICT

Salida doesn't have any major sights, but its downtown contains around 100 brick buildings that date to the turn of the last century, making it the largest historic district in Colorado. If you're visiting other historic towns in Colorado, like Aspen or Breckenridge, you'll likely notice that the buildings are all made of wood. Salida's all-brick construction is due to two successive fires, one in 1886 and the other in 1888, which convinced local businessmen that building with timber was simply too dangerous.

Another historic landmark to look out for is the 365ft smokestack northwest of town, off Hwy 291. Once the tallest smokestack west of the Mississippi, it belonged to a mineral smelting plant.

J. NORMAN REID/SHUTTERSTOCK

Arkansas River rafting (p238)

the muscles after a hard day's play or warming the cockles of your frozen swimsuit on a winter night, they both deliver.

Mt Princeton Hot Springs *(mtprinceton.com; day pass from $40)* is a sprawling, four-star hot-springs resort, which is popular with families and spa-goers. There are 30 natural pools on the property that differ in size and atmosphere, including soaking pools, an expansive swimming pool and a 400ft water slide. Don't let that last feature scare you off: the full-service spa will ensure you bliss out in peace. Many guests stay the night. It's located in the shadow of Mt Princeton, off County Rd 321.

Cottonwood Hot Springs *(cottonwood-hot-springs.com; day pass from $30)* is the New Agey option, but we mean that in the best possible way. It's more intimate, and the leafy grounds, gushing fountains and wind chimes evoke a more contemplative atmosphere. While it's a cheaper soak, it is in need of a renovation and the lodging options are just OK. Both springs are about 15 minutes from Buena Vista and 30 minutes from Salida.

EATING IN BUENA VISTA: OUR PICKS

Louie's: Hands-down the best ice cream and sorbet in the valley, with a fun playground and patio, too. *noon-8pm Thu-Tue* **$**

Olive: A reggae food truck and a patio – perfect for gyro sandwiches, tabbouleh bowls and salads. *11am-4pm Mon-Wed, to 8pm Thu-Sun* **$**

House Rock Kitchen: A fire pit, sofa, live band and horseshoes – dinner here is like hanging out at a backyard BBQ. *11am-9pm* **$$**

Simple Eatery: Sharing a space with outdoor store Trailhead is this welcoming soup and salad cafe. *10:30am-8pm* **$$**

Drive Cottonwood Pass

High-altitude adventure

Ever wonder what it's like to drive to the moon? Then wind your way 19 gorgeous miles on County Rd 302 to **Cottonwood Pass** (12,126ft). After passing Cottonwood Hot Springs, you'll reach the Avalanche Trailhead on the north side of the road, Mt Yale's summit flickering in and out of the trees (9.5 miles round trip). Further uphill you'll come to Denny Creek Trail (4.6-mile round trip to Hartenstein Lake), then Ptarmigan Lake Trailhead (6.8 miles round trip). The drive to the pass goes from moderately sinuous to downright jagged as you approach the edge of the timberline, the Collegiate Peaks spread out before you against the big blue sky. It's far more scenic than Monarch Pass (p239), and if you're headed west to Gunnison or Crested Butte (p243) it's a far superior route – descending past the Taylor Park Reservoir is simply gorgeous.

From the pass's parking lot, take the short 0.2-mile trail up to the Continental Divide lookout for a great photo-op – it's worth the huffing and puffing. The pass is open June through October.

Hike in the Collegiates

Standardized tests not required

Who said the Ivy Leagues had to be stuck-up and stressed out? Laced with 105 miles of trails, the Collegiate Peaks has the highest average elevation of any wilderness area in the US: eight peaks exceed 14,000ft, including the state's third- and fifth-highest summits, **Mt Harvard** and **La Plata Peak**. (Princeton, Yale, Oxford and Columbia rank 20th, 21st, 26th and 35th respectively.)

Huron Peak (14,012ft), meanwhile, doesn't have the name recognition of its neighbors, but it is arguably the top climb. But the best hikes here don't necessarily involve peak bagging. Easier day trips include **Ptarmigan Lake** (6.6 miles; 14 miles from Buena Vista on County Rd 306), **Kroenke Lake** (8 miles; access County Rd 365) and as much of the Colorado Trail as you want to do (access Avalanche Trailhead, 9 miles from Buena Vista on County Rd 306). You can also pick up the Continental Divide Trail atop both Monarch (p239) and Cottonwood Pass.

Remember that storms in the Collegiates can blow in fast, so don't hesitate to turn back if the weather gets dicey. For detailed descriptions and maps, stop by the ranger office in Salida.

BUENA VISTA HERITAGE

Before Salida was named county seat in 1933, the honor belonged to Buena Vista, as evidenced by the 1882 Chaffee County Courthouse on Main St. However, in true Wild West fashion, the court records didn't come to Buena Vista willingly. No sir, it required a posse of local men, who rode a locomotive 17 miles north to the rival town of Granite in the dark of night. They held the sleep-addled sheriff at gunpoint and loaded all the Chaffee County records and court furniture onto the train's flatbed car, then returned home to stash their haul until the new courthouse was built three years later. Today the building holds the **Buena Vista Heritage Museum**, whose exhibits introduce different aspects of regional history.

 DRINKING IN BUENA VISTA: OUR PICKS

| **Buena Vista Roastery:** Hatch plans for the day over a cup of organic fair-trade coffee and a giant blueberry scone. *7am-3pm* | **Buena Viking:** The Viking food truck has graduated to full-on gastropub, with burgers, cocktails and draft beer. *11am-9pm Wed-Mon* | **Deerhammer:** Single-malt whiskey, gin and brandy are the winners at Buena Vista's distillery. *3-8pm Thu, Fri & Mon, 11am-10pm Sat, 11am-6pm Sun* | **Eddyline Restaurant & Brewery:** With a sunny patio just steps from the Arkansas River, this brewpub is a local hangout. *11:30am-8pm Tue-Sun* |

THE CONTINENTAL DIVIDE TRAIL

Both Cottonwood and Monarch Pass offer easy access to the longest and least-developed trail in the Triple Crown: the Continental Divide Trail (CDT). Unlike its more famous counterparts, the Appalachian Trail and the Pacific Crest Trail, the Continental Divide Trail is still incomplete, adding an extra challenge for through hikers. As if they needed it: at 3028 miles in length, and running along the spine of the Rockies with few markers, this is not a challenge for novice backpackers. And that's before you consider the grizzlies, mountain lions, rattlesnakes, lightning strikes and other risks. Colorado in particular is considered to be the most challenging state, with an average elevation above 10,000ft, deep snowpack and multiple 14ers to summit along the way.

ATMOSPHERE1/SHUTTERSTOCK

St Elmo

Explore St Elmo Ghost Town

A prospector's faded dreams

An old gold-mining ghost town tucked amid the Collegiate Peaks, **St Elmo** makes for a fun excursion. The drive is the best part: the road wends its way past stands of redolent ponderosa pine, a wildlife-viewing meadow and jagged peaks before petering out at what is Colorado's best-preserved ghost town.

Of course, it wasn't about the scenery back in the good ol' days – there was gold in this here creek! Most buildings were built in or around 1881: the schoolhouse, an old mercantile building and a miners exchange are among the best kept of the bunch.

The only catch to this spectacular setting is that St Elmo is also a staging point for ATV and snowmobile enthusiasts, who follow the Forest Service road up to Tincup Pass. The revving of not-too-distant engines can take away some of the charm, so try to avoid weekends.

If you've got the time and energy, you can continue on 5 miles to **Hancock**; the turnoff is just before St Elmo. From here it's a 3-mile hike up to the **Alpine Tunnel** – a failed attempt to get a railroad through the mountain – and amazing views from the Continental Divide.

If you want to have the place to yourself, stay the night: the **Ghost Town Guest House** (*ghosttownguesthouse.com*) is a local B&B (really!) and there are three popular USFS campgrounds on the way up. They're all nice, but Chalk Lake has a choice location with views of Mt Princeton. Reservations via *recreation.gov* are essential. Just before the turnoff to the campground is a parking lot for the Agnes Vaille trail (on your right), a short half-mile hike up to a waterfall. It's the perfect spot to stretch your legs.

St Elmo is on County Rd 162, 11.5 miles past Mt Princeton Hot Springs (p240). The road turns to dirt about halfway up. In summer it's not a problem, but in winter or muddy conditions you'll want an AWD.

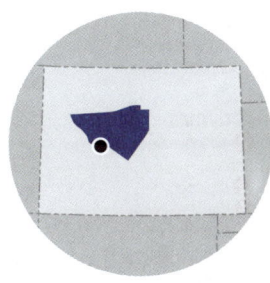

Crested Butte

SKIING | MOUNTAIN BIKING | WILDFLOWERS

Crested Butte (8865ft) is one of the best mountain towns in the United States, and thanks to its remote location, it's managed to retain much of its renegade charm. Looming above it all is the pyramid-shaped Mt Crested Butte itself (12,162ft) – an extreme powder-filled playground, punctuated by some of the steepest lines in Colorado.

This was also one of the birthplaces of mountain biking, and you can ride or hike for hundreds of miles on the smooth, wildflower-laden trails that traverse the wilderness areas surrounding town. And the scenery is off-the-charts gorgeous, with aspen-choked hillsides, scenic alpine lakes and towering snowcapped peaks in every direction.

In the quaint old town center, well-preserved Victorian homes and storefronts now house art galleries, excellent restaurants, shops and more. The locals here are carefree and unassuming, and you get a sense that this is a real community. In Crested Butte, everybody has a good time.

Ski the Steeps

Brave the Teocalli Bowls

It might not be Aspen, but that suits the locals just fine: Crested Butte remains one of Colorado's best **ski resorts** *(skicb.com; adult/child day pass $195/127)*. It's known for its stomach-lurching steeps, with infamous runs like Rambo and the Banana Chute bestowing bragging rights onto

GETTING AROUND

Crested Butte is roughly a 4½-hour drive from Denver. In summer, opt for the wild and scenic Cottonwood Pass across the Sawatch Range. In winter, traffic needs to cross the mountains at Monarch Pass, on Hwy 50. There are also flights to Gunnison-Crested Butte Regional Airport, usually at least once a week, sometimes more in winter, which is 45 minutes south of town in Gunnison.

Rocky Rides *(rockyrides.com; $115 per person)* offers a shuttle service between DIA and Crested Butte. Denver's **Bustang** *(ridebustang.com; $45)* also serves Crested butte once daily, though the trip takes nearly six hours.

☑ TOP TIP

Before your next trip to the Butte, be sure to watch the short film *Born from Junk*, an entertaining account of the origins of mountain biking in the 1970s, back when the boys from Aspen would ride into town on motorcycles and steal all the women.

SIGHTS

1 Crested Butte Mountain Heritage Museum

ACTIVITIES

2 Adaptive Sports Center
3 Alpineer
4 Big Al's Bicycle Heaven
5 Crested Butte Mountain Resort
6 Crested Butte Nordic Center
7 Lupine Loop
● Mountain Bike Park (see 5)

SLEEPING

8 Crested Butte Hostel
9 Elk Mountain Lodge

EATING

10 Breadery
11 Frank's Deli
12 Secret Stash
13 Sunflower

EATING

14 Dogwood
15 Eldo Brewery
16 Montanya
17 Uley's Cabin Ice Bar

TRANSPORT

18 Silver Queen Express

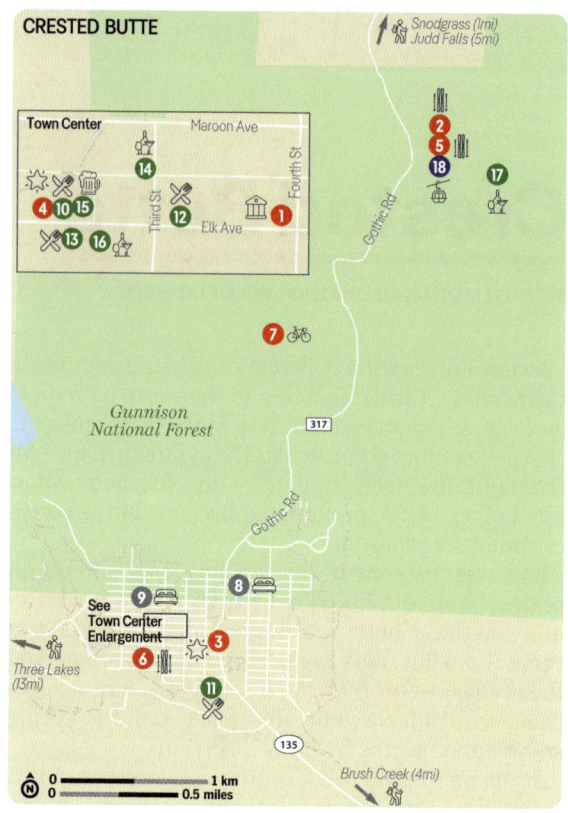

survivors. The Teocalli Bowls near the summit offer more extreme lines, including a backcountry-esque 20-minute hike out at the bottom.

It's not all daredevil plunges, though – regardless of your level, everyone loves the short lift lines, irreverent spirit and stunning scenery.

The town also has a terrific **Nordic Center** (*cbnordic.org; day passes $25*) with 50km of groomed trails and a special ski-in gourmet dinner at Magic Meadows Yurt (reserve). The **Adaptive Sports Center** (*adaptivesports.org*), meanwhile, promotes mountain access for people of all abilities.

 EATING IN CRESTED BUTTE: OUR PICKS

Frank's Deli: Local fave serving hearty sandwiches and breakfast burritos perfect for the trail. Ask about the specials! *9am-6pm Mon-Sat* $

Secret Stash: Award-winning pizzeria with boho vibe, teahouse seating and tapestries included. Cocktails pack a serious punch. *11am-9pm* $$

Sunflower: Inventive, locally sourced dishes served in a homey cabin-like setting. Menu changes with seasonal ingredients. *6-10pm Wed-Sat* $$$

Breadery: Chewy sourdough flatbreads meet shared plates (pear ricotta ravioli) and soups and salads for a family-style meal. Fresh bread to go. *5-9pm Wed-Sun* $$$

The Birthplace of Mountain Biking

Get your flow on

Crested Butte is one of the places that brought mountain biking to the world and it absolutely lives up to the hype. Take your pick between a fantastic **mountain bike park** *(skicb. com; day pass from $65)* or 450 miles of smooth-flowing single-track crossing wildflower- and aspen-clad hills and meadows.

The **Lupine Loop** is a great first trail, with outrageous views across the Slate River Valley. The 13-mile intermediate-level ride has just enough climbing to keep you honest, interspersed with fun, flowing descents.

Local outfitters **Big Al's Bicycle Heaven** *(bigalsbicycle heaven.com)* and **Alpineer** *(alpineer.com)* have rentals, maps, gear and more. Figure on $55 for a full-suspension bike for half a day.

After your ride, stop by the **Crested Butte Mountain Heritage Museum** *(crestedbuttemuseum.com; by donation)* for everything you ever wanted to know about local biking.

Wildflower Trails

A hiker's paradise

If you're after more of a stop-and-smell-the-flowers type of vibe, then you're in luck: this is the official wildflower capital of the state. Hiking trails are saturated in color, from purple lupines and columbines to yellow glacier lilies. **The Wildflower Festival** is mid-July and peak season is late July, though anytime from mid-June through early August will do.

Top hiking trails for flowers include **Snodgrass** (5.8 miles) and **Brush Creek** (4.25 miles). Farther out of town is **Judd Falls** (2.2 miles), which features a waterfall and alpine lake. If alpine hiking is more your thing, ride the **Silver Queen Express** *(adult/child $45/39)*. From the top, the summit of Mt Crested Butte (12,162ft) is a 2-mile round trip.

Finally, for a gorgeous drive, head up Kleber Pass west of town, where numerous campgrounds and trailheads like **Three Lakes** offer access to the spectacular high country.

FAT-TIRE REVOLUTIONARY

In April 1998 Neil Murdoch – local CB eccentric and the founder of mountain biking as the world knows it – slipped out town with just his clothes and a bike, hours before federal marshals closed in. Murdoch, aka Richard Barrister, had settled in little-known Crested Butte in 1974 after skipping bail on a cocaine-smuggling charge in New Mexico. A consummate tinkerer, Murdoch began outfitting old Schwinn bikes to be ridden off-road, including adding low gears and wide knobby tires – thus the 'Fat Tire Revolution' was born. When he disappeared, Crested Butte rallied behind Murdoch in absentia, even establishing a fund for his legal defense. He was eventually caught in 2001 but is still revered as the godfather of mountain biking.

 DRINKING IN CRESTED BUTTE: APRÈS-SKI

Dogwood: Cocktail lounge in a historic miner's cabin. Innovative drinks feature house-infused liquors, which pair well with the good appetizers. *4-10 Wed-Sun*

Montanya: Artisanal rum distillery serving potent mixed drinks, sippers and flights in a midcentury-modern tasting room. Reservations recommended. *3-9pm Tue-Sun*

Eldo Brewery: Low-key brewery serving pints and Himalayan eats. Outdoor deck and live music most nights. *3-11pm Mon-Fri, from noon Sat & Sun*

Uley's Cabin Ice Bar: The ski resort's ice bar – snow-covered bar top included – at the bottom of Peanut and Twister. *11am-3pm*

Places We Love to Stay

$ Budget $$ Midrange $$$ Top End

Winter Park   p192

Idlewild Campground $ Just outside of town and connected to the Fraser River Trail, this is an awesome location for cyclists and hikers.

Snow Mountain Ranch $ The YMCA has the best family digs around, from yurts to cabins and hotel rooms. It's 14 miles north of Winter Park.

Devil's Thumb Ranch $$$ The cowboy-chic lodge is a must for a romantic weekend escape.

Breckenridge   p196

Bivvi Hostel $ A modern hostel with a log-cabin vibe, the Bivvi wins points for style, friendliness and affordability. Four- to six-person dorms and a gorgeous deck.

Fireside Inn $ This long-running hostel and B&B has cozy private rooms and dorms, plus the requisite hot tub. Ten-minute walk from the gondola.

Gravity Haus $$ Sleek modern rooms for adventurers at the base of Peak 9, with fitness classes, sauna and even a cold-plunge pool.

Lodge at Breckenridge $$$ High above town off Boreas Pass Rd, this hotel's draw is the breathtaking panoramas.

Frisco   p202

Peak One Campground $ Frisco's main campground is located on the southwest shore of Dillon Reservoir; has 80 sites.

Frisco Lodge $$ Receiving guests since it first opened as a log-cabin stagecoach stop on Main St in 1885.

Inn on Galena $$$ Friendly B&B with serene atmosphere and 15 wonderfully comfortable rooms. On-site spa, afternoon *aperitivo* and a gourmet breakfast up the appeal.

Dillon & Silverthorne   p203

Prospector Campground $ Dillon's main USFS campground (107 sites) is located on the south side of Dillon Reservoir.

The Pad $ A variety of rooms are available at this hip Silverthorne hostel, from dorms to private shipping containers with kitchenette.

Homewood Suites $$ Located near the Dillon Marina, all rooms here come with kitchens; also has an indoor pool.

Vail   p207

Gore Creek Campground $ Twenty-four tent sites are nestled in the woods by Gore Creek, 6 miles east of Vail village.

Sebastian Hotel $$$ Deluxe and modern, this sophisticated hotel showcases tasteful contemporary art and an impressive list of amenities, including a mountainside ski valet and luxury spa.

Arrabelle $$$ The grand dame of Lionshead, the Arrabelle is a massive, chalet-style resort with a stone-and-marble lobby, top-shelf service and a variety of accommodations.

Austria Haus $$$ Both hotel rooms and condos feature charming details such as Berber carpets and marble baths.

Mountain Haus $$$ One of Vail's better deals is near the village entrance; rooms have fireplaces, king-sized beds and balconies.

Minturn   p213

The Bunkhouse $ The Ikea-chic Bunkhouse features 30 custom-built pods – cozy, enclosed bunk beds – for the cheapest digs near Vail.

Minturn Inn $$ Set in a 1915 log-hewn building, this cozy B&B turns on the mountain charm with handcrafted log beds and river-rock fireplaces.

Leadville   p215

Inn the Clouds Hostel $ Guests get the run of this hostel, which includes two common areas, a Ping-Pong table and a large kitchen.

Tennessee Pass Sleep Yurts (p215) **$** Sleeping in the backcountry has never been so luxurious, with room service and even luggage delivery. Yurts sleep up to six.

Delaware Hotel $$ Antique-strewn Victorian hotel that dates back to 1886, with high ceilings and lace curtains.

Aspen   p218

Difficult Campground $ The largest campground near Aspen and one of four sites at the foot of Independence Pass. Reserve well ahead.

St Moritz Lodge $$$ Come ski season, this simple European-style lodge is one of the cheapest deals in town.

Tyrolean Lodge $$$ Spacious personalized rooms, some with kitchenettes and fireplaces. Another affordable choice.

Mollie Aspen $$$ Make like Rihanna and book a room at Aspen's coolest new digs, with understated minimalist design and rooftop pool.

Limelight Hotel $$$ Sleek and trendy, rooms here are spacious with stylish accoutrements. Mountain views too.

Hotel Jerome $$$ Superb service and relaxed elegance are the trademarks of this historic landmark. Expect period antiques and fluffy, feather-down comforters.

Glenwood Springs   p230

Hotel Maxwell Anderson $$ Convenient downtown location and charming interior makes this century-old property (formerly the Hotel Denver) a seductive choice.

Glenwood Hot Springs Lodge $$$ If you're coming here specifically for the hot springs, the on-site hotel is the top pick. Pool access included.

Basalt   p233

Chapman Campground $ One of six campgrounds along the Fryingpan River, 29 miles east of Basalt.

Basalt Mountain Inn $$ One of the most affordable places to stay in the Aspen area; only 20 minutes from Snowmass.

Salida   p236

Simple Lodge & Hostel $ It may be simple, but it's got a full kitchen and a comfy communal area that feels just like home.

Amigo Motor Lodge $$ This cool motel is not only Southwestern stylish, it's got five retro Airstream trailers to sleep in.

Palace Hotel $$ The atmospheric redbrick Palace is a 1909 landmark with six personalized vintage suites.

Buena Vista   p236

Chalk Lake Campground $ One of three campgrounds by the Mt Princeton Hot Springs; 13 miles southwest of Buena Vista.

Railroad Bridge Campground $ Six miles north of town, past a series of blasted tunnels, is this gorgeous site by the Arkansas River. No water.

Surf Chateau $$$ Funky and modern, this river-stone property has split-level lofts in row houses and more traditional rooms overlooking the river.

Crested Butte   p243

Crested Butte Hostel $ The most luxurious hostel in Colorado is this beauty with a restaurant-grade kitchen, crackling fireplace and mix of dorms and private rooms.

Elk Mountain Lodge $$$ Historic 1919 miner's hotel with comfortable modern rooms. Easy access to main street and the ski shuttle.

Lodge at Breckenridge

For places to stay in Mesa Verde & Western Colorado, see p296

RON KARPEL/SHUTTERSTOCK

Independence Monument (p291)

Mesa Verde & Western Colorado

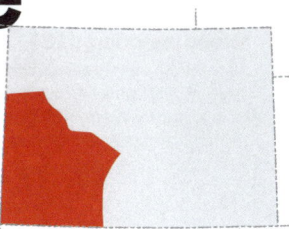

HISTORY AND OUTDOOR ADVENTURE

From red-rock desert to towering peaks, the landscape is as diverse as the history of the region itself: welcome to western Colorado.

DANITA DELIMONT/SHUTTERSTOCK

Western Colorado is the stuff of dreams, with magnificence at every turn: rugged snowcapped mountains and otherworldly red-rock desert, sweeping alpine meadows and deep, dark canyon floors. It was the home of the Fremont people and Ancestral Puebloans and, later, the Ute, who lived atop its mesas and hunted through its valleys. Gold and greed pushed the Utes out – an American storyline – replaced by soldiers, miners, farmers and ranchers, all looking for a new life in the Wild West. Modern times have added a new set of locals – people seeking outdoor adventure by boot, bike, ski and more.

The influences of the myriad people who have walked these lands is still visible today in the cliff dwellings in and around Mesa Verde National Park, the petroglyphs in Canyon Pintado, the historic mining towns such as Ouray and Silverton, the small-town wineries and hot-spring spas, and the tony ski resort of Telluride. Then there are the vast spaces in between, such as Colorado National Monument and its miles of backcountry trails, the stark desert beauty (and not-so-hidden bones) of Dinosaur National Monument, the still untamable, vertigo-inducing drops of the Black Canyon of the Gunnison, and the boundless DIY adventures to be had in Weminuche Wilderness. Western Colorado's real pull, however, might well be its independent spirit, which has drawn people to the area for millennia.

THE MAIN AREAS

MESA VERDE NATIONAL PARK
Ancient cliff dwellings. **p254**

OURAY
History, hiking and hot springs. **p266**

BLACK CANYON OF THE GUNNISON NATIONAL PARK
Epic canyon views. **p279**

GRAND JUNCTION
Small town base camp. **p285**

Grand Junction, p285

A small town with old-school charm that's an optimal base for outdoor adventure in the nearby high desert, red-rock canyons and wine country.

● Grand Junction

Black Canyon of the Gunnison National Park, p279

A little-visited national park with 2000ft-high walls and dramatic craggy spires. Winding roads along both rims makes visiting easy.

Black Canyon of the
Gunnison National Park

Ouray, p266

A historic mountain town located in a dramatic box canyon with hot springs, ice climbing, high-altitude hikes and more.

Mesa Verde National Park, p254

A one-of-a-kind national park and UNESCO World Heritage Site, Mesa Verde's cliff dwellings inspire awe and respect.

Book Cliffs
Mountains

○ Parachute

70

○ Fruita

○ Collbran

Colorado River

Colorado
National
Monument

Grand Mesa
National
Forest
○ Grand
Mesa

Cedaredge ○

50

Gunnison River

● Delta

○ Gateway

Uncompahgre
National
Forest

Montrose ○

550

○ Paradox
○ Bedrock

Dolores River

○ Naturita

Ridgway ○

○ Slick
Rock

Mt Sneffels
Wilderness
○
Telluride

Lizard Head
Wilderness

○ Dove
Creek

San Juan
National
Forest

○ Rico

Pleasant
○ View

San Juan
National
Forest

San Jaun
Skyway

550

Animas River

McPhee
Reservoir

○ Dolores

San Juan
Mountains

Canyons of the
Ancients National
Monument

○ Cortez

○ Mancos

○ Durango

Towaoc ○

● Mesa Verde
National Park

Ute Mountain
Indian Reservation

Mancos River

Mancos
Canyons

Southern Ute
Indian Reservation

UTAH

ARIZONA

NEW MEXICO

0
0
50 miles
100 km

Find Your Way

Western Colorado is a vast and varied region extending from Mesa Verde's cliffs and Grand Junction's wine country to the high desert surrounding Dinosaur National Monument. The San Juan Mountains form a verdant, rugged spine.

CAR

To fully explore the region, bring or rent a car. It'll give you the freedom to stop in small mountain towns, tour archaeological zones, access trailheads and pop into wineries, all at your own pace. For sites off the beaten path, consider a high-clearance 4WD vehicle.

BUS

Bus service is limited in the region. Bustang Outrider will get you to hubs such as Grand Junction, Montrose and Durango, as well as the popular ski town of Telluride. Local bus service is nonexistent or geared toward commuters.

PLANE

There are several small airports in the region: Grand Junction, Montrose, Telluride, Cortez, Durango and Pagosa Springs. There are plenty of commercial flights to and from Denver and a handful of cities beyond Colorado. There are few flights within the region itself.

Plan Your Days

Travel options vary immensely by season, and few top attractions are available year-round. Decide on the main thing you want to do – wine tasting, skiing, visiting archaeological or dino sites – and base your trip around that.

NIKO BONO/SHUTTERSTOCK

Bridal Veil Falls (p272)

If You Only Do One Thing

● Head straight to **Mesa Verde National Park** (p254), an impressive Native American archaeological site known for its elaborate and well-preserved cliff dwellings. Take a **ranger-led tour** (p256) to Cliff Palace or Balcony House and prepare to climb ladders, crawl through tunnels and descend ancient stone steps. Spend the rest of the day **hiking to petroglyphs** (p257) and exploring other structures along the **Mesa Top Loop Road** (p257); if you have energy, head to Wetherill Mesa for a self-guided tour of impressive **Step House** (p257).

● Stay after sunset for **tribal performances** (p257), celebrating the culture of the modern-day descendants of the people who once lived here. End the day **stargazing** (p257), either as part of a ranger-led program, at a pull-off on Mesa Top Loop Rd, or just by stepping outside of your tent.

SEASONAL HIGHLIGHTS

Winter is ski and snow season, while spring is green, especially at lower elevations. Summer is best for hiking and fall brings golden colors and cooler weather.

JANUARY

Ski season is in full gear. Head to the resorts – Telluride , Purgatory and Powderhorn. Check out also the **Ouray Ice Festival** (p268), which attracts ice climbers from near and far.

FEBRUARY

Take in quirky winter festivals such as Durango's **Snowdown** (p262) and Silverton's **Skijoring** (p277), which showcase the region's fun-loving character. Consider skiing Wolf Creek for, historically, the deepest powder of the year.

JUNE

Telluride Bluegrass Festival (p274) kicks off the summer festival season. The San Juan Mountains fill with hikers, bikers and campers. Or walk instead through a sea of purple in Palisade's **Colorado Lavender Festival** (p294).

Three Days to Travel Around

● Once you've seen Mesa Verde National Park, drive to **Telluride** (p272), a magnificent mountain town tucked into a box canyon. Spend the morning hiking to Colorado's tallest waterfall, **Bridal Veil Falls** (p272), or challenge your fear of heights (and upper body strength) on the spectacular **via ferrata** (p274). In the afternoon, kick around town, have a nice meal and take a sunset ride on the **gondola** (p273).

● On your last day, beeline to Ridgway for an early-morning soak at **Orvis Hot Springs** (p276) – no worries if you forgot your bathing suit!. Relaxed, head north, stopping at the must-see **Ute Indian Museum** (p283). Grab some lunch in Montrose, then straight-shot it to **Black Canyon of the Gunnison National Park** (p279) for an afternoon of spectacular canyon vistas along the park's South Rim Rd.

If You Have More Time

● From Black Canyon, head to **Grand Junction** (p285), a good base for touring the red-rock landscape in **Colorado National Monument** (p290) or wine tasting in **Palisade** (p293).

● Spend a day hiking through the alpine beauty of **Grand Mesa** (p294) or taking in the Jurassic fossils at **Dinosaur National Monument** (p292). Head back south, stopping at **Fort Uncompahgre** (p284) to learn about life in the Old West or to see the petroglyphs in **Shavano Valley** (guide required). Continue to historic **Ouray** (p266). If you have energy, hike a portion of the **Perimeter Trail** (p266) before hitting the **Ouray Hot Springs** (p267) for a well-deserved soak.

● In the morning, head to Durango on the epic **Million Dollar Highway** (p271). End your trip on the historic **Durango & Silverton Narrow Gauge Railroad** (p261), taking in majestic mountain views.

JULY

Wildflowers are in full bloom in the mountains and the weather is near perfect. **Hiking** trails around Telluride, Ouray and Grand Mesa take on an almost otherworldly feel. The **peach season** kicks off in Palisade.

SEPTEMBER

Cooler days begin and crowds disperse – a good time to visit Mesa Verde National Park and Dinosaur National Monument . It also means harvest season and **wine tasting** in Palisade and Paonia.

OCTOBER

Aspen groves paint the landscape in brilliant yellows and golds. The Million Dollar Hwy is epically beautiful, bringing photographers from near and far. The red-rock canyons cool off, making them optimal for outdoor adventure.

DECEMBER

Powder hounds hit the slopes, though the snow can be hit or miss (discounted lift tickets make up for it). **Hot springs** around the region – Ouray, Durango, Pagosa – provide an easy way to warm up!

Mesa Verde National Park

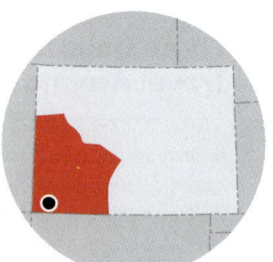

ANCIENT CLIFF DWELLINGS | RANGER TOURS | STARGAZING

GETTING AROUND

There is no public transportation in Mesa Verde. Plan on driving yourself and allot plenty of time to explore the park. Expect about an hour's drive from the main visitor center, near the highway turnoff, to sites on either Chapin Mesa or Wetherill Mesa – it's about 45 minutes between the two mesas. Roads are steep, narrow and winding, so even a short distance can be slow going. Avoid passing vehicles until there's a pull-off and watch for cyclists, wildlife and rocks on the road. If you're low on fuel, there's a gas station at Morefield Campground, open mid-May to mid-October.

Mesa Verde National Park is one of the US's largest archaeological sites and certainly the best preserved. Nestled into a stunning landscape of canyons and mesas, it holds more than 5000 ancient structures and 600 elaborate cliff dwellings. Inhabited by the Ancestral Puebloans for more than 750 years, it was abruptly abandoned in 1300 CE. No one knows exactly why.

Mesa Verde sat undisturbed until 1888 when it was 'discovered' by two white ranchers following a tip from a local Ute Native American. Their family, the Wetherills, proceeded to sell artifacts from the site and to serve as guides. In 1906, with increasing visitor numbers, it was designated a national park and eventually became a UNESCO World Heritage Site. Today, Mesa Verde is both an archaeological wonderland and a sacred site to the descendants of the Ancestral Puebloans. It's a place to respect and to explore, to learn about and to delve into the mysteries of ancient America.

☑TOP TIP

If you find an artifact – say, a fragment of pottery – leave it untouched. Once removed from its original context, an artifact is incredibly difficult for archaeologists to analyze. Instead, take a photo or create a drawing and alert a ranger to its location.

DON MAMMOSER/SHUTTERSTOCK

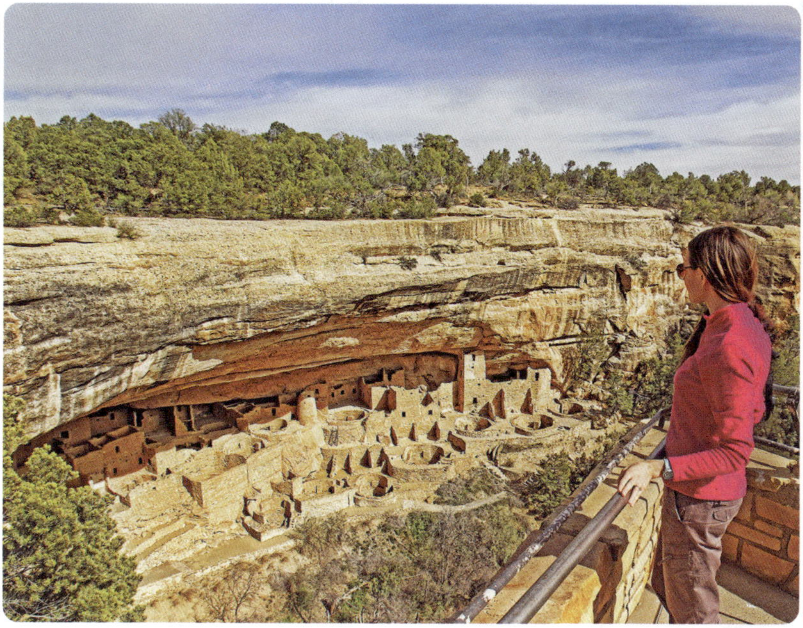

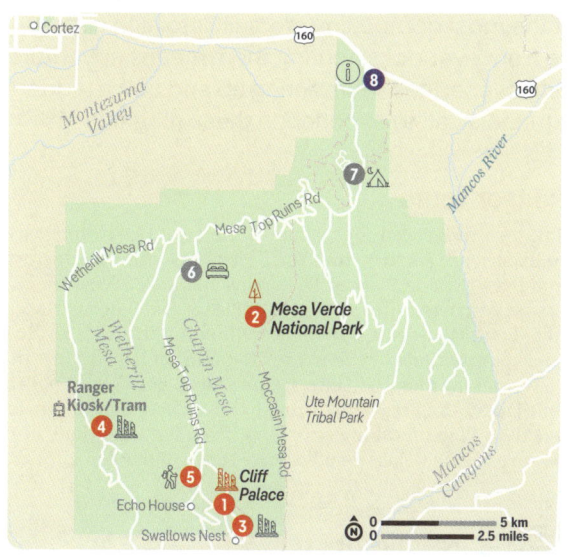

Cliff Palace (p257)

HIGHLIGHTS
1 Cliff Palace
2 Mesa Verde National Park

SIGHTS
3 Balcony House
4 Step House

ACTIVITIES
5 Petroglyph Point Trail

SLEEPING
6 Far View Lodge
7 Morefield Campground

INFORMATION
8 Mesa Verde Visitor & Research Center

WANDERLUSTER/GETTY IMAGES

Balcony House

Experiencing Mesa Verde

Mesa Verde National Park *(nps.gov/meve)* spans 81 sq miles over two broad mesas, both rife with Ancestral Puebloan dwellings. Some are on the mesa tops, but the most compelling are built into high cliffs. While many are visible from overlooks, touring them means adventure at great heights, peering over edges, clambering up and down ladders and crawling through tunnels...all to experience these magnificent dwellings up close.

Ranger Tours

Taking a ranger-led tour is one of the most rewarding ways to experience Mesa Verde. You'll deep dive into the history and lives of the Ancestral Puebloans and have access to otherwise restricted sites such as Cliff Palace and Balcony House plus Long House, a sprawling dwelling in the park's rugged backcountry. But they're not for the faint of heart! Most involve walking along cliff edges, climbing up and down wooden pole ladders and crawling through tight spaces. But they're so worth it. Plan on taking two tours if you have the time. And be sure to buy tickets in advance – they sell out fast.

> **DON'T MISS**
>
> Cliff Palace
>
> Balcony House
>
> Step House
>
> Petroglyph Point Trail
>
> Mesa Top Loop Rd
>
> Long House

PRACTICALITIES
Scan this QR code for prices and opening hours.

Cliff Palace

Cliff Palace is the largest known cliff dwelling in the American southwest, a grand engineering achievement with 151 rooms and 23 kivas (ceremonial enclosures) that once housed 25 families. It's remarkable for its fine construction and efficient design. Walk through it on a 45-minute tour, retracing the paths taken by the enclave's original inhabitants. In summer, twilight tours are offered, too. If you can't join a tour, check out the site from afar from the Sun Temple overlook on the Mesa Top Loop Rd.

Balcony House

The Balcony House tour requires you to descend a 100ft staircase, climb a 32ft ladder and crawl through a 12ft tunnel... and that's just to get there. There are more ladders and steps on the way out. It's well worth the effort: the 38-room village is built in a cliffside alcove with a long arching roof, and offers views of Soda Canyon, 600ft below.

Step House

Wetherill Mesa has the park's only self-guided cliff dwelling: **Step House**. A short but steep 0.8-mile trail leads to a two-in-one village, with 7th-century pit houses standing alongside 13th-century multistoried dwellings. Information booklets are available near the trailhead; a ranger is typically at the site to answer questions.

Mesa Top Loop Road

A complement (or alternative) to scrambling through the cliff dwellings is a 6-mile driving tour along the Mesa Top Loop Road. At various pull-offs, you can enjoy magnificent overlooks of Cliff Palace and other cliff dwellings, or take short paths to a dozen different surface sites (no teetering ladders on this route). A free **audio tour** (nps.gov/podcasts/podcasts-mtl-audiotour.htm), played on any smartphone, guides the way.

Petroglyph Point Trail

The 2.4-mile loop Petroglyph Point Trail follows a leafy footpath once used by the Ancestral Puebloans. Dropping below the canyon rim, it's occasionally steep and rocky before making a short scramble back to the top of the mesa. Look for the petroglyphs at the 1.4-mile mark – a 35ft-wide wall with almost three dozen human and animal figures, spirals and handprints. A gate at the trailhead is locked in the evenings. If you arrive in the early morning, begin the trail in reverse.

Dances & Demonstrations

In summer, the park hosts cultural dances and pottery demonstrations by native peoples with ancestral connections to Mesa Verde. Fascinating and educational, the events are a way to learn about Mesa Verde's ancient inhabitants and their modern-day descendants. Events are in the **Morefield Campground** amphitheater or the main **visitor center**, typically in the evening.

STARGAZING IN MESA VERDE

An International Dark Sky Park, Mesa Verde's remote location, high elevation and arid climate make it one of the best places in the country to enjoy the night skies. Rangers offer regular nighttime programs, from lectures and star parties to astrophotography workshops, all for free. Alternatively, stop at an overlook (or step out of your tent) to take in the sky on your own.

TOP TIPS

● Visit mid-May to mid-October. Winter and spring bring closures to several areas and amenities, and tours are suspended.

● Tickets for ranger tours can only be purchased online (recreation.gov) or by phone, up to 14 days in advance. Tours often sell out, so reserve early.

● Information booklets are stocked in metal bins around the park.

● Fill your tank before you arrive – you'll be driving a lot! In a pinch, there's a gas station at Morefield Campground.

● Cellphone service is limited; download audio tours and maps ahead of time.

● Except for holiday weekends, Morefield Campground almost always has walk-up availability.

Beyond Mesa Verde National Park

Rich in archaeological sites and outdoors opportunities, Mesa Verde's surroundings beckon explorers of all stripes.

Places

Brimming with archaeological sites and natural beauty, Mesa Verde's surroundings are an ideal for exploration and to learn about the ancient peoples who made this high desert home. Small towns pepper the landscape, offering traveler amenities as well as insight into the area's modern-day life and residents – the Native Americans, the ranchers, the artists, the big-city expats. Woven through it all is a treasure trove of trails leading hikers and bikers (and historic-train riders) through high desert, red-rock canyons and the state's largest mountain wilderness. Hot springs and homegrown ski areas are the cherries on top.

Ute Mountain Ute Reservation

TIME FROM MESA VERDE NP: **30 MINS** 🚗

Backroad archaeological tour

Ute Mountain Ute Tribal Park (*utemountaintribalpark. info; half/full day adult $35/49, child 15/8 and under $16/10*) is a dramatic landscape of towering mesas and buttes, and visiting is a unique and unforgettable way to learn about Ancestral Puebloan communities. Ute tribal members guide visitors on half-day or full-day tours, following a network of rough dirt roads to reach several cliff dwellings and petroglyph sites, hiking along narrow cliffside trails and clambering up ladders to access them. Along the way, guides share in-depth interpretation of the ruins, relating them to their present-day culture. If your budget can swing it, opt for the park-provided transportation ($16 per person); it'll save you 40 to 80 miles of tough driving and give you that much more time to learn about the place and the people from the guide, who doubles as the driver. The 125,000-acre park belongs to the Weeminuche band of the Ute Nation of Indians, one of seven Ute bands that once inhabited the entire state (and beyond). It neighbors Mesa Verde National Park. Tours run April to October; cash only.

GETTING AROUND

The region has three small airports: Cortez Municipal Airport, Durango-La Plata County Airport and Pagosa Springs' Archuleta County Airport. Towns are small enough to navigate on foot, though Durango and Pagosa Springs have public buses to reach further afield. you'll You'll need your own vehicle to reach archaeological sites and trailheads. Rentals are available at the airports.

Canyon of the Ancients National Monument

TIME FROM MESA VERDE NP: **20 MINS**

Explore Ancestral Puebloan ruins

Visually stunning and imbued with ineffable historical and spiritual energy, **Canyon of the Ancients National Monument** *(blm.gov/visit/canyons-ancient-national-monument; free)* is home to the largest known concentration of archaeological sites in the country – more than 6000 at last count. The sites, accessible off rough roads and remote trails, are spread over 170,000 acres of public land and span 12,000 years of human history. They range from singular hogans to entire ancient pueblos – once-thriving population centers that grew and persisted for thousands of years.

The **Canyon of the Ancients Visitor Center and Museum** *(blm.gov/visit/canyons-ancients-national-monument-visitor-center-and-museum; museum adult/child $6/free)* is an important first stop. A fascinating museum and research center, it has informative films and exhibits about the national monument. It also hosts periodic events such as Indigenous art markets and stargazing parties. Touch base with the rangers here; they can recommend specific sites and supply maps. A high-clearance vehicle is needed to access trailheads for most of the national monument's sites. The **Southwest Colorado Canyons Alliance** *(swcocanyons.org; half/full day from $50/84)* also runs recommended tours led by experienced guides.

If you don't have a 4WD, the easiest ruin to visit is **Lowry Pueblo**, about 25 miles northwest of the visitors center on (mostly) paved roads. Dating to 1060 CE, the site has several stone structures and nine kivas, including the 47ft-wide Grand Kiva, believed to have been used for spiritual rites.

Alternatively, head to the southern entrance of **Sand Canyon Trail**, a relatively flat 6.5-mile (one way) trail through the breathtaking **McElmo Canyon**, with several cliff dwellings tucked into natural alcoves along the way. The largest, **Saddlehorn Pueblo**, is 1 mile from the trailhead. For a post-hike treat (charcuterie and wine, anyone?), stop at the lovely **Sutcliffe Vineyards** *(sutcliffewines.com)*, just down the road. It's open noon to 7pm.

Cortez

TIME FROM MESA VERDE NP: **15 MINS**

Learn about Native customs

The modest **Cortez Cultural Center** *(cortezculturalcenter. org; free)* is well worth a stop, especially on summer evenings

 EATING IN CORTEZ: OUR PICKS

Silver Bean: Full line-up of caffeinated drinks and burritos, sold from an old-school Airstream trailer. *6am-2pm Mon-Fri, 7am-1pm Sat & Sun* **$**

WildEdge Brewing Collective: Healthy-ish pub grub pairs well with the ever-changing brews on tap (plus local ciders and wine). *3-9pm Tue-Sat, to 7pm Sun* **$**

Farm Bistro: Made-to-order comfort food prepared with (mostly) local ingredients...even yak. Plenty of vegan and gluten-free options. *11am-9pm Mon-Fri* **$$**

Stonefish Sushi: Classic sushi menu with Southwest touches like prickly-pear chili sauce and Colorado seared beef. *11am-9pm Mon-Sat, 3-9pm Sun* **$$$**

MCPHEE RESERVOIR

Before it was filled with water and named **McPhee Reservoir**, the Dolores River Canyon was an important agricultural area, supplying beef and vegetables to surrounding mining towns. It was also home to McPhee, a town built by the New Mexico Lumber Company. For centuries before that, Native Americans lived and hunted here. Archaeologists, historians and photographers raced to document the canyon's rich history before it was flooded in 1984 – more than two million artifacts were collected and preserved, and they are today housed at the Canyon of the Ancients Visitor Center and Museum (p259). Much was left behind and, when water levels are low, it's possible to see artifacts half-buried along the shoreline.

when Ute, Navajo, Lakota and Hopi tribal members give dance performances and craft demonstrations to showcase and celebrate their cultures. Stay on to check out the **Fulks' Collection**, an exhibit of Ancestral Puebloan artifacts found over the course of 50 years on a local 320-acre family farm, home to more than two dozen archaeological sites.

Work alongside archaeologists

If you're interested in archaeological digs, the nonprofit research institute **Crow Canyon Archaeological Center** *(crowcanyon.org; prices vary)* offers week-long educational programs to nearby excavation sites. Students work alongside experts, learning excavation and lab techniques while deepening their understanding of the Ancestral Puebloans. Free archaeological webinars are offered every Thursday afternoon, too.

Four Corners
TIME FROM MESA VERDE NP: 1 HR

Four places at once

Don't be shy. Everyone at **Four Corners Monument Navajo Tribal Park** *(discovernavajo.com/four-corners-navajo-tribal-park; entry $8)* lies down on the marker so they're in four states at once. It's a good photo, even if inaccurate – the marker should be almost 2000ft east – though it's still the official border of Arizona, New Mexico, Utah and Colorado. Ironically, the site is in, and managed by, the Navajo Nation.

Backcountry biking

The Four Corners area offers some epic mountain biking on Bureau of Land Management (BLM) and US Forest Service (USFS) lands: miles and miles of singletrack and dirt roads, climbing to high mesas, through rolling woodlands and over exposed slickrock. A favourite is **Phil's World**, a 32-mile trail system with one-way (clockwise) tracks for all levels through a beautiful piñon juniper forest. Other popular spots include **Boggy Draw Loop**, a shady 8.5-mile trail north of Dolores (watch for cow patties!), and **Stoney Mesa Loop**, with gorgeous views and a rocky, technical descent. Stop in Cortez' **Kokopelli Bike & Board** *(kokopellibike.com; rental from $50 a day)* for trail talk and rentals.

Hovenweep National Monument
TIME FROM MESA VERDE NP: 1¼ HR

DIY ruin-hopping

Hovenweep National Monument *(nps.gov/hove; $20 per vehicle)* is a collection of five Ancestral Puebloan villages peppered across the red-rock canyons of Colorado, Utah and the Navajo Nation. Built between 1200 and 1300 CE, the archaeological sites are known for their impressive towers, most perched on canyon rims. The largest and easiest to access is the **Square Tower Community**, a clutch of well-preserved structures lining a beautiful sandstone canyon near the visitor center (Utah). A relatively flat loop trail (2 miles) leads you through the site. The other ruins are located 4 to 9 miles

DAVE G. HOUSER/GETTY IMAGES

Four Corners

away, most along unmaintained dirt roads. High-clearance 4WD vehicles are recommended, especially after heavy rains.

Mancos

TIME FROM MESA VERDE NP: **10 MINS** 🚗

Afternoon of art

With a flourishing art scene, chilled vibe and cattle drives right through town, Mancos (MAN-cuss), just west of Mesa Verde, has a special brand of cowboy quirk. The intersection of Grand Ave and Main St is the heart of the action, with galleries, bohemian boutiques and murals dotting the small town's streets. Duck into spots featuring local artists, such as **Artisans of Mancos** *(artisansofmancos.com)* and **Raven House Gallery** *(ravenhousegallery.com)*, then meander to **Mancos Common Press** *(mancoscommonpress.org)*, a restored historic letterpress selling quirky prints and cards – if you have time, consider taking an artsy workshop in its new, adjoining education space. Afterwards, stop at **Fenceline Cidery** *(fenceline.co)* for a hard cider or homemade apple juice, both made from wild apples. The cidery's food truck provides tasty meals on its idyllic riverfront patio.

Durango

TIME FROM MESA VERDE NP: **40 MINS** 🚗

Breathtaking mountain train ride

Whether or not you're a train buff, don't miss riding the **Durango & Silverton Narrow Gauge Railroad** *(durangotrain.com; Silverton route adult/child from $114/75, Cascade Canyon route $89/64)*. A National Historic Landmark, it has hauled more than $300 million in gold and silver on its tracks since 1882. Today, vintage locomotives carry passengers in Victorian-era carriages and open-air gondolas on a spectacular 45-mile route along the Animas River to Silverton (p276), one jaw-dropping mountain vista after another.

WHY I LOVE CANYON OF THE ANCIENTS

Liza Prado, Lonely Planet writer

Hiking solo through McElmo Canyon, the sky bright, the red earth dotted with yucca plants and sage brush, I can almost see them. The people who once called this red canyon home, carrying woven baskets filled with plants and berries, passing me on their way to their adobe brick homes that, remarkably, still stand in the alcoves. I can almost smell the smoke from their cooking fires and hear the sounds of their everyday life carried through the canyon – the chatter, the chopping of wood, the children playing. This place transports me, fills me with wonder and reminds me that, regardless of time or circumstance, we're all connected. For me, that's what travel is all about.

DURANGO ART BRIGADE

Walking through Durango, you'll see sculptures and art installations all around, transforming ordinary locations such as street corners, parking lots, planters and even dumpsters into visually engaging and thought-provoking spaces. The works, by local artists, often draw on the area's diverse cultural heritage, as well as Durango's landscape, from mountain vistas to the Animas River. Much of the art is thanks to the Durango Art Brigade, a community-driven initiative, launched in 2020, to promote economic recovery and resiliency in the city's business districts. It has also served to beautify the town. The initiative has expanded in the years since, integrating art workshops, open community events and public input on proposed artworks.

The trip takes nine hours, including two hours in Silverton (to lop off 1½ hour, return by bus for an extra $29). Those looking to access the backcountry and several fourteeners (peaks over 14,000ft) can arrange to step off at the **Needleton** or **Elk Park** stops – to return, hikers must flag down passing trains. In winter, the line only extends 26 miles to **Cascade Canyon**, with deep snow limiting the train's reach. The excursion lasts 5½ hours, with an hour lunch break to step out into the frozen wilderness (wear boots!). Regardless of the season, reserve early.

Ziplining through the forest

If the train ride to Silverton doesn't pack enough punch, stop midway at **Soaring Tree Top Adventures** (*soaringcolorado. com; $600*), home to the world's longest zipline course (and perhaps, the most expensive!). The 27 ziplines range from 56ft to 1400ft in length, running through the dense San Juan National Forest. The full course takes 5½ hours to complete, including a gourmet lunch. There's no road access, but admission includes train travel in a 1st-class car.

Festival in the sky

Durango's **Animas Balloon Rally** (*animasvalleyballoon rally.com; free*) is a quintessential southern Colorado fest, with colorful hot-air balloons soaring high above the San Juan Mountains. The three-day October event is a photographer's dream. Come in the early morning for the 'mass ascension' – two to three dozen balloons launching against the autumn backdrop. Evenings bring 'balloon glows,' with the giant balloons illuminating Durango's Animas Valley and downtown area. Free tethered rides are especially fun for little ones.

Quirky winter fun

Dubbed the 'Cure for Cabin Fever,' Durango's weeklong **Snowdown** (*snowdown.org*) coaxes thousands to its streets for lighthearted fun. Held in late January/early February, the theme changes yearly – Intergalactic, Superhero, Shakespearean – with costumed festival-goers partaking in quirky and hilarious events such as beard-growing contests, joke-offs, theater performances, cat yoga, even kickball in skis.

 EATING IN DURANGO: OUR PICKS

Cream Bean Berry: Award-winning ice-cream shop with inventive flavors, gluten-free waffle cones and vegan frozen treats. *noon-9pm* **$**

11th Street Station: Culinary collective serviced by food trucks, a bar and a coffee stand. *11am-11pm Sun-Thu, to midnight Fri & Sat* **$**

Taco Libre: Mexican street food in a wrestler-themed diner. Aguas frescas are a must. *11am-9pm Sun-Thu, to 10pm Fri & Sat* **$**

College Drive Café: Breakfast fave serving classic American dishes with Southwest flavors such as green chile and chorizo. *7:30am-1pm* **$**

Steamworks Brewing Co: Industrial meets ski lodge – pub grub with Cajun influences. *11am-10pm Sun-Thu, to 11pm Fri & Sat* **$$**

James Ranch Grill: Farm-stand grill showcasing organic grass-fed beef, artisanal cheeses and fresh produce. *11am-7:30pm Wed-Sun* **$$**

El Moro Tavern: Gastropub serving innovative small plates and good cocktails to Durango hipsters. *4-11pm daily, 9am-2pm Sat & Sun* **$$$**

Eolus Bar & Dining: Serving beautifully composed surf-and-turf dishes. Save room for the decadent desserts. *5-9pm Mon-Fri* **$$$**

Durango & Silverton Narrow Gauge Railroad (p261)

All-ages soaking

Durango Hot Springs *(durangohotspringsresortandspa.com; adult/child 2hr $39/19)* is the go-to for a good soak after a day of activity. Its 32 pools (99°F to 112°F; 37°C to 44°C) bubble with healing minerals and infused oxygen. Adults-only pools are set in tranquil hillside spots with views of Durango's red sandstone mountains; live music adds ambience. Those with children will also appreciate the resort-style swimming pool, kid-friendly soaking pools and a rain tower that periodically drops steaming water on willing victims. Reservations required.

Close to heaven

One of Colorado's best values – and one the best resort names anywhere – **Purgatory Resort** *(purgatory.ski; lift tickets adult $9-89, under 12yr free; mountain-bike passes half/full day $39/49)* has outstanding terrain, a friendly local vibe and none of the lines and hassle of Front Range resorts. Lift-ticket prices vary with demand. The mountain is evenly split between greens, blues and serious blacks, plus terrain parks and snowcat skiing. Purgatory is blanketed by 260in a year of that famous San Juan deep stuff – pure heaven! If you're here in summer, rent a bike on-site (adult/child from $100/35) and cruise the resort's 20 trails, from mellow to technical, or head into the backcountry, where 400 miles of singletrack awaits.

FORT LEWIS COLLEGE

Overlooking Durango, Fort Lewis College is a well-respected school with a notable Native American student population – more than 27%, representing 113 tribes. A reason? Native Americans attend tuition-free as part of the school's 1911 charter. Prior to becoming a college, Fort Lewis was an Indian boarding school aiming to eradicate student tribal identity and force assimilation into mainstream culture. Little was officially known about the treatment of students until a 2023 state-issued report revealed what most assumed: students suffered physical and sexual abuse, living in conditions so dangerous that 31 children died. Time will tell how this informs the college and its future efforts to right the wrongs of the past.

DRINKING IN DURANGO: OUR PICKS

Ska Brewing: Award-winning craft brewery with a laid-back tasting room. Live music most Thursdays. Full menu and food trucks, too. *11am-8pm*

Bookcase & Barber: Modern speakeasy hidden behind a bookcase. Enter through the barbershop and bring the password! *5pm-midnight Mon-Sat*

Starlight Lounge: LGBTIQ+-friendly bar and lounge with outdoor stage. Weekly drag nights and lip-synching competitions. *4:30pm-2am*

Diamond Belle Saloon: Old-timey bar with waitresses in Wild West barmaid getups. Live ragtime packs the house most evenings. *11:30am-11pm Mon-Fri*

HOT SPRINGS 411

The hot springs dotting western Colorado are a result of the genesis of the Rocky Mountains themselves – the massive tectonic shifts that pushed the land into the towering peaks and caused deep cracks in the earth's crust. When rain and surface water seep into the ground, they travel toward the earth's mantle and become superheated. When the hot water hits one of these fissures, it returns to the surface as a hot spring, collecting healing minerals en route. And the rotten-egg smell? It's hydrogen sulfide that is naturally released when the water interacts with sulfur-containing minerals deep within the earth's crust. Smelly or not, the hot springs provide the perfect place to soak and relax.

Chimney Rock
National Monument
TIME FROM MESA VERDE NP: 1½ HR

Wander past ancient ruins

Chimney Rock National Monument *(fs.usda.gov; $20 per vehicle)* is a fascinating archaeological site perched on a forested mesa just outside Pagosa Springs. Built in the 11th century at the foot of two rocky pinnacles (Chimney Rock and Companion Rock), it was a thriving commercial center and key lunar observatory of the Ancestral Puebloans. Today, 200 structures remain, and many are impressive examples of Chacoan architecture. Two trails head through the site: the lower one is an easy quarter-mile paved loop past pit houses and the Great Kiva; the upper one is a moderately strenuous hike along a narrow ridge to a 35-room Great House. There's no access to either pinnacle. For a deeper dive, book a tour with **Chimney Rock Interpretive Association** *(chimney rockco.org; tours from $12)* – full-moon and night-sky visits are especially rewarding. Don't miss the museum. Open mid-May to mid-October.

Pagosa Springs
TIME FROM MESA VERDE NP: 1¾ HR

Soaking in town

Pagosa Springs is all about hot springs. Its aptly named wellness resort, the **Springs Resort** *(pagosahotsprings.com; adult/child day pass $67/35)*, has 25 artificial pools fed by the mineral-rich waters of the Mother Spring, the world's deepest known geothermal spring. Wander its terraces, all overlooking downtown, dipping into pools of varying size and temperature (45°F to 114°F; 7°C to 45°C). A few even have direct access to the icy San Juan River – perfect for cooling off between soaks. If the admission fee is onerous, two smaller nearby spas are fed by the same hot spring but charge way less: **Overlook Hot Springs Spa** *(overlookhotsprings. com; adult/child day pass $30/24)*, with rooftop and indoor tubs; and **Healing Waters Resort & Spa** *(pshotsprings. com; adult/child day pass $20/15)*, with a swimming pool and clothing-optional areas.

Waterfalls galore

At 780 sq miles, **Weminuche Wilderness Area** *(fs.usda.gov)* is the most extensive wilderness in Colorado. Though it offers myriad opportunities for backcountry hiking and camping, waterfalls take center stage near Pagosa Springs. For a mod-

EATING IN PAGOSA SPRINGS: OUR PICKS

Kip's Grill & Cantina: Bustling local hangout serving Baja-style street tacos and strong margs. Sit at the bar for the full experience. *11am-10pm* **$**

Riff Raff on the River: Brewery outpost serving geothermically brewed beers, tasty burgers and monster salads. Grab a seat on the riverside patio. *11am-9pm* **$**

Rose: Homey cafe serving hearty breakfast and to-die-for green chile (go ahead, smother your meal in it). *7am-2pm Mon-Fri, to 1pm Sat & Sun* **$$**

Alley House Grill: Upscale restaurant in a restored 1912 cottage. Come for seafood and steak, but consider the elk and lamb dishes instead. *4-9pm Tue-Sun* **$$$**

HEIDI BESEN/SHUTTERSTOCK

Pagosa Springs

MAJOR LUNAR STANDSTILL

Like many ancient peoples, Ancestral Puebloans were supremely attuned to celestial phenomena, including those that unfold over years, not merely weeks or months. Moonrise, for example, shifts north and south in a cycle lasting 18.6 years. It includes two 'pauses,' when the moon rises in the same place for roughly three years (known today as the major and minor lunar standstills). At Chimney Rock National Monument, the Great House was built such that, during the major lunar standstill, the full moon appears to rise exactly between the site's twin stone spires. Archaeologists point to this as evidence of the immense skills – in astronomy, engineering and more – of the Ancestral Puebloans.

erate hike, **Four Mile Falls** (6.2 miles round trip) is a memorable double cascade ranging from wispy to thundering, depending on the season. Or look for the 100ft-high **Treasure Falls** – it's visible from Hwy 160 but a short steep hike (1 mile round trip) to the observation area is a mist-soaked pleasure. (It's also stunning when frozen in winter.) **Piedra Falls** (1 mile round trip) is another beauty, reached following a scenic backroads drive on County Rd 637.

Epic powder

One of Colorado's best-kept secrets, **Wolf Creek Ski Area** (*wolfcreekski.com; adult/child day pass $91/45, half-day $75/38*) has the deepest average annual snowfall in the state – a whopping 430in. Steep and deep, it's geared toward advanced skiers and boarders, with terrific chutes and tree skiing, though there are some decent groomers and greens, too. Come after a big storm for waist-high powder and an incomparable white-carpet ride. Almost best of all, Wolf Creek's distance from a big city and lack of on-site lodging (the nearest is in Pagosa Springs, 25 miles away) has kept it happily isolated, meaning short lift lines and plenty of opportunities to lay first tracks. Don't expect anything fancy, though – the lodge and lifts are old school! Located 120 miles east of Mesa Verde, it makes for a doable but long day trip.

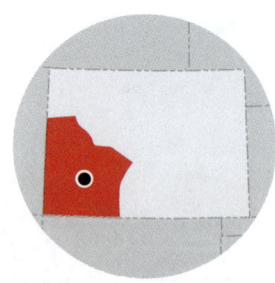

Ouray

OUTDOOR WONDERLAND | EPIC DRIVES | HOT SPRINGS

GETTING AROUND

Getting to Ouray by public transportation isn't easy; there's commuter bus service *(allpointstransit. com/ourway; $4)* from Ridgway and Montrose on weekdays only. Beyond that, private vehicle or driver service are the only options. Once here, Ouray is easily navigated on foot – it's a small, relatively flat town and most businesses are on or near the main drag. Despite the lack of paved streets, there are sidewalks throughout town and the streets are regularly graded to keep them maintained. Having a 4WD vehicle makes it easy to explore the surrounding area (rentals available), though tour agencies easily fill in the gaps. For those arriving by car, there's plenty of free street parking.

With gorgeous waterfalls draping the box canyon and soothing hot springs dotting the valley floor, Ouray (you-RAY) is a privileged spot, even by Colorado standards. It's a world-class ice-climbing destination, while for hikers and 4WDers, it's a playground of rugged terrain and stunning landscapes. Ouray sits on what was for centuries the summer hunting grounds of the Uncompahgre Utes. In the 1870s, the Utes were pushed out by the crush of miners who descended on the San Juan Mountains in search of silver and gold (and federal policies that favored them). Ouray soon became one of the region's fastest-growing towns; at its height it had more than 30 active mines and a population above 2500. Today, it's a well-preserved mountain village with just 1000 full-time residents. Its only fully paved street, Main St, is registered as a National Historic District, and houses most of the town's gift shops, cafes and inns.

Heart-Pumping Views

Hiking high above Ouray

Forming nearly a complete loop around Ouray, the 6-mile **Perimeter Trail** is one of the most scenic ways to experience the 'Switzerland of America.' Beginning across from the **visitor center** *(visitouray.com)*, the clockwise trail charts an up-and-down path through forests and aspen groves, across creeks and bridges and even a one-time miners' potato patch turned alpine meadow. Highlights include the spectacular **Cascade Falls**, **Baby Bathtubs** (a series of smooth tub-like rock divots) and the Ouray Via Ferrata (p269) and Ice Park (p268), where you can spy people clambering along sheer rock (or ice) faces. The coup de grace is **Box Cañon Falls** *(visitouray.com/box-canyon-falls; adult/child $7/5)*, a thundering 285ft waterfall that drops into a spectacular quartzite canyon. There's a modest fee to enter the canyon – a small park rich in birdlife – but you also can stay on the trail and admire it from a sky bridge. The full circuit takes four to five

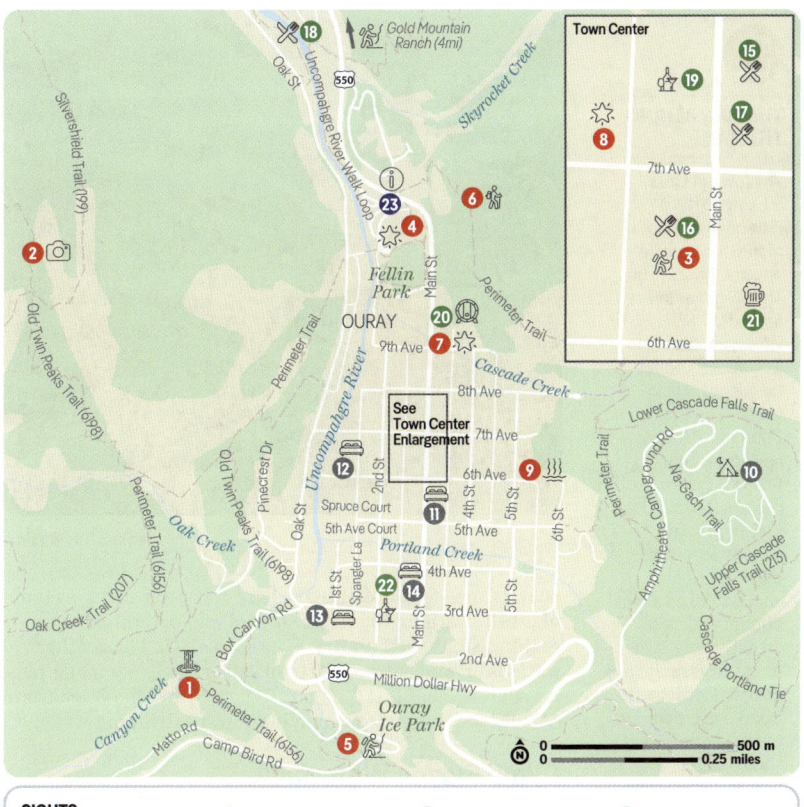

SIGHTS
1 Box Cañon Falls
2 West Gold Hill Dinosaur Trackway

ACTIVITIES
3 Basecamp Ouray
4 Ouray Hot Springs
5 Ouray Ice Park
● Ouray Via Ferrata (see 5)

6 Perimeter Trail
7 San Juan Mountain Guides
8 San Juan Scenic Jeep Tours
9 Wiesbaden Hot Springs Spa & Lodgings

SLEEPING
10 Amphitheater Campground

11 Beaumont Hotel & Spa
12 Black Bear Manor
13 Box Canyon Lodge & Hot Springs
14 Ouray Main Street Inn

EATING
15 Brickhouse 737
16 Kami's Samis

17 Maggie's Kitchen
18 The Smokehouse

DRINKING
19 Full Tilt Saloon
20 KJ Wood Distillers
21 Ouray Brewery
22 Ouray Wine Garden

INFORMATION
23 Ouray Visitor Center

hours to complete; for a shorter hike, there are several entry points along the outskirts of town.

Soak in Historic Springs

Relax in Ouray Hot Springs

For a healing soak or kiddish fun, try the **Ouray Hot Springs** (*visitouray.com/ourayhotspringspool; adult/child $26/16*). The springs were used and considered sacred by the Ute people before they were pushed from the region; later, miners soaked in the same waters to help their tired bodies. Today, the springs are a year-round water park surrounded by 13,000ft

☑**TOP TIP**

Being situated at the bottom of a box canyon means that most of Ouray's hikes involve steep elevation gains. Consider carrying trekking poles – they'll help steady your footing on both the uphills and downhills.

THE MAN BEHIND THE NAME

The town of Ouray is named after a 19th-century chief of the Uncompahgre band of the Ute tribe. The US government named Ouray, a known peacekeeper who spoke several languages, 'Head Chief' of all Utes in Colorado, despite having no authority to do so. Ouray represented the Utes in several treaty negotiations with the US, his more conciliatory positions often at odds with other Ute chiefs. All of which makes for a complicated legacy: Ouray's decisions are credited with having saved his people from the death and destruction that befell so many other Native American tribes, but at the cost of losing vast swaths of ancestral lands and, ultimately, the removal of the Utes to far-off reservations.

Yankee Boy Basin

peaks. Come for the eight-lane lap pool, water slides, a climbing wall overhanging a splash pool and several adults-only soaking areas (74°F to 106°F; 23°C to 41°C). The geothermal water is crystal clear and free of sulfur smells – a major plus. It's sourced near Box Cañon Falls (p266) and the Weehawkin Spring, the latter also supplying Ouray's drinking water.

Climb Frozen Waterfalls

Get belayed at Ouray Ice Park

Even if you're just mildly curious, don't miss the world's largest artificial public **Ice Park** *(ourayicepark.com; free)* – 2 miles of frozen cascades in Uncompahgre Gorge. The ice climbing is world class, but the spectacle alone is worth bundling up to see. With more than 150 routes, there's a sublime (if chilly) experience for climbers of all skill levels. Newbies should get instruction through local outfitters such as Basecamp Ouray (p270); equipment rentals are available at local shops. In mid-January, the park hosts the **Ouray Ice Festival**, a popular three-day event with climbing competitions, clinics and nightly parties.

DRINKING IN OURAY: OUR PICKS

Ouray Brewery: Bustling brewery with chairlift bar stools and a sunny rooftop deck. Try the award-winning Camp Bird Blonde Ale. *11am-8pm*

Ouray Wine Garden: Casual garden seating at a historic home turned B&B, serving local wines and hefty charcuterie boards. Stay for s'mores. *5-7:30pm late May–mid-Oct*

KJ Wood Distillers: Atmospheric tasting room serving gin, whiskey and vodka made with local barley and blue corn. Live music most nights. *3-9pm Thu-Sat*

Full Tilt Saloon: Popular pub with a no-frills mountain vibe, two patios and free billiards. Live music and happy-hour specials are serious draws. *11:30am-late*

Pull Yourself Across Mountains

Take on Ouray Via Ferrata

Traversing the same dizzying terrain as the Ice Park, the **Ouray Via Ferrata** *(ourayviaferrata.org; free)* is its summertime counterpart. Created for the adventurous and vertigo-free, this series of steel cables, metal rungs and suspension ladders allows you to traverse the steep mountain walls that line the Uncompahgre River. The reward: magnificent alpine views, the sound of the raging waters below and a feeling of serious badassness. The via ferrata has two routes but, unless you're experienced with via ferratas, hire a guide from a company such as **San Juan Mountain Guides** *(mtnguide.net)*.

Soak Underground

Bliss out at Wiesbaden vapor cave

The **Wiesbaden Hot Springs Spa & Lodgings** *(wiesbaden hotsprings.com; entry $25)* boasts Ouray's only 'natural' vapor cave. Carved into the mountain (and under the main lodge), it's fed by two hot springs – one seeping steaming water into a shallow soaking pool (107°F to 109°F; 41°C to 42°C); the other providing a cooling mineral-rich cascade (78°F; 25°C). The dim lighting, rough walls and dripping water are more reminiscent of a mine shaft than a spa, but it's still a treat. Outside there's a small spring-fed pool and a private, clothing-optional soaking tub with a waterfall (reservation only; from $75 per hour).

See the Backcountry

Jeeping in the San Juans

A vast network of old mining roads zigzagging through the spectacular San Juan Mountains makes Ouray ground zero for some of the state's best 4WD touring. Routes follow rugged backroad trails, through isolated alpine basins and past towering snowcapped peaks, with ghost towns and abandoned mines making for fascinating stops. Popular routes include **Yankee Boy Basin** (18.8 miles), known for its waterfalls and wildflowers; **Imogene Pass** (17.5 miles), for its steep and rocky ride; and **Alpine Loop** (65 miles), for its variety of alpine passes, some pushing 13,000ft. If you're experienced driving rough mountain roads, rent a Jeep in town from a handful of agencies (from $220 per day). Otherwise, book a tour with **San Juan Scenic Jeep Tours** *(sanjuanscenicjeeptours.com; half-day adult/child from $69/34, full day from $138/68)*. Hiking, hunting and fishing drop-offs easily arranged, too.

SPOTTING THE BLACK SWIFT

Migrating more than 4300 miles from northwestern Brazil to the western US, the protected black swift is notoriously difficult to spot. It could be the days it spends flying so high it's beyond sight. Or its flight speeds, which can exceed 100mph. Or its habit of nesting high on isolated waterfall ledges or deep inside coastal caves. Committed ornithologists go to extremes to find black swifts, exploring deep into wilderness to catch a glimpse. The exception? Ouray's Box Cañon Falls (p266), a once-remote waterfall, now accessible by bridge, staircase and walkway, where summertime visitors can spy these elusive birds and their one-egg nests camouflaged against the dark canyon walls.

 EATING IN OURAY: OUR PICKS

Maggie's Kitchen: Graffiti-bombed hole-in-the-wall known for delicious burgers and onion rings. Nab a seat on the deck. *11am-8pm Thu-Sat, to 6pm Sun* **$**

Kami's Samis: Bright, modern spot with breakfasts, hearty burritos and gourmet sandwiches. Loads of vegan, gluten- and dairy-free options. *7am-2pm* **$$**

The Smokehouse: Finger-lickin' BBQ joint serving generous portions of goodness smoked 'low and slow.' Perfect for post-hike. *7-11am daily, 11:30am-9pm Thu-Sun* **$$**

Brickhouse 737: Cozy, upscale restaurant with contemporary American cuisine, served with flair. Creative top-shelf cocktails. Reservations recommended. *5-9pm* **$$$**

PATHFINDER OF THE SAN JUANS

Otto Mears, often called the 'Pathfinder of the San Juans,' was an entrepreneur who played a pivotal role in developing Colorado's southwest region in the late 19th century. A Latvian orphan and Civil War veteran, he created a network of roads and narrow-gauge railroads to support the mining industry across the rugged mountains. He financed them by charging hefty tolls. Arguably the most famous road he built was the Million Dollar Hwy. Mears began work on it in 1883, at the behest of mining interests in Ouray and Silverton. Construction through the beautiful yet treacherous terrain reportedly cost $10,000 per mile, which some say led to the road's name. The toll? Five dollars per wagon – $150 in today's money.

West Gold Hill Dinosaur Trackway

Walk in the Footsteps of Giants

Hike to mountain-top dino tracks

Hike high above Ouray to the world's longest-known dinosaur trackway, a set of 134 footprints made by a sauropod, one of the largest creatures to have ever walked on the planet. During the Late Jurassic period, when Colorado was a flat, marshy place crisscrossed by rivers, the massive, long-necked herbivore made a 270-degree turn that was imprinted, fossilized and eventually pushed 8000ft skyward during the creation of the Rocky Mountains. Glaciers later swept away the overburden, revealing the footprints – a paleontological miracle.

The **West Gold Hill Dinosaur Trackway** is newly accessible via the **Silvershield Trail** (the land was purchased by the USFS in 2024). The 4-mile hike starts on the north edge of town, cutting through the forest and up the side of a mountain. It's strenuous, with a 1600ft elevation gain and patches of scree here and there. But even taking it slow, about a half-day is all you need to be able to see the one-of-a-kind dino site.

Traverse & Scale Mountains

Navigate a sky-high via ferrata

Gold Mountain Ranch (*goldmountainranch.com*) is a one-time mining district, now home to a challenging via ferrata. Accessible through **Basecamp Ouray** (*basecampouray. com; without/with guide $119/220*), the via ferrata uses steel rungs, cables and wobbly sky-high cable bridges to traverse the mountain, mimicking rock climbers to scale about 1800 vertical feet. The route peeks into an abandoned, century-old mining operation – from the tunnel entrance to its blacksmith shop. If the spectacular San Juan views are enticing but hanging off a mountain isn't, 2½-hour **trail rides** (*$180*) also are offered. They're a nod to the miners who long ago traveled these mountains on horseback.

MILLION DOLLAR HIGHWAY DRIVE

Drive the Million Dollar Hwy through Uncompahgre Gorge, where hairpin turns past snow-covered peaks reveal quintessential Colorado landscapes.

START	END	LENGTH
Ouray	Silverton	25 miles; 4 hours

South from Ouray, **1 Bear Creek Falls** is a dramatic waterfall plunging 200ft from below a highway bridge. Late spring/early summer bring thundering water and often, a second waterfall, **2 Ralston Creek Falls**, across the gorge. A viewing platform makes for an easy stop.

Continue south, past the entrance to **3 Alpine Loop**, a popular 4WDing route, to **4 Crystal Lake**, a photographer's dream. A 0.3-mile out-and-back walk provides spectacular views over the water to Brown Mountain, Red Mountain 1 and Red Mountain 2, the latter pair named for the hue of oxidized minerals on their surface. In fall, the landscape is highlighted with golden aspens.

Just south, follow signs down a rugged dirt road to the ghost town of **5 Ironton**. Built in the 1880s, its dilapidated buildings formed the heart of a booming travel hub, linking Ouray with surrounding mining camps. Stretch your legs along the town's creek to a 1.5-mile round-trip trail through the forest to the **6 Colorado Boy Mine**, one of the region's only vertical mineshafts.

Continue to **7 Red Mountain Pass**, with a parking area at 11,018ft with spectacular 360-degree views. Peek into the now-closed **8 Treasury Tunnel**, once the entrance to 100 miles of mining tunnels, some stretching to Telluride. From here, the roadway snakes its way to an end at Silverton.

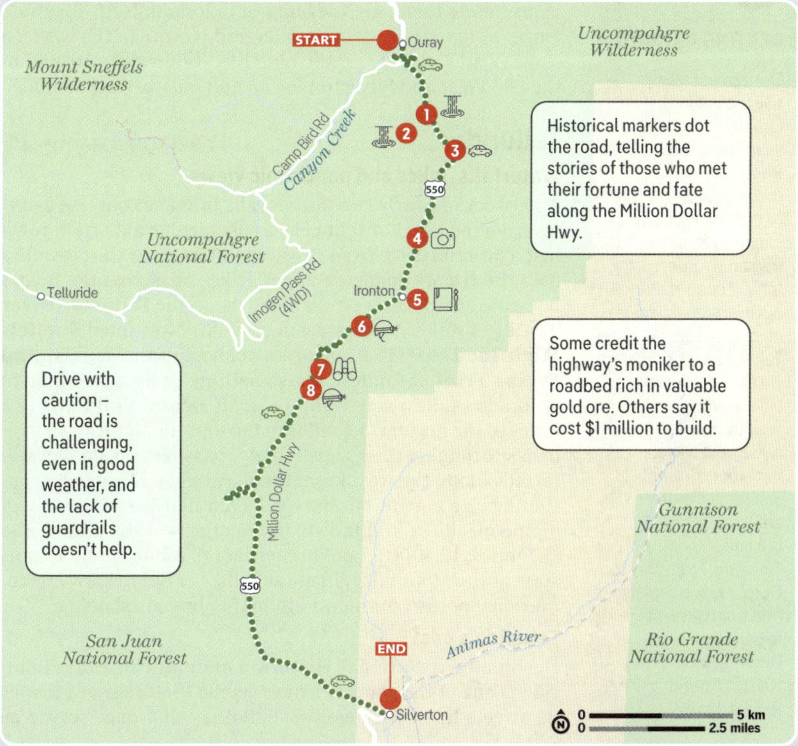

START ○ Ouray

Uncompahgre Wilderness

Mount Sneffels Wilderness

Camp Bird Rd

Canyon Creek

550

Uncompahgre National Forest

Imogen Pass Rd (4WD)

○ Telluride

Ironton

Historical markers dot the road, telling the stories of those who met their fortune and fate along the Million Dollar Hwy.

Some credit the highway's moniker to a roadbed rich in valuable gold ore. Others say it cost $1 million to build.

Drive with caution – the road is challenging, even in good weather, and the lack of guardrails doesn't help.

Million Dollar Hwy

550

Gunnison National Forest

San Juan National Forest

END

Animas River

Rio Grande National Forest

○ Silverton

N

| 0 | 5 km |
| 0 | 2.5 miles |

Beyond
Ouray

Ouray's surroundings offer awe-inspiring mountainscapes and appealing small-town vibes, with recreational opportunities (and some good old-fashioned fun) at every turn.

Places

Telluride p272
Ridgway p275
Silverton p276

GETTING AROUND

The easiest way to access the region is by plane, using **Telluride Regional Airport** (*tellurideairport.com*) or the nearby, often cheaper, Montrose Regional Airport (p282). Long-distance buses (*ridebustang. com*) only service Telluride and Ridgway via Grand Junction. Once here, having your own wheels is the best way to get around; rentals, including 4WDs, are available at the airports and in Telluride. From May to October, you can also ride from Silverton to Durango on the Durango & Silverton Narrow Gauge Railroad (p261).

In the heart of the spectacular San Juan Mountains, the towns surrounding Ouray are quintessential western Colorado: old-time mining outposts turned picture-perfect mountain towns offering countless opportunities to ski, bike, hike, fish or just bask in some high-altitude sunshine. You'll find high-end restaurants and rooftop bars, thriving arts communities, free-spirited festivals and shops ranging from fine boutiques to kitschy gift shops. The area is imbued with history, too: the lives of early miners and ranchers, and the Ute Native Americans before them, are the story of Colorado itself. Together, Ouray's surroundings paint a layered picture of the western slope. Visit Telluride for the high life, Ridgway for its nod to the Old West and Silverton for its no-holds-barred attitude.

Telluride

TIME FROM OURAY: 1 HR

Waterfalls, lakes and panoramic views

A network of nearly two dozen trails branches out like arteries from the heart of Telluride, a spectacular mountain town just a 50-mile drive from Ouray (or 10 miles as the crow flies over the craggy Sneffels Range). Hikes crisscross the town's box canyon, from easy strolls along the scenic **Telluride River Trail** (4.4 miles) to the strenuous, wildflower-filled **Sneffels Highline Trail** (12.5 miles), an offshoot of the popular **Jud Weibe Trail** (3.1 miles). For something in between, hike to Colorado's tallest waterfall, the 365ft **Bridal Veil Falls** (2.5 miles to the bottom, 3.4 miles to the top), along rocky switchbacks through a thick aspen forest, passing two smaller waterfalls along the way. From there, extend your hike by continuing up a narrow mining road, eventually passing through alpine meadows and forests to the otherworldly **Blue Lake** (5.7 miles, 12,400ft). Looking for more? A dozen other trails start at the Mountain Village at Telluride Ski Resort, including some perfect for mountain biking or snowshoeing.

Telluride's past

Designated a National Historic Landmark in 1961, Telluride is one of the country's most iconic Victorian-era towns, its streets lined with elegant buildings that once served as flophouses and saloons, schoolhouses and churches. Stop in the Smithsonian-affiliated **Telluride Historical Museum** *(telluridemuseum.org; adult/child $9/6)*, the town's one-time hospital, to deep dive into Telluride's mining past, its beginning as Ute hunting grounds and its transformation into a world-class ski town. Maps of a self-guided walking tour of Telluride are available at the front desk. Or take a **guided walking tour** *($15)*, offered on summer and fall afternoons, with Ashley Boling, a local historian and storyteller who has led engaging town tours for more than 20 years.

Ski and board in style

Known for plunging runs and deep powder, while boasting gorgeous San Juan Mountain views and a certain high-society je ne sais quoi, **Telluride Ski Resort** *(tellurideski resort.com; day pass adult/child from $245/125)* is a truly special place. Decently sized in terms of lifts and acres – it has three distinct areas served by 19 lifts – Telluride has an outsize supply of advanced and expert terrain, from steeps to trees to wide-open cirques, and even more if you are willing to hike for it, including iconic Palmyra Peak. There are also ample options for beginners and intermediate cruisers, including the playful, 4.6-mile Galloping Goose run. Telluride's Achilles heel is the snowpack: it takes an especially deep blanket of snow for the resort to open fully.

Epic views

A **gondola** ('The G') links Telluride and the ski resort's Mountain Village, providing a free 12-minute ride that affords stunning box-canyon panoramas as it transports you up and over 10,540ft Coonskin Ridge. Get off midway at **Station San Sophia** for easy access to the slopes in the winter, or hiking and biking trails in the summer. Or wander through the station to mountain-chic restaurant-bar **Allreds** *(allredsrestaurant. com)*, a local hot spot for sunset drinks (don't miss the handcut truffle fries!). Built in 1996 to improve the town's air quality, the wind-powered gondola transports almost three million people yearly.

TRANSFER WAREHOUSE

Dating to 1906, the **Transfer Warehouse** served as Telluride's transportation hub for everything from gold to groceries until its roof caved in under the weight of snow in 1979. Left virtually untouched for almost 40 years, Telluride Arts acquired the building in 2017 with the vision of preserving its structural beauty while transforming it into an open-air cultural center. Today, the Transfer Warehouse is a place where art exhibits, film screenings, concerts, dance parties and more are held year-round, all under the open sky. Plans to add indoor spaces, including a rooftop bar, are in the works. This fusion of heritage and creative repurposing is a thread seen throughout Telluride's streets, a reflection of its resilience.

EATING IN TELLURIDE: OUR PICKS

Brown Dog Pizza: Buzzing joint known for award-winning Detroit-style pizza. Come early or prepare to wait for a table. *11:30am-9pm* **$**

Uno Dos Tres Telluride: Casual Mexican place serving inventive tacos and quesadillas from a repurposed little house. *11am-9pm* **$**

Butcher & Baker: Cute breakfast spot with generous to-go sandwiches and sides for the trail. *7am-8pm Mon-Sat, 8am-2pm Sun* **$$**

Strong House Brewpub: Family-friendly brewery in an 1892 building; pub grub such as elk brats and pork green chile. *noon-8pm Thu-Mon* **$$**

Wood Ear: Ramen meets Texas smokehouse at this inventive underground spot. Creative cocktails to go in reusable plastic flasks. *5-9pm* **$$$**

Petit Maison: Inviting French bistro serving classics such as *moules frites* and coq au vin. Save room for the crème brûlée. *5-9:30pm* **$$$**

221 South Oak: New American cuisine by chef Eliza Gavin. Dine in the cozy historic home or the leafy patio. *5-9:30pm daily, 10am-1pm Sun* **$$$**

Chop House: Old-school steakhouse; Western fare from savory elk steaks to dry-aged bison ribeye. *8am-2pm & 5:30-9pm* **$$$**

Sky-high adrenaline rush

Suspended 500ft in the air on Telluride's **via ferrata**, pulling yourself across the eastern face of the box canyon on thick cables and iron rungs, you might wonder what you've gotten yourself into. But one look around says it all: bird's-eye views of the craggy San Juan peaks, a thick carpet of aspen and fir trees all around, the iconic Bridal Veil Falls on one end and the oh-so-tiny-looking town grid on the other. It's high adventure in a harness. Allot about five hours for the 2-mile trek, and go with a guide unless you're an experienced climber. Try **Mountain Trip** *(mountaintrip.com; $209 gear included)*, a reputable company with experienced guides. Note: climbers under 5ft in height will have to stretch to their limits (or create work-arounds) to reach some rungs.

Banjos, hula hoops and more

The **Telluride Bluegrass Festival** *(bluegrass.com/telluride)* is the town's most famous fest, a summer-solstice celebration of folk music and mountain life. It draws big-name bands and more than 10,000 revelers each day – many donning hula hoops as dance partners. The main stage is set in the leafy town park, with stalls selling all sorts of food and local brews. Late-night concerts and free workshops are held in smaller venues around town. Tickets sell out fast for the June event – buy early (like December early) and consider a combo ticket-and-camping package for an all-in experience. Kids under 12 are free.

If you can't make the bluegrass fest, don't fret – Telluride hosts some two dozen other festivals throughout the year. Faves include **Mountainfilm** *(mountainfilm.org)*, a documentary film festival; **Telluride Mushroom Festival** *(telluride institute.org/telluride-mushroom-festival)*, a celebration and education on all things fungi (don't miss the parade!); the internationally renowned **Telluride Film Festival** *(telluride filmfestival.org)*; and the season-ending **Blues & Brews Festival** *(tellurideblues.com)*.

Year-round performance art

Telluride has a vibrant performing-arts scene, showcasing everything from live music and theater productions to comedy shows and film screenings on several stages. At the center of it all is the historic **Sheridan Opera House** *(sheridan operahouse.com)*. Built in 1913, it originally served as a vaudeville theater to entertain Telluride's growing population. Today, the beautifully restored theater hosts big-name artists, its 238 seats making every ticket in the house a good one. If

DRINKING IN TELLURIDE: OUR PICKS

there Telluride: Bohemian social alcove serving creative cocktails and nibbles to share, with an East meets West bent. *4-10pm*

Telluride Brewing Co: Popular no-nonsense brewery with a Western warehouse vibe; don't miss the celebrated Facedown Brown brew. *2-7pm Mon-Sat*

Last Dollar Saloon: Shoot pool and spin stories at 'The Buck,' a longtime locals' haunt. Views from the rooftop patio can't be beat. *3pm-1am*

Telluride Distillery Company: Mountain Village tasting room serving spirits. Billiards, TVs and couches lend it a rec-room feel. *2-8pm Wed-Sat, 11am-7pm Sun*

Telluride's via ferrata

FLY FISHING KNOW-HOW

Most of fly fishing's etiquette boils down to not crowding other anglers or spooking the fish they're targeting. A few pointers.

Anglers working upstream (which will be most of them) generally have the right of way.

Avoid 'high holing' (stepping into the water directly upstream of an angler) or standing on the bank opposite someone – this can spook rising fish.

If someone is at a nice spot but not fishing, they may be 'resting the hole.' Ask if they plan to keep fishing there; if so, move on.

By the same token, don't monopolize good spots.

Be kind to folks who are still learning, especially kids – we've all been there once.

tickets are scarce, pop into the Transfer Warehouse (p273), a historic building turned cultural center, to see what's on deck on its open-air stage, head to Mountain Village for live music at the glitzy **Club Red** *(clubredtelluride.com)*, or check out the varied performances at the state-of-the-art **Palm Theater** *(telluridepalm.com)*.

Ridgway

TIME FROM OURAY: **15 MINS**

True grit

An alpine beauty with a ranching vibe, the town of Ridgway has been the site of several Hollywood Westerns, including the 1969 classic, *True Grit*. Several of the film's buildings and props – the railroad depot, courthouse, saloon, jail wagon and more – remain part of the town's landscape. Film buffs will especially enjoy the **True Grit Café** *(truegritcafe.com)*, a kind of shrine to John Wayne, who played a tough, one-eyed US marshal in the film, a performance that won him his only Oscar. Free one-hour True Grit tours are offered in the summer through Ridgway's visitor center, or download a self-guided tour from *ridgwaycolorado.com* instead.

EATING IN RIDGWAY: OUR PICKS

Tacos del Gnar: Fusion riff on street tacos in a fast-casual setting. Loads of vegan and gluten-free options. Booze served, too. *11am-8:30pm Tue-Sat* **$**

Kate's Place: One of the best breakfast joints around, in a cute and colorful spot. Perfect for a post-hike bite. *7am-2pm Fri-Wed* **$**

Eatery 66: Food truck turned trendy restaurant with a changing menu of sandwiches, salads and treats. Airstream burger bar open afternoons only. *11:30am-8pm Thu-Tue* **$$**

Hearth at the Old Firehouse: Historic firehouse, now an upscale farm-to-table restaurant. Open-flame cooking dominates the offerings. *5-10pm Wed-Sun* **$$$**

AVALANCHE SAFETY

Colorado is famous for its pristine backcountry skiing and snowmobiling, but also for its extreme avalanche danger – one-third of the country's avalanche deaths (an average of six per year) occur in Colorado. But there are literally thousands of slides every winter in Colorado's backcountry, and dozens of people are partially or fully buried in them. It's mostly luck that determines who lives or dies in an avalanche, but technology and education can help – avalanche beacons aid in locating buried victims, and courses can help you identify dangerous conditions. Before you head on a backcountry ski trip, consider taking an avalanche class – it could save your life. Recommended schools include San Juan Mountain Guides (p269) and **Silverton Avalanche School** *(avyschool.org)*.

One-stop water play

Fishing aficionados should head to **Ridgway State Park** *(cpw.state.co.us; $10 per vehicle)*, home of Paco, the Blue Ribbon–rated tailwater of the Uncompahgre River. This gorgeous stretch of river, 14 miles from Ouray, is stocked with native trout, including browns, rainbows and cutthroat; catch and release only. Fishing not your thing? The park's turquoise **reservoir**, with its jaw-dropping views of the Sneffels Range, has a swim beach and is a popular for paddleboarding and kayaking. Self-service **rentals** *(wheneverwatersports.com; paddleboards and kayaks per hour from $20)* are available on-site through an app. For fishing gear, try **Rigs Fly Shop & Guide Service** *(fishrigs.com)*.

Clothing-optional soaking

Even if baring it all makes you uncomfortable, the steaming rock pools and garden setting make the clothing-optional **Orvis Hot Springs** *(orvishotsprings.com; day pass adult/child $28/12)*, 2 miles outside Ridgway, hard to resist. Yes, it does get its fair share of nudists, but the variety of soaking areas (65°F to 112°F; 18°C to 44°C) means you can scout out the perfect spot. On-site accommodations, even camping, include two days of unlimited soaking...a sweet deal!

Overnight in the backcountry

Spend your days exploring the mountains and your nights in the **San Juan Huts** *(sanjuanhuts.com; from $275 per person)*, a series of basic cabins owned and operated by their namesake outfitter and extending 215 miles from Durango through Ridgway, Ouray and Telluride to Moab, Utah. You can base yourself in one hut, or travel hut to hut by foot, skis or bike, accessing trails rarely used by others, the great outdoors seemingly all yours. Rental includes basic supplies and amenities; mountain-bike trips include food, too.

Silverton

TIME FROM OURAY: **45 MINS**

Experts only

Silverton Mountain Resort *(silvertonmountain.com; unguided/guided lift ticket from $109/279, heliskiing from $199)* is unlike any other Colorado resort, with a motto that says it all: No Frills, All Thrills. There are no condos, no grooming, not even any proper runs and only one dinky lift. And yet that lift puts you at the top of hundreds of acres of backcountry bowls, chutes, trees and steeps – even more if you're up for hiking. It's North America's steepest and highest resort (the peak is over 13,000ft) with arguably the best powder lines and expert-only terrain anywhere. The guided option is the most popular, with expert skiers leading groups of eight to the best snow on the mountain. Add in heliskiing – available in single drops or six-drop passes – and it's no wonder Silverton is the stuff of legends. Avalanche gear is required (and available for rent). Located 23 miles south of Ouray.

Silverton Mountain Resort

Snow-cat skiing and riding

More accessible to families and intermediate skiers than big bad Silverton Mountain Resort, **Silverton Powdercats** *(silvertonpowdercats.com; $750)* is a friendly and professional operation running guided ski and snowboard trips on **Molas Pass**, just outside of Silverton. A snow cat delivers your group to great drop-in points – most groups get about 10 runs in for the day. The guides know the best powder stashes, drop-offs, tree runs and more, all while keeping everyone safe and smiling. Avi beacon and lunch included. Reserve well ahead of time. Most trips depart from Molas Lake Trail, 1 mile north from Molas Pass.

Adrenaline-filled fest

Every February, rowdy crowds descend on Silverton's historic streets for **Silverton Skijoring** *(silvertonskijoring.com; free)*, a popular two-day competition where galloping horses pull skiers by a tow rope at 35 to 45mph through snow-covered streets-turned-courses with jumps, slalom gates and obstacles. The goal: to complete the courses as fast as possible, often grabbing rings along the way for extra points. The winner gets a cash prize. It's a thrilling competition to watch, with live music, food and street vendors adding to the festive vibe.

NOTORIOUS BLAIR STREET

Lined in historic buildings and wooden boardwalks, Notorious Blair St is a quiet, charming street. But at the height of the mining boom, it was the epicenter of Silverton's vibrant vice trade, home to brothels, dance halls, variety theaters and saloons. Miners from camps around the region came to Silverton for supplies, but stayed to blow off steam on Notorious Blair St. It was infamous for its lively, wild atmosphere, with high-stakes gambling, rowdy drinking and frequent brawls earning it a reputation as one of the wildest parts of Colorado. Today, though some rowdiness returns during Silverton Skijoring, it's better known for its restaurants and antique shops – a place to stroll and imagine what life was once like here.

DRINKING IN SILVERTON: OUR PICKS

Avalanche Brewing Co:
Longtime local brewery that pulls a crowd; look for the skis inside and out. Pizza served, too. *11am-8pm*

Lacey Rose Saloon:
Historic Old West bar with ornate fixtures, stamped-tin ceiling and bullet hole. Live ragtime piano most days. *11am-10pm Mon-Sat, to 9pm Sun*

Coffee Bear Silverton:
Modern coffeehouse with Western flair. Known for its square-shaped breakfast burritos and epic rooftop views. *6:30am-3pm*

Columbine Roadhouse:
Popular music venue with open-air bar and stage. Located on the edge of town, where the Million Dollar Hwy ends. *hours vary*

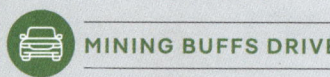

MINING BUFFS DRIVE

An active mining town for well over a century, Silverton's 'rich' history is well worth a day of exploring.

START	END	LENGTH
One Hundred Gold Mine	Mining Heritage Center Museum	24 miles; 5½ hours

Start 8 miles east of Silverton at the ① **One Hundred Gold Mine**, donning a hard hat and riding a vintage mining tram 500yd into a once-active mine. Former miners lead the tours, sharing fascinating anecdotes about life underground; they often perform drilling demonstrations with old-school equipment.

Take the gravel road north to ② **Animas Forks Mine**, a ghost town sandwiched between towering mountains. Several cabins and structures still stand, offering a glimpse into daily life at this hub for hard-rock silver and gold mining. Interpretive signs give context.

Head back toward town, stopping at ③ **Mayflower Gold Mill**, the longest-running mill

in the San Juans. Learn how gold, silver and other metals were extracted, using the imposing and still-intact machinery. The Aerial Tram House is a highlight, with tram buckets that once carried men and ore hanging on cables leading from the mill to now-closed mines. Don't miss the Guard Shack and its exhibits on the creative robberies the mill experienced.

End at the ④ **Mining Heritage Center Museum**, a sprawling 14,000-sq-ft complex with well-conceived exhibits, including a re-creation of the Sunnyside Mine, an actual miners' boarding house and rare train memorabilia. The museum is attached to the meticulously restored 1902 county jail.

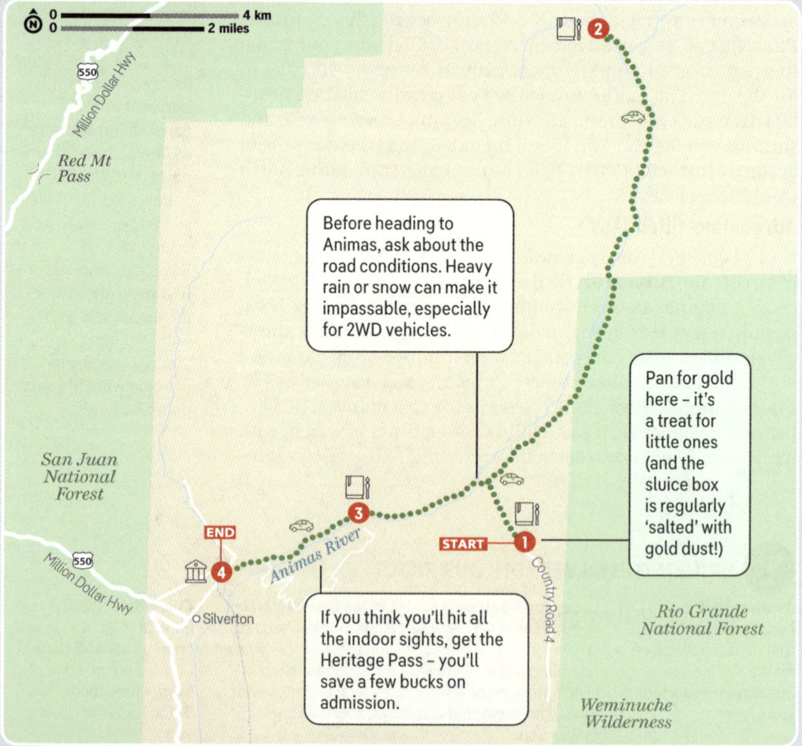

Before heading to Animas, ask about the road conditions. Heavy rain or snow can make it impassable, especially for 2WD vehicles.

Pan for gold here – it's a treat for little ones (and the sluice box is regularly 'salted' with gold dust!)

If you think you'll hit all the indoor sights, get the Heritage Pass – you'll save a few bucks on admission.

Red Mt Pass

San Juan National Forest

Million Dollar Hwy

Animas River

Silverton

Country Road 4

Rio Grande National Forest

Weminuche Wilderness

Black Canyon of the Gunnison National Park

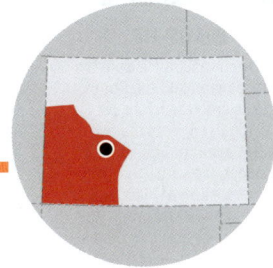

JAW-DROPPING VIEWS | WORLD-CLASS FISHING | MULTILEVEL TRAILS

Steep, narrow and utterly spectacular, the Black Canyon of the Gunnison National Park is a massive 2700ft-deep gash in the earth, etched over millions of years by the Gunnison River and volcanic uplift. Declared a national park in 1999, it offers breathtaking views, challenging hikes and myriad climbs – no matter how you experience it, you're sure to leave with a sense of awe (and a little vertigo).

Black Canyon has proven a formidable obstacle to humans trying to best it. Though early Utes had settlements along its rim, no people have lived within the chasm itself. Efforts to create a train route through it were limited (some say, doomed) and eventually abandoned. Only its river has been tamed – a water-diversion tunnel and a series of upriver dams keep the river at a predictable flow, while providing water and electricity to surrounding communities.

Easy Driving, Thrilling Views

Cruise along South Rim Rd

With views of 2000ft-high canyon walls and colorful craggy spires, a drive along the rim of the Black Canyon of the Gunnison is the most accessible and popular way to experience the national park. For 7 miles, the flat, winding and paved **South Rim Rd** *(nps.gov/blca/planyourvisit/southrim.htm)* hugs the canyon's edge with a dozen pullouts and overlooks offering heart-stopping vistas. Hit them all in a day, or just select a few and leave time for hiking. Good options include **Pulpit Rock Overlook**, a fingerlike outcropping with expansive river views; **Devil's Lookout**, at the end of a long path with spectacular views over the canyon rim (plus the North Rim's winding road in the distance); **Chasm View**, the canyon's narrowest point; **Painted Wall**, Colorado's tallest vertical cliff (2250ft), named after the magnificent pink pegmatite stripes that stretch half a mile across; and **Sunset View**, with dramatic vistas at the day's end. There are information placards at each overlook, providing insight into the park's geology and history. Many also have picnic tables for an easy break.

GETTING AROUND

Black Canyon of the Gunnison National Park is only accessible by private vehicle. For both rims, Montrose is the nearest transportation hub, with an airport and long-distance bus service. In the park, there's plenty of parking at the visitor center and ranger station as well as at pullouts along the South Rim and North Rim roads. In winter (late November to late April), the South Rim Rd is only open to vehicles up to the visitor center; the remainder is only open to cross-country skiers and snowshoers. The East Portal and North Rim roads are entirely closed in winter.

☑TOP TIP

The national park is split by the canyon into the South Rim and North Rim. No bridge connects the two sides even though, at their closest, they are just 1100ft apart. Allow at least two hours to drive between the two areas – about 80 miles on (mostly) paved roads.

SAFETY IN THE PARK

With dizzying heights and fast-moving waters, it's worth keeping a few Black Canyon pointers in mind.

There are few guardrails, even near the steepest drops – keep small children close and watch your step, especially while taking selfies. Don't throw anything into the canyon – even a small rock could prove fatal to someone hiking or climbing below. Paddling on the Gunnison River is highly discouraged – it's swift, rocky and cold. Head instead to neighboring Curecanti (p282). And to protect wildlife, pets must be leashed and are prohibited on trails, the inner-canyon wilderness, or ranger-led walks. During the summer, dogs cannot be walked around the South Rim Campground due to potentially aggressive mule deer defending their fawns.

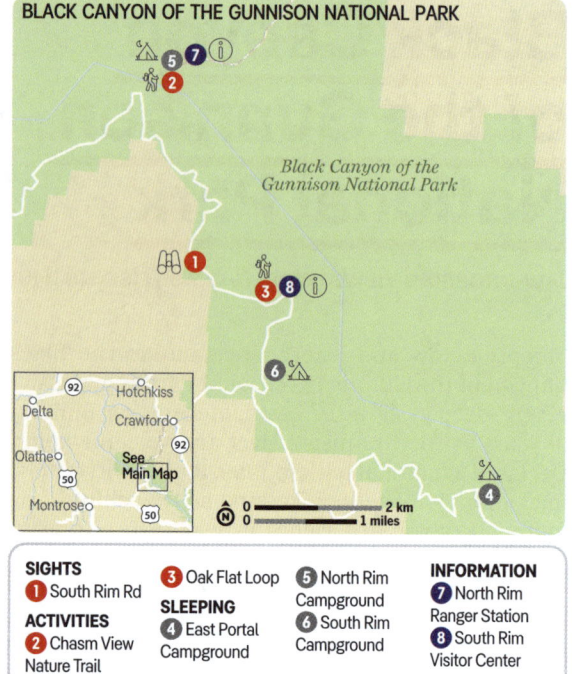

BLACK CANYON OF THE GUNNISON NATIONAL PARK

Black Canyon of the Gunnison National Park

See Main Map

0 — 2 km
0 — 1 miles

SIGHTS
1 South Rim Rd

ACTIVITIES
2 Chasm View Nature Trail

3 Oak Flat Loop

SLEEPING
4 East Portal Campground

5 North Rim Campground
6 South Rim Campground

INFORMATION
7 North Rim Ranger Station
8 South Rim Visitor Center

Leafy Hike with Views

Trek just below the rim

If you're looking for a below-the-rim hike without going clear to the canyon bottom, **Oak Flat Loop** *(nps.gov/thingstodo/oak -flat.htm)* is a good option. Starting at the **South Rim Visitor Center**, the 2-mile trail loops through aspen and fir forest, with openings in the trees providing spectacular views. It's a moderately strenuous hike with a 400ft drop before the trail meanders back to the rim (for an easier ascent, hike counterclockwise from the visitor center). Plan on hiking for 45 to 60 minutes and be sure to carry water. (Note: water stations are available at the visitor center during the summer months only.)

Scrambling to Rock Bottom

Inner canyon wilderness

Hiking to the bottom of the Black Canyon (and back up!) is a punishing but rewarding way to spend a day. There are six routes through the inner canyon – three from each rim – ranging from 1800 to 2700 vertical feet, and promising untrammeled wilderness, magnificent canyon views and solitude. All are primitive hiking experiences on unmarked and unmaintained trails, involving scrambling over boulders and loose rocks and navigating by natural landmarks. Most routes end at riverside campsites – it's a treat to stay overnight if you're up for carrying the extra gear and supplies.

Hikers must have a **wilderness use permit** *(nps.gov/blca/planyourvisit/innercanyon.htm)* to descend into the inner canyon – only eight to 23 permits per route are allotted each day, and they go fast. Permits are free and available at the South Rim Visitor Center or **North Rim Ranger Station** from 3:30pm the day prior. If the latter is closed, there's a self-service permit-registration kiosk near the front door. Whichever route you take, start early and bring items such as hiking shoes, a headlamp, snacks and water filter. Wear long pants – there's lots of poison ivy. The South Rim Visitor Center also has helpful binders listing additional recommended supplies as well as step-by-step photos of each route – peruse them before heading out.

Casting on Gold Medal Water

Fishing on the Gunnison River

Driving down the steep, hairpin-curved East Portal Rd to the canyon floor, anglers will find some of Colorado's best fishing. Designated Gold Medal Water, the Black Canyon's section of the Gunnison River is a top spot for rainbow (catch and release) and brown trout (bag limit of four). The water runs deep and fast, the rocky banks and pocket water loaded with hearty, self-sustaining trout. The road runs alongside the river for about 2 miles, bookended by the East Portal Campground and Crystal Dam; anglers can continue on foot in either direction. Be sure to get a Colorado fishing license before your first cast, and use lures and flies only. Casting is permitted anywhere along the river, except 200yd downstream of Crystal Dam.

Scaling Sheer Walls

Climbing on the North Rim

The North Rim is all about rock climbing. Much less traveled but reachable by gravel road, the area has 145 multipitch climbing routes rated between 5.9 and 5.13, including along the **North Chasm** and to the top of the Painted Wall. Wilderness permits are required, available for free at the North Rim Ranger Station; be sure to check out – and add your info to – the whiteboard near the front door, listing the day's climbers; it helps prevent traffic jams on any given route. Unless you're an experienced climber, a guide is a must. Try Mountain Trip (p274) or **IRIS** *(irisalpine.com)*, an outdoors company catering to women, non-binary and trans people.

Stroll along the Edge

Meander on a forested trail

The North Rim's picturesque **Chasm View Nature Trail** is well worth the 20 to 30 minutes it takes to complete. A flat, rocky half-mile walk, it begins in thick juniper forest near the campground, with placards describing the park's flora and fauna. Nearing the canyon's edge, the trees open onto a spectacular view of the 1800ft-tall North Chasm. From there, follow the snaking rim, taking in views of the rushing river below flanked by the almost-vertical canyon walls. Continue to the dramatic overlook of Painted Wall, where guardrails allow for picture-perfect selfies, before circling back into the forest.

INTERNATIONAL DARK SKY PARK

Black Canyon of the Gunnison is an outstanding place for stargazing, thanks to its clear dry weather and exceptionally dark skies. In 2015 the park became one of Colorado's first International Dark Sky Places (the state has 10), thanks to its dark skies and the park's work to limit light pollution and educate visitors on astronomy, nocturnal ecosystems and more. Summer brings loads of **free astronomy programs** by park rangers and members of the Black Canyon Astronomical Society. In September, the park hosts **AstroFest**, with nightly telescope viewings, constellation tours, guest lectures by astronomers and info on the park's nocturnal animals.

Beyond
Black Canyon of the Gunnison National Park

Places

Curecanti National Recreation Area p282

Montrose p283

Delta p284

From museums to backcountry adventure, the Black Canyon's surrounds provide historical context and outdoor fun year-round.

The region surrounding Black Canyon of the Gunnison National Park is as diverse as the canyon is deep. On its western edge, Montrose is a nondescript town whose main role is supplying goods to the surrounding communities. But it also happens to have some archaeological sites and museums that are worth a stop. Just north, in Delta, a re-created trading post gives a sense of life here during its earliest settlement days. On the region's eastern edge lies the stark beauty of Curecanti National Recreation Area, a huge reservoir system formed by the damming of the Gunnison River and a popular place for water play.

Curecanti National Recreation Area

TIME FROM BLACK CANYON OF THE GUNNISON NP: **25 MINS**

Adventure on the water

Impossible to miss from Hwy 50, **Blue Mesa Reservoir** is Colorado's largest body of water, with nearly 100 miles of shoreline edged by sweeping mesas, volcanic spires and secluded canyon walls. This is the heart of the **Curecanti National Recreation Area** *(nps.gov/cure; free)*. An otherworldly playground neighboring the Black Canyon of the Gunnison National Park, it was created from a series of dams and reservoirs where the Gunnison River once flowed freely. Explore the waters by boat and rent fishing gear – it's Colorado's largest kokanee salmon and lake-trout fishery. Paddlers will especially enjoy the calm waters at the **Bay of Chickens**, but beware of strong afternoon winds. For rentals, gear and guides, head to the **Elk Creek** and **Lake Fork marinas** *(thebluemesa.com; paddleboards half/full day $35/60, kayaks $45/80, guided fishing trips from $550)*. If you'd rather stay on dry land, hike the moderately easy **Dillon Pinnacles Trail** (4 miles round trip), offering close-up views of the area's striking volcanic spires, with the reservoir always in view.

GETTING AROUND

Montrose is the transportation hub for the Black Canyon region, serviced by long-distance **Outrider** *(ridebustang.com)* buses and **Montrose Regional Airport** *(montroseairport. com)*. Once here, public transportation is extremely limited, so the best way to explore is in your own vehicle (there are car rental agencies at the airport); 4WD is especially useful in the winter or if you're planning to head into the backcountry. Be sure to gas up each day – long stretches of empty roads are commonplace here.

Paddling through Black Canyon

For a DIY kayaking tour, head to **Morrow Point Reservoir**, a 12-mile stretch of the Gunnison River between the Blue Mesa and Morrow Point dams in Curecanti. Paddling through its calm, clear waters, you'll be surrounded by dramatic canyon walls highlighted by waterfalls, hidden coves and volcanic spires, including the 700ft-tall **Curecanti Needle**. There are a handful of primitive boat-in **campsites** (free; first come, first served). To access the reservoir, prepare to carry your kayak down the staircase at the start of **Pine Creek Trail** (off Hwy 50) – approximately 232 steps to a put-in spot (the trail continues for another mile alongside the river). Kayak rentals are available at Lake Fork Marina, about 2.5 miles from the trailhead. Be sure to fill out a free backcountry use permit, available at the trailhead. Note: water levels can fluctuate dramatically, making it difficult to navigate – check reservoir levels at *usbr.gov* before setting off.

Montrose

TIME FROM BLACK CANYON OF THE GUNNISON NP: **20 MINS**

Mosey back in time

For an authentic-as-it-gets Wild West museum, Montrose's **Museum of the Mountain West** (*museumofthemountain west.org; adult/teen/child $12.50/7.50/5, guided tour adult/ child $2.50/free*) doesn't disappoint. A recreated Old West town, its grounds feature 28 buildings relocated from nearby towns, including a saloon, clinic, jail, chapel, numerous storefronts, even the original building where boxing champ Jack Dempsey trained. Each one is overflowing with memorabilia, from prosthetic eyeballs to bank safes. For a few extra bucks, docents in period dress will guide you through the museum for 1½ hours, adding interesting and wacky anecdotes along the way. Especially fun for kids.

Learn about the Ute

One of the few American museums dedicated to a single tribe, the **Ute Indian Museum** (*historycolorado.org/ute-indian -museum; adult/child $7/free*) examines the many cultural and historical layers of Colorado's longest continuous residents. Artifacts, displays, videos and hands-on exhibits paint a powerful portrait of the Ute people, past and present. There are regular speaker series and film screenings, too. The museum sits on the homestead of legendary Ute Chief Ouray (p268) and his wife, Chipeta; she's buried in the adjoining **Ouray Memorial Park**.

BLACK CANYON TRAIN TRACKS

From 1882 to 1949, the Denver & Rio Grand (DRG) train traveled through the Black Canyon's upper reaches, showcasing its 2000ft-high canyon walls and the raging Gunnison River. Part of a Denver–Salt Lake City line, the 15-mile track proved a dangerous and expensive construction endeavor, claiming numerous lives and costing an astounding $165,000 per mile. Once completed, the track was plagued by rock falls and avalanches. It was eventually abandoned, with a safer route built through Grand Junction. Today, the train tracks are almost entirely gone, submerged beneath the waters of the Curecanti National Recreation Area. A railyard exhibit at the **Cimarron Visitor Center** is the only reminder of what once was here.

✕ EATING IN MONTROSE: OUR PICKS

Bluecorn Cafe & Mercantile: Hearty sandwiches and salads in a bright, airy space doubling as a candle shop. *7am-4pm* **$**

Horsefly Brewing Co: Popular brewhouse known for its Tabano Red and extensive pub-grub menu, including 16 varieties of wings. Live music most weeks. *11am-9pm* **$**

Colorado Boy Pizzeria & Brewery: Creative pizzas and craft beers served at this casual spot in historic downtown. Gluten-free crust available. *4-9pm* **$**

Camp Robber: Fine dining meets strip mall. Come for Americana with New Mexican and Italian twists. *11am-8:30pm Mon-Sat* **$$**

DRY MESA DINOSAUR QUARRY

Uncompahgre National Forest is home to Dry Mesa Dinosaur Quarry, the site of the most diverse cache of Jurassic-period dinosaur specimens ever found. More than 4000 dinosaur bones were unearthed here, belonging to everything from colossal crocodiles and turtles to winged lizards and fierce carnivores – there was even the 8ft shoulder blade of a 120ft-long herbivore dubbed Supersaurus. And yet an entire skeleton was never found – the bones were deposited haphazardly atop each other, the likely result of periodic droughts and flash floods washing them to this spot from near and far over millennia. Today, after three decades of excavation, the quarry is covered up, with only a couple of signposts remaining where an epic discovery was once made.

DAVID A EASTLEY/ALAMY STOCK PHOTO

Fort Uncompahgre Interpretive Center

Petroglyph tour

Just west of Montrose, **Shavano Valley** (p253) is home to a spectacular petroglyph site dating to 1000 BCE. The 37 well-preserved panels are on private land, set in red sandstone cliff faces and boulders. Many depict plants and animals, people and anthropomorphic figures, and there are even representations of the still-celebrated Ute Bear Dance. The site is accessible by private **tour** *($20)*, arranged through the Ute Indian Museum (p283). Tours last two hours, along a short trail.

Delta   TIME FROM BLACK CANYON OF THE GUNNISON NP: **40 MINS**

Life in the Old West

Sitting on the bank of the Gunnison River, about 20 miles north of Montrose, **Fort Uncompahgre Interpretive Center** *(fortuncompahgre.com; adult/child $3/free, guided tour $2/free)* is a faithful reconstruction of an 1828 trading post that once stood nearby (it was never used or intended to be a military fort). Strategically located on the Old Spanish Trail, it was an early hub of commerce and cultural exchange for trappers, Ute and Navajo people, Mexicans and Anglo settlers. Today, Fort Uncompahgre showcases life during the mountain-man era, offering tours with guides in period dress, living-history demonstrations and hands-on activities such as blacksmithing, beading and hide tanning. You can also freely explore the traditional log and adobe buildings. It's a fun and interesting way to spend an afternoon learning about the Old West.

Grand Junction

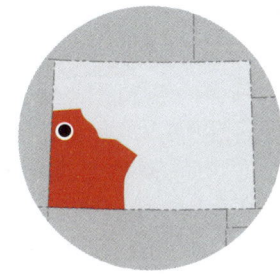

CHARMING DOWNTOWN | RELAXED PACE | OUTDOOR ADVENTURE

Named for its location at the confluence of the Colorado and Gunnison Rivers, Grand Junction is an agricultural hub and a right-of-center stronghold in an increasingly left-leaning state. As a travel destination, Grand Junction's backers quip that the city's motto could be 'Gas and Gatorade' as many road-trippers view the city as a convenient pit stop between the better-known destinations of Moab and the Colorado Rockies. Even Coloradans seem unaware of what Grand Junction has to offer. But anonymity has its advantages: Grand Junction has small-town charm but also engaging places to visit, and you'll often have them to yourself. And with loads of traveler amenities, Grand Junction makes a convenient base camp for the myriad surrounding outdoors options – from stunning red-rock vistas and hikes past dinosaur bones to wild horse reserves and even Colorado's very own wine country.

Art, Antiques & More

Downtown stroll

Soak in Grand Junction's small-town charm with an afternoon stroll through the heart of downtown. Start on Main St, between 3rd and 7th Sts, where colorful murals brighten large brick walls and the wide walkways host **Art on the Corner** (*gjcreates.org/aotc*), an outdoor exhibit of more than 115 sculptures, ranging from whimsical to historic – new pieces (most for sale) are rotated in each year. Peruse the quirky

GETTING AROUND

Grand Junction is a breeze to get to: it's a straight shot from Denver on the I-70 – either by car or bus (*ridebustang. com, greyhound. com*) – and there's the **Grand Junction Regional Airport** (*gjairport.com*). Once here, downtown is very walkable: it's flat with well-maintained sidewalks and most businesses are located around a four-block section of Main St. Beyond downtown, driving is the most convenient way to get around (and good news – there's not much traffic). Vehicle rentals are available at the airport and street parking is either free or cheap ($0.50 to $1 per hour, 8am to 4pm Monday to Friday). Alternatively, renting a bike is easy from a handful of downtown shops.

☑️**TOP TIP**

Grand Junction has western Colorado's largest airport and best selection of car rentals. Flying to Denver is going to be cheaper, but requires at least a four-hour drive on busy I-70. Check for flight deals to Grand Junction; it may be a better hub for your Colorado adventures.

shops along the way – **A Robin's Nest of Antiques and Treasures** *(robinsnestgj.com)*, the largest vintage shop on the western slope, is jam-packed with treasures and finds – or search for that missing vinyl in your collection (or disc golf needs) at the long-standing **Triple Play Records** *(facebook.com/TriplePlayRecords)*. From there, stop at the **Museum of Western Colorado** *(museumofwesternco.com; adult/child $7/4)*, which has a fascinating range of exhibits, from Ancestral Puebloan pottery to Wild West firearms. Wrap it up with a pint at **Ramblebine Brewing** *(ramblebinebrewing.com)*, a warehouse-style taproom serving everything from IPAs to sours.

Singletrack near Downtown

Shred red-rock trails

Just 2.9 miles from downtown, **Lunch Loops Bike Park** *(blm.gov; free)* is a favorite singletrack park close enough for locals to squeeze in a ride during their lunch hour (hence, the name). Bikers of all levels enjoy loop-de-loop fun through the red-rock landscape, while advanced riders can tackle the famous **Tabeguache/Lunch Loop Trail System**. The bike

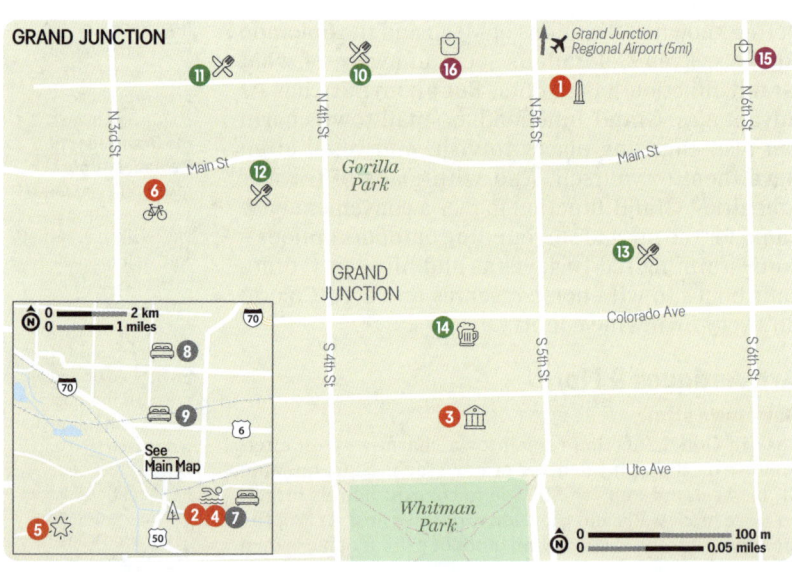

SIGHTS
1 Art on the Corner
2 Las Colonias Park
3 Museum of Western Colorado

ACTIVITIES
4 Grand Junction Adventures

5 Lunch Loops Bike Park
6 Ruby Canyon Cycles

SLEEPING
7 Camp Eddy
8 Castle Creek Manor
9 Hotel Maverick

EATING
10 Bin 707 Foodbar
11 Dream Cafe
12 Pablo's Pizza
13 Tacoparty

DRINKING
14 Ramblebine Brewing

SHOPPING
15 A Robin's Nest of Antiques and Treasures
16 Triple Play Records

CLAUDIA G COOPER/SHUTTERSTOCK

Cyclists, Colorado National Monument (p290)

park, located at the beginning of the trail system, has rollers, berms and singletrack of various sizes and pitches – a great place to hone your balance and gear management. Longer trails, including a 142-mile ride to Montrose, offer tough biking and spectacular views in equal measure. For quality rentals, try **Ruby Canyon Cycles** *(rubycanyoncycles.com).*

Floating on the Colorado River

Water play in Las Colonias Park

Created in the late 1980s as the last 'pearl' on a 21-mile riverfront trail, **Las Colonias Park** provides easy access to the Colorado River, with a small beach and boat ramp. Stand-up paddleboarders and kayakers put in at this spot – you can rent both (plus inner tubes) on-site from **Grand Junction Adventures** *(gjadventures.com; per hour from $25),* honing your paddling skills on Butterfly Lake before navigating the river's currents. Or if chillax is more your vibe, float down a protected section of the river running beside the beachfront. Rent an inner tube (from $15 per hour) or grab a free life jacket (available at the boat ramp) and while away the afternoon.

 EATING IN GRAND JUNCTION: OUR DOWNTOWN PICKS

Dream Cafe: Diner with to-die-for breakfast, from eggs Benedict and quiche to chocolate-hazelnut French toast. Come early or prepare to wait. *7am-2pm* **$**

Pablo's Pizza: With sidewalk seating and a small-town vibe, these creative thin-crust pies are easily the best in town. *10am-8:30pm Mon-Sat, from noon Sun* **$**

Tacoparty: Trendy taco joint showcasing locally sourced ingredients, from produce to proteins. *11:30am-8pm Sun-Thu, to 9pm Fri & Sat* **$$**

Bin 707 Foodbar: Chef Josh Niernbern pays homage to western Colorado's seasonal flavors at this mid-century-chic restaurant. *4:30-10pm Mon-Sat* **$$$**

Beyond Grand Junction

Grand Junction's surrounds are brimming with outdoors options, from trails and climbing routes to quiet vineyards and agritourism offerings.

Places

Fruita p288

Canyon Pintado National Historic District p289

Palisade p293

Grand Mesa p294

GETTING AROUND

Accessing the region is easy via Grand Junction, which is serviced by long-distance buses and Grand Junction Regional Airport. Once here, **Grand Valley Transit** *(gvt.mesacounty. us)* provides limited bus service between Grand Junction, Fruita and Palisade. Beyond those towns, you'll need your own vehicle. Rentals are available at the airport; consider getting a 4WD in the winter, or if you want to explore the backcountry.

The high-desert landscape surrounding Grand Junction is often overshadowed by flashier parts of the state. But set out to explore and you'll find a place rich in beauty and outdoors activities. From wine tasting and picking your own lavender to dramatic red-rock hikes and some of the best singletrack biking in the west, it's a surprisingly layered part of Colorado (and don't even get us started on all the dino sites!). Almost best of all, the region is conveniently compact, with most of its sights and activities just a few miles apart, making it possible to have a full day of activities without spending half of it in your car.

Fruita

TIME FROM GRAND JUNCTION: **20 MINS**

Hike a hidden treasure

Twenty miles from Grand Junction in the stunning high desert of **McKinnis Canyons National Conservation Area** *(blm. gov; free)*, where **Rattlesnake Arches Trail** (12.4 miles round trip) leads visitors past nearly three dozen natural arches – the most in the US outside Arches National Park. The trail begins on a scenic sagebrush mesa and splits – a lower trail gets you up close and personal with eight of the largest arches, including **Cedar Arch**, measuring 76ft across, while an upper trail offers views from above and (if you dare) a walk across some of the sandstone arches. Be sure to take plenty of water and keep your eyes peeled for wildlife such as desert bighorn sheep and golden eagles. The trail's namesake, the midget faded rattler, is venomous but rarely seen. The access road, off Rimrock Dr, is rough, especially the last 2 miles – visitors in 4WD or high-clearance vehicles can reach the main trailhead, while most park and walk once the road becomes impassable.

High-desert biking

Fruita is home to some of the best mountain biking in the west and has a fraction of the crowds of nearby Moab, Utah. The riding is incredibly scenic, with exhilarating and challenging singletrack through desert, rocky canyons and river valleys. The dry desert climate allows for a long riding season that stretches from late April to mid-November, though the summer temperatures can hit the 100s Fahrenheit. **Kokopelli's Trail** *(blm.gov/visit/kokopellis-trail)* is Fruita's most famous ride, with 142 miles of ruggedly beautiful advanced-level riding leading all the way to Moab. Closer to town, the **18 Road** *(blm.gov/visit/18-road-north-fruita-desert)* area in the North Fruita Desert has more than 40 miles of trails that offer a mix of fast descents, flowy berms and challenging climbs. Check out **Over the Edge Sports** *(otefruita.com)*, a full-service bike shop and Fruita biking institution. It offers guided rides and advocates for responsible trail use.

Paleontologist for a day

The best of four interpretive dinosaur trails around Fruita, **Trail Through Time** is a 1.5-mile loop in the high desert of **Rabbit Valley Research Natural Area** *(blm.gov; free)*. You'll learn loads about the prehistoric landscape from interpretive signs, touch in-situ bones and, in summer, check out the active Mygatt-Moore Quarry, where more than 2000 dinosaur bones have been unearthed since the 1980s. Better still, join paleontologists on full-day digs in the quarry ($175), a program offered through the Paleontology Division of the Museum of Western Colorado (p286); children over six welcome.

Canyon Pintado National Historic District
TIME FROM GRAND JUNCTION: 1¼ HR 🚗

Ancient messages

On an unforgiving and arid stretch of Hwy 139 sits **Canyon Pintado National Historic District** *(blm.gov; free)*, a 15-mile treasure trove of rock art. The spectral, mysterious images – ghostly birds, life-size flutists and more – are attributed to two communities: the Fremont Culture (100 to 1150 CE) and the Ute (1300 to 1881). They were first written about in 1776 by Silvestre Vélez de Escalante, a Franciscan missionary who came through on the famed Dominguez-Escalante Expedition, naming the corridor Cañon Pintado (Painted Canyon).

Of the 50 sites flanking the road, 17 are indicated by BLM road signs. Dirt parking lots, pull-offs and well-maintained trails lead to the petroglyphs and pictographs, most with information placards. Highlights include **East Four Mile Site** (milepost 61.3), a one- to two-hour walk past panels scattered across ledges and caves; **Kokopelli Site** (milepost 56), its Fremont-era art visible from the road; and **Waving Hands**

Continued on p293

MIKE THE HEADLESS CHICKEN FESTIVAL

In 1945 Fruita farmer Lloyd Olsen chose a bird named 'Mike' for dinner and, hoping to preserve as much of the tasty neck as possible, lopped off the chicken's head, but missed the all-important brain stem. Mike the (newly) Headless Chicken didn't fall over and die – to the contrary, he stayed alive for another 18 months, fed grain and water through an eyedropper, and became the subject of news reports, magazine covers and scientific studies. He even toured Atlantic City with his owner and his severed head, preserved in alcohol. Naturally, the townspeople of Fruita created a festival in Mike's honor. Celebrated every June, **Mike the Headless Chicken Festival** *(fruita.org/mike)* includes chicken-themed contests, chicken dances, live music and more.

EATING IN FRUITA: OUR PICKS

Hot Tomato Pizza:
Bustling pizza joint and cyclist hangout. Hand-stretched dough, big salads and a good selection of beers. *11am-9pm Tue-Sat* **$**

Camilla's Kaffe:
Charming little breakfast spot serving up classic American brekkie, from egg dishes and pancakes to oatmeal and burritos. *8am-2pm Wed-Sun* **$**

Base Camp Provisions:
Sprawling brewpub with rotating taps, cocktails and elevated pub fare. *3-9pm Mon-Wed, 11am-9pm Thu, 11am-10pm Fri & Sat, 11am-8pm Sun* **$$**

Karma Kitchen:
Family-run restaurant serving Indian and Nepali comfort food. On weekends, expect a wait. *11am-2:30pm & 5-9pm Mon-Sat* **$$**

RON KARPEL/SHUTTERSTOCK

Independence Monument

TOP EXPERIENCE

Colorado National Monument

Don't let the mundane name fool you, nor your eagerness to reach more famous destinations: Colorado National Monument *(nps.gov/colm)* is a stunning natural area. Just 16 miles west of Grand Junction, it's a warren of canyons, their sheer walls painted a gorgeous cedar red and punctuated by long rocky fins, dramatic sandstone spires and massive overhangs. It's an adventurer's (and photographer's) dream.

DON'T MISS

Rim Rock Drive

Scenic Overlooks

Independence Monument views

Devil's Kitchen

Coke Ovens Overlook

Stargazing

Driving Past Red Rocks

The most popular way to experience Colorado National Monument is the paved 23-mile **Rim Rock Drive**, which weaves along the cliff edges, with 19 pullouts offering vertiginous vistas of the red sandstone cliffs, monoliths and formations carved by millions of years of erosion. Pullouts have interpretive signage explaining the park's various aspects: its history, geology, flora and fauna. Plan on two to three hours for the drive with stops at scenic overlooks, including loads of opportunities to take photos and selfies.

PRACTICALITIES
Scan this QR code for prices and opening hours.

Hiking Through the Park

Forty-six miles of trails make for outstanding and varied hikes, allowing visitors to appreciate the park's formations close-up. Trails range from 400yd to take in a view, to a challenging 14-mile trek through red-rock canyons. Many trailheads are near the Rim Rock Dr pullouts, so it's easy to combine the scenic drive with a hike. Popular trails include **Devil's Kitchen** (1.9 miles round trip), a short hike and scramble to a natural 'room' inside a large stone outcrop; and **Monument Canyon Trail** (11.6 miles round trip), which passes many of the park's most interesting natural features, including the **Kissing Couple**, **Independence Monument** and the **Coke Ovens**.

Climbing Sandstone

Colorado National Monument is a dream for rock climbers, with towering sandstone spires of smooth rock interspersed with cracks, chimneys and ledges. The park is known for its 'trad' climbing routes, which require climbers to place their own protection as they ascend (and remove it as they descend), making it ideal for more experienced climbers. Some climber faves include **Otto's Route** on Independence Monument, the park's iconic 450ft sandstone monolith, with a very doable 5.9 rating; and **Sentinel Spire**, just across the valley, with beautiful crack routes such as West Face (5.11 rating), with steep, challenging terrain and breathtaking exposure. Alternatively, intermediate climbers will find giant slabs and long cliff lines throughout the park that offer scenic bouldering, scrambling and top-roping. Spring and fall are optimal for climbing as summer can be scorching, with temperatures often over 90°F (32°C), and winter can be cold and snowy. Head to **Gearhead Outfitters** (*gearheadoutfitters.com*) in Grand Junction for equipment, maps and route recommendations.

Sleeping under the Stars

Camping in Colorado National Monument is sublime, with dark starry skies and a nighttime orchestra of crickets and coyotes. While the park has one established campground, Saddlehorn (p297), campers can find a spot just about anywhere along the park's extensive trail system. Pitch a tent in **Monument Canyon** for its rock sculptures, **Black Ridge** for its vistas and **No Thoroughfare Canyon** for its isolation. Wherever you spend the night, be sure to get a backcountry permit; they're free and available at the visitor center. Remember to set up camp at least 100ft off the trail and out of sight and hearing of others. Bring plenty of water too, and note that fires, bikes, drones and pets are prohibited.

JOHN OTTO'S VISION

John Otto arrived in Grand Junction in 1906 and was astounded by the red cliffs and sandstone spires west of town, famously calling them 'the heart of the world.' He campaigned tirelessly for federal recognition of the canyonscape. Otto also cut a network of trails, mostly by himself with a shovel and pickax, so when President Taft signed an order creating Colorado National Monument in 1911, it was ready for visitors.

TOP TIPS

● Rim Rock Dr can close in winter or after storms – check the website for current conditions before heading out.

● Rim Rock Dr is popular with cyclists. Stay alert and give them space on the narrow, curvy road.

● For wildlife sightings, arrive early. Morning is the best time to spot creatures such as bighorn sheep, mule deer and golden eagles.

● This is a high desert. On trails, carry at least a gallon of water per person per day to stay hydrated.

● Don't forget sunscreen, a hat and sunglasses – sunny days are the norm and trails are often totally exposed.

Dinosaur National Monument

At the end of desolate stretches of blacktop, Dinosaur National Monument *(nps.gov/dino)* is arguably Colorado's most remote destination. But for travelers fascinated by prehistoric life, it's worth every lonely mile. Spanning the Colorado–Utah border, it's one of the few places on earth where you can reach out and touch a dinosaur skeleton, snarling in its final pose, petrified eternally in rock and stone.

ERIC POULIN/SHUTTERSTOCK

Steamboat Rock

TOP TIPS

● The Utah and Colorado entrances are 28 miles apart – about a 30-minute drive. Plan accordingly, especially to include a quarry visit.

● Services are few and far. Before heading out, fill your tank and be sure to carry drinks and snacks.

PRACTICALITIES

Scan this QR code for prices and opening hours.

The Fossils

The park's indoor highlight is in Utah – the 150ft-long **Dinosaur Quarry Wall** with some 1500 dinosaur bones embedded in it. Part of an ancient riverbed where the remains of Jurassic-era dinosaurs were deposited and later fossilized, you'll see bones from allosaurus to stegosaurus.

Just outside, the **Fossil Discovery Trail** is one of the world's most spectacular open-air collections of fossils, with dinosaur bones, marine creatures and plants visible in the rocks. The moderate 1.2-mile trail has interpretive signs explaining the sights and distinct geological stages.

Panoramic Views

In Colorado, **Harpers Corner Trail** is a moderate 2-mile hike through juniper forests that eventually open to vistas of the park's winding canyons. At the trail's end, hikers are rewarded with spectacular views of the confluence of the Yampa and Green Rivers at jutting **Steamboat Rock**. The trailhead is off Harpers Corner Rd, a scenic drive in itself.

Rafting

Rafting the Green and Yampa rivers is a popular way to experience the park. Expect Class III and IV rapids, red-hued canyons, sandstone formations and petroglyphs. **Adrift** *(adrift. com; adult/child from $120/99)* and **OARS** *(oars.com; from $1049)* offer single and multiday trips, beginning in Utah.

Continued from p289

(milepost 53.5), a combination of rock art from both eras with fantastical characters (including one that appears to be waving), horses, arrows and outlined hands, visible at the end of two short separate trails. More sites can be found along the parallel **Dragon Trail** on Country Road 23, directly south of Rangely. A visit to the historic district is easily paired with a trip to Dinosaur National Monument, 25 miles north. Fill your tank and bring provisions – services are nil.

Palisade

TIME FROM GRAND JUNCTION: **20 MINS**

Taste Colorado wines

Twelve miles east of Grand Junction, Palisade's warm, dry microclimate and volcanic soil aren't just great for growing peaches – turns out, they're ideal for grapes as well. The town has more than 25 vineyards, mostly small-scale family farms with spectacular views of the surrounding **Little Book Cliffs** and Grand Mesa (p294). While no Napa Valley, the low-key ambiance is part of the attraction; many vineyards also offer free tastings and some have extensive tours. Visit the vineyards along the **Fruit and Wine Byway**, with three routes ranging from 5 to 25 miles. Bike rentals are available with **Palisade Cycle & Shuttle** *(palisadecycle.com; per day $40-65),* or book **Palisade Pedicab** *(palisadepedicab.com; per day $85)* to pedal you around instead. Favorite stops include the award-winning **Colterris** *(colterris.com; tour $55),* known for its *vitis vinifera* wines and cave tastings; **Maison La Belle Vie** *(maisonlabellevie.com; tasting from $15),* a country-casual winery specializing in small-batch wines; and **Sauvage Spectrum** *(sauvagespectrum.com; tour $65),* a relative newcomer known for its sparkling wines.

All about alpacas

If cute were currency, the McDermott family would be sitting on a Palisade gold mine with its alpaca farm, **Suncrest Orchard, Alpacas & Fiber Mill** *(suncrestorchardalpacas.net; tours $5, treks $20).* Meet the fuzzy, inquisitive creatures (a smaller cousin of the llama) and then take a tour of the fiber processing plant. Or turn up the cute and pair off with your own alpaca for a 45-minute trek through the peach orchard.

Hike past wild mustangs

Little Book Cliffs *(blm.gov; free)* is home to one of the last protected bands of wild mustangs in the US – about 100 horses on 36,000 acres of craggy canyons and plateaus. Several

PREHISTORIC MAMMALS

Twenty-ton dinosaurs weren't the only creatures walking present-day Colorado during prehistoric times. In 2024, paleontologists from the CU Boulder discovered fossilized remains of a small prehistoric mammal near Rangely. The creature, dubbed *Heleocola piceanus* ('swamp dweller'), resembled a muskrat and lived in the swampy margins of the inland sea that covered much of the American West at that time, around 70 million years ago. The animal weighed around 2lb – pretty hefty for a mammal of the Late Cretaceous period – and was an ancestor of today's marsupials. Dinosaurs get most of the attention when it comes to Colorado's fossils, but it was the little guys who clearly survived the test of time.

 EATING IN PALISADE: OUR PICKS

Palisade Brewing Company: Craft brewery serving up seasonal pints and hearty pub grub. Sit on the patio for spectacular mesa views. *11am-10pm* **$$**

13 Brix Cider Bistro: Sunny bistro pairing classic deli faves with fruit-forward hard ciders. *11am-3pm Mon, to 5pm Fri & Sat, 10am-2pm Sun* **$$**

Fidel's Cocina & Bar: Boho taqueria serving creative tacos plus other Mexican standards. *11:30am-9pm Mon, Thu & Fri, 4:30-8pm Tue & Wed, 10am-9pm Sat & Sun* **$$**

Pêche: Elegant changing menu showcasing Grand Valley ingredients in globally inspired dishes. Reservations recommended. *5-9pm Tue-Sat* **$$$**

PALISADE PEACHES

Of all the fruits grown on Colorado's western slope, the Palisade peach is perhaps the most famous. It was introduced in the late 19th century when early settlers realized the combination of warm summer days, cool nights and a long frost-free season could support fruit orchards. Using a system of irrigation canals fed by the Colorado River – no small feat itself – Palisade became a fruit-growing center. After some trial and error, it soon became clear that peaches were best suited to the region's unique climate. They're harvested in late summer – look for them in grocery stores, on menus and celebrated in local fests – their exceptional sweetness, juiciness and rich flavor standing the test of time.

trails run through the reserve, making it possible to see different families of horses – either studs with a small harem of mares, or bands of young stallions. The easiest access is via the **Main Canyon Trail** (8 miles round trip), off I-70 (Cameo exit), 16 miles east of Grand Junction. The trail runs through a spring-fed canyon – its vegetation and fresh water are a draw for the mustangs, especially in winter and spring. Alternatively, split off onto **Spring Creek Trail** (10 miles round trip) with towering voodoos, flowering cacti and a gurgling creek. If you see horses, don't approach or pet them – they are wild, after all – and give foals especially a wide berth.

Pick your own lavender

Each summer, a sea of purple greets you at **Sage Creations Organic Farm** (*sagecreationsfarm.com; free*) a 6-acre lavender farm. Take a free self-guided tour to learn about lavender varietals and pick a basketful of your own from its gorgeous fields (basket and scissors provided; $8 per bundle). In late June, the farm also participates in the **Colorado Lavender Festival** (*coloradolavender.org/annual-lavender-festival*), a multiday event integrating farm tours, cooking demos and loads of lavender goods.

Grand Mesa   TIME FROM GRAND JUNCTION: **45 MINS**

Water everywhere

Rising over the region like a sleeping giant, the 10,000ft-high, 500-sq-mile Grand Mesa is one of the world's largest flat-top mountains. Its dense forest landscape and wildflower-filled meadows stand in stark contrast to the red rocks and canyonlands below. Add in its 300 lakes and it's altogether another world. Hwy 64 winds through it, with forest roads and trails providing access to harder-to-reach spots. In summer, come for the hiking (bring mosquito repellent) – the **Mesa Lakes Loop Trail** is a gorgeous, relatively flat, 3.2-mile walk past crystal-clear Mesa and Lost Lakes (in autumn, aspens paint the trail in bright yellow). Or kayak on tranquil and glassy **Island Lake**, the largest lake on Grand Mesa – rentals are available at Grand Mesa Lodge (p297). In winter, **Powderhorn Mountain Resort** (*powderhorn.com; lift ticket adult/child from $99/54*) is a popular locals' hill, known for its tree skiing and powder stashes. Year-round, this is a go-to fishing spot (even ice fishing), with most lakes stocked with rainbow, brook and cutthroat trout. For trail maps, stop by the **visitor center** (*fs.usda.gov/gmug*), next to Cobbett Lake.

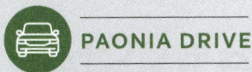

PAONIA DRIVE

Spend a day exploring Paonia, a charming little town known for its organic farms, vineyards and vibrant arts community.

START	END	LENGTH
Azura Cellars	The Blue Sage Center for the Arts	5.7 miles; 4 hours

Nestled at the foot of the West Elk Mountains, Paonia has spectacular views of towering mesas and snowy peaks all around.

Start at **1 Azura Cellars**, a one-time miniature burro farm turned Tuscan-style winery. Enjoy a charcuterie board and a flight of wines on the patio overlooking the gorgeous North Fork Valley. Don't miss the gallery, showcasing the modern art of the owners and artists Ty and Helen Gillespie. Beeline to **2 Big B's Delicious Orchards** for some fruit picking – depending on the season you'll find the orchards brimming with organic apples, pears, plums or apricots (and locals filling their baskets). Stay for a

hard-pressed cider, live music and to soak in the festive community vibe. Next, head toward Paonia's historic **3 Grand Ave**, which is lined with boho boutiques and thrift shops between 2nd and 3rd Sts. Stop in at **4 Horse Cow 57**, a 6000-sq-ft warehouse of thought-provoking sculptures and paintings. Window shop your way to **5 The Refinery**, a consignment shop selling handmade goods made by women or women-owned businesses, and the **6 Cirque Boutique**, showcasing artisanal jewelry and home goods. Finish up at the **7 Blue Sage Center for the Arts** to check out the art gallery and, if you can swing it time-wise, to buy tickets to an evening concert.

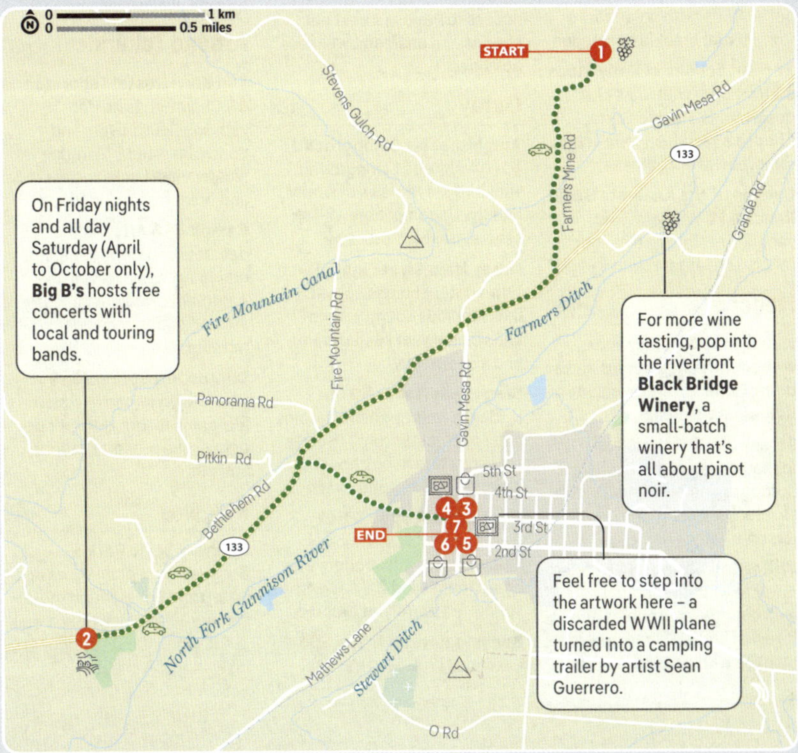

On Friday nights and all day Saturday (April to October only), **Big B's** hosts free concerts with local and touring bands.

For more wine tasting, pop into the riverfront **Black Bridge Winery**, a small-batch winery that's all about pinot noir.

Feel free to step into the artwork here – a discarded WWII plane turned into a camping trailer by artist Sean Guerrero.

Map labels: 1 km / 0.5 miles; Stevens Gulch Rd; Gavin Mesa Rd; 133; START; Farmers Mine Rd; Grande Rd; Fire Mountain Canal; Fire Mountain Rd; Farmers Ditch; Gavin Mesa Rd; Panorama Rd; Pitkin Rd; Bethlehem Rd; 133; 5th St; 4th St; 3rd St; 2nd St; END; North Fork Gunnison River; Mathews Lane; Stewart Ditch; O Rd

Places We Love to Stay

$ Budget $$ Midrange $$$ Top End

Mesa Verde National Park
p254

Morefield Campground (p257) **$** Full-service campground in a grassy canyon, 5 miles from the visitor center. General store sells basics. Open April to October.

Far View Lodge $$ Comfortable though outdated hotel rooms in the heart of the park, all with balcony views. Open April to October.

Cortez
p259

Retro Inn at Mesa Verde $ Classic roadside motel decked out in 1950s retro splendor. Continental breakfast included.

Ancient Echoes at Kelly Place $$ Rare gem with ruins and desert trails outside Cortez. Choose a tasteful adobe-lodge room, casita or campsite.

Canyon of the Ancients Guest Ranch $$$ Western-chic vacation rentals on a historic ranch. The largest sleeps eight.

Mancos
p261

Mancos Inn $ Homey spot with country-style rooms and a dorm. Common areas include a fully stocked kitchen.

Jersey Jim $ Historic fire-lookout tower with a kitchen, outhouse and epic forest views. No electricity or running water. Reserve early.

Willowtail Springs $$$ Idyllic 60-acre wildlife sanctuary with country-chic cabins and lakeside home. Kitchens come stocked with goodies.

Durango
p261

General Palmer Hotel $$ Victorian-era hotel decorated in period style. Cozy library and rooftop terrace are pluses.

Rochester Hotel $$$ Boutique hotel with a Hollywood-meets-cowboy vibe. Enjoy the garden lounge with a cocktail.

Pagosa Springs
p264

Fireside Inn Cabins $$ Cozy, well-appointed log cabins along the San Juan River, perfect for families.

Springs Resort & Spa $$$ Modern hotel rooms with 24/7 access to Pagosa's best hot springs and unlimited wellness activities.

Ouray
p266

Amphitheater Campground $ High-altitude campground with bird's-eye views of Ouray and the Uncompahgre Valley; several trailheads nearby.

Ouray Main Street Inn $ Three 19th-century homes converted into spacious country-style units, some with kitchens. Pet- and 420-friendly.

Black Bear Manor $$ Cozy B&B with well-appointed rooms and spectacular views. Hearty breakfast and happy hour included. Fifteen and over only.

Box Canyon Lodge & Hot Springs $$ Geothermically heated motel with modern pine-board rooms and 24/7 access to spring-fed barrel hot tubs.

Beaumont Hotel & Spa $$$ Luxurious 19th-century hotel decked out in magnificent period furnishings with great views. Sixteen and over only.

Telluride
p272

Telluride Town Park Campground $ Creekside campground in the heart of Telluride, with showers, wi-fi, a pool and tennis.

Camel's Garden $$$ Ski-in, ski-out condo-hotel at the base of the gondola. Hit the 25ft Jacuzzi at sunset.

Lumière $$$ Ski-in, ski-out luxury lodge in Mountain Village; breathtaking views of the San Juans included.

Around Telluride
p272

The Bivvi Hostel Telluride $$ Chalet-style hostel with spacious private and bunkrooms and Coloradan hipster vibe. Lockers, gear room and breakfast included.

CampV $$$ Artsy high-desert escape with camping, glamping, cabins, even luxe Airstreams. Regular concerts, art workshops and yoga retreats.

Dunton Hot Springs $$$ Ghost town turned exclusive log-cabin resort. Hot springs pepper the property, indoor and out.

Ridgway
p275

Ridgway State Park $ Gorgeous mountain views and waterfront access from three campgrounds, including a walk-in site along the Uncompahgre River. Yurts available.

Hotel Palomino $$ Charming Western-motif hotel with bright, stylish rooms opening onto a pleasant courtyard. Contactless check-in is a breeze.

Silverton
p276

Alma House Inn $$ Cozy rooms in an 1800s hotel off Notorious Blair St. Flower-print decor and lacy curtains add to the old-timey feel.

Red Mountain Alpine Lodge $$$ All-inclusive rooms and semi-private lofts in a gorgeous lodge. Backcountry adventure year-round. Just outside town.

Black Canyon of the Gunnison National Park
p279

South Rim Campground $ Large campground in a high-altitude scrub forest, 1 mile from the visitor center. Running water available during summer only.

East Portal Campground $ Leafy riverside campground accessible by a steep paved road. Tents only. Open mid-May to mid-October. First-come, first-served.

North Rim Campground $ Remote rim-side campground off a well-maintained gravel road, a half-mile from the ranger station. Open May to November. First-come, first served.

Montrose
p283

Minecart Motor Lodge $ Modern motel with mid-century modern flair; a grassy courtyard makes for pleasant lounging. Basic brekkie included.

Canyon Creek B&B $$ Immaculately restored B&B with three cozy rooms. Happy hour and an outdoor hot tub are perks.

Grand Junction
p285

Camp Eddy $ Surprisingly charming RV park on the Colorado River. Fully equipped tiny homes and Airstreams lend a hipster vibe.

Castle Creek Manor $$ Suburban B&B with five tasteful rooms, each with Jacuzzi and independent entrance. Adults only.

Hotel Maverick $$$ Plush, modern rooms with spectacular views of the Grand Mesa. Located on Colorado Mesa University's campus, with students working the front.

Fruita
p288

James M Robb Colorado River State Park $ Pleasant lakeside campground with clean facilities; on Fruita's outskirts.

Balanced Rock Motel $ Tidy, stylish motel popular with mountain bikers. Continental breakfast included.

Colorado National Monument
p290

Saddlehorn Campground $ The park's only drive-up campground; potable water and flush toilets available. Open year-round.

Dinosaur National Monument
p292

Echo Park Campground $ Gorgeous, primitive Colorado-side campground at the confluence of the Yampa and Green rivers. 4WD highly recommended. First-come, first-served.

Moosehead Lodge $ Comfortable country-style rooms and cabins in Rangely. Hot tub, sauna and basic brekkie are pluses.

Palisade
p293

Spoke and Vine Motel $ Modern motel with boho flair. Expect breakfast delivered, bike storage and contactless check-in.

Wine Valley Inn Palisade $$ Victorian B&B with wraparound porch, fireplace and clothing-optional hot tub. Adults only and LGBTIQ+ friendly.

Grand Mesa
p294

Jumbo Campground $ Gorgeous forest campground between Jumbo Reservoir and Sunset Lake. Most sites have reservoir views. Potable water available; vault toilets only.

Grand Mesa Lodge $$ Simple log cabins on Island Lake. Easy access to trails and backcountry adventure; equipment rentals available. Open year-round.

Paonia
p295

Big B's Delicious Orchards $ Lovely campsites under apple trees and alongside orchard ponds. Wi-fi, potable water and coin-op showers.

Local Nomad $ Charming hostel with cozy private rooms with shared bathroom. Fully equipped guest kitchen plus several lounge areas. Open May to October.

For places to stay in Southeast Colorado, see p333

LANGELL//SHUTTERSTOCK

Manitou Springs (p311)

Southeast Colorado & the San Luis Valley

PEAKS AND VALLEYS OF POSSIBILITY

Behold arresting landscapes that once guided travelers across the Great Plains and connect with the vein of creative souls inspired to live here today.

Colorado's arid southeast comprises high deserts set among craggy peaks and flat-topped mesas, where scraggly juniper morphs into the quaking aspens and hardy pines of the central mountains.

With its signature landmarks – Pikes Peak, the Great Sand Dunes, the Royal Gorge and the Garden of the Gods – southern Colorado interweaves dramatic vistas and hardscrabble history, threaded through with art as a mirror in unexpected and powerful ways.

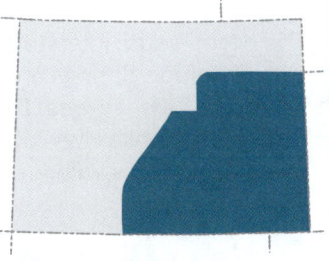

GALYNA ANDRUSHKO/SHUTTERSTOCK

Fossilized dinosaur footprints, massive petrified sequoia stumps and the volcanic vestiges of the Spanish Peaks serve as stark reminders of a geological timescale in which human life is no more than a heartbeat.

But a fascinating human element lingers here too, in the people inspired to live and create where the energy of these southeastern towns is anything but fossilized. Discover a time when the area was part of Mexico and played host to the Santa Fe Trail, intersecting the lives of Native Americans, Hispanic settlers, French trappers, grizzled prospectors and the covered wagon trains of hope-filled American homesteaders.

From the mysteries of the San Luis Valley to the divinely etched summits of the Sangre de Cristo range, whether rafting the rapids of the Arkansas River, riding historic steam trains to the vistas of Pikes Peak, or driving the treacherous routes of old stagecoach roads, a magnificent journey through the parched wilds of southeast Colorado awaits.

THE MAIN AREAS

COLORADO SPRINGS
Museums meet the great outdoors.
p304

GREAT SAND DUNES & THE SAN LUIS VALLEY
Ecological wonder and Hispanic heritage.
p313

CAÑON CITY & THE ROYAL GORGE
Cliffs, rivers, railroads and prisons. **p323**

TRINIDAD
Old forts and tall grasses. **p327**

Find Your Way

The north–south interstate I-25 links Denver with Colorado Springs and down to Pueblo and Trinidad. The east–west Hwy 50 stretches to Cañon City, while Hwy 160 extends west to the massive San Luis Valley.

SOUTHEAST COLORADO & THE SAN LUIS VALLEY

CAR

With minimal public transportation in the area, renting a car is the way to go. Several scenic byways and backroads have unpaved sections – depending on your level of interest, you may want to rent an AWD vehicle.

BUS

Bustang runs between Colorado Springs, Denver and Pueblo, with another west-bound route running from Pueblo with stops in Cañon City, Salida and Alamosa. Greyhound runs along the I-25 corridor, with stops in Colorado Springs, Pueblo and Trinidad.

TRAIN

Amtrack's *Southwest Chief*, running from Chicago to LA, stops in Trinidad, near the New Mexico border. A handful of historic steam trains are still in operation, but are not useful for getting around.

Cañon City & the Royal Gorge, p323

Thrills await in Royal Gorge Bridge & Park, tour dinosaur quarries and former gold mines, or explore 150-plus years of prison history.

Great Sand Dunes & the San Luis Valley, p313

An expansive dune field draws visitors to the San Luis Valley, embraced by the jagged Sangre de Cristo and San Juan mountain ranges.

Colorado Springs, p304

Drive or hike up a fourteener, scramble over red-rock formations, assemble in heavenly gardens and learn something new at numerous museums.

Trinidad, p327

Soulful Trinidad, tucked against the high mesas of New Mexico, is rife with frontier history and home to Corazón de Trinidad Creative Art District.

Bennett

Last Chance

Idalia

Bonny State Park

Agate

Castle Rock

Limon

Burlington

70

Matheson

Colorado Springs

Fountain

Kit Carson

25

Great Plains Reservoirs

Pueblo

Fowler

Lamar

Colorado City

La Junta

Walsenburg

Houghton

Springfield

Trinidad

Trinidad State Park

0   100 km
0   50 miles

Plan Your Days

Many visitors will get no further than Colorado Springs and Pikes Peak, though adventures to the Royal Gorge, San Luis Valley and Trinidad are unexpected and rewarding journeys.

MARTINA BIRNBAUM/SHUTTERSTOCK

Garden of the Gods (p308)

If You Only Do One Thing

● Greet the day in **Colorado Springs** (304) with a sunrise trip to the **Garden of the Gods** (p308). Stroll through the park and admire the wafer-thin red-rock formations, but don't lose sight of the majesty that towers in the background: Pikes Peak. Drive to **Manitou Springs** (p311), from where you can either take the cog railway up the Pikes Peak mountainside or follow the 19-mile serpentine highway thousands of feet up to the wind-whipped summit.

● All that elevation change will likely leave you knackered, so enjoy a lazy afternoon strolling through Manitou's historic downtown, playing in the penny arcade and stopping for a proper tea at the castle, or return to Colorado Springs and replenish your calories in style.

SEASONAL HIGHLIGHTS

Late spring and early fall are the perfect times to explore low-elevation destinations, while the height of summer offers an idyllic window of opportunity to hike the high country.

JANUARY
Have leftover fruitcakes? Bring them on down for the **Great Fruitcake Toss** (p311) in Manitou Springs' Memorial Park. Bear witness to the Fruitcake Terminator, a locally made fruitcake cannon that really goes the distance!

MAY
Welcome summer in the mountains with festivals such as **MeadowGrass** (p307), a forest celebration of music and community, and **Territory Days** (p307) with live music, Native American dancers and a cowboy church service.

JUNE
Explorers, get it while it's (not too) hot, which the Great Sand Dunes soon will be! Make sure to take in a trip to the 'beach,' created by the **Medano Creek** (p314) snowmelt, while you're here.

A Few Days to Travel Around

● From Colorado Springs, drive southwest to **Cañon City** (p323) and the **Royal Gorge** (p324). Let loose in the adventure park up top, or venture off-road to local mountain-biking trails and sport climbing at nearby **Shelf Road** (p326), and delve into more than 150 years of prison history at the **Museum of Colorado Prisons** (p323).

● The next day, adventure seekers can follow the **Golden Loop Historic Parkway** (p326) to Cripple Creek and back, while those looking for nourishment can ease their way to **Joyful Journey Hot Springs Spa** (p318) in Mosca. From here, it's a 50-minute drive through San Luis Valley to the **Great Sand Dunes** (p313), one of the more surprising and most ecologically diverse national parks. Return to Colorado Springs via La Veta and the **Spanish Peaks** (p332).

Road-Tripping Across the State

● Instead of zipping through the plains on I-70, why not hitch your wagon and lumber along the old Santa Fe Trail on Hwy 50 instead? The first site is the Japanese internment camp at **Amache** (p331); a detour north will take you to the **Sand Creek Massacre** (p331) memorial.

● Back on Hwy 50 in Las Animas are the **Boggsville** (p331) homestead and **Bent's Old Fort** (p331). Bear left at the fork to follow Hwy 350 through the **Comanche National Grassland** (p332), where a full-day detour brings you to the country's largest dinosaur track site and the ruins of an abandoned mission. From here, it's another hour southwest to **Trinidad** (p327), with its museums, the Corazón de Trinidad Creative Art District, local eats and live music, beside the New Mexico border.

JULY	SEPTEMBER	OCTOBER	NOVEMBER
Always dreamed of rafting the Arkansas River? Warmer temperatures and smaller waves make the challenging **Royal Gorge** (p324) white-water experience more friendly for first timers.	Art lovers visit downtown Manitou for the **Labor Day Arts and Crafts Festival** (p311). Arachnophiles, see firsthand how far our eight-legged friends will travel for love at La Junta's **Tarantula Fest** (p331).	The aspens shimmer gold and the **Emma Crawford Coffin Race** (p312) is back just in time for Halloween. Lore has it that, in 1995, Manitou Springs created the nation's first coffin race to honor a beloved resident.	Waste not, want not! As temperatures drop, learn about traditional meat processing at the Everything but the Oink workshop at **Rock Ledge Ranch** (p309), seeing how pioneers wasted not a bit of the hog.

Colorado Springs

POIGNANT LANDSCAPES | OLYMPIC INSPIRATION | PIONEER HISTORY

GETTING AROUND

Colorado Springs is 70 miles south of Denver and can be divided into two distinct neighborhoods, bisected by I-25 and connected by the east–west Colorado Ave and Hwy 24. The downtown area lies to the east, while Old Colorado City, the original 1860s settlement, lies to the west. A sprawling city, it's easiest navigated with your own wheels, though Pike Ride operates an electric-bike share program, and Mountain Metropolitan Transit buses run between Colorado Springs, Old Colorado City and Manitou Springs. There is also an abundance of parking meters.

One of the nation's first destination resorts, Colorado Springs is the state's second-largest city and a multifaceted one. Strong military presence underpins the city's economy and population, with veterans comprising nearly 17% of the population and 45,000 active troops living in the area.

The Air Force Academy is the city's most well-known military institution, followed closely by the controversial Space Command and NORAD (North American Aerospace Defense Command). NORAD's 30-megaton-proof nuclear bunker, buried deep in Cheyenne Mountain (yes, that Cheyenne Mountain) is the stuff of urban legend and has been fodder for Hollywood filmmakers for decades. Alas, the facility is not open to tourists. Most visitors, however, aren't here for the army bases, but the natural landscape – the arresting Garden of the Gods and the anthem-inspiring Pikes Peak – juxtaposed against a lively downtown rife with art, history and good eats.

Climb, Bike & Wander over Ancient Formations

A red-rock playground

A former quarry, this 1474-acre park was nearly developed into a golf course and townhouses. Thanks to committed residents who fought the good fight, **Red Rock Canyon Open Space** *(redrockcanyonopenspace.org)* is now a fabulous park. It's a continuation of the sandstone rock formations of the better-known Garden of the Gods (p308) to its north, allowing you to spend the day hiking, mountain biking or rock climbing in a setting that is less a marquee tourist site, but surrounds you with jaw-dropping vistas just the same.

With 11 marked trails catering to all levels (including two off-leash dog loops), there is something for every type of visitor. Plenty of trails, such as Sand Canyon, Mesa and Contemplative, loop through and can be combined for walks of 2 miles

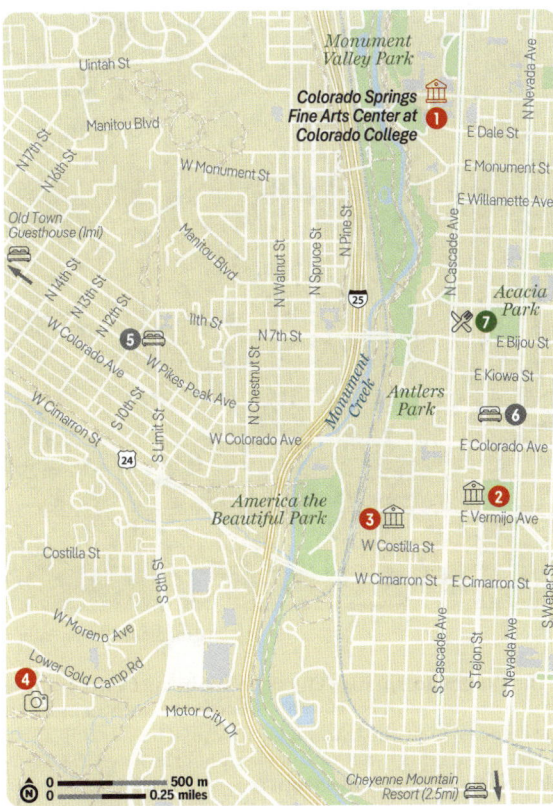

SOUTHEAST COLORADO & THE SAN LUIS VALLEY COLORADO SPRINGS

HIGHLIGHTS
1 Colorado Springs Fine Arts Center at Colorado College

SIGHTS
2 Colorado Springs Pioneers Museum
3 US Olympic & Paralympic Museum

ACTIVITIES
4 Norris Penrose Event Center

SLEEPING
5 Holden House
6 Mining Exchange

EATING
7 Birdtree Cafe

to 6 miles. Rock climbers have access to more than 90 bolted routes. Sign up with **Front Range Climbing** *(frontrange climbing.com)* or the **Pikes Peak Alpine School** *(pikespeak alpineschool.com)* for a guided day out, or visit the Garden of the Gods visitor center for your technical climbing permit if climbing independently.

Museum-Hopping
Stories of the unbridled spirits who made the town

The expansive **Colorado Springs Fine Arts Centerat Colorado College** *(fac.coloradocollege.edu)* is one of the state's best, with compelling Latin American art and photography and rotating exhibits drawing from the 20,000 pieces in its permanent collection. While Richard Diebenkorn's *Urbana No 4* is the museum's most renowned work, there's a strong focus on Native American, Hispanic and Spanish Colonial art. Expect to see Mexican clay figures, Native American basketry and quilts, and wood-cut prints from social-justice artist Leopoldo Mendez. The 400-seat theater has excellent year-round performances.

☑️**TOP TIP**

Parking kiosks make for user-friendly downtown parking. Rates vary from $1 to $1.50 per hour, depending on the zone, and most meters accept coins and credit cards, or can be paid using a mobile app. Once parked, the downtown is very strollable.

THE BROADMOOR

Spencer Penrose dreamed of creating the most compelling and intricate resort imaginable in the Pikes Peak area. Founded in 1918, and often referred to as the Grande Dame of the Rockies, the **Broadmoor's** opulence is unmistakable. Colorado's most famous luxury hotel is set against the mosaic blue-green slopes of Cheyenne Mountain. Flamingos once frolicked in its fountains, and everything is exquisite and drips with discernment: acres of lush grounds, world-class golf and shopping, award-winning restaurants, a lavish spa, elegant rooms. No surprise that Hollywood stars, celebrities, athletes and many presidents have made it a point to visit – notable patrons have included John Wayne, Jimmy Stewart, Kevin Bacon, Babe Ruth and President Eisenhower.

RAMOLEMON/SHUTTERSTOCK

Broadmoor Seven Falls

The **Colorado Springs Olympic Training Center** *(usopc .org/training-centers)* is one of just three such centers in the country. Tour the training facility (maybe spotting a few Olympic hopefuls in action), or check out the new **US Olympic and Paralympic Museum** *(usopm.org)* 2.5 miles away. The museum's spectacular and accessibly designed complex houses 12 galleries capturing Olympic history through memorabilia, athlete profiles and interactive training exhibits.

Aviation buffs can discover 27 beautifully restored planes, plus others undergoing restoration, at the **National Museum of World War II Aviation** *(worldwariiaviation.org)*, including biplanes, B-25 bombers, twin-engine fighters and amphibious craft. Archives, maps and interpretive narratives paint a fuller picture of wartime aviation.

The 1903 El Paso County Courthouse is home to the **Pioneers Museum** *(cspm.org)*, which holds 60,000 regional artifacts and displays hundreds of items from the Ute, Cheyenne and Arapaho Nations. Exhibits are thoughtfully presented, often incorporating engaging questions for young learners. Don't miss the restored courtroom on the 3rd floor and '50% of the Story: Women Expressing Creativity,' a one-of-a-kind curation giving long-overdue recognition to the artistry of women.

The larger-than-life lore of America's cowboys and cowgirls is alive and well at the **ProRodeo Hall of Fame and Museum of the American Cowboy** *(prorodeohalloffame.com)*, with '45 Years of Memories' honoring the Hall of Fame's preservation of rodeo history. Catch the movie explaining how rodeo came to be, stroll through the Hall of Famers' memorabilia or outdoor sculpture garden, and say hi to the rodeo livestock out back.

Old-car and carriage aficionados should visit the **Penrose Heritage Museum** *(elpomar.org)* at the Broadmoor hotel.

Family Fun
Cascading falls and the country's highest zoo

Cheyenne Mountain Zoo *(cmzoo.org),* the highest in the country (6700ft), is a can't-miss family destination. Opened in 1926 from the private animal collection of Spencer Penrose, founder of the **Broadmoor** *(broadmoor.com),* today the zoo is home to some 750 animals, including Amur leopards and bears. Most famous are the reticulated giraffes, which kids can feed. The Mountaineer Sky Ride provides a bird's-eye view of the city. Just behind the zoo is the unusual Will Rogers Shrine of the Sun, a stone tower named after the 1930s Hollywood star.

Colorado's grandest mile is at the **Broadmoor Seven Falls** *(sevenfalls.com),* a series of tumbling cascades located in South Cheyenne Canyon. There's a free shuttle from the **Norris Penrose Event Center** *(norrispenrose.com).* From the shuttle drop-off, it's a 1300yd hike to the base of the falls (mobility-accessible options exist to the Eagle's Nest viewing platform). Gauge your courage and choose your adventure: climb or take the Mountain Elevator to the **Eagle's Nest** platform for panoramic views, or climb to the top of the falls themselves. Additional hiking trails can be accessed from the top. Caveat: those shaky with heights, don't look down on the way up! Don't miss the cave-like entrance to the elevator, adorned with facts and history about the falls and South Cheyenne Canyon.

Ring in summer with festivals like **MeadowGrass**, celebrating world-class music in the Pikes Peak region and full of family-friendly activities including hiking, workshops, and yoga, or visit Old Colorado City's **Territory Days**, touted as Colorado's largest street fair.

50% OF THE STORY

Leah Davis Witherow, curator of history at the Pioneers Museum, offers deeper context to the museum and its powerful exhibit, 50% of the Story: Women Expressing Creativity. The Colorado Springs Pioneers Museum centers people and stories in all that we do, endeavoring to serve as a mirror to our community, so that everyone can see a bit of their story reflected back. 50% of the Story uses historic artwork, contemporary pieces and artifacts from the collection to create a complex conversation between women across time, demonstrating how they've always told their stories through art and creativity. Approximately 90% of all artworks held by museums were created by men; this exhibit seeks to shift that narrative.

 EATING & DRINKING IN COLORADO SPRINGS: OUR PICKS

Birdtree Cafe: Lively, with all-day breakfast and lunch. Veg/vegan options, rich coffee, gorgeous cocktails and a patio across from Acacia Park. *hours vary* **$$**

TAPAteria: Beautifully rendered, gluten-free Spanish tapas, with extensive Spanish wine list. There's a 'secret' patio out back. *noon-10pm* **$$**

Uchenna: Homestyle cooking and a warm family vibe at this Ethiopian restaurant, tucked in a shopping mall. *11:30am-2:30pm & 5-9pm Tue-Sat* **$$**

Westside Cantina: Vibrant and festive (the patio is lovely), offering cocktails and tacos with distinctive flavors and fresh ingredients. *hours vary* **$$**

JOHN HOFFMAN/SHUTTERSTOCK

TOP EXPERIENCE

Garden of the Gods

The moment the red-rock cathedrals of the Garden of the Gods come into view, you'll understand. In 1859, the tale goes, two Denver surveyors happened upon these exquisite sandstone formations. Surveyor Beach suggested it 'a capital place for a Biergarten!' His poetic-natured partner, Rufus Cable, countered that it was a fit place for the gods to assemble. The rest, they say, is history.

DON'T MISS

Visitor center

Perkins Central Garden Trail

Three Graces

Kissing Camels

Segway tours

Rock Ledge Ranch

Mesa Rd Overlook

Enhance Your Learning

Begin your Garden of the Gods visit in the **visitor center**. Not a place to be skipped, it has a museum-like exhibit that offers greater depth and understanding to what you'll see. Interact with exhibits about the park's geology, wildlife and history. Need to know if it was a bear or a bat that shared your path recently? Take the 'scat exam,' and you'll learn. If visual learning is your style, the movie at the **Geo-Trekker Theater** (children five and under are free) travels back in time to the formation of these red-rock wonders.

PRACTICALITIES
Scan this QR code for a color map of the park's rock formations, trails and parking.

Explore Veins of Red Sandstone

Exquisitely thin cathedral spires (about 290 million years old) are hair-raising up close. Gazing from the base of the highest rock formations on the **Perkins Central Garden Trail** inspires awe and humility. From there, choose from numerous paved trails to explore central formations such as the **Kissing Camels**, **Three Graces** and **Montezuma's Tower**. Depending on your timing, you could easily spend an hour or two here. For a more fluid experience, Segway tours run from 9am to 1pm. If you're inclined to see a bit more, you can explore 21 miles worth of trails on an e-bike, or sign up for a horseback ride or rock climbing (though we recommend the routes at Red Rock Canyon Open Space (p304) for the latter).

Nourish at the Gateway Cafe

Located on the visitor center's 2nd floor, the **Gateway Cafe** has pre-hike snacks, granola bars and coffees, or you can choose from its wide variety of food options, including vegetarian choices, to replenish after your hike. The dining room directly overlooks the park.

Step Back in Time at Rock Ledge Ranch

Tucked behind the trees adjacent to the overflow parking lot is **Rock Ledge Ranch** (rockledgeranch.com), listed on the National Register of Historic Places. Stepping onto the ranch grounds feels immediately like a stroll back in time. The grounds are open from dawn to dusk, though buildings are only open during the Living History Museum Program and other special events. The main summertime attraction is the Living History Museum Program, where you can learn about the lives of the Utes and visit a 19th-century homesteader cabin, blacksmith's shop, the Orchard House, barn and general store. Enjoy peanuts, popcorn and cracker jacks at the 1880s Labor Day Vintage Baseball Game, celebrate Native American cultures and history through song and dance at the Annual Powwow in September, or learn about traditional hog processing at **Everything but the Oink** as temperatures drop in November. The Summer Living History Program runs from the beginning of June through the middle of August (10am to 5pm Wednesday to Saturday, 1pm to 5pm Sunday).

A Park for All

The visitor center and many trails in the central garden are mobility accessible. Driving through the park is free and a great option – most of the main formations are visible from the roads. There is also a shuttle bus that runs between the overflow lot, the visitor center and the park.

FOREVER FREE

The 480 acres comprising the Garden of the Gods were gifted by Charles Perkins' children in 1909 to the city of Colorado Springs. The conveyance ensured the land would be accessible to all and 'shall remain free to the public, where no intoxicating liquors shall be manufactured, sold, or dispensed, where no building or structure shall be erected except those necessary to properly care for, protect, and maintain the area as a public park.'

TOP TIPS

● From the overflow parking near the garden entrance at the bottom of the park, it's a short walk to the paved paths leading to the formations.

● There is an underground tunnel leading to the visitor center (and bathrooms!) from the park entrance, which is mobility-friendly.

● Shade is limited, so remember hats, water and sunscreen. Sunburn at 6400ft is real!

● A short drive to the Mesa Rd Overlook, about 2.5 miles north, outside the garden, will reward you with breathtaking views and sunsets over the park.

Beyond Colorado Springs

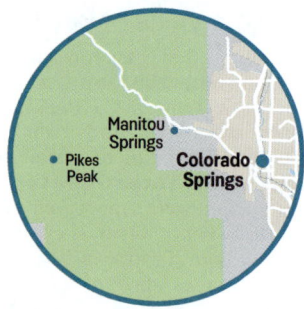

Ascend Pikes Peak by car, railway or on your own two feet to claim views that have inspired millions.

Places

Pikes Peak p310
Manitou Springs p311

GETTING AROUND

Manitou Springs is 6 miles west of Colorado Springs along Hwy 24. A highly walkable city with plenty of metered parking, it's easiest to use a parking spot as your 'base' for strolling to shops, restaurants, sipping springs and the castle. Payment options include Manitou's Text2Park system and parking kiosks. All paid spots have 30 minutes of free parking, but make sure you register at a kiosk to take advantage. Free shuttle buses running from the Field's Park lot help ease parking woes.

Pikes Peak is the most summited mountain in Colorado and, by some accounts, the country. You can drive the Pikes Peak Hwy, travel by rail, hike or even grab your bike. With 7800ft of elevation gain, this is the steepest bottom-to-top ascent in the state, so prepare for the effects of altitude and changes in the weather and temperature. (Layers are key to most Colorado adventures!) However you ascend, all paths to Pikes Peak leave from Manitou Springs, the small town at its base just a stone's throw west of Colorado Springs. Walkable and friendly, Manitou has its fair share of lovely sites, art and great eats, and makes a good alternative base to Colorado Springs.

Pikes Peak

TIME FROM COLORADO SPRINGS: 1 HR

Summiting the mountain

Pikes Peak (14,115ft) may not be the tallest of Colorado's 54 fourteeners, but it's certainly the most famous. The Ute called it the Mountain of the Sun, an apt description for the majestic peak that crowns the southern Front Range. Rising 7800ft from the plains, it's summited by more than 500,000 visitors every year. Its location as the easternmost fourteener has contributed heavily to its place in American myth. Katherine Bates, a guest lecturer at Colorado College in 1893, wrote the original draft of 'America the Beautiful' after reaching the summit.

There are three ways to ascend the peak: Pikes Peak Hwy, built in 1915 by Spencer Penrose, winds 19 miles to the top from Hwy 24 (about a three-hour round trip; timed-entry reservations are required late May to September – book at *coloradosprings.gov/drivepikespeak*); the cog railway (three hours round trip; reservations necessary), opened in 1891; and on foot on the **Barr Trail**, which most hikers split into a two-day trip due to the elevation gain, stopping overnight at Barr Camp (10,200ft), the halfway point.

MARGARET.WIKTOR/SHUTTERSTOCK

Pikes Peak cog railway

Manitou Springs TIME FROM COLORADO SPRINGS: **15 MINS** 🚗

A bewitching stroll

The gateway to Pikes Peak, Manitou is the counterweight to Colorado Springs' conservative, evangelical leanings. Urban legend has it this unassuming town is populated by pagans and witches – we'll leave that for you to decide, but the magic of this little town is undeniable. Downtown is nostalgic and festive, peppered with myriad shops, art, sweet treats and watering holes. Old-fashioned fun awaits at the **Manitou Penny Arcade**, don't tell your dentist you visited the **Candy Bar**, and don't miss the celebration of local and regional art at the **Commonwheel Artists Co-op** *(common wheel.com)*, celebrating its 50th year of highlighting local artists and hosting the **Labor Day Arts and Crafts Festival** each September.

On the National Register of Historic Places, Miramont – meaning to look at the mountain – is the vantage point of **Miramont Castle** *(miramontcastle.org)*. Walkable from downtown, the castle features nine architectural styles and is home to 30 rooms depicting Victorian times, as well as gardens. The museum is reading-heavy, and may be better enjoyed by older children and adults, but everyone can enjoy the **Queen's Parlour Tea Room**, serving traditional high teas and lunches (reservations required, closed Monday). Should you wish, fun, fancy tea hats are included. The castle has two chairlifts for mobility access to most exhibits and the tea room.

Despite its fanciful entrance, **Cave of the Winds** *(caveof thewinds.com)* is a real-deal cave (reservations required) full of the stalactites and stalagmites of your dreams. Most visitors opt for the 45-minute Discovery Tour, but the Lantern Tour is twice as deep, twice as dark and lasts twice as long. Above ground is a kids' challenge course, ziplines and, for

THE GREAT FRUITCAKE TOSS

Through the years it's been suggested that leftover fruitcakes (are there fruitcakes that are not leftover?) reincarnate as anything from doorstops to science experiments to an ecofriendly answer to street paving. Manitou has the answer: the **Great Fruitcake Toss** *(manitousprings.org)*, held each January in Memorial Park. Tosses are assessed for distance, balance, accuracy and aim, and fruitcakes are launched into space by mechanical devices. For staunch defenders of the edibility of fruitcakes, there's a bake-off for the best organic, non-GMO, natural fruitcake. The event supports the Manitou Springs Food Pantry and the tossed leftovers go to Jezebel the pig at Sun Mountain, so everyone is a winner.

EMMA CRAWFORD COFFIN RACE

The promise of a cure for tuberculosis lured many, including Emma Crawford, to Manitou Springs in 1889. Lore has it she loved the town so much that she wished to be buried atop Red Mountain. When TB took Emma's life two years later, her then-lover honored her request with the help of 11 others. They carried Emma's coffin up a 7200ft climb, where she was laid to rest...for a time. After years of harsh rains and winters, Emma's coffin 'raced' down the mountain in 1929 – it was identified by only a nameplate, the handles to the casket and some of her bones. In 1995 the Manitou Springs Chamber of Commerce created the Emma Crawford Coffin Race to honor the beloved Emma.

NATALIEJEAN/SHUTTERSTOCK

View from Cave of the Winds (p311)

adrenaline junkies, the Terror-dactyl ride, which launches you 150ft into the canyon at nearly 100mph!

Sample the springs

Manitou's namesakes are the mineral springs that bubble up from limestone aquifers beneath Manitou Ave. They rise to the surface, picking up minerals and elements such as lithium (a natural mood stabilizer), calcium, potassium and iron. Many, such as **Shoshone** and **Cheyenne**, have sipping fountains where you can sample the distinctive-tasting naturally carbonated water. Stop by the **visitor bureau** *(manitou springs.org)* for a map and cup, and visit *manitousprings .org/tour-the-mineral-springs* for a self-guided sipping tour.

Aim high at the Air Force Academy

Founded in 1954, this elite **military academy** *(usafa.edu)* trains a select group of 4000 cadets to serve in the Air Force or Space Force. Visits to the 18,500-acre campus offer a limited but fascinating look into the lives of these elite students. From the visitor center, you can walk over to the rocket-esque modernist chapel (1962) or embark on a driving tour of the expansive grounds. Plane buffs will enjoy glimpses of aircraft such as the B-52 Stratofortress or the sleek T-38 Talon. The entrance is north of Colorado Springs; ID required.

EATING IN MANITOU SPRINGS: OUR PICKS

The Loft: Slow-moving ceiling fans mirror the pace; thoughtful food with a side of whimsy. Hand-rolled bagels, emphasizing organic and local. *8am-4pm* **$**

Sahara Cafe: Bustling, authentic Middle Eastern restaurant with shawarmas, mezze plates, falafel and fresh tabbouleh. Vegetarian friendly. *hours vary* **$**

Adam's Mountain Cafe: Slow-food cafe, with global and local cuisines – Senegalese veggies to cashew chicken salad. *breakfast & lunch daily, dinner Wed-Sat* **$$**

Dining Room at the Cliff House: Award-winning American and international cuisine, with an elegant atmosphere. *11:30am-2:30pm & 5-9pm* **$$$**

Great Sand Dunes & the San Luis Valley

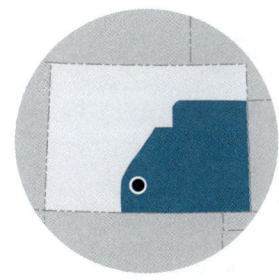

OPTICAL ILLUSIONS | GEOGRAPHIC WONDER | DUNE ADVENTURES

A standout even in a state that boasts a tapestry of jaw-dropping natural sights, the surreal Great Sand Dunes National Park will ignite wonder and curiosity as boundless as the dunes themselves. A place of stirring optical illusions that pull at the mind's reason, this veritable sea of sand, bound by jagged peaks and scrubby plains, is a place where nature's magic is on full display.

Throughout the day, sunlight paints shifting shadows upon the canvas of the dunes' angles. The ceaseless wind works like a disconsolate sculptor, forever casting and carving the landscape. Hike past the edge of the dune field to experience the shifting sand up close. Most visitors limit their activities to the area around where Medano Creek divides the main dune mass from the towering Sangre de Cristo Mountains. The remaining 85% of the park's area is designated wilderness: not for the unprepared or fainthearted.

Get Curious at the Visitor Center

Mysteries unraveled

From the park entrance, you'll first come to the **visitor center** on your left. Our suggestion: don't drive by. The moment you enter, intentional and thoughtful displays offer cultural background and context to your experience. An extensive curation of history, geology and wildlife information, expertly shepherded by the park's rangers, it's well worth your time. Rangers are happy to guide and offer suggestions for hikes and making sense of the park map. There's a 20-minute film that plays on a loop (so you can come and go as you please), which is free and highlights the park's unexpected and exceptionally diverse ecosystems. There's an additional night-sky video, also free, shown in an adjacent exhibit. The view from the outdoor deck is breathtaking and you may just see a few artists trying their hand at capturing the ethereal. The center also houses the park's gift shop. The center is also your restroom stop.

GETTING AROUND

Great Sand Dunes National Park is 33 miles northeast of Alamosa, the closest town. Be sure to fuel up and buy any food before arriving. If traveling along Hwy 160 east or west, keep an eye out for the signage directing you to Hwy 150 – it's easy to miss. Visitors with high-clearance 4WD vehicles can travel to more remote trailheads in the park, though getting stuck in sand is all too easy.

☑TOP TIP

Regardless of your chosen activity, or where you venture in the park, always take a hat, closed-toe shoes, sunscreen, water, a small snack and a bandanna to protect your face if winds pick up. Always check conditions at the park visitor center before setting out.

WHY ALL THE SAND?

On your first glimpse of the dunes, you can't help but wonder: where did all this sand come from, and why does it stay here?

The answer lies in the unique geography and weather patterns of the San Luis Valley. Streams and snowmelt have been carrying eroded sand and silt out of the San Juan Mountains, about 60 miles to the west, to the valley floor for millions of years. There, prevailing winds from the southwest gradually blow the sand into the natural hollow at the southern end of the Sangre de Cristo range, causing it to pile up into what are now North Americas' highest dunes.

SIGHTS
1 High Dune
2 Star Dune
3 Zapata Falls

ACTIVITIES
4 Montville Nature Trail
5 Mosca Pass Trail

SLEEPING
6 Great Sand Dunes Lodge
7 Great Sand Dunes Oasis
8 Pinyon Flats Campground
9 Zapata Falls Campground

INFORMATION
● Great Sand Dunes National Park Visitor Center (see 4)

Exploring the Dunes

Sand-tastic

By day, they're the tallest dunes in North America; by night, an International Dark Sky Park. A short trail from the visitor center toward the Mosca Picnic Area, or from the dunes parking, leads to ankle-deep Medano Creek, which you must ford (when the creek is running) to reach the dunes. Check both creek conditions (the creek usually begins to dry up in July) and park weather at *nps.gov/grsa/planyourvisit/medano-creek.htm*.

There are no trails through the 30-sq-mile field of sand, though two DIY hikes afford excellent views. The first is to the 700ft **High Dune** (ironically, not the highest dune in the park). It's roughly 2.5 miles out to the dune and back, but be warned: it's likely a different measure from any 2.5-hike trek you've taken. Slogging up towering hills of sand will present moments where you wonder if you moved forward at all. Those with more energy can push on to a second worthy goal – 750ft **Star Dune**, the tallest dune in North America. In midsummer, hikers should plan to hit the dunes during the early morning or evening, as the sand can reach 150°F (66°C) during the heat of the day. Although you might think

GREAT SAND DUNES & SAN LUIS VALLEY

sandals would be the footwear of choice, closed-toe shoes provide better protection against the heat. If you're hiking with children, keep them in your sight. It's easy to get separated.

Tubing & Sandboarding
A new kind of beach
One of the most curious spectacles in the entire park is the snowmelt-fed **Medano Creek**, flowing down from the Sangre de Cristos and along the eastern edge of the dunes. Peak flow is usually late May or early June. The rippling water over the sand creates a temporary beach, which is extremely popular with families. When the water is high enough, you can even float down the creek on an inner tube.

Sandboarding is another wildly popular activity. The heavy wooden sled may seem like a bad idea when dragging it out to the dunes, but the gleeful rush down the slopes is worth every footstep. Sand conditions are best after recent rain; too dry and you'll simply sink. The less weight on the sled, the zippier the ride, so if you've been bulking up on microbrews, don't expect to zoom down the hill. You'll need to rent a board outside the park. **Kristi Mountain Sports** (*kristi mountainsports.com*) in Alamosa or the Great Sand Dunes Oasis (p333; *greatdunes.com*) at the edge of the park are two options.

Hike to a Different Perspective
Explore divine mountains and firmer ground
Lost in all the excitement over the dunes is the park's backdrop: the rugged Sangre de Cristo Mountains, which are so magnificent you expect a director to yell 'Cut!' at any given moment. Across from the visitor center parking lot is the **Montville Nature Trail**, a family-friendly, well-marked, half-mile loop that's mostly shaded, has lovely spots for reflection and offers a grand view of the dunes along the way. It's a perfect warm-up for hiking the dunes or forging ahead to the **Mosca Pass Trail** (7 miles round trip), which follows an old Ute path up Mosca Creek, providing fabulous bird's-eye views of the dunes. The 9747ft pass offers the lowest passage through the Sangres. From 1871 to 1911, it was used as a toll road ($1 horse and rider). Built in the 1830s by fur trader Antoine Robidoux, who transported supplies to posts in western Colorado and eastern Utah, the Montville Store once stood at the foot of the trail.

Hike to Zapata Falls
Family fun on the way to the falls
This short half-mile hike higher in the Sangre de Cristos leads to **Zapata Falls** (*alamosa.org*), hidden at the end of a slot canyon. The last 150yd are loads of fun (though not without risk), as you scramble through ankle-deep, ice-cold water and over slippery rocks. Grippy water shoes will enhance this good family hike. Extend your adventure by continuing on to **South Zapata Lake** (8 miles round trip).

WHY I LOVE GREAT SAND DUNES

Nicole Hagg, Lonely Planet writer
More than a national park, I found an unexpected metaphor for life. The magnificence and duality of the dunes – serene and wild, staid and ever-changing, ancient and new – take time to process. Determined to reach the top, I chose my 'route,' but trails change with the wind, or are erased entirely. Illusory images painted with false summits.

One step forward felt like two back, charting imagined paths, leading to questions: Is this where I thought I'd be? Can I do this? What's my best next step? My mind, looping endlessly about a 'finish line,' falsely promised the next dune would be it. It was a powerful reminder to pause, be fiercely present to your process and embrace the wonder surrounding you now.

Beyond the Great Sand Dunes

The serene yin to Colorado's notorious peaks, the San Luis Valley's agricultural flatland cradles troves of history and unexpected sights.

Places

GETTING AROUND

Alamosa, the region's largest city and transport hub, is located at the intersections of Hwys 17, 160 and 285. A car is essential for ease of navigating the valley. Common directions might include turning onto County Rd T or County Rd B or La 6. These roads are often long, straight stretches across the valley marked by smaller signs. Pay close attention to your fuel tank in advance and watch for wildlife always.

Quiet and mysterious, the San Luis Valley is the driest part of Colorado, hemmed in by the San Juan Mountains to the west and the Sangre de Cristos to the east. This expansive and stark landscape is the world's largest alpine valley and holds many surprises, including a mystical, palpable energy and healing hot springs. The ethereal nature of the land inexplicably beckons passersby and seems to only deepen the bond of community and creativity in the hearts of the people who live here.

This was the first part of Colorado to be permanently settled, and the influence of the Hispanic pioneers who set out from Taos in the mid-19th century to find new homesteads still defines valley culture today.

Alamosa
TIME FROM GREAT SAND DUNES: 1 HR

Explore downtown Alamosa

The largest town in the San Luis Valley, Alamosa (Spanish for 'cottonwood') was built along the banks of the Rio Grande, running for some 450 miles to the south. Hidden behind its unassuming highway presence is an inclusive enclave of history, culture, art and literature fueled by the love of community. Nearby Adams State College students keep the vibe fresh. It's a strategic stop for travelers to fuel up, buy groceries, or spend the night if you'd rather not camp.

On arrival, you'll likely spot **Engine No 169** (next to the library), one of the oldest enduring locomotives from the Denver & Rio Grande Western Rail (D&RG). From there, it's less than a half-mile walk to the **Welcome Center** *(alamosa.org),* housed in the former Alamosa train depot.

Though modest in size, the **San Luis Valley Museum** *(ala mosa.org)* exudes a wide-ranging air of intention and engagement. Displays include well-curated collections of then-and-now photographs, relics from early valley mercantile and farm life, and exhibits highlighting Native American artifacts, Hispanic settlers and the Japanese-American community. The museum is home to numerous community events,

Alamosa National Wildlife Refuge

FORT GARLAND

Fort Garland, which operated between 1858 and 1883, was established to protect early settlers in the San Luis Valley from Ute raids. Union troops stationed here marched in a campaign against Confederates in Texas during the Civil War. In 1862, to put an end to Confederate attempts to hold New Mexico and stave off invasion from Colorado, Fort Garland soldiers participated in the Battle of Glorieta Pass. For a short time, the outpost was under the direction of famed frontier scout Kit Carson. Though Carson successfully negotiated a period of peace with Utes, all hell broke loose after the Meeker Incident in 1879. After that, the fort became a major base of operations in the forcible removal of Utes from the area.

including weekly veteran's coffee socials, artist of the month and lectures, and it participates in the Alamosa Arts Festival each September.

Cross the threshold of the **Narrow Gauge Book Cooperative** *(narrowgaugebooks.com)* and you know you've wandered into something special. When the Narrow Gauge Newsstand of 40 years closed its doors in 2018, the community stepped in. Six years later, as the only traditional bookstore in the valley, the NGBC has more than 100 owners, and its shelves, according to its website, 'hold the heartbeat of the community.' Pick up a newsletter to find story slams, book giveaways, author events and Indie Press Book Club happenings.

Wildlife and wetlands

The **Alamosa National Wildlife Refuge** *(fws.gov),* on the banks of the Rio Grande, southeast of town, is a special preserve that will give you some idea of what the valley must have looked like before it was developed for agriculture. It's best to visit at dawn or dusk, when wildlife is most active and when you'll hear the sonorous soundscape of bird calls and whistles. A 2.5-mile trail along the river and a panoramic overlook on the east side of the refuge give visitors views of the marshes, ponds and river corridor.

EATING IN ALAMOSA: OUR PICKS

Milagro's Coffee House: Delicious, simple, healthy eats at this nonprofit increasing awareness around hunger and homelessness in the valley. *7am-4pm Mon-Sat, to 2pm Sun* **$$**

All Valley Cafe: Adjacent to the Dunes Inn, serving breakfast and brunch comfort food. Friendly and casual atmosphere. *6am-1pm Tue-Sat, to 2pm Sun* **$**

Calvillo's: Family-owned and serving delicious 'homemade food with love.' The Mexican buffet is perfect for families, the famished and the indecisive. *10am-8pm Wed-Sun* **$**

Friar's Fork: You may want to confess your order on entering this 1926 adobe church with gorgeous exterior courtyard. Upscale Italian fare in intimate surrounds. *hours vary* **$$**

HEALING HOT SPRINGS

Joyful Journey Hot Springs Spa:
A sanctuary *(joyful journeyhotsprings. com)* of three soaking pools, open year-round, with breathtaking views of the Sangre de Cristo Mountains, protected from the elements. Delicious, healthy breakfast and light dinner are included in stays.

Sand Dunes Recreation:
This family oasis *(sanddunespool. com)*, know locally as the Hooper Pool, includes a larger main pool for all, a separate kiddie pool, a water slide and four additional adult pools.

Valley View Hot Springs: These Orient Land Trust pools *(olt.org)* allow guests unrivaled views of a diverse ecosystem. A steep 400yd hike brings you to natural rock ponds. There are options for pool soaking, a kids' pool and a sauna. Note that this is a clothing-optional facility.

Walsenburg
TIME FROM GREAT SAND DUNES: **30 MINS**

Mine for history in an old jail

About 2.5 miles off I-25 along US 160, in the town of Walsenburg (known historically as the City Built on Coal), is the small **Walsenburg Mining Museum** *(huerfanohistory.org/ mining-museum)*. The museum, housed in the old county jail, packs a punch, with mining history and information on the Ludlow Massacre of 1914.

Not far past Walsenburg is **Lathrop State Park** *(cpw.state. co.us)*, Colorado's first state park. Nestled against the backdrop of the Spanish Peaks, the park is home to two lakes with every imaginable water recreation available. For those who haven't caught the cold-plunge bug, these lakes are warmer than most mountain lakes – around 75°F (24°C) in summer) – due to their positioning between the foothills and the plains. Don't miss the visitor center, which has excellent maps for hiking and birdwatching.

West of La Veta Pass, along US 160, is the **Fort Garland Museum** *(museumtrail.org/fort-garland-museum)*. The museum is in the original fort (p317) and contains five of its original 22 buildings. Learn about the Buffalo Soldiers of the 9th Cavalry and check out the Civil War and the West exhibit. Active military and veterans get free admission from Memorial Day through Labor Day.

Hooper
TIME FROM GREAT SAND DUNES: **30 MINS**

A hidden valley oasis

The sign where you turn from County Rd B left to County Rd 63 simply reads 'Pool,' and is as unassuming as the location of this local treasure. **Sand Dunes Recreation** *(sanddunespool.com)*, affectionately known to locals as the Hooper Pool, is a delightfully unexpected oasis. The large main pool is family-friendly. Near the main pool is the **Mile Deep Grille**, with food for all tastes. For those seeking a more grown-up experience, wander down the darkened hall with an almost speakeasy vibe to the Green House, a 10,000ft tropical paradise with four separate soaking pools, the Steel Box Bar with an upscale small-plates menu, and a sauna, all for the 21-plus crowd (there's a small additional fee for this portion of the pool). An on-site gift shop and water-toy rentals round out the experience.

Mosca
TIME FROM GREAT SAND DUNES: **20 MINS**

Eat, drink and shop local

About 20 miles southwest of the Great Sand Dunes is the **Mosca Pit Stop** *(moscapitstop.com)*, the only locally owned general store between Salida and Alamosa and a gem of convenience. In addition to sundries and snacks you might expect, there is a focus on local products, produce and meats. Also convenient is the fuel pump; good to remember along these stretches of valley roads.

Housed in a revived 1933 gymnasium, the **Dune Valley Distillery** *(dunevalleydistillery.com)* is far from your grade-school PE class. A gorgeous, one-of-a-kind offering created by

DAVID RADZIETA/GETTY IMAGES

Lathrop State Park

UFO WATCHTOWER

The San Luis Valley is one of the top areas in the world for alien sightings and abductions – don't say we didn't warn you! But don't panic: visiting aliens are harmless (well, mostly). If you're eager for a glimpse (or to leave an offering for a weary interstellar hitchhiker), then the **UFO Watchtower** *(theoriginalufo watchtower.com)* is a must. At about 15ft in height, the tower will certainly not improve your chances of spotting a flying saucer (though there are two large energy vortexes located here, so...), but the garden and its assorted treasures are something to behold. The watchtower is off Hwy 17, near Hooper.

Nick Chambers, it's sophisticated in experience, yet grounded in its vision of celebrating the San Luis Valley – think local potatoes and quinoa. Organic potato vodka is the primary spirit, though quinoa vodka and local fruit rakias round out the lovingly made craft cocktails. Lore has it that family patriarch Anthony Carbone received Colorado's first post-Prohibition liquor license in 1933. You'll find Anthony's legacy offered in quality local wines bearing the family name. DVD is also home to a restaurant space for events. The stage that once held school plays is graced by valley musicians, comedians and performers. Look for buzz-worthy, locally focused, monthly five-course dinners from June through October, including the Fall Gala, which supports the Crestone Energy Fair (p321*)*.

San Luis

TIME FROM GREAT SAND DUNES: **45 MINS** 🚗

Learn the settlement's Hispanic history

Southeast of Alamosa, San Luis is Colorado's oldest settlement (1851). Its character – today and historically – is largely the result of its isolation. For Spain, the upper Rio Grande was a lost province best left to the nomadic Native American tribes that the Spanish were unable to dominate. Under the threat of Ute raids, and far from the mercantile and spiritual centers at Taos and Santa Fe, San Luis developed as a self-sufficient outpost and largely escaped the 'progress' that revoked Hispanic tenure in other parts of the valley following the arrival of the railroad. The town remains almost 90% Hispanic.

San Luis' main attraction is the **Stations of the Cross** *(alamosa.org)* installation, situated along a 1-mile path up a small hill. Local sculptor Huberto Maestas' 15 dramatic life-sized statues of Christ's crucifixion are a powerful testament to the Catholic heritage of communities near the 'Blood of Christ' Mountains.

LONESOME SONG OF THE PENITENTE

Of the characters who populate the early stories of Colorado's south, none are more mysterious than **Los Hermanos Penitente**, a secretive religious sect that thrived in the early 19th century. Some say the Penitente's membership drew from a servant class of Native Americans working as housekeepers and shepherds, called *genízaros*. Gathering in humble meeting houses known as *moradas*, their ceremonies sought spiritual awakening through the suffering of the Passion of Christ. The mournful songs of Los Hermanos Penitente *(alabados)* are haunting, unaccompanied hymns that blend Hispanic *folclórica* with elements of droning Native American song. Often sung at funeral processions and burials, *alabados* have themes that are, like the group itself, fixated on the suffering and torture of Jesus.

West of town is the 1863 adobe-walled **Capilla de San Acacio**, one of the oldest churches in Colorado. It was dedicated to St Agathius, who is said to have protected the women and children of the Hispanic settlement during a Ute attack in 1853, when the men were away herding sheep.

Cumbres Pass   TIME FROM GREAT SAND DUNES: **2 HRS** 🚗

Riding the Cumbres & Toltec Railroad

One of several narrow-gauge trains in Colorado, the impressive **Cumbres & Toltec Railroad** *(cumbrestoltec.com)* is a chance to tackle the Cumbres Pass (10,022ft) by power of steam.

In 1880 the Denver & Rio Grande Western Rail completed a track over this pass, linking Chama, NM, with Denver, and this particular section is now the longest and highest steam railroad in North America. The twisting, mountainous terrain was suited to narrow-gauge track, which is only 3ft wide instead of the standard gauge of 4ft 8in. The slopes of pine and aspen and expansive views of the high plains and mountains make an excellent way to spend a day. Trains run daily, roughly from July to mid-October. Dress warmly as the unheated cars, both enclosed and semi-enclosed, can get quite chilly. Most trips require a full day and include lunch (there are also half-day express options). Alternatively, you can drive a similar route on Hwy 17 west of Antonito, which provides an abundance of hiking, camping and fishing opportunities in the remote South San Juan Wilderness.

Penitente Canyon   TIME FROM GREAT SAND DUNES: **1 HR** 🚗

Hike the canyon

Penitente Canyon *(fs.usda.gov)* offers the chance to climb, hike and mountain bike among tumbles of strangely shaped giant boulders covering four separate canyons. The haunting landscape was birthed by one of the largest volcanic explosions in history, ejecting 1000 cubic miles of ash some 27 million years ago.

The main canyon, named after Los Hermanos Penitentes, is symbolized by the fading, blue-cloaked **mural of the Virgin of Guadalupe** painted on a canyon wall. Local legend has it that the mural was painted by three men, one of whom descended sitting on a suspended tire. The inscription reads *'Consuelo y Espíritu'* (Comfort and Courage).

Look for pictographs on the canyon walls, painted by Ancestral Puebloans, Apache and Ute, who possibly used the area for game drives. Most are hard to find, though you can easily see one at the entrance to the main canyon, near the parking lot.

The surrounding desert landscape makes for excellent hiking, but remember that this is rattlesnake country, so watch your step. The **Penitente Canyon Loop** (2 miles) follows the lush canyon, shaded by groves of aspen and thickets of chokecherry, before climbing back up into the desert, where you'll be rewarded with glorious views across the valley to the Sangre de Cristo Mountains. Along the way, you can detour to view some old wagon *(carreta)* tracks grooved into the stone.

Crestone Ziggurat

FAINA GUREVICH/SHUTTERSTOCK

Crestone

TIME FROM GREAT SAND DUNES: 1 HR 🚗

See into the future at the Crestone Energy Fair

Each September for more than three decades, the **Crestone Energy Fair** *(crestoneenergyfair.org)* has exemplified many core values of this tight-knit mountain town: strong community engagement, health and wellness, and deep spiritual and reverent connection to the environment. While the population of Crestone municipality tops out at about 150, nearby Bacca Grande is home to another 1200 residents, many of whom live off-grid.

Set against the backdrop of the Sangre de Cristo Mountains, the Energy Fair – one of the country's longest-running fairs of its kind – provides education, insight and hands-on demonstrations around alternative building methodologies and materials, including home tours. It's a weekend catalyzed by community and filled with art, music, yoga, an artisan marketplace and youth activities.

A spiral to the divine

The only spiritual monument of its kind in the US, the **Crestone Ziggurat** is a reflection of monuments from ancient Mesopotamia thought to connect the earth upwards to the divine. It's roughly a 20-minute drive from the center of town (some of the dirt roads require slower speeds) followed by a half-mile hike. From the ziggurat's base, you can ascend the spiral structure, which affords lovely 360-degree views of the dunes and mountains, especially at sunset.

Spirituality for all

Considered a spiritual heart in the US, Crestone is home to more than 20 sacred landmarks, spiritual centers and monuments. Those who call this sacred land home tell stories with a similar, magical thread about the heart and energy that drew

CRESTONE END OF LIFE PROJECT

Located off County Rd T, and denoted by a small one-board sign marked 'Pyre,' is Colorado's only legal, open-air cremation site. The **Crestone End of Life Project** (CEOLP, *crestoneendoflifeproject.org*) is a non-denominational, not-for-profit service that's open to Sauguache residents only. Following a trend in private, open-air cremations, CEOLP, after many hours of public discourse, obtained its permit and held its first official cremation in January 2008. It aims to offer options in a natural burial ground and compassionate education to the community around making informed end-of-life choices. Using a half cord of wood, a stretcher and a shroud, the pyre provides an ancient way for residents to return their bodies to the elements of fire and air.

Crestone Artisans Gallery

them here. **Haidakhandi Universal Ashram** *(babajiashram.org)* and Maha Lakshmi Temple, created in 1986, is the ashram built around the teachings of Haidakhan Babaji and focuses on karma yoga, or the yoga of service. Visitors are welcome daily from 7am to 7pm to join in meditation, karma yoga, prayers or ceremonies, such as the Havans or fire ceremonies. The ashram is located off-grid on dirt roads – the driveway is steep, so take your time.

Living creatively

In a town teeming with artistry in every direction, from the painted side of a building to a lovely little gallery on Cottonwood St, you will find the **Crestone Artisans Gallery** *(crestoneartisansgallery.com),* with its inviting covered porch and fanciful garden. The light-filled gallery is a cooperative of about 20 local artists who create using beautifully diverse mediums, each of exceptional quality. Founded in 2004, the gallery hosts a number of events throughout the year, highlighting new artists such as the Art Lovers Brunch and the Champagne and Dessert Party.

EATING IN CRESTONE: OUR PICKS

Elephant Cloud Cafe: Local, organic, healthy comfort food. Gluten-free and vegan options. Locals meet here on the porch or patio, or for live music. *8am-7pm* **$$**

Our Food Is Art: It's in the name! Local, organic food, and Colorado craft beers, served with creative flair. Vegan and vegetarian options. Porch dining available. *hours vary* **$$**

T-Road Brewing Company: Burgers and pizza-type fare featuring artists and musicians. Patio seating. Don't miss poetry nights. *hours vary* **$$**

Mountain Laurel Apothecary: Handcrafted elixirs, herbal remedies and varied food offerings steeped in loving magic. *hours vary* **$$**

Cañon City & the Royal Gorge

HEART-STOPPING SCENERY | EXHILARATING RAPIDS | PRISON HISTORY

Tucked away in the juniper-and-piñon-dotted scrub of the Arkansas River Valley is the Royal Gorge, a 1000ft-deep gash where bighorn sheep balance precariously on the sheer walls and rattlesnakes lie coiled in the summer sun. There are only two ways to see the bottom: rafting the rapids, or chugging along the historic railway. Echoes of the Wild West resound along Shelf Rd, a former stagecoach route that runs past limestone cliffs and legendary dinosaur quarries to the one-time gold mines of Cripple Creek.

At the heart of it all is Cañon City, a town that appears sleepy enough, until you learn that it's home to 13 prisons, including the Supermax, where some of the country's most notorious criminals serve life sentences. While it's not open for tours, the town does have a prison museum that shares a wall with the Supermax, bringing all that hair-raising history to life.

Doing Time

Explore the history of Colorado's prison system

The bright sun against a silhouette of barbed-wire coils is the first tip you've arrived. While that wire isn't there to keep patrons of the museum in, it is used by the active Supermax facility next door, the Colorado Territorial, adding to the hair-raising museum experience. The last gas chamber used in a Colorado execution, displayed in the front yard, is your second tip. Housed in the former Colorado Women's Correctional Institution, built in 1935, the **Museum of Colorado Prisons** *(canoncitycolorado.com)* is a non-profit organization with a mission to 'collect, preserve, conserve, exhibit and interpret the historical heritage of the Colorado Prison System.' While certainly a bit macabre, it soundly achieves its mission. Exhibits are meticulously curated cell by cell with extensive history, artifacts and photos. Many stories aren't for the faint of heart. Downstairs, you'll find the original kitchen and dining-room areas, as well as the laundry where the sewing of uniforms and cobbling took place. Notable is a room full of heart-rending inmate art.

GETTING AROUND

The Royal Gorge is 8.5 miles northwest of Cañon City along Hwy 50. You'll need a car. Be forewarned: If heights make you queasy, Skyline Dr is a one-way, 2.8-mile stretch with no shoulders, no guardrails and steep drop-offs on both sides. This detour off Rte 50 is like a rollercoaster for your car. If heights aren't an issue for your crew, then the sky's the limit! FYI, you don't need to drive Skyline Dr to visit the Royal Gorge.

☑**TOP TIP**

Cañon City's geography protects it from the worst of Colorado's weather. Summer is the high season, but note that the absence of daily thunderstorms means it can get blistering hot. We recommend a spring or fall visit for the most comfortable temperatures.

CAÑON CITY & THE ROYAL GORGE

HIGHLIGHTS
① Royal Gorge Bridge & Park

SIGHTS
② Museum of Colorado Prisons

ACTIVITIES
③ Royal Gorge Route Railroad

SLEEPING
④ Best Western Cañon City

EATING
⑤ Bean Pedaler
⑥ El Caporal
⑦ Nirvana Culinary Paradise
⑧ White Water Bar & Grill

The Suspense of the Gorge

Choose your own adventure

Most will experience the gorge via the private **Royal Gorge Bridge & Park** *(royalgorgebridge.com)* up top. Is it a theme park? Yes. But like most theme parks, it's fun, with a gondola, zipline, skycoaster and via ferrata all upping the ante to see which can provide the most thrills. If walking is more your speed, stick with the general admission, which is focused on the historic 1260ft-long suspension bridge 1000ft above the gorge floor. If you have more time to explore, the bottom of the gorge beckons. The **Royal Gorge Route Railroad** *(royalgorge route.com)* makes the trip along the historic D&RG line, the one-time site of explosive railroad wars in 1879. Options range from simple open-air cars to more eventful journeys with lunch, dinner, wine and even a murder, and leave from Cañon City.

The most adrenaline-inducing way to see Royal Gorge is on a raft, but the 7 miles of Class IV and V white water are not for the timid. Tour operators typically require rafters to be over 18 years of age in the early season (May to June), or over 12 years when the flow diminishes by midsummer (July to September). There's a large gathering of rafting operators near the Royal Gorge turnoff, 8 miles west of Cañon City, and several others upstream in Salida and Buena Vista.

EATING IN CAÑON CITY: OUR PICKS

Bean Pedaler: Family-owned, boutique coffeehouse with homemade baked goods, simple breakfast and lunch fare. *hours vary* $

White Water Bar & Grill: A festive, string-lit patio with cornhole, horseshoes, a playground and (feeling lucky?) axe-throwing. *hours vary* $$

El Caporal: Down-to-earth and lively Mexican diner. Smothered tamales, chili Colorado and chicken en mole. *11am-9pm Mon-Sat, to 8pm Sun* $$

Nirvana Culinary Paradise: North Indian – fresh, non-GMO ingredients, with vegan, veg, gluten-and dairy-free options. *9am-11pm* $$

Beyond
Cañon City
& the Royal
Gorge

Cañon City &
the Royal Gorge

Drive your trusty steed along the Gold Belt Scenic Byway, which loops to the Old West of Cripple Creek and back.

Just a 90-minute drive from Cañon City, yet worlds away, Cripple Creek hurls you back into the dusty Wild West of yore. This 'once-lucky lady' (read, 'mine') produced a staggering $413 million in gold by 1952. The booze still flows and gambling thrives, but yesteryear's saloons and brothels are now modern casinos. A gold-mine tour will keep nongamblers entertained, but the real treasure is the drive here.

A further 15 miles north is the Florissant Fossil Beds National Monument. Although there is little here aside from petrified sequoia stumps, the location is gorgeous and it's a great place for a hike through wildflower-freckled meadows, boulder-crusted hills and views of the back of Pikes Peak.

Teller County
TIME FROM CAÑON CITY: **1 HR** 🚗

Ancient impressions at Florissant Fossil Beds
In 1873 Dr AC Peale was on his way to survey and map the South Park area, when he discovered ancient lake deposits, buried by a series of volcanic eruptions. Located 17 miles north of Cripple Creek and 48 miles north of Cañon City, the **Florissant Fossil Beds National Monument** *(nps.gov)* has been recognized as one of the greatest collections of Eocene fossils (34 million years old) on the planet.

Explore fossils of insects, leaves, seeds, fish and a few mammals and birds in impressive detail. Because weathering is a factor in preservation, visitors can find a small sampling of the 50,000 fossils that have been excavated (including the only known fossilized tsetse flies), as well as an educational film to learn about and better appreciate what you're seeing. Out in the open is a collection of spectacular petrified redwood stumps, including one that's 38ft in circumference and can be viewed on 1-mile and half-mile self-guided interpretive trails. For those wanting to stretch their legs, there are 15 miles of hiking trails.

Places
Teller County p325

GETTING AROUND

Cripple Creek is 27 miles from Cañon City along the unpaved Shelf Rd, though the fastest route is Hwy 9, which is twice the mileage. Formerly used to transport goods by stagecoach, Shelf Rd includes narrow spots, ruts from wagon wheels of yore and rocks. An AWD is not necessarily needed, but do check road conditions in advance.

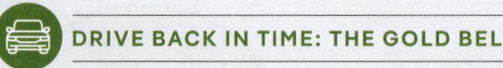

DRIVE BACK IN TIME: THE GOLD BELT

This rugged combo of a former stagecoach road and railroad grade is a drive not to be missed.

START	END	LENGTH
Phantom Canyon	Marsh Dinosaur Quarry	17 miles; 2–3 hours

The Golden Loop Historic Parkway, dating back to the 1890s, was used to connect the Cripple Creek and Victor mining sites and communities. Red earth, low-growing piñon pines, juniper and sheer cliffs transport you to the set of an old Western. Looping from Cañon City to Cripple Creek, it can be driven in either direction.

Start at ❶ **Phantom Canyon** and follow a sinuous old railroad grade (the Florence & Cripple Creek, which ran from 1894 to 1912) through gorgeous sandstone cliffs and blasted-out tunnels for 35 miles to historic ❷ **Victor**, climbing 4500ft in elevation. Although unpaved, you don't need AWD, weather permitting.

Returning from Cripple Creek, just beyond Victor, try your driving hand at ❸ **Shelf Road**. The first 8 miles are unpaved and definitely not for those with vertigo – it's called Shelf for a reason. At the bottom is the ❹ **Shelf Road Recreation Area**, one of the top sport-climbing destinations in the state.

Marsh Dinosaur Quarry, at the ❺ **Garden Park Fossil Area** *(canoncity.org)*, 6 miles past the rock-climbing area, is one of the Jurassic graveyards that spawned the Bone Wars, which produced stars such as stegosaurus, diplodocus and allosaurus back in the late 1800s. They're still standing in the Smithsonian today.

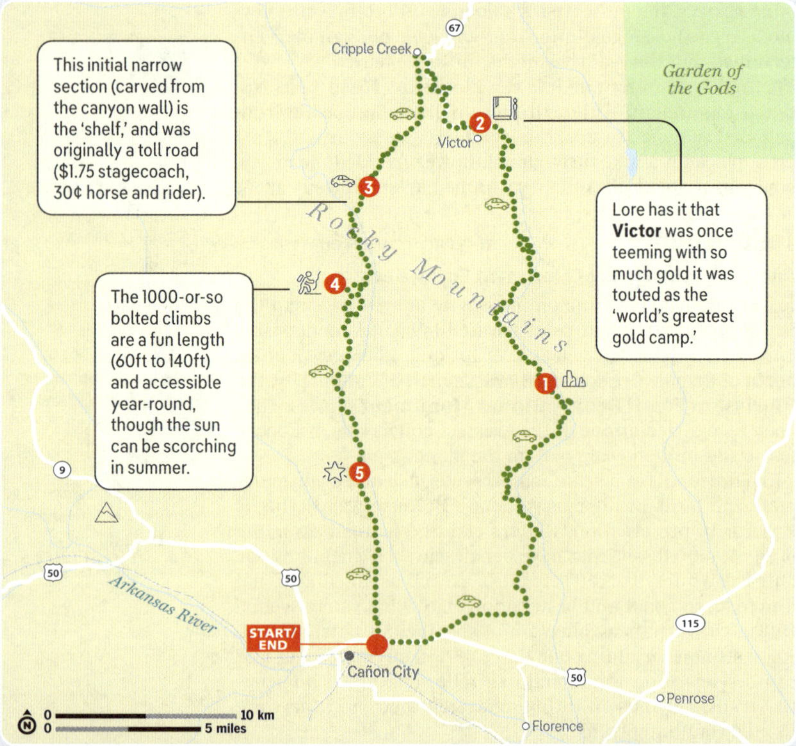

This initial narrow section (carved from the canyon wall) is the 'shelf,' and was originally a toll road ($1.75 stagecoach, 30¢ horse and rider).

The 1000-or-so bolted climbs are a fun length (60ft to 140ft) and accessible year-round, though the sun can be scorching in summer.

Lore has it that **Victor** was once teeming with so much gold it was touted as the 'world's greatest gold camp.'

Cripple Creek · 67

Garden of the Gods

Victor · ❷

❸

❹

Rocky Mountains

❶

9

❺

50

50

Arkansas River

115

START/END

50

Cañon City

○ Penrose

○ Florence

0 — 10 km
0 — 5 miles

Trinidad

HISTORY | ART | SPANISH PEAKS

Tucked into a chimney-top mesa along the Purgatoire River (sometimes Anglicized as the Picketwire River), which flows down from the heights of the Sangre de Cristo Mountains and the Spanish Peaks in the west, lies Trinidad, where a quiet renaissance is afoot. The energy simmers with creativity and revival. The town's past – from its origins as a Spanish outpost and Santa Fe Trail stopover to its coal-mining days when it played a central role in a groundbreaking labor dispute – is documented in its museums and on the brick-paved streets.

Road-trippers will smell adventure on the pine-tinged winds streaming down Rte 12 from Cucharas Pass on the Highway of Legends, the scenic drive that passes through the Spanish Peaks Wilderness, or along Hwy 350, which follows the Santa Fe Trail.

Although the nearby city of Pueblo may be larger, Trinidad has a more dramatic, movie-like setting and makes a convenient base.

Step into Local History

The New Mexico border

The **Trinidad History Museum** *(historycolorado.org)*, which takes up a full city block on Main St, is comprised of the adobe Baca House (1870), the French-style Bloom Mansion (1882) and the Baca-Bloom Heritage Gardens. Early settlers Felipe and Dolores Baca, who came to Trinidad in the 1860s, bought the unusual two-story Baca House for 22,000 pounds of wool in 1873. The real prize here is the **Santa Fe Trail Museum**, a featured exhibit set in the Bacas' workers cottage. Displays trace the course of early Trinidad – an interesting mix of Mexicans and settlers from as far off as Nova Scotia – through its Santa Fe Trail heyday to its transformation as a railroad and mining town.

GETTING AROUND

Trinidad is 130 miles south of Colorado Springs, right at the New Mexico border. Amtrak operates a daily *Southwest Chief* train service between Los Angeles and Chicago that stops here. Greyhound also offers daily, limited round-trip bus service between Colorado Springs and Trinidad (2½ hours). While the most convenient mode of transport to, from and around is a car, the city itself is highly walkable.

☑TOP TIP

Some sites along the Santa Fe Trail have limited opening hours or require advance reservations, such as tours of the Picketwire Dinosaur Tracksite. Even if you're just passing through, it's a good idea to check ahead to ensure that you're getting the most out of a visit.

Art is the Heart

Immerse yourself in Trinidad's creativity

A vein of creativity runs through this storied town. You can see it from its brick-paved sidewalks to its architecturally rich skyline. But, mostly, you can see it in the sparkle of the eyes of the energetic souls who live here. The **Corazón de Trinidad**, listed on the National Register of Historic Places in 1973, earned designation as a Creative District in 2016. The Corazon was birthed to support artists and entrepreneurs through cultural and creative initiatives, adding life to the economy through art and innovation, and honoring the rich and sometimes mercurial history of Trinidad.

Downtown is richly dense with art for the viewing. The **Arthur Roy Mitchell Memorial Museum of Western Art** *(armitchellmuseum.com)* is a standout. Housed in a 1906 Western-style building with a spacious horseshoe-style mezzanine, the museum – originally the historic Jamieson Dry Goods Store – honors its namesake and displays an extensive collection of Western landscapes, cowboys, horses, Hispanic and Native American art. There's a rotating exhibition space and terrific collection of historic Trinidad photos.

The **Corazon Art Gallery** *(corazongallery.org)* offers a not-for-profit, co-op format for local working artists. The art is of excellent quality and varied in medium. The artists (typically more than a dozen in the co-op) take turns tending the shop and participating in various shows and events, including classes for the public. You'll find more local artists and crafts at the weekly, seasonal **Trinidad Farmers Market** *(trinidadcofarmersmarket.com)*. Held June through September in Cimino Park, it features artisans and craftspeople along-

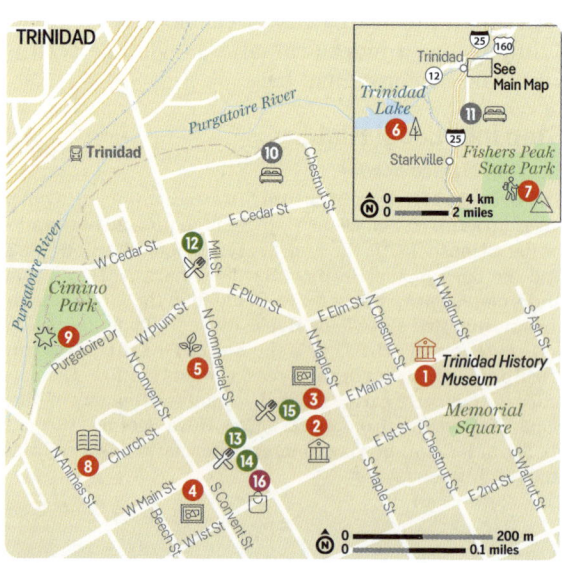

J.C. CLINE/SHUTTERSTOCK

Downtown Trinidad

THE SANTA FE TRAIL

The Santa Fe Trail (p331) linked Missouri with New Mexico (a Mexican province from 1821 to 1848), bringing manufactured goods west and Mexican silver and Native American jewelry and blankets east. The 800-mile route took seven to eight weeks to cross in a covered wagon, and was defined by monotony and hardship. Near Dodge City in Kansas, the route divided: the southern road (Cimarron Route) cut down into New Mexico, and was shorter but more dangerous, while the northern road (Mountain Route) continued through Bent's Fort and Trinidad, and was longer but safer. With the expansion of the railroad west, trade along the route eventually diminished, coming to a close in 1880.

side local produce, educational programs around fresh food and health, and live music.

Downtown Nuggets

Find new-to-you books or peace in a wellness garden

Strolling down North Commercial St, you happen upon **Books & More, Friends of the Trinidad Carnegie Library** (*library bookstore-trinidadcolorado.org*). Tin ceilings and gorgeous architectural detail provide a fitting home for this not-for-profit secondhand bookstore, with its mission for educational and charitable purposes and to support the **Trinidad Carnegie Public Library** (*trinidadpubliclibrary.org*). The library stands as grand today as when it opened in 1904. A stone's throw from the bookstore, it's the perfect place to sit and find a peaceful spot to read, reflect or enjoy a quiet moment.

The **Sister Blandina Wellness Gardens** (*mtcarmelcenter. org*) were created to nurture mind, body and spirit of community. Offerings include wellness programs, cultural festivities, a reflection pool, picnic tables and gorgeous gardens. Check out the calendar for events and live music.

Stroll Back In Time

Downtown architectural walking tour

You don't need to be an architect to discern the striking and varied architecture that comprises downtown Trinidad. The Trinidad Historical Society presents **A Walk Through Historical Trinidad** (*visittrinidadcolorado.com/walking-tour*), written by Gerald Stokes, who created a storytelling, historical narrative around Trinidad's rich and notable architecture. This DIY tour includes 40-plus buildings of note; see some or all and stroll at your pace.

A DHARMA TALE

Jess McCorkle, owner of Sita's Kitchen, shares the importance of dharma (purpose).

We moved to Trinidad after my husband retired from the military. It's such a kind and genuine community – what you see is what you get. I was teaching yoga and selling baked goods out of the studio. People kept asking when I'd open a restaurant. I had zero restaurant experience. I sensed the universe saying *'you need to feed the people physically'* – it chose me. It didn't matter that it was a vegan restaurant in a small ranching town. A lot of people didn't think it would work. That was just over six years ago.

Food is medicine. It's about feeling good. Watching people learn how that impacts their wellbeing is transformative.

WESTEND61/GETTY IMAGES

Fishers Peak

The Great Outdoors at Your Doorstep

Mountain views and a lake as blue as a Colorado sky

For hiking adventures, the distinctive 9633ft **Fishers Peak** (*fisherspeakstatepark.com*) is only a 10-minute drive south of town. It was named a state park in 2020 and is now accessible via a relatively new trail to the summit. Note that there is no water on the trail and little shade for the first half, so come prepared. The 360-degree views at the mesa top are worth every step.

Around 10 minutes west of town is **Trinidad Lake State Park** (*cpw.state.co.us*). Strikingly blue in appearance due to low algae content, the 800-acre lake is mild in temperature – 70°F (21°C) degrees in summer – and a great place to enjoy some peace or adventure, whatever your flavor that day. For anglers, trout, largemouth bass and catfish (to name a few) await. Water-sport enthusiasts can swim, jet ski, kayak and stand-up paddleboard.

 EATING IN TRINIDAD: OUR PICKS

Sita's Kitchen: Family-owned vegan restaurant and bakery with floor-to-ceiling plants. Locally sourced organic bowls, salads, soups and sandwiches. *hours vary* **$$**

The Cafe: Gourmet egg wraps, tantalizing soups and sandwiches and daily fresh-baked goods in the charming Danielson Dry Goods building. *10am-2pm* **$**

The Marketplace Food Court and Bar: Tin ceilings, exposed brick and ductwork for a fun, festive vibe and something for everyone. *hours vary* **$$**

Perkatory: Fun flower, skull and steampunk atmosphere, serving Colorado roasted coffee, breakfast and other eats. Extensive selection of teas. *hours vary* **$**

Beyond Trinidad

If you fancy following the old wagon ruts of history, the Santa Fe Trail beckons.

For some people, the Santa Fe Trail is no more than a lonely drive with a series of don't-blink-or-you'll-miss-'em historical markers. Others will find themselves thrown back to a time when finding yourself in this part of the world meant a daily fight for survival.

Either way, this slice of Colorado is one of great natural beauty and contrasts. From the wild, sun-drenched prairie around Bent's Fort to the high mesas and billowing clouds on the New Mexico border and the ancient volcanic walls of the twin Spanish Peaks near La Veta, these long-traveled routes provides a mix of history and natural wonder.

Santa Fe Trail

TIME FROM TRINIDAD: 1½ HR

Driving the historic Santa Fe Trail

Drive along Hwy 350 and experience the fabled western reaches of the Great Plains and the Santa Fe Trail. Just north of the Arkansas River (the original border between the US and Mexico) is **Bent's Old Fort National Historic Site** (*nps.gov*). The beautifully restored adobe fort, used between 1833 and 1849, was once a cultural crossroads and the busiest settlement west of the Missouri.

Further east is the 1862 **Boggsville Historic Site** (*bent countyheritage.org*), a one-time store, trading post and homestead for frontiersmen Thomas Boggs and Kit Carson. Northeast of Boggsville is Fort Lyon, where on November 29, 1864, John Chivington led the Colorado Volunteers in a dawn attack on Chief Black Kettle and his band. More than 150 Cheyenne and Arapaho men, women and children were slaughtered, an event commemorated at the **Sand Creek Massacre National Historic Site** (*nps.gov*), northeast of Fort Lyon.

Drive through Granada to the **Amache National Historic Site** (*nps.gov*). This WWII Japanese internment camp once held 7567 prisoners, most of whom were US citizens, all brought here from the farmlands of central California.

Places

Santa Fe Trail p331
Timpas p332
Highway of Legends p332
Pueblo p332

TARANTULA FEST

What's brown, furry, has eight legs and falls in love every September? If you guessed Oklahoma brown tarantulas, you'd be right! Of-age male tarantulas roam more than 443,000 acres of the Comanche National Grassland annually to find their mate. Their goal: be quick about it and don't get eaten (roughly 20% don't make it). The city of La Junta celebrates the **Tarantula Fest** (*visitlajunta.net*) each September with parades, food vendors, movies (*Arachnophobia*, anyone?) and tours.

HOW THE SPANISH PEAKS CAME TO BE

The staggering appearance of the twin Spanish Peaks makes clear that these are mountains of import. The magma that formed the peaks was congealed in the earth's crust 24 million years ago. The 17-million-year-old formations above ground, which the Ute aptly called *wahatoya* (meaning 'breasts of the earth'), were once critical landmarks for travelers crossing the Great Plains. The East Peak is 12,708ft high, while the West Peak soars to 13,625ft. With hundreds of incredible vertical stone dikes (ancient magma) radiating outward like some kind of primordial fence line, these mountains are ripe for hiking adventures.

Timpas

TIME FROM TRINIDAD: **1 HR** 🚗

Walk the wild Comanche National Grassland

Along Hwy 350 is the unassuming settlement of Timpas, one of the gateways to the **Comanche National Grassland** *(fs. usda.gov)*. Walking through the unforgiving wilderness of hip-high grasses, it's easy to imagine the challenges that traders and settlers faced.

Follow backroads from Timpas 45 minutes to the **Withers Canyon Trailhead**, where a 5.6-mile (one way) hike along the Purgatoire River leads to the ruins of the late-19th-century Dolores Mission and the **Picketwire Dinosaur Tracksite** *(fs.usda.gov)*, the largest dinosaur-track site in North America, where some 1300 dinosaur prints are visible. Alternatively, reserve a trip with **Picket Wire Guided Auto Tours** *(recreation.gov/ticket/facility/234166)*.

Highway of Legends

TIME FROM TRINIDAD: **5 MINS** 🚗

Hiking the Spanish Peaks

West of Trinidad, the Highway of Legends (Hwy 12) is a stunning scenic route wrapping around the west side of the volcanic Spanish Peaks for 66 miles before reaching La Veta.

Hikers, take heart! At Cuchara Pass (9994ft), you can take a forest service road 6.5 miles east to the **Cordova Pass Trailhead**. It's a steep 2.5-mile climb to the summit of the West Peak over scree and stones; this is the most popular route up. Figure on 2½ hours up and make sure you're off the summit by noon.

The 12-mile (one way) **Wahatoya Trail** traverses the saddle between the peaks. As you approach the peaks, you may see remnants of the 2013 wildfire that burned the north side of the East Peak. There are three campgrounds in the area, including reservable sites at Purgatoire.

Pueblo

TIME FROM TRINIDAD: **1½ HR** 🚗

Learn about life on the plains

Urbanites should enjoy a stay in Pueblo, 85 miles north of Trinidad. This one-time railroad hub and steel-manufacturing center along the Arkansas River is home to the **El Pueblo History Museum** *(historycolorado.org)*, set at the original site of Fort Pueblo, used from 1842 to 1854, and telling the story of life on the plains in the 1800s. Exhibits include a family tipi and a cut from a massive tree, ominously called the hanging tree, that once stood over present-day Union Ave. Constructed in 1893, the **Rosemount Museum** *(rosemount.org)*, designed by New York architect Henry Hudson Holly, is grandeur not to be missed. Aerophiles will delight in the **Pueblo Weisbrod Aircraft Museum** *(pwam.org)*.

Places We Love to Stay

$ Budget $$ Midrange $$$ Top End

Colorado Springs   p304

Mining Exchange $$ Set in the stately turn-of-the-century bank where Cripple Creek prospectors traded gold for cash. Vibrant atmosphere and chic decor, with dining from craft coffeehouse to classic cocktails and small plates. Italian fare is slated for 2025.

Holden House $$ Three Victorians make up this 1902 B&B in Old Colorado City. Well-appointed rooms, full breakfast and afternoon refreshments. This is a 21-plus-only accommodations.

Old Town Guesthouse B&B $$$ On a Victorian block, with elegant, variously themed rooms with balconies. Some include hot tubs, sauna/steam showers or fireplaces. Full breakfast included.

Cheyenne Mountain Resort $$$ Boasting a glorious position overlooking Cheyenne Mountain, this woodsy resort has an air of indulgence. Golf, a spa and lake activities.

Manitou Springs   p311

Cliff House at Pikes Peak $$$ Historic 1873 hotel, once a stagecoach stop for gamblers and miners. Elegant 1800s period furnishings. Valet or street parking.

Great Sand Dunes   p313

Pinyon Flats Campground $ Official park campground, with a great location not far from the dune field. Reserve months ahead.

Zapata Falls Campground $ Seven miles south of the park, up a dirt road, with glorious views of the valley floor from its 9000ft perch. Reserve ahead.

Great Sand Dunes Oasis $ Store, restaurant, campground and motel at the park entrance. Fairly minimal, with slightly smaller but adequate camp spots. Has showers and a kids' playground.

Great Sand Dunes Lodge $$ Located near the park's entrance, with clean, comfortable rooms that have everything you need and nothing you don't. Patios out back of the rooms overlook the dunes for memorable sunrises and sunsets. Hot breakfast and continental fare included. Buy-n-bake pizza for additional cost.

Moffat

Joyful Journey Hot Springs Spa (p318) **$$** Indulge in this healing, year-round hot-spring setting. Spacious rooms with patios out back, healthy breakfast and light dinner, and soaks included in the price of your stay. Additional spa services available.

Alamosa   p316

Dunes Inn $ Budget-friendly, family-owned hotel in the heart of downtown Alamosa. Simple and clean rooms with complimentary comforting breakfast at the cafe next door.

Rustic Rook Resort $$ Glamping with unobstructed views of the Sangre de Cristo Mountains. Tents, showers and some in-tent bathrooms. Nightly campfire and s'mores and hot breakfast are included.

Fairfield Inn & Suites $$$ The newest and best kept of the chain hotels west of town.

Clean and spacious rooms with fitness center and hot tub.

Antonito

Elk Creek Campground $ Twenty-three miles west of Antonito, off Hwy 17, this is an off-the-grid location with 38 forested sites. The campground is well-kept, with exceptionally clean facilities.

Mogote Campground $ Shaded spot along the Conejos River, with 41 sites and friendly staff. Watch for mosquitoes on the lower loop near the river.

Rainbow Trout Ranch $$$ Turn back time amid the natural beauty of this five-star, family-friendly dude ranch with horseback riding and fly-fishing adventures.

Cañon City   p323

Best Western Cañon City $$ Clean rooms, friendly staff, and great location just a few miles from the Royal Gorge History Museum and a 25-minute drive to Royal Gorge Bridge.

Trinidad   p327

La Quinta Inn & Suites $ Friendly staff and spacious, clean and fresh rooms, with breakfast and on-site pool included. Conveniently located near I-25 and Trinidad State Lake.

Hilton Garden Downtown $$ Conveniently located off I-25 near the Trinidad Riverwalk. Walkable to downtown museums and restaurants. On-site fitness center and restaurant serving breakfast and dinner for dine-in and takeout.

TOOLKIT

The chapters in this section cover the most important topics you'll need to know about in Colorado. They're full of nuts-and-bolts information and valuable insights to help you understand and navigate Colorado and get the most out of your trip.

Arriving
p336

Getting Around
p337

Money
p338

Accommodations
p339

Family Travel
p340

Health & Safe Travel
p341

Food, Drink & Nightlife
p342

Responsible Travel
p344

LGBTIQ+ Travelers
p346

Accessible Travel
p347

Cannabis
p348

Nuts & Bolts
p349

Crested Butte (p243)
LIZA PRADO/LONELY PLANET

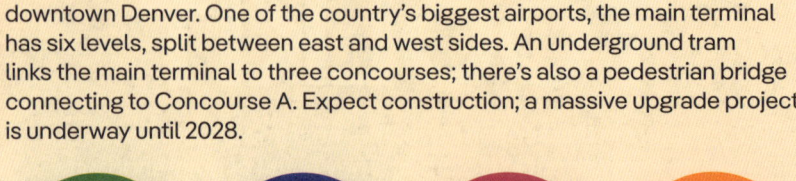

Arriving

Most visitors arrive through Denver International Airport (DIA), 24 miles from downtown Denver. One of the country's biggest airports, the main terminal has six levels, split between east and west sides. An underground tram links the main terminal to three concourses; there's also a pedestrian bridge connecting to Concourse A. Expect construction; a massive upgrade project is underway until 2028.

Visas

Most foreign visitors to the USA must have a visa. Exceptions include citizens of Canada and Bermuda and citizens of countries participating in the **Visa Waiver Program** (esta .cbp.dhs.gov/ esta).

Biometrics

Every person entering the USA at DIA has their photo taken by a US Customs & Border Protection agent, which is validated against an existing passport or visa photo.

Cash

ATMs are located throughout the DIA. There are currency exchange booths in Concourses A and B as well as on level 5 of the main terminal, just outside the international arrivals area.

Wi-Fi & Charging

Free wi-fi is available at DIA; choose 'DEN Airport Free WiFi' on your device (no registration or ad-viewing required). Hundreds of charging stations dot the airport.

Airport Transportation

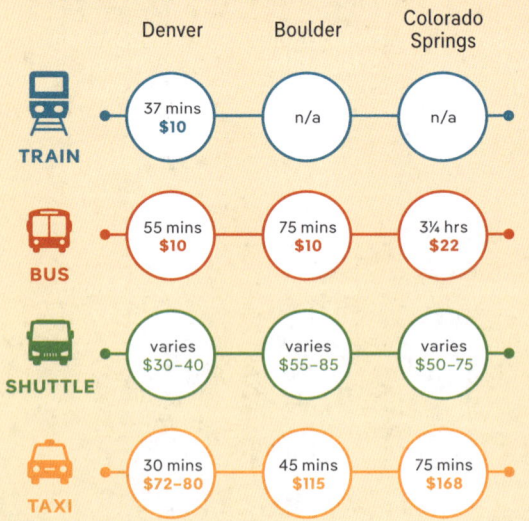

	Denver	Boulder	Colorado Springs
TRAIN	37 mins **$10**	n/a	n/a
BUS	55 mins **$10**	75 mins **$10**	3¼ hrs **$22**
SHUTTLE	varies $30–40	varies $55–85	varies $50–75
TAXI	30 mins **$72–80**	45 mins **$115**	75 mins **$168**

AIRPORT ART

Thanks to a public art fund, DIA is draped in a robust collection of murals, photos and large-scale sculptures. You can't miss *Kinetic Air Light Curtain* in the tram tunnels, a nod to Denver's mile-high elevation, with 5280 tiny propellers that spin with each passing train. Or listen for Native American songs as you walk Concourse A's pedestrian bridge. As you leave, keep an eye out for the most (in)famous: *Mustang/ Mesteño*, nicknamed 'Blucifer,' a 32ft-high blue stallion with gleaming red eyes. In a bizarre tragedy, the artist, Luis Jimenez, died after the 9000lb structure fell on him during its creation.

Getting Around

There are lots of options for getting around Colorado, but a car is essential for exploring beyond the Front Range or ski resorts.

TRAVEL COSTS

Car rental
From $62/day

Petrol
Approx $3.40/ gallon

EV charging
Free–$0.45/ kWh

Mountain shuttle
From $79

Car Hire & Costs

Car-rental agencies are available at most Colorado airports, offering everything from tiny sedans to mammoth SUVs. But they don't come cheap! Save some cash by booking off-site, which cuts out hefty airport taxes and fees. A quick cab or bus ride to the nearest town can save you hundreds on a week-long rental.

Road Conditions

City roads and highways are generally paved and well maintained; smaller mountain towns and rural areas often have dirt or gravel roads. Some mountain passes close seasonally or when driving conditions are hazardous. Before heading out, check with **Colorado Department of Transportation** (codot.gov/travel) for road closures and weather warnings.

TIP

Wildlife often wanders onto roads – deer, elk and moose are common sights, especially in the mountains. Drive cautiously!

TRACTION LAW

From September to May, along mountainous sections of I-70, Colorado law requires two-wheel-drive vehicles to have snow tires, all-weather tires or to carry tire chains or autosocks. Plus all vehicles have minimum tread requirements of 3/16ths of an inch. The law is in place to reduce accidents in hazardous winter conditions. If disregarded, you could face a substantial fine or, much worse, injure or kill yourself or others.

Mountain Shuttles

Epic Mountain Express (epicmountainexpress. com) and **Peak 1 Express** (mountain shuttle.com) provide door-to-door shuttle service from Denver airport to Aspen and major resort towns along I-70, including Vail, Beaver Creek, Copper, Breckenridge and Keystone. Both offer shared shuttles and private charters.

Bus

Bustang (ridebustang. com) is the regional bus service. It serves cities along I-70 and I-25 as well as destinations like Telluride, Crested Butte and Trinidad via their **Outrider** routes. In winter, it runs **Snowstang**, with routes from Denver to several different ski resorts, geared toward day trippers.

Plane

Several small commercial airports dot Colorado. Flights tend to be expensive and often involve connecting through Denver. But flying regionally can help you avoid the cost and hassle of renting a car. In winter, many carriers offer direct flights from major US cities to popular ski towns.

DRIVING ESSENTIALS

Drive on the right

Speed limit is 25–35mph in urban areas, 20–40mph on mountain roads and 55–75mph on highways

Blood alcohol limit is 0.05% (DWI) and 0.08% (DUI)

Money

CURRENCY: US DOLLAR ($)

Credit Cards

Credit cards are the most common way to pay for goods and services in Colorado, used from corner stores to ski resorts. But consider cash. A 2022 state law allows businesses to offset their credit card processing costs by adding a surcharge to customer bills, typically around 2%.

Sales Tax

Sales tax is added to most goods sold in Colorado, including state tax (2.9%) and a city and/or county tax (typically around 7% to 8%). There are some exceptions – groceries and prescription medications – but plan on paying as much as 11.2% extra for your mementos.

Tipping Etiquette

Generally, tipping is expected in restaurants, and anytime a service has been provided.

Breweries $1–2 per pour
Coffee shops $1 per drink
Dispensaries $2 per purchase
Guides 15%–20% of tour cost
Luggage attendants $2–5 per suitcase
Hotel housekeeping $5 per night
Restaurants and bars 15–20% of the bill

HOW MUCH FOR A...

Museum entry
Free–$30

National Park pass
(unlimited)
$80

Ski-lift ticket
$70–275

Denver CityPASS
Adult $46–64
Child $37–54

HOW TO... Save Cash

Don't be shy about asking about discounts! Children often pay half-price for tours, sights and public transportation. Ditto for students, seniors and military personnel. Museums around the state, too, often offer a free day each month. And if you're traveling to Denver, consider purchasing a **CityPASS** (*citypass.com/denver*), a prepaid ticket package that offers significant discounts for some of the city's top attractions.

RESTAURANT SERVICE CHARGES

Hiring and retaining food service workers has become challenging since the COVID-19 pandemic struck. Many quit or were laid off and never returned. To make the work more appealing, Colorado restaurants are increasingly adding a 'service charge' or 'cost-of-living fee' to bills. Added pre-tax, it's typically a percentage of the bill, designated to supplement staff wages or benefits. Often it's directed to non-tipped kitchen staff but sometimes it's for everyone. Read the menu's fine print or simply ask the server. Typically, if the charge is 12% or less, a gratuity is still expected and appreciated.

LOCAL TIP

Many small businesses such as tour companies and B&Bs don't accept credit cards. Be sure you have access to digital cash through Venmo, Apple Pay, PayPal or Zelle to cover your costs.

Accommodations

Boutique on a Budget

A growing number of Colorado's cities and mountain towns have modern hostels, still catering to travelers on a budget yet featuring swanky style and boutique amenities. Most offer private rooms (with shared bathrooms) though if you're looking for the ultimate bargain, dorms are where it's at. Most hostels include breakfast and have kitchens for making your own meals too.

Pitch a Tent

Camping is one of the most popular ways to experience Colorado. It's easy, too, with hundreds of established private and public campgrounds spread across the state. Most have shared bathrooms and fire pits; some have showers and camp stores. Or try dispersed camping, a free back-to-the-basics experience, where you set up camp on public lands, away from the crowds.

Backcountry Huts

Colorado has an extensive system of backcountry huts that are accessible year-round by foot, ski or mountain bike, using trails and fire roads. Some are basic dry cabins while others are nicer affairs with solar-powered lights, wood-burning stoves and even eco-compost toilets. Hut-to-hut travel is a fun option and sometimes includes pre-stocked food. Reserve early for winter stays!

Historic Hotels

Many Colorado cities are home to historic hotels, most dating to the turn of the 20th century. Stepping inside is like stepping back in time, the communal areas decked out in antique furnishings, Victorian-era decor and art. Guest rooms feature modern amenities (no outhouses here!) and some occupy modern buildings attached to the original structure.

VIDI STUDIO/SHUTTERSTOCK

Vacation Resorts

From working ranches to posh alpine lodges, Colorado offers a wide range of resorts. Many are geared toward families and include long activity lists that feature guided hikes, horseback riding, fly-fishing, mountain biking, cross-country skiing and more. Accommodations run the gamut from rustic log cabins to cushy suites; meals also range from DIY cooking to four-course tasting menus.

HOW MUCH FOR A NIGHT IN A...

Campsite
Free–$40

Hostel (dorm bed)
$45–90

Vacation resort
From $115

COMPETITIVE CAMPING

With the growing number of Colorado residents and the state's popularity among travelers, camping can feel like a competitive sport. Campgrounds fill up fast, especially on summer weekends; some are completely booked months ahead of time, so reserve early. Try *recreation.gov* for campsites on federal land and **Colorado Parks & Wildlife** (*cpw.state.co.us*) for state parks. For dispersed camping near popular destinations like Crested Butte or Aspen, camp midweek or arrive by Friday morning to secure a spot. For more information, stop at ranger stations or a **Bureau of Land Management** (*blm.gov*) office.

Family Travel

Colorado is a welcoming place for families, especially for exploring the great outdoors with endless blue skies and adventure galore. But the state is also bursting with history and culture, from prehistoric finds and ancient ruins to modern-day museums.

Discounts for Kids

In Colorado, discounts for children and youth often apply for tours, admission fees and public transportation; discounts can be as much as 50% off the regular rate, while infants under two are typically free. If traveling to Denver, consider purchasing a **CityPASS** *(citypass .com/denver)*, a bundled ticket package that offers discounts for several family-friendly attractions.

Facilities

Colorado's cities and ski resorts are well equipped for traveling kids. Most restaurants, diners and cafes offer highchairs for toddlers; many also have kids' menus and offer crayons and coloring books to pass the time. Breweries often welcome children, sometimes even offering juice boxes and snacks.
Hotels have cots and cribs for traveling families.

Nursing Rooms

Private nursing or lactation rooms are few and far between in Colorado but their prevalence is on the rise. Look for them at large facilities like airports, auditoriums and hospitals as well as at child-centered destinations like children's museums and zoos.

Diaper-Changing

Diaper-changing stations are found in most public restrooms in Colorado. Museums and airports typically have 'family restrooms' – single-user bathrooms with changing tables that are roomy enough for a parent, a couple of children and even a stroller to enter at once.

TOP CHILD-FRIENDLY SIGHTS

Dinosaur National Monument (p292)

Touch dinosaur skeletons and see thousands of prehistoric bones up close.

Children's Museum of Denver (p67)

Come for imaginative play, maker spaces and even cooking classes.

Woodwar Barn (p204)

Practice gnarly moves at Copper Mountain's action sports playground.

Bent's Old Fort (p33l)

Learn about the Old West at this one-time trading post from staffers in costume.

Ouray Hot Springs (p267)

Splash year-round at this water park featuring geothermically heated water.

SKI SCHOOL

Ski and snowboard lessons can be a great way for everyone in the family to make the most of a mountain vacation. Beginners can get quality instruction, while advanced skiers and riders have a few hours to hit the double-blacks. Consider half-day lessons, which allow for a good balance of instruction and family together-time and are available for all ages. If you opt for full days, kids' lessons typically include lunch. Some ski school packages include lift tickets and rentals too – often a great deal. Above all, remember to have fun and keep your expectations reasonable: skiing and boarding are tough to master!

 # Health & Safe Travel

HIGH ALTITUDE

Altitude sickness is a serious health risk in Colorado. Stay hydrated, take it easy and allow a few days to acclimatize before going really high – like to the top of a fourteener. A little light-headedness, slight headaches and sluggishness are normal. But if you experience severe and continued nausea, headache and dizziness, consult a doctor and/or get to lower altitudes.

Drinking Water

Colorado has great tap water – you can drink out of the faucet pretty much anywhere in the state. When camping, be sure to purify any water you collect to kill disease-causing viruses, bacteria and parasites. If you choose to boil the water, be sure it's roiling for at least a minute, or for three minutes at altitudes over 6500ft.

Bites & Stings

Being proactive is effective against bites and stings.

Wear long sleeves and pants, and use bug repellent, to ward off ticks, spiders and mosquitoes; check for ticks at the end of the day.

If you're bitten or stung, stay calm and seek treatment.

THE SUN

High elevation and blue skies mean increased exposure to the sun's rays. Cover up, slather on sunscreen and wear a hat!

WILDLIFE ROAD SIGNS

Bear Crossing

Moose Crossing

Cattle & Livestock Crossing

Deer Crossing

Elk Crossing

Insurance

Getting basic travel insurance is a good idea, especially for flight cancellations, luggage theft and loss. International travelers should consider adding coverage for medical emergencies, including hospital stays and emergency flights home. While the US offers some of the best-quality healthcare in the world, it can be prohibitively expensive.

WILDFIRES

Wildfires are all too common in Colorado, particularly during summer when conditions are hot, dry and windy. They're often sparked by lightning strikes or unattended campfires, and can spread quickly, causing devastating damage. Even distant communities can be affected by the poor air quality. Always heed fire bans! And if there's a wildfire, follow evacuation orders and road closure signs.

Food, Drink & Nightlife

When to Eat

Breakfast (7am–10am) is filling, focused on eggs, fruit, orange juice and coffee.

Brunch (9am–1pm) is a leisurely weekend meal, combining breakfast and lunch dishes. Mimosas and bloody Marys are common.

Lunch (11am–2pm) is quick, often sandwiches and salads with iced tea or soft drinks.

Dinner (5:30pm–9pm) is substantial, varying from takeout to multicourse meals served with wine or beer. Dessert is common.

Where to Eat

Casual dining Relaxed restaurant with moderately priced meals and counter or table service.

Cafe Unhurried locals' spot that serves breakfast, lunch, pastries and hot drinks.

Diner Inexpensive, casual eatery, typically lined with booths and serving American staples; open late.

Food truck Kitchen on wheels, serving fast, made-to-order food that's taken to go.

Food halls Collection of indoor eateries with a variety of cuisines in a classed-up food-court-style setting.

Fine dining Upscale restaurant often featuring farm-to-table and ethically raised ingredients.

MENU DECODER

À la carte A menu of individually priced dishes, Colorado's most common.

Blue plate An old-school term meaning 'daily special,' typically used in diners.

Buffet An array of all-you-can eat dishes, typically hot and cold, offered for a set price.

Du jour A French term indicating 'daily special' (eg soup du jour)

Family-style A larger-portioned dish, typically enough for two to four people, that is centrally placed for diners to serve themselves.

Prix fixe A set-price meal, including two or more predetermined courses.

Shareable menu A selection of small plates, several of which are ordered and shared to create a meal for two or more diners.

Tasting menu A multicourse meal with small, often bite-sized, portions that showcase the chef's talent.

HOW TO…

Eat at a Food Hall

Food halls are taking Colorado by storm: collections of eateries, sometimes a bar, surrounding communal tables. The options can be overwhelming and the ordering process confusing. Here are some tips.

Before you sit down, peruse the options. It's easy to see what's being made and if it looks appetizing.

If you see a menu, order at the counter and find a seat. You'll receive a pager that will buzz when your food is ready.

If there aren't any menus visible, find a seat and look for a QR code at the table. Scan the QR code for menus and order from your phone. If you're able to enter a table number, the food will be brought to you; if not, you'll receive a text when your food is ready.

Occasionally, roving waiters take and bring your drink orders.

Payment may be taken by mobile scanner or QR code.

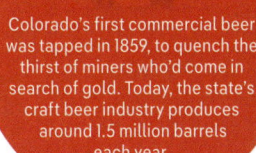

HOW MUCH FOR A...

Cup of coffee
$3–5.50

Breakfast burrito
$8–12

Sandwich
$8–14

Scoop of ice cream
$4–6

Dinner for two (without drinks)
$30–120

Pint of craft beer
$7–10

Glass of wine
$9–16

Happy-hour cocktail
$5–10

HOW TO...

Order a Craft Beer

With over 400 craft breweries, enjoying a glass of beer is a quintessential Colorado experience. Across the state, beer aficionados sip and savor beer as they would wine, and some restaurants even have 'beer sommeliers.' It's not surprising, then, that stepping into a tasting room or brewery means navigating lots of options. Here are a few tips for handling it like a loca.

Ales Full-bodied with complex flavor profiles and a pronounced aroma.

Flavored Brewed with flavors that lend unique tastes like raspberry and jalapeño.

IPAs Meaning 'India Pale Ale,' bitter, hoppy and known for its high alcohol content.

Lagers Light-bodied, crisp and clean tasting.

Stouts and porters Dark, rich and full-bodied. Often brewed with roasted malt and barley, lending a coffee or chocolate flavor.

Sours Tart, crisp and often layered with fruity flavors.

Colorado's first commercial beer was tapped in 1859, to quench the thirst of miners who'd come in search of gold. Today, the state's craft beer industry produces around 1.5 million barrels each year.

COLORADO WINE COUNTRY

Colorado isn't the first place you'd think of when you hear the phrase 'wine country.' But vineyards have been in the region since the late 1800s, when miners planted grapevines to make homegrown wine, a common practice in the era. It wasn't until the 1960s that Colorado produced its first commercial wine. It began with Gerald Ivancie, a Denver periodontist, who started making wine as a hobby in his three-car garage using California grapes and wine-making knowledge he'd gained from his European parents. Ivancie's homemade wine was such a hit with friends and family, he decided to scale up his operation: Ivancie Cellars, in Denver, became the state's first winery in 1968. With an eye to growing the business and focusing on Colorado-grown grapes, Ivancie enlisted the help of Warren Winiarski, a

rising Californian winemaker. Together, they scouted out and approached farmers in the Grand Valley, near Grand Junction, to plant wine grapes. The red rocks and high desert surroundings seemed unusual but the fertile soil, sunny days, cool nights and low humidity proved ideal. The vineyards also proved record-breaking – growing between 4000ft and 7000ft above sea level, they are the highest vineyards in North America.

Ivancie Cellars eventually folded, but it sparked a movement and an industry. Today, there are over 140 Coloradan wineries, mostly small family-owned estates. Many are in the Grand Valley and the nearby West Elks regions. Winery tours and tasting rooms abound in **Palisade** (p293) and **Paonia** (p295), while areas around Cortez and the Front Range are developing.

Responsible Travel

Climate Change & Travel

It's impossible to ignore the impact we have when traveling; Lonely Planet urges all travelers to engage with their travel carbon footprint, which will mainly come from air travel. While there often isn't an alternative, travelers can look to minimize the number of flights they take, opt for newer aircrafts and use cleaner ground transportation, such as trains. One proposed solution – purchasing carbon offsets – unfortunately does not cancel out the impact of individual flights. While most destinations will depend on air travel for the foreseeable future, for now, pursuing ground-based travel where possible is the best course of action.

The **UN Carbon Offset Calculator** shows how flying impacts a household's emissions

The **ICAO's carbon emissions calculator** allows visitors to analyse the CO2 generated by point-to-point journeys

Support Local

Nibble your way through some of the state's best locally produced food at **Boulder County Farmers Market** (p112), where there's a strict sell-only-what-you-grow-or-make policy. Most only offer organic, non-GMO food. All waste is recycled or composted too.

Learn More

Take a free guided hike of Hallam Lake nature preserve with a naturalist from **Aspen Center for Environmental Studies** (p225) and learn all about the creatures that call this 25-acre wildlife sanctuary home.

Pedal your way around **Denver** (*lyft.com and li.me*), **Fort Collins** (*spin.app*) and **Colorado Springs** (*pikeride.org*) using their e-bike and e-scooter share programs; most are accessibly priced by the minute or day.

Travel the mountains on foot, ski or bike, staying in off-the-grid huts along the way. Good options include **10th Mountain Division Hut Association** (p226), **Summit Huts Association** (p201) and **San Juan Huts** (p276). Reserve early!

STARGAZE

Take in the twinkling night sky at **Black Canyon of the Gunnison National Park** (p279) and **Great Sand Dunes National Park** (p313), two of Colorado's 11 Dark Sky Parks, whose light reduction efforts benefit wildlife and nature conservation.

GIVE BACK

Help with food prep or wash dishes at **SAME Café** (p91), a donation-based cafe in Denver that strives to provide access to wholesome food for everyone, regardless of their ability to pay.

Bottoms Up
Go ahead, have another. **Dune Valley Distillery** (p318) uses local organic potatoes and quinoa to create its small batch vodka. And did we mention it hosts five-course farm-to-table dinners in its tasting room, a repurposed school gymnasium?

Treat Yo' Self
Splurge on an overnight stay at the luxurious **Populus Hotel** (p99), the country's first carbon-positive hotel, removing more carbon from the atmosphere than it emits. Among many efforts, a tree is planted for every night booked!

Pick Your Own
Pick your own lavender at **Sage Creations Organic Farm** (p294), a sea of purple on the western slope. Or head to **Big B's Delicious Orchards** (p295) for fruit and veggie picking, from peaches to cucumbers.

Do Good Outdoors
Join **Volunteers for Outdoors Colorado** *(voc. org)* for a day or more to help protect and preserve Colorado's public lands. Projects are statewide and include trail construction, habitat restoration and preservation of historic structures.

Eat Up
Support immigrant and refugee women, most from Latin America, by enjoying a meal at **Comal** (p88), a training ground for aspiring restauranteurs. The menu integrates culturally significant dishes to the participants, most locally sourced.

Learn all about the atmosphere, from pollution to climate change, at Boulder's **National Center for Atmospheric Research** (p123).

Practice Karma yoga – selfless service – at Crestone's **Haidakhandi Universal Ashram** (p322) through a day of volunteering.

No 1
Colorado is a leader in renewable energy, ranking eight in the nation for most LEED-certified buildings per person. Standing for 'Leadership in Energy and Environmental Design,' these buildings use less energy and water, reducing carbon emissions.

RESOURCES

lnt.org
'Leave no trace' resources and volunteer opportunities in Colorado

cpw.state.co.us
Deep dive into Colorado's State Parks' offerings

wwoofusa.org
Volunteer opportunities on small-scale organic farms

LGBTIQ+ Travelers

Colorado is a mixed bag for LGBTIQ+ travelers. In general, cities and college towns are more progressive – Denver, Boulder, Fort Collins and Durango are especially accepting. Rural areas and smaller mountain towns are characterized by conservative attitudes toward sexual and gender identity; the more affluent ski towns like Aspen, Telluride and Breckenridge are exceptions.

Pride Festivities

Rainbow flags come out in full force in Denver every June, when the city hosts **PrideFest** (p74), a two-day celebration with over 550,000 attendees partying in the streets, and **City Park** (p89) – Colorado's largest queer fest. **Boulder County** *(rmequality.org)*, **Fort Collins** *(nocoequality.org)*, **Avon** *(mountainpride. org)*, **Colorado Springs** *(pikespeakpride.org)*, **Manitou Springs** *(ucppe.org)* and **Alamosa** *(slvpride.org)* also host Pride festivals from June to August, celebrations marked with entertainment, food and parades. If you'll be here beyond summer, **Durango Pride** *(thealliance.gay)* means LGBTIQ+ parties in September and February that include movies, dances and late-night drag shows.

Denver's **Capitol Hill** (p70) LGBTIQ+ neighborhood with a thriving queer scene. Neighboring **Cheesman Park** is another gathering spot, and is ground zero for Denver's PrideFest parade. Other LGBTIQ+ inclusive areas include **Downtown Boulder** (p106) and **Fort Collins' Old Town** (p172), with queer and trans-friendly locales.

Gay Rodeo

The **Colorado Gary Rodeo Association** *(cgrarodeo.com)* is among the country's biggest and best gay-centric rodeos, featuring traditional events like bull riding and barrel racing as well as not-so-traditional events like wild drag racing and goat dressing. Any gender can compete together, a nod to non-binary and trans cowfolk. Held every July in Denver.

LEGAL PROTECTIONS

Though parts of Colorado are still quite conservative, it consistently ranks as one of the best states for LGBTIQ+ equity. This reflects hard-fought laws that protect the rights of individuals and prohibits discrimination based on sexual orientation or gender identity, from hate crimes to same-sex marriages.

RESOURCES & VOLUNTEERING

The Center on Colfax (p75) is the largest LGBTIQ+ community center in the Rocky Mountain region, offering programming, resources and events in Denver. **Rocky Mountain Equality** *(rmequality. org)* provides similar services on a smaller scale in Boulder County. Both offer several volunteer opportunities. Beyond the Front Range, **IRIS** (p281) provides outdoors guiding and instruction catering to women and non-binary and trans people.

Goings-On

For the latest LGBTIQ+ news and goings-on in Denver and beyond, check out the cheeky and smart online magazine **Out Front Colorado** *(outfrontonline. com)*. For a general overview of LGBTIQ+ friendly events and businesses in the state, peruse **PrideGuide Colorado** *(gaycolorado.com)*.

LEFT: ZMOTIONS/SHUTTERSTOCK, RIGHT: MARKUS MAINKA/SHUTTERSTOCK

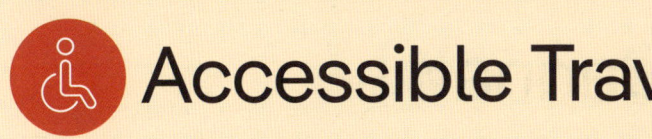

Accessible Travel

Travel within Colorado is getting easier for people with disabilities, with accessible facilities, attractions and accommodations plus adaptive outdoors activities. Challenges still exist in off-the-beaten-track places and rural areas.

National Parks

Colorado's National Parks have accessible visitor centers, overlooks, campgrounds and picnic areas. **Rocky Mountain National Park** (p146) also has wheelchair-friendly trails and **Great Sand Dunes National Park** (p313) loans special sand-friendly wheelchairs.

RESOURCES

Adaptive Sports Center *(adaptive sports.org)* provides opportunities for people with disabilities to participate in adventure sports in Crested Butte.

National Sports Center for the Disabled *(nscd.org)* is a Colorado-based organization providing access to various sports and outdoors activities statewide.

Society for the Advancement of Travel for the Handicapped *(facebook. com/SATHTRAVEL)* offers resources for travelers with disabilities.

TrailLink (traillink. com) has a list of wheelchair-accessible trails in Colorado.

Airport

Denver International Airport is well equipped, with accessible elevators, restrooms and seating areas as well as wheelchair assistance. Assistive technology and interpreter services are provided throughout. Ground transportation providers are required to have wheelchair-accessible vehicles.

Accommodations

Colorado offers a variety of accommodations for travelers with disabilities, ranging from wheelchair-accessible campsites to hotels with specially designed rooms. Vacation rental websites often can be filtered by accessibility features like step-free access and wide-width doors.

SIDEWALKS

Generally, Colorado's cities have well-maintained sidewalks with curb ramps; crosswalks are wide and easily visible. Small towns often limit sidewalks to the main commercial areas while dirt roads and parking areas are common.

Braille & Audio Signals

All public buildings are required to have braille signage and tactile maps – expect them in places like airports, hotels, restaurants, banks and museums. Many busy intersections also have audible crossing signals.

Public Transportation

Public transportation must be made accessible to all, including priority seating and wheelchair securement. Drivers typically are trained to assist passengers with disabilities to board or exit. Expect braille signage and stop announcements too.

Many Colorado ski resorts offer programs specifically designed for visitors with cognitive and physical disabilities. Ski and snowboarding instruction are provided using specialized equipment; some resorts also offer family lessons to teach relatives how to assist with the adaptive equipment.

Cannabis

In November 2012 Colorado and Washington became the first US states – and, arguably, the first jurisdictions in the world – to legalize recreational marijuana. But you can't just walk into a restaurant, roll a joint and light up. You will need to smoke at home or in designated places.

BUY FROM A DISPENSARY

Dispensaries are the only businesses licensed to sell cannabis products. Sales fall into two categories: recreational (21+ only) and medicinal (prescription required).

Bring cash. Since the sale of marijuana is illegal under federal law, most banks won't allow their credit cards to be used. Note: debit cards are increasingly being accepted with an added $3 to $5 surcharge.

With over 1000 dispensaries in Colorado, you're sure to find one near you, especially in cities and ski towns. They often sport a green cross or cannabis leaf image.

Bring government-issued ID. You must prove you're 21+ to even step inside.

Rely on the budtender. They know the stock. Remember to tip a couple of bucks!

Dispensaries have ATMs on-site; while convenient, expect a $3 to $5 surcharge.

PARTAKE IN PRIVATE OR SPECIALLY DESIGNATED AREAS

Smoking marijuana in public is not permitted, including in parks, on sidewalks and at concert halls.

- Some hotels and vacation rentals are '420 friendly,' but not all. Check before lighting up, or you may face steep clean-up charges.
- Blazing a doobie in a private residence is legal, but not where you can be seen by the public (like on a front porch). Head inside or to the backyard.
- You can partake in specially designated vehicles, like those on a cannabis tour.
- Enjoying MJ in your own car (or even having an open container of it) is illegal.
- Marijuana social clubs were recently legalized but few exist.
- Cannabis remains illegal on federal property, including national parks and some ski resorts.

Cannabis Culture

Though there's plenty of marijuana around the state, Denver is ground zero for everything cannabis. It has around 240 dispensaries alone and hosts the **420 Festival** (75), the largest marijuana fest in the world. It's also home to the **International Church of Cannabis** (80), with guided meditations and laser shows for the general public as well as **Tetra Cannabis Lounge** (tetralounge.com), a marijuana social club with one-day memberships. Several cannabis tours operate in Denver-metro too, ranging from customized experiences to party bus excursions with **Colorado Cannabis Tours** (coloradocannabistours.com).

Don't drive if you're high. You could really hurt someone and face a DUI charge too. Take an Uber or taxi instead.

Nuts & Bolts

OPENING HOURS

High-season hours follow. In the mountains and rural areas, many businesses close on Sunday.

Banks 8:30am–5pm Monday to Friday, 9am–noon on Saturday

Bars 4pm–midnight, to 2am Friday and Saturday

Breweries noon–10pm Thursday to Saturday, to 8pm Sunday to Wednesday

Nightclubs 9pm–2am Thursday to Saturday

Restaurants 7am–2:30pm and 5pm–9:30pm

Stores 10am–6pm Monday to Saturday, noon–5pm Sunday

Supermarkets 7am–10pm

Smoking

Smoking, including vapes and cannabis, is prohibited in all public spaces except in specially designated areas.

Electricity

120V/60Hz

GOOD TO KNOW

Time zone
GMT/UTC minus 7 hours early Nov to mid-Mar, GMT/UTC minus 6 hours rest of year

Country code
1

Emergency number
911

Population
5.8 million

PUBLIC HOLIDAYS

On the following national public holidays, banks, schools and government offices (including post offices) are closed; transportation and other services operate on a Sunday schedule. Holidays falling on a weekend are usually observed the following Monday.

New Year's Day January 1

Martin Luther King Jr Day Third Monday of January

Presidents' Day Third Monday of February

Easter March or April

Memorial Day Last Monday of May

Independence Day July 4

Labor Day First Monday of September

Mother Cabrini Day Second Monday of October

Veterans Day November 11

Thanksgiving Fourth Thursday of November

Christmas Day December 25

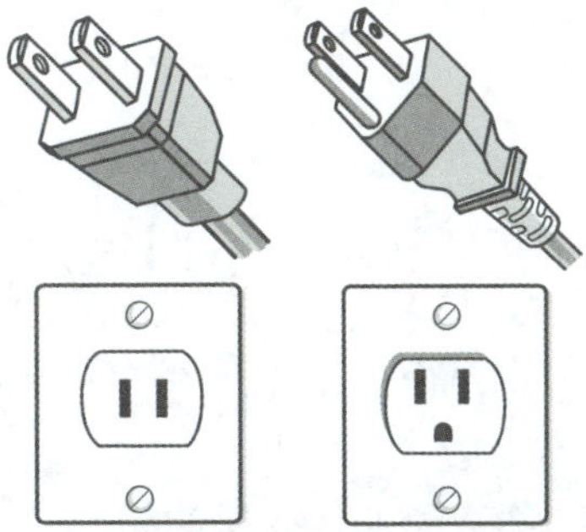

Public toilets can be hard to find. Try gas stations, libraries, big box stores and supermarkets.

Cellphone coverage can be unreliable in mountain regions; use internet-based services like WhatsApp to communicate.

349

STORYBOOK

Our writers delve deep into different aspects of Colorado life

A HISTORY OF COLORADO IN
15 PLACES

Colorado's history is written in fossils, petroglyphs, gold dust and ski tracks. It's marked by discovery and domination, vision and modernization, with natural beauty woven throughout. Ultimately, it's a story about change, and how the force of nature and human hands created the Colorado we see today. By Liza Prado

THE NAME 'COLORADO' evokes images of towering mountains, swooshing skiers and fly-fishers. And for good reason: Colorado is an outdoor wonderland. But that's not all – it's a state with a rich culture and complex history. Knowing how it has developed, who has lived here and how they have shaped the social and physical landscape, speaks volumes. Context is everything.

Colorado history dates to prehistoric times; it's home to some of the world's best fossil beds, dinosaur bones telling a story of a once lush land. Human archaeological sites also dot the state, remnants of ancient communities that whisper about life on the plains, mesa tops and mountain valleys. The discovery of gold brought thousands to this vast wilderness, building cities, mountain towns, mines and railroads. The native people who'd lived in the Rockies for countless generations were killed or pushed out, relegated to a tiny corner of the state. And still Colorado continued to grow: the land mined and farmed, parks created and scenic roadways built; along the way, Colorado became a tourist destination.

Today, Colorado is a diverse and thriving state, and its population continues to change, its complex history revisited and rediscovered. All the while, its natural beauty remains ever present.

1. Dinosaur National Monument
WHERE DINOSAURS ROAMED

Present-day Colorado was a very different place 150 million years ago, during the Jurassic era. It was closer to the equator for one thing, and was mostly low plains, crisscrossed by languid rivers. Dinosaurs of many kinds and sizes lived and died beside those rivers; their bones were covered in successive layers of sediment, forming what became known as the Morrison Formation, arguably the richest dinosaur fossil bed in the world. Its 1877 discovery in Colorado, and the subsequent formation of Dinosaur National Park in 1915, brought world attention to the state. Colorado remains an important center of paleontological research today.

For more on Dinosaur National Monument, see p292

2. Mesa Verde National Park
THE FIRST COLORADANS

The incredible cliff dwellings of Mesa Verde National Park were built during the 12th century CE by the Ancestral Puebloan people. By that time, they had already occupied southwest Colorado for over 1100 years, living and farming the valleys and mesa tops. The dwellings, built in vertiginous natural alcoves and exhibiting sophisticated masonry, were accessed via wood-pole ladders, stairways cut into the cliffs and narrow tunnels. The site was abruptly abandoned in 1300 for reasons still unknown. Today, Mesa Verde is the largest and best-known archaeological site in Colorado, but by no means the only one.

For more on Mesa Verde National Park, see p254

3. Santa Fe Trail
WESTERN EXPANSION

The Santa Fe Trail was a 19th-century trade route that connected Missouri to New Mexico. Officially opened in 1821 and used until the arrival of the railroad in 1880, it was a lifeline for pioneers and merchants, providing a direct link between the goods of the American frontier and the resources of Mexican and Native American territories. Today, parts of the Santa Fe Trail are protected and preserved along a National Scenic Byway in southeast Colorado. Sights along the route, like Bent's Old Fort National Historic Site, provide insight into the cultural crossroads of the Old West.

For more on the Santa Fe Trail, see p331

4. Larimer Square
DENVER'S BEGINNINGS

The discovery of gold near the confluence of the South Platte River and Cherry Creek in 1858 sparked the Colorado Gold Rush. Thousands of fortune-seekers descended on the area known today as Conflu-

Mesa Verde National Park (p254)

STEVEN GROUP/SHUTTERSTOCK

ence Park. An astute land developer from Kansas named William Larimer staked a claim on a square-mile parcel of land near the site, laid out streets and sold plots to settlers. He called it Denver City. Larimer also created the city's first commercial center with a bank, a jail, a city hall and even a bookstore and named it after himself. In 1971 Larimer Sq became Denver's first historic district.

For more on Larimer Sq, see p60

5. Sand Creek Massacre National Historic Site
MEMORIAL TO NATIVE AMERICANS

On November 29, 1864, around 700 volunteer soldiers attacked a peaceful Cheyenne and Arapaho encampment in southeastern Colorado. More than 150 people, mostly elders, women and children, were killed and mutilated; body parts of the victims were later paraded through Denver in grisly celebration. The massacre reflected the fear of (and utter disregard for) Native Americans held by the US government and, by extension, white settlers. Not surprisingly, it only served to increase conflict in the region. In 2000 the Sand Creek Massacre National Historic Site was established to commemorate the horrors of that day and to raise awareness about the region's history.

For more on Sand Creek Massacre National Historic Site, see p331

6. Durango & Silverton Narrow Gauge Railroad
RAILROADS AND MINING

Railroads were the lifeblood of Colorado's early development, connecting the young state to the rest of the country and greasing the wheels of economic growth. Rails were especially critical to Colorado's burgeoning mining industry. Beginning in 1882, the Durango & Silverton Narrow Gauge Railroad served mines in the San Juan Mountains, carrying over $300 million in gold and silver on its tracks; when gold and silver mining ended, it began hauling coal. The railroad was pivotal to the growth of the modern-day towns of southwest Colorado and today is a National Historic Landmark that can be ridden May through October.

For more on the Durango & Silverton Narrow Gauge Railroad, see p261

7. Matchless Mine
SILVER BOOM AND CRASH

Opened in 1878, Matchless Mine in Leadville became one of the richest silver mines in Colorado, the source of an estimated $7.5 million ($245 million in today's dollars). It was owned by Horace Tabor, Colorado senator and eventually one of the wealthiest individuals in the state. But his success and that of Matchless Mine didn't last. In 1893 the repeal of the Sherman Silver Purchase Act led to the collapse of the silver mining industry and Tabor, like many others, lost everything. He died penniless, leaving Matchless Mine to his widow, Baby Doe. She lived out her life impoverished, in a small cabin at the mine.

For more on Matchless Mine, see p216

8. Colorado Chautauqua
A NEW IMAGE

In 1898 Boulder won the bid to create a 'Chautauqua' for the Texas Board of Regents, which was searching for a desirable summer school locale for its teachers. Part of a nationwide Chautauqua movement, Boulder's location aimed not only to provide a summer school but also to create year-round educational and cultural experiences for its community with lectures, concerts and social activities, all designed to bridge the perceived cultural gap between urban and rural America. Colorado Chautauqua proved a success. It quickly rose to be the preeminent educational retreat of the West, putting Boulder – and Colorado – on the map as a sophisticated destination.

For more on Colorado Chautauqua, see p118

9. St Elmo Ghost Town
THE END OF AN ERA

By the 1920s, hundreds of once-thriving mountain communities in Colorado, founded during the gold and silver rushes, were abandoned, the mines closed or residents moving to more prosperous areas. St Elmo, a gold-mining town in the Collegiate Peaks, became one of the best-preserved of these 'ghost towns.' Around 40 of the town's buildings remain standing – a saloon, billiards hall, courthouse, jail and more – most dating to the 1880s when the town had over 2000 residents. In 1922 the train stopped running and the last mine closed, leaving the town empty save for modern-day tourists.

For more on St Elmo Ghost Town, see p242

10. Colorado National Monument
THE BUILDING OF PARKS

The Great Depression had a profound impact on Colorado, with rampant unemployment and families struggling to make ends meet. In 1932 President Roosevelt introduced the New Deal, a series of programs and policies that provided much-needed relief. Colorado National Monument was among many parks where men were put to work, building infrastructure to promote tourism and earning precious wages in the process. Among the projects in the park was the construction of Rim Rd, the epically beautiful 23-mile road that winds through the park, including tunnels and overlooks, offering breathtaking views of the Colorado National Monument's towering red-rock formations.

For more on Colorado National Monument, see p290

11. Amache National Historic Site
WWII INJUSTICE

Camp Amache, located on a desolate windy prairie in southeastern Colorado, was one of 10 Japanese internment camps established during WWII between 1942 and 1945 under Executive Order 9066, a racist response to the bombing of Pearl Harbor that forced the relocation and incarceration of people of Japanese descent, mostly US citizens. Against all odds, Amache's residents grew enough food to feed the entire camp (which was woefully undersupplied) and provided millions of pounds of surplus produce to the military. What's more, over 400 men from Amache enlisted, and 31 died, fighting overseas. Amache became a National Historic Site in 2022.

For more on Amache National Historic Site, see p331

12. US Air Force Academy
MODERN MILITARY PRESENCE

The start of the Cold War highlighted the US' need for more professional and specialized training for its military pilots. In 1954 the US Air Force Academy was opened in Colorado Springs, integrating military training with

Colorado State Capitol (p73)

academic rigor in the sciences. The city was chosen for its central location and favorable climate. It marked the beginning of a major US Air Force presence in the state, which today includes five bases, one of which houses the North American Aerospace Defense Command (NORAD).

For more on the US Air Force Academy, see p312

13. Vail

COLORADO'S SKI INDUSTRY

The opening of Vail Ski Resort in 1962 marked the beginning of Colorado's rise as a major ski destination. The brainchild of locals Peter Seibert and Earl Eaton, the ambitious resort quickly became known for its world-class ski slopes, stunning mountain scenery and luxurious amenities. Vail was one of the first ski resorts in the United States to offer high-speed lifts, on-mountain restaurants and a wide variety of ski runs for all skill levels. Today, Vail is widely recognized as one of the premier ski resorts in the world, attracting almost three million visitors each year.

For more on Vail, see p207

14. Coors Field

REVITALIZATION OF DENVER

Downtown Denver's transformation from dreary and dangerous to lively and livable can be traced to one thing: Coors Field. The stadium (a terrific brick throwback) opened in 1995 and was soon followed by a vibrant mix of bars, restaurants, shops and residential buildings. Change was already afoot with artists turning warehouses into lofts in what would become RiNo and future-governor John Hickenlooper opening Denver's first brewery at 18th and Wynkoop Sts. Mayor Federico Peña, elected in 1983, worked tirelessly for a stadium downtown, rightly understanding its potential. Colorado was awarded an expansion team – named the Rockies – in Peña's last year in office.

For more on Coors Field, see p62

15. Colorado State Capitol

PURPLE STATE

Overlooking downtown Denver`, the gold-domed Colorado State Capitol houses the Governor's Office, Senate and House of Representatives. Built in the late 1800s, its ornately decorated walls have seen innumerable laws debated and enacted, reflecting the societal attitudes and perspectives of Coloradans over the course of its history. Large portions of Colorado are solidly conservative, but recent statewide elections and legislation have swung decidedly leftward, including the legalization of recreational marijuana and same-sex civil unions. In 2018 Colorado elected Jared Polis, the US' first openly gay governor; he was re-elected in a landslide victory in 2022.

For more on the Colorado State Capitol, see p73

MEET THE COLORADANS

A growing and ever-changing people, most of today's Coloradans were born out-of-state. And while they may not agree on politics, they all love the outdoors. LIZA PRADO introduces her people

DRIVING WEST FROM Denver on I-70, especially on a weekend, there's no doubt Colorado is a fast-growing state. A highway that was a cruiser 15 years ago is now bumper-to-bumper at 8am, packed with city-dwellers headed for mountain fun. Since 2010 Colorado's population has exploded, adding over 800,000 people for a total of 5.8 million – a 15% growth rate, most of it in Colorado's big cities. Denver has repeatedly topped the 'Fastest Growing Cities in the US' lists. With all the new apartment buildings being built these days, it's no surprise. And frankly, neither is the traffic.

The 'Native Coloradan' bumper stickers I so often saw on my commute years ago are now almost a relic. Today, about 58% of Colorado residents were born outside of Colorado, either in another state or another country. Over 160 languages are spoken in the city of Aurora alone. The most commonly spoken language after English is Spanish, of course; it reflects the Latinx population that has immigrated to the state for work as well as those that were here before Colorado even existed (a quarter of the state was once part of Mexico after all). In fact, the Latinx population is the fastest-growing segment of Colorado, projected to hit 26% by 2030. But still, that stereotype about Colorado being really white...? Yeah, it holds water. White Coloradans make up 66% of the population. The percentage of African Americans, Asian Americans and Native Americans are all in the single digits.

Politically, the state is diverse. It has an almost equal mix of Democrats (41%) and Republicans (42%) with Independents (17%) rounding it out. A longtime swing state, voters have leaned blue in recent elections. Colorado's progressive policies on issues such as cannabis legalization, environmental protection and same-sex unions are a nod to that. Geographically, Denver and Boulder are the state's liberal hubs. Mountain towns can go either way; ski towns tend to be blue while most others lean red. Colorado Springs, Grand Junction and farming communities are decidedly conservative. As you drive through the state, political billboards and yard signs are prominent. They'll tell you immediately where people stand. Tread lightly. Coloradans value courtesy but can have strong, vocal opinions if pushed, especially on their home turf.

One thing all Coloradans agree on, though, is outdoor recreation. We love it. It's a major reason why people move here. It's no wonder, with so many people hiking, climbing, skiing and more, that Colorado is often ranked among the healthiest states (if not the healthiest) in the US. Even in big cities, bikers and joggers are a typical sight and green spaces are filled with people playing in the sun.

Religion

Religion isn't a common topic among Coloradans, though the numbers speak volumes: 64% identify as Christian, and of those 41% are Protestants. Only 2% are Jewish, and less than 1% are Muslim or Hindu. Almost 33% of Coloradans have no religious affiliation at all.

Pictured clockwise from top left: Skiers on a chairlift, Vail (p207); Hiker, Rocky Mountain National Park (p146); Young people eating tacos; Colorado cowboy

A TRANSPLANT WITH COLORADO ROOTS

Like most Coloradans, I was born out-of-state. In Buffalo, NY, to be exact. And like many Coloradans, my parents are Mexican immigrants. I love my parents, I love Buffalo, but never, not once, did I think I'd stay in western New York. After college I bounced from coast to coast and lived all over Mexico, but when I moved to Colorado on a whim, I unexpectedly found my home. Like so many other transplants, the mountains called to me. I didn't understand it, but I listened and stayed. About a decade after moving to Denver, I learned my great-grandfather had lived here too; Papa Lalo had come with tens of thousands of other Mexican *traqueros* (track workers) to help build the railroads. He'd lived in a shantytown near Union Station. It suddenly made sense. This pull to Colorado had as much to do with snowcapped mountains as with family ties, with my great-grandfather, who helped build the state.

COLORADO'S
CHANGING CLIMATE

In the parched Rocky Mountains, water is everything. How is climate change impacting the region's long-term prospects?
By Christopher Pitts

THE MOST VISIBLE indication of the effects of climate change in Colorado are not in the state itself, but further downstream along the Colorado River. In 2022 water levels at Lake Mead, the massive reservoir formed by the Hoover Dam outside Las Vegas, fell to their lowest level ever, at just one-fourth of its capacity.

The infamous bathtub ring, a chalky white coating on the reservoir's cliffs, is a reminder of just how far the water's surface has dropped in the past two decades. At its all-time low in 2022, the ring extended 150ft down to the water's surface – or 26.63% capacity. Even after two historically wet winters, in 2024 the reservoir had only risen to 34% capacity. If the water in the Colorado River continues to be used at the same rate as today, the US Bureau of Reclamation concluded that the water level in the reservoir will soon drop so low that Hoover Dam will no longer be able to generate electricity. And after that? There remains the possibility that one day, the reservoir could reach 'dead pool,' when the level in the dam drops so low that the river stops flowing entirely, and Arizona, Nevada, southern California and northwestern Mexico will be cut off from their main source of water.

The Colorado River

But what does all this have to do with Colorado? In a word: snowpack. The Colorado River, whose headwaters lie on the western slope of Rocky Mountain National Park and whose tributaries are scattered across the Rockies, is largely fed by snowmelt. Approximately 90% of all the water in the river comes from the mountains of Colorado, Wyoming and Utah, with the lion's share coming from Colorado watersheds. The equation is simple: the less snow that falls in the Rockies, the less water there is in the river, and the less water that's available for one of the most important agricultural regions in the country – not to mention the 40 million people who live in the Colorado River basin (including Los Angeles, San Diego, Las Vegas and Phoenix).

Of course, as any skier will tell you, snowpack varies from year to year. Some years may be above average, others below. But data from the Environmental Protection Agency (EPA) indicates that overall, there has been a downward trend over time: across the West, snowpack has declined an average 23% since 1955. More importantly, the date of peak snowpack has been moving steadily backward. That is, the largest amount of snow in the Colorado

Rockies used to be measured in mid-April; over the past decade, that date has been inching toward March.

What does that tell us? That because of climate change, winters are slowly getting shorter. Meanwhile, summer temperatures in the Southwest have risen faster than in any other part of the United States. In Colorado, they've risen by 2.5°F since the beginning of the 20th century. Higher temperatures mean increased aridity and higher rates of evaporation throughout the landscape. Soils in particular have dried out to such an extent that when the spring runoff begins, much of that snowmelt is sucked straight into the ground, leaving increasingly less water that makes it into the river system – even in years when snowpack is average.

Factor in the 20-plus-year megadrought that is currently gripping the region (the worst in 1200 years), and a flawed seven-state compact that draws more water from the Colorado River than there is annual flow, and you have all the ingredients for what has become a monumental crisis – albeit in slow motion. At this point, it seems highly unlikely that nature will re-plenish the Lake Mead or Lake Powell (on the Utah–Arizona border) reservoirs on its own. Barring an end to the drought, the only other way to avoid dead pool is to reduce consumption.

Considering that roughly one-half of all the water that flows out of the spigots in Los Angeles, San Diego and Phoenix comes directly from the Colorado River (in Vegas it's upwards of 90%), drastically reducing consumption in what is one of the fastest-growing regions in the US may seem like a tall order. But city dwellers aren't even the primary consumers. That would be agriculture, which sucks up 80% of the allotted river flow. And yet, reducing agricultural demand for irrigated water is easier said than done. With only 3in of annual rainfall, Yuma (Arizona) and the Imperial Valley (southern California) might seem like some of the world's most improbable farmland, but they're actually the nation's primary producer of winter fruit and vegetables. When farmland in the rest of the nation is on winter vacation, 90% of all the carrots, lettuce and other greens you find at the supermarket are being grown in the always-sunny desert, irrigated directly with Colorado River water.

Climate change is not the only reason the Southwest's most important water source is drying up. Flawed planning, stubborn special-interest groups, outdated water rights and a naturally occurring drought cycle all play their own role. But as in so many other situations, climate change makes an already serious problem that much worse. As the Colorado snowpack continues to decline and summer temperatures continue to rise, eventually, there can only be one outcome. And sure enough, in 2023 an agreement on the first round of water restrictions was finally reached: the three Lower Basin states agreed to cut 3 million acre-feet of water use per year through 2026, in return for $1.2 billion in payments from the federal government. A critical first step in establishing a permanent agreement when the temporary deal expires.

Wildfires

Beyond the consequences for all the people who live downstream, climate change has a direct impact on Coloradans as well.

Wildfire-fighting efforts in Boulder (p100), 2022

MICHAEL CIAGLO/GETTY IMAGES

Colorado's mainstay of the tourism economy, skiing ($5 billion in annual revenue), seems to be headed for a day of reckoning, though the impacts of warming weather are less immediately visible for high-altitude ski resorts in the Rockies than in lower-elevation resorts in the Alps or along the East Coast, where winter rainfall is already commonplace. While Colorado ski resorts are nonetheless preparing for shortened seasons and less natural snowfall, there is another less obvious threat on the near horizon: wildfire.

In 2021, just miles from the residential sprawl around Lake Tahoe, California, the Caldor Fire raced through the mountains with such startling speed and ferocity that it's a miracle that firefighters were able to stop the blaze before it reached the lakeside settlements. One of the casualties of the fire, however, was the Sierra-at-Tahoe ski resort, where roughly 80% of the terrain was burned; the shocking photos of empty ski lifts being swallowed up by a raging orange inferno seemed to encapsulate all fire-mitigation challenges the West is currently facing.

While California's fires may get more coverage in the media, this is a region-wide phenomenon. Over the past decade, unusually hot and dry conditions have led to an increase not only in the number of wildfires per year, but also in their intensity. Warming conditions have stressed forests, making them more susceptible to disease and infestations of spruce, fir and pine beetles. Huge stands of dead trees – anyone who drives up Trail Ridge Rd in Rocky Mountain National Park will spot the gray- and rust-colored stands of deadwood – combined with exceptionally dry grasses, low humidity and high winds have resulted in increasingly massive fires. Of the 20 largest fires in Colorado history, 16 occurred after 2011, and the other four took place in the 2000s. The three largest ever, Cameron Peak, East Troublesome and Pine Gulch, all took place in 2020, filling the skies outside several major cities with raining ash and a terrifying red glow.

Another change is that there is no longer a wildfire season. What used to be a late-summer event might now happen at any time of year, as evidenced by the most destructive fire in Colorado history, the Marshall Fire, which sprang up at the edge of Boulder on December 30, 2021. Fueled by 115mph gusting winds and a complete absence of snowfall that year, the grassland fire swept through a dense residential community in a matter of hours, completely destroying over 1000 homes and businesses, taking two lives and causing $2 billion in damages.

There's no question that decades of overly aggressive fire suppression on public lands is partially to blame for the blazes, as the Smokey the Bear strategy resulted in the accumulation of huge amounts of fuel and dense understory vegetation throughout the West. While no one wants unplanned fires to happen (campfires are off-limits in many places throughout Colorado), local officials today are passing on a different sort of message. It's no longer one of fire suppression, but fire adaptation. As the Boulder City Wildfire Preparedness Guide reminds its residents: 'We live in a location where the wildfire threat is real. Wildfires happen frequently. A wildfire that threatens your home is not a matter of if, but when.' Residents in the West are learning to be prepared, because they are now living in an environment where people have to accept wildfires and mandatory evacuations as an inevitable part of their lives.

THE LESS SNOW THAT FALLS IN THE ROCKIES, THE LESS WATER THERE IS IN THE RIVER, AND THE LESS WATER THAT'S AVAILABLE FOR ONE OF THE MOST IMPORTANT AGRICULTURAL REGIONS IN THE COUNTRY.

Lake Isabelle trail (p161)
FRANCISCO BLANCO/SHUTTERSTOCK

LESSONS FROM LEADVILLE

Nothing's easy in an alpine mining town at over 10,000 ft. As Leadville 100 founder Ken Chlouber would say, that's when you 'dig deep.' By Nicole Hagg

BEFORE MOVING TO Colorado, I don't know that I'd have called myself 'super outdoorsy,' and that's being generous. A New Yorker by birth, my childhood camping experience involved a yellow Girl Scout poncho and a standard-issue mess kit. My survival expertise? Mad s'mores-making skills. From there, my young adulthood found me in a succession of large east-coast cities. Put me in a moving tube 200ft underground with coffee and paper, and I was good. Truth.

Twenty-one years of living in Colorado changed that. Not overnight, but it was undeniable. Colorado has the magical power to catalyze the staunchest urbanite among us. I came for the city of Denver; its theater and shops, world-class eats, and omnipresent views of the mountains. The majestic views felt like living on a movie set. I watched them for a while, like the shy

new kid surveying the party from the sidelines. And, for a while, that was enough.

Until it wasn't.

Trail Running in Colorado

For me, the gateway drug was trail running. I've been a runner more on than off for 30-plus years. It's my soul's salve, my muse, and my bond with others so inclined to chat about their VO2 max at social events. I've completed five marathons and nearly as many triathlons, which makes me the least-decorated amateur athlete in this state.

Over time, I became curious. I began to notice fellow Colorado runners' higher-elevation adventures; the well-documented Gram-moments with puffer jackets and beanies, wildflowers, and super-cool shoes I knew would make me run with goat-like agility. They regaled their trail war stories around the yoga studio where I taught and in the local running store, my second home.

That's where I first saw the buckle. Phil worked at the store and hobbled over wearing said buckle: large, silver, ornate, and did I say large? Phil explained he'd just run the Leadville 100. Thinking I misheard, I asked, 'What's that?'

'It's a 100-mile race across the sky up in Leadville, Colorado,' he calmly replied, like he was relaying the day's weather. 'One hundred miles?' My lips parted silently with unformed words. He smiled and nodded. 'Like, US customary system measurement miles?' I uttered. Mind. Blown.

Phil, or Leadville Phil (as he was known among trail-running fam), planted the seed that day. I place all the blame for the wonder that was to follow squarely on his inspirational shoulders!

In the 15 years since, I've learned a lot. Much of it the hard way, but all of it life-changing.

First Steps on the Trail

It started innocently enough in the foothills at Matthew Winters Park, right by Red Rocks. 'Just a couple of miles up!' they said. 'Families hike there all the time!' they reassured. Two important clarifications to this well-intended guidance: 1) running up trails that top out just under 6800ft, with large rocks, switchbacks and the very real possibility of rattlesnakes will feel unlike any 2 miles you've known; and 2) hiking is not trail running. I know, I know, it seems like it might be, but I'm here to confirm it's not. Also, babies don't hike; they're carried.

'Matty Winters' and I became good friends. For years, I'd make the early drive to the dusty parking lot, trail shoes and many Goo flavors in tow. It was a level of presence I'd never known or seen in the subway, that's for sure. Wildflowers grew with casual magnificence, and I began to memorize the rocks like the faces of old friends. It's a moving meditation, a live video game, and a call to the moment all at once.

And then, one day, Matty pulled me aside, 'I think we both know what you need to do next.' The trail is gracious that way; it wants you to grow.

The Leadville 100

The genesis of the Leadville 100 'Race Across the Sky' is as storied and raw as the mountain town itself. The closure of the Climax Mine put unemployment at the highest in the country in the 1980s. The creativity and grit of Ken Chlouber, a miner and would-be Colorado state senator with good business sense, and Merilee Maupin gave birth to the legendary race. They figured overnight stays to run 100 miles would revitalize the economy with tourism, and where the mining boom had waned, the race boom flourished!

So, for my 50th birthday, I joined the countless hopefuls in the Leadville Race lottery system and signed up for the Heavy Half, a race on my bucket list for over a decade. I learned Leadville is a mystical and historic town with the truest and kindest people, the most breathtaking, badass mountains, and very little oxygen. The race is 15.7 miles long, about 7.5-ish up and down, with incline grades reaching just under 14%, and topping at Mosquito Pass some 13,284ft in the sky.

It's More than a Race

Everything about this race monster-under-the-bed scared me: the physicality, the altitude, driving there (I looked – no subway), the rocks to the summit – so many! The week prior, I talked myself out of going a bazillion times; endless internal chatter about lightning strikes, throwing up, and those who don't finish. A mind-loop of 'can't': there is no way you're going to finish this course, you are under-trained, things with more legs than you live up there, oxygen masks will not drop from the sky, you may die an untimely middle-aged death etc.

A few days before the race, I figured it out! The surest way to validate all of that – to know I would 100% not complete the course – was not to go.

So, I went.

And, I finished.

Colorado's ancient landscapes whisper (and often thunder) their wisdom: show up in this world and witness miracles. And, in the famous words of Mr Chlouber, 'You are better than you think you are, you can do more than you think you can.'

INDEX

"Standing on the edge of the Sun Up Bowl in Vail (p207) on a brisk February morning, the sun glinting off icy peaks in the distance and miles of untracked powder spread out beneath you, is the stuff that Colorado dreams are made of."

"A trip through Rocky Mountain National Park (p146) will take you from riparian meadows, favored by herds of grazing elk and deer, up through the forests of ponderosa and spruce, before topping out on the windswept tundra."

Mapping data sources:
© Lonely Planet
© OpenStreetMap http://openstreetmap.org/copyright

THIS BOOK

Destination Editor
Melissa Yeager

Coordinating Editor
Michael MacKenzie

Cartographer
Dorothy Davidson

Alex Conroy, Melanie Dankel

Production Editor
Kate James

Book Designer
Megan Cassidy

Assisting Editors
Janet Austin,
Andrew Bain,
Imogen Bannister,

Cover Researcher
Gerilyn Attebery

MIX
Paper | Supporting responsible forestry
FSC™ C021741

Paper in this book is certified against the Forest Stewardship Council™ standards. FSC™ promotes environmentally responsible, socially beneficial and economically viable management of the world's forests.

Published by Lonely Planet Global Limited
CRN 554153
5th edition – Aug 2025
ISBN 978 1 83758 375 1
© Lonely Planet 2025 Photographs © as indicated 2025
10 9 8 7 6 5 4 3 2 1
Printed in China